CH
CRAFT
WORKS

KNIGHT KING ROOK QUEEN BISHOP PAWN

VOL. 12

PRESENTED BY RYU MIZUNAGI

CONTENTS

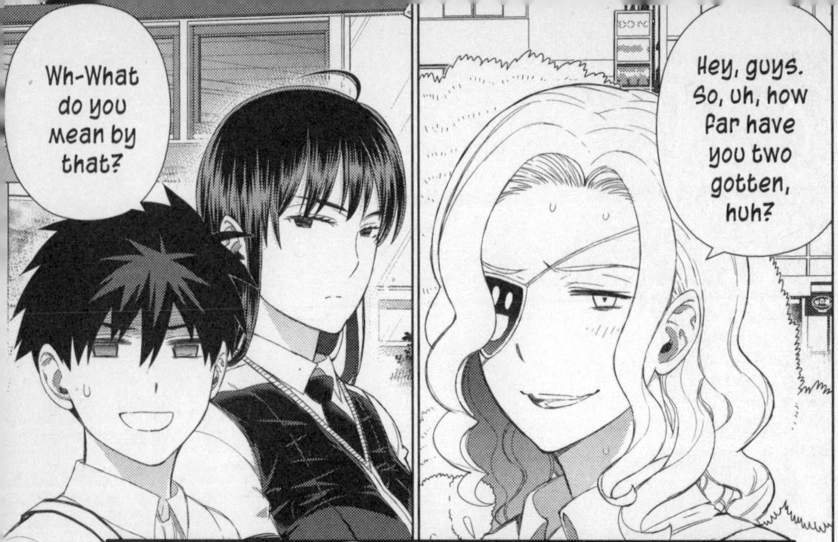
Hey, guys. So, uh, how far have you two gotten, huh?
Wh-What do you mean by that?

CHAPTER 62 Takamiya and the Summer Break Dinner

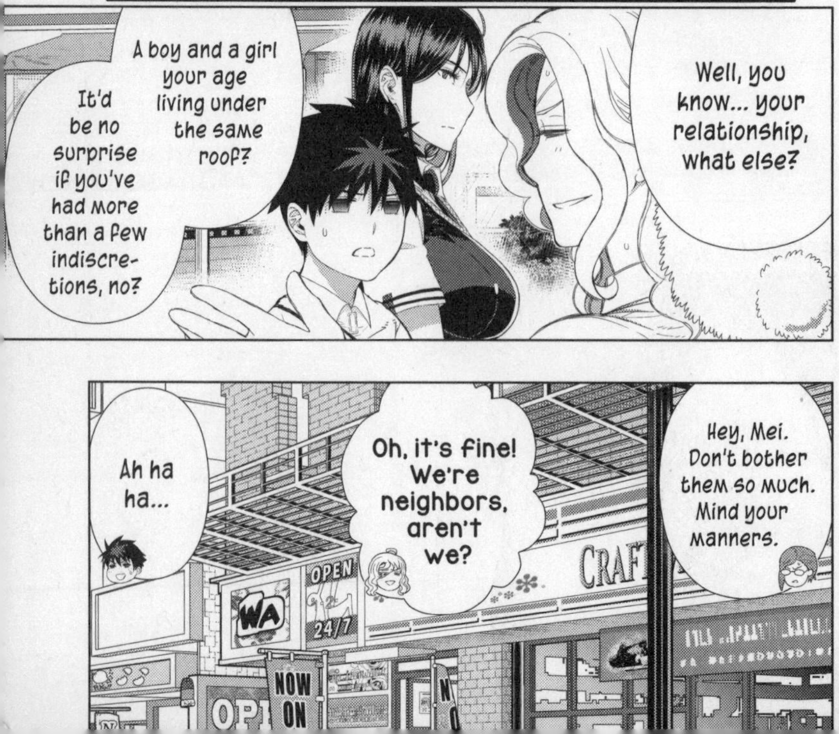
Well, you know... your relationship, what else?
A boy and a girl your age living under the same roof?
It'd be no surprise if you've had more than a few indiscretions, no?
Hey, Mei. Don't bother them so much. Mind your manners.
Oh, it's fine! We're neighbors, aren't we?
Ah ha ha...
OPEN
24/7
WA
NOW ON

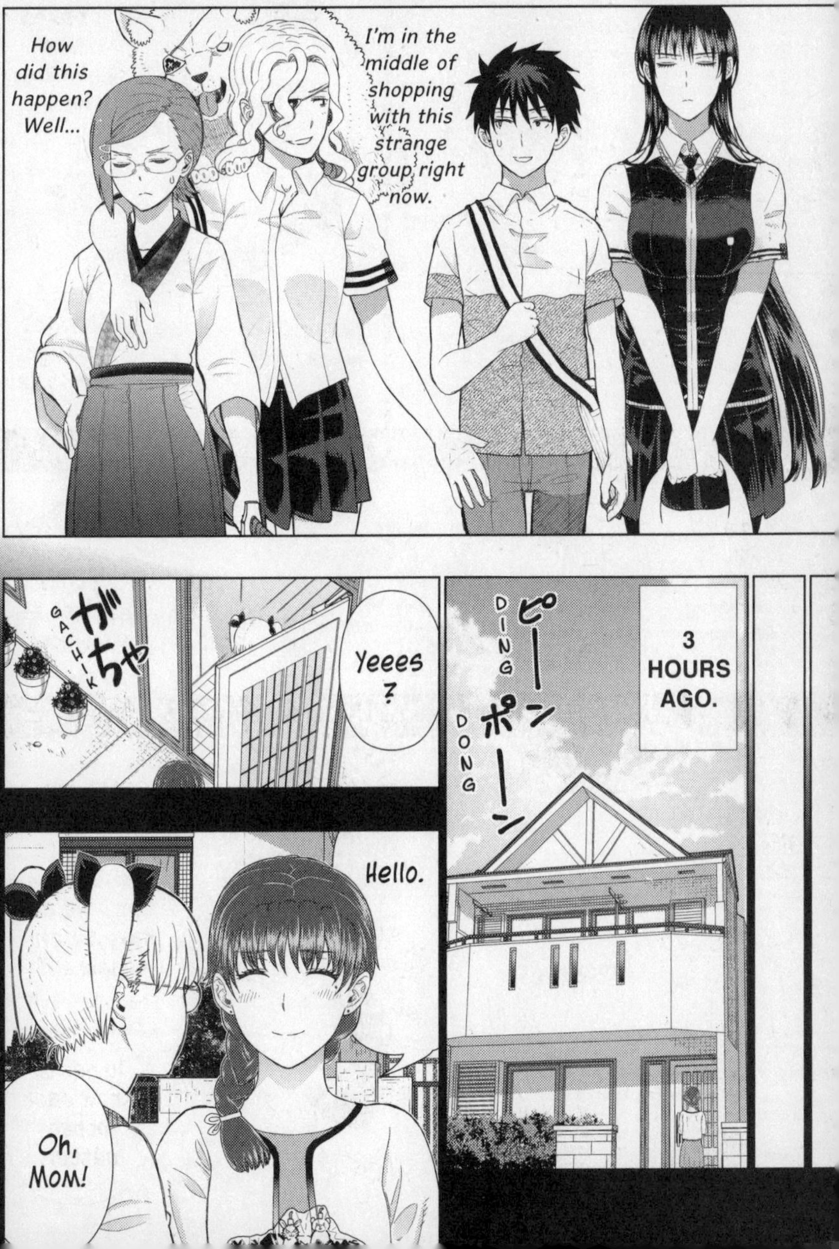
I'm in the middle of shopping with this strange group right now.
How did this happen? Well...
3 HOURS AGO.
ピーンポーン
DING DONG
Yeeees?
がちゃ
GACHIK
Hello.
Oh, Mom!

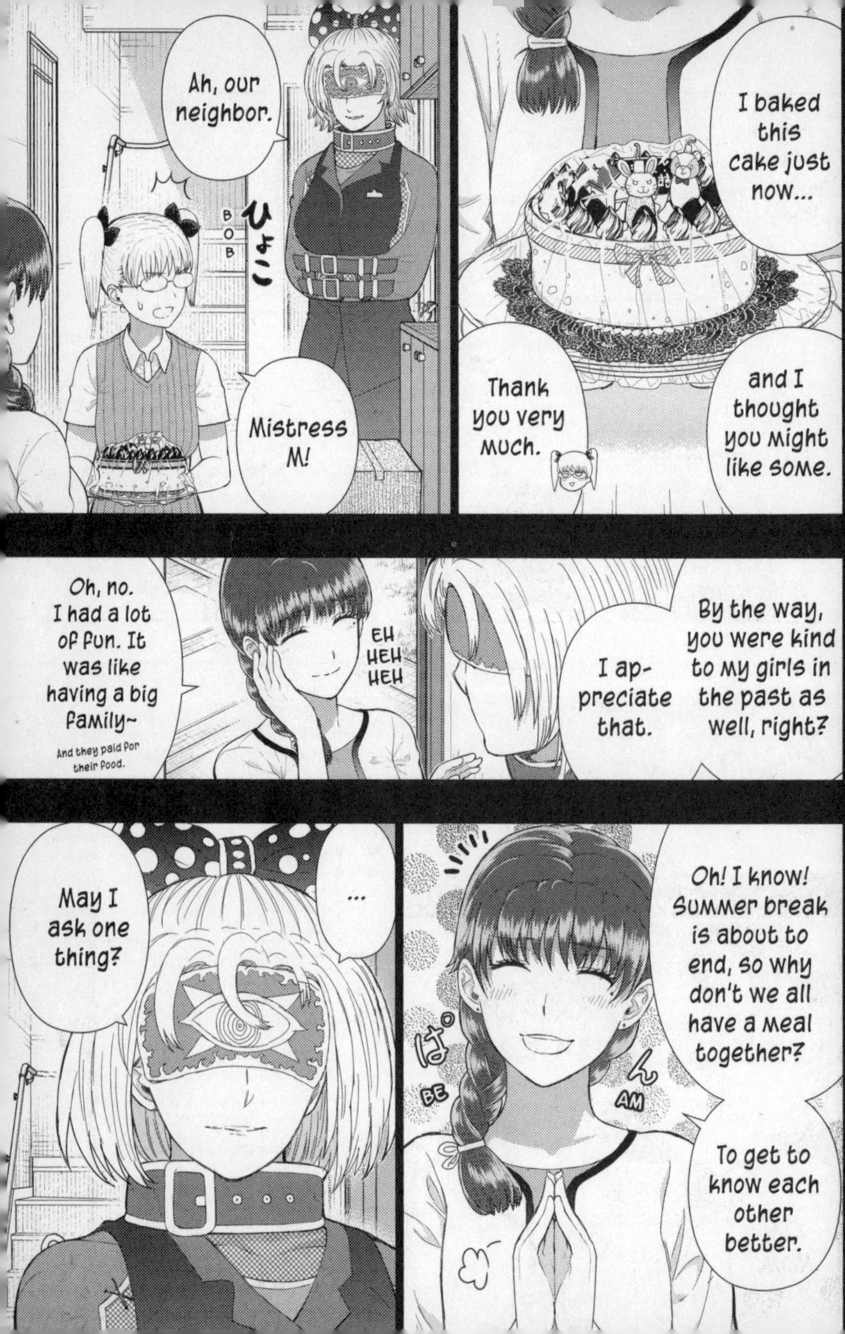
I baked this cake just now...
and I thought you might like some.
Thank you very much.
Ah, our neighbor.
ひょこ
BOB
Mistress M!
By the way, you were kind to my girls in the past as well, right?
I ap-preciate that.
EH HEH HEH
Oh, no. I had a lot of fun. It was like having a big family~
And they paid for their food.
Oh! I know! Summer break is about to end, so why don't we all have a meal together?
ぱ
BE
ん
AM
To get to know each other better.
...
May I ask one thing?

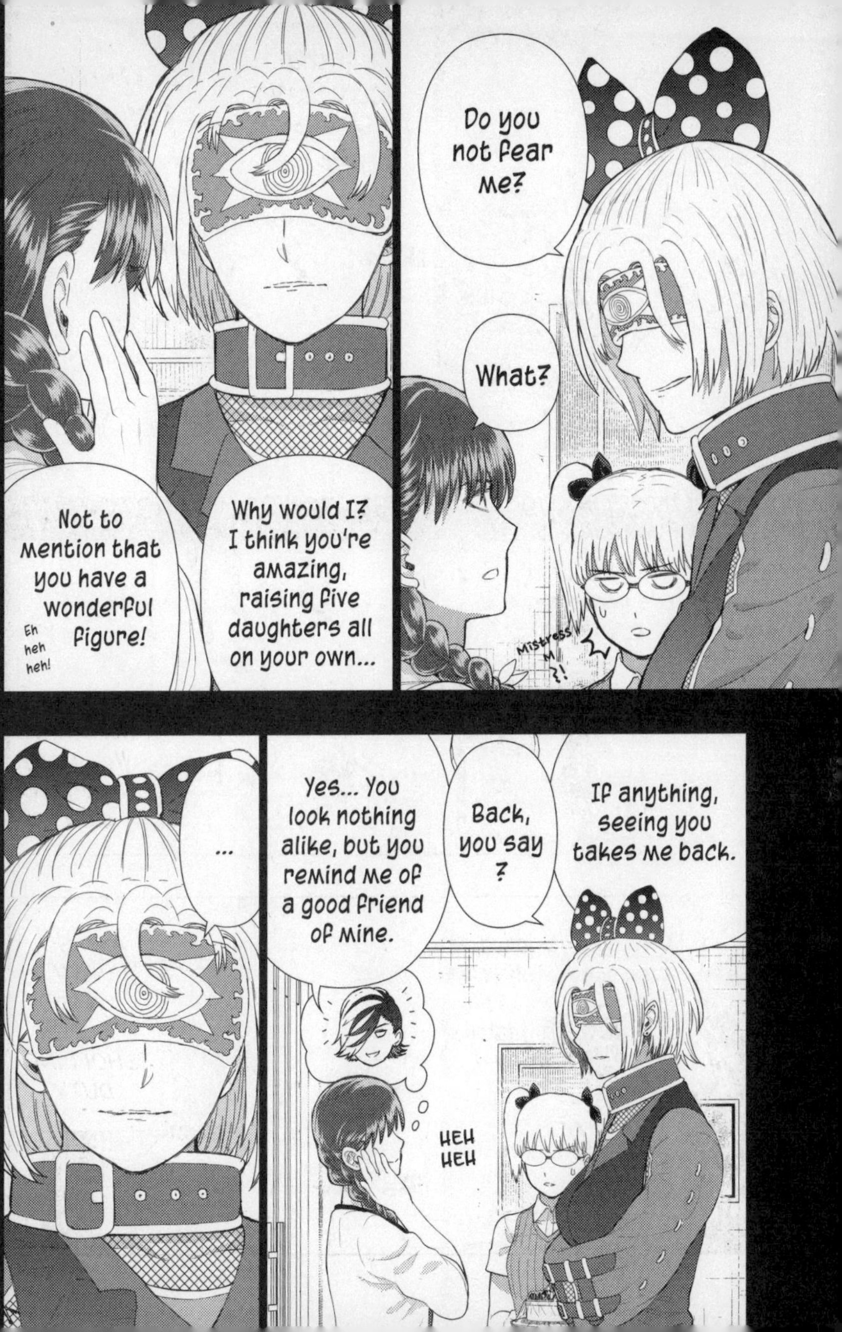
Do you not fear me?
What?
Mistress M?!
Why would I? I think you're amazing, raising five daughters all on your own...
Not to mention that you have a wonderful figure!
Eh heh heh!
If anything, seeing you takes me back.
Back, you say?
Yes... You look nothing alike, but you remind me of a good friend of mine.
HEH HEH
...

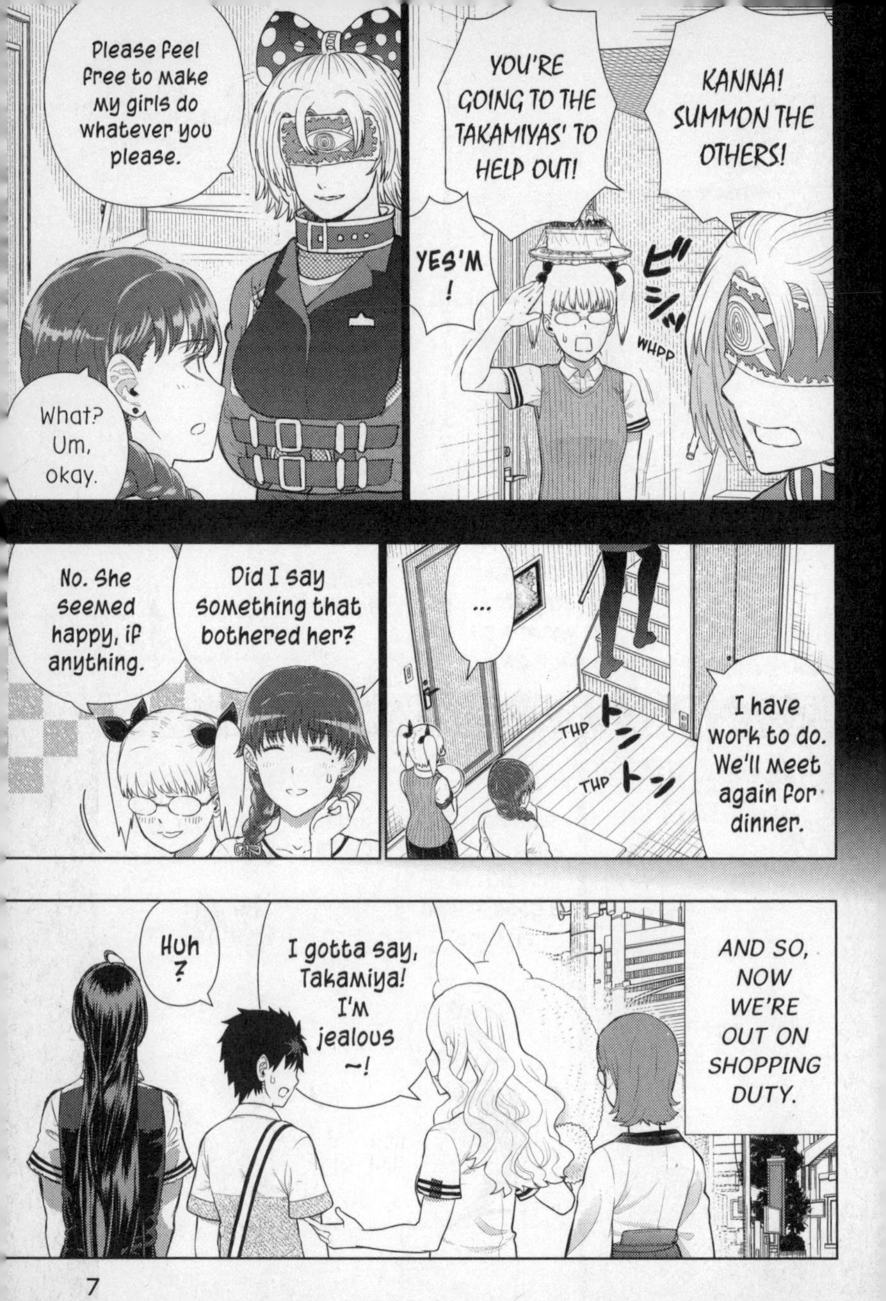
KANNA! SUMMON THE OTHERS!
YOU'RE GOING TO THE TAKAMIYAS' TO HELP OUT!
YES'M!
ビシッ
WHPP
Please feel free to make my girls do whatever you please.
What? Um, okay.
...
I have work to do. We'll meet again for dinner.
トン
THP
トン
THP
Did I say something that bothered her?
No. She seemed happy, if anything.
AND SO, NOW WE'RE OUT ON SHOPPING DUTY.
I gotta say, Takamiya! I'm jealous~!
Huh?

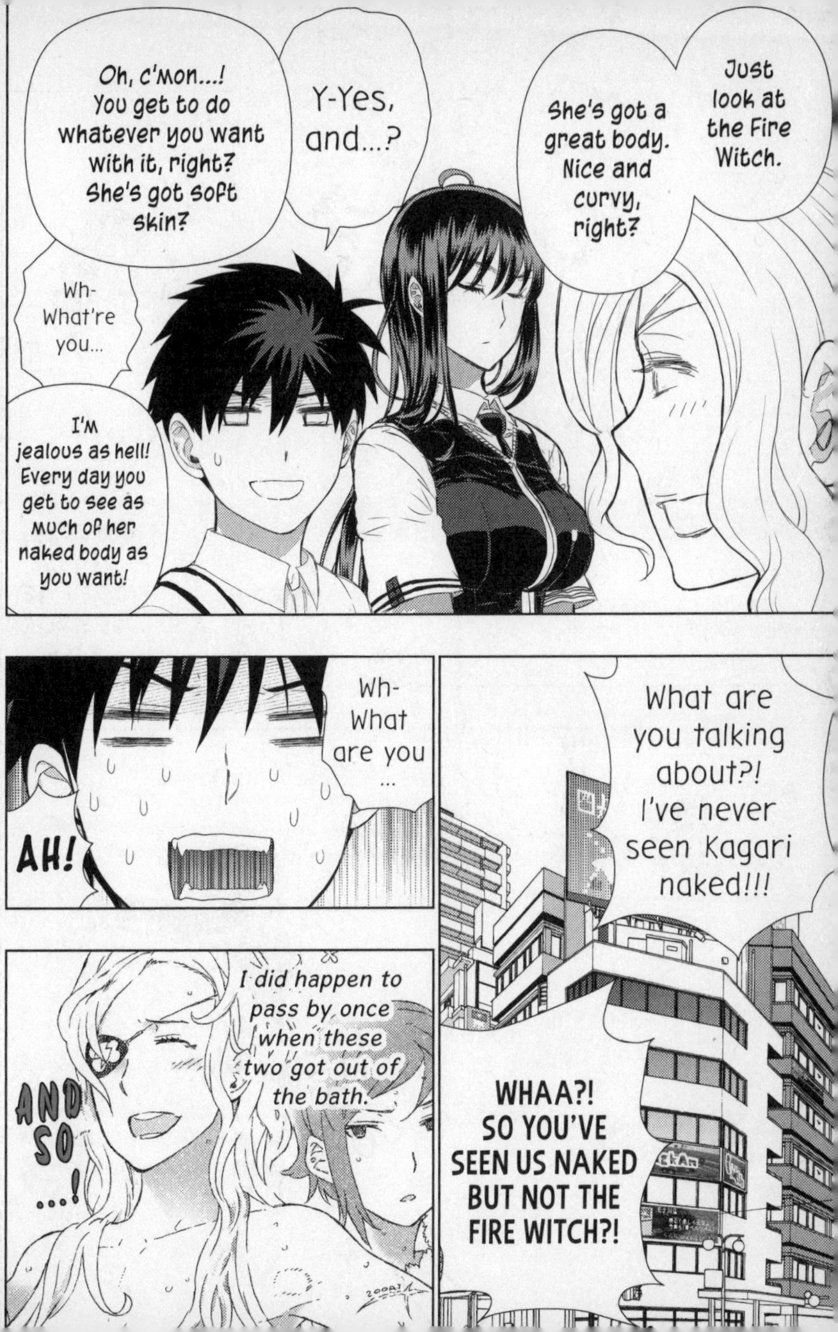
Just look at the Fire Witch.
She's got a great body. Nice and curvy, right?
Y-Yes, and...?
Oh, c'mon...! You get to do whatever you want with it, right? She's got soft skin?
Wh- What're you...
I'm jealous as hell! Every day you get to see as much of her naked body as you want!
What are you talking about?! I've never seen Kagari naked!!!
WHAA?! SO YOU'VE SEEN US NAKED BUT NOT THE FIRE WITCH?!
Wh- What are you ...
AH!
I did happen to pass by once when these two got out of the bath.
AND SO ...!

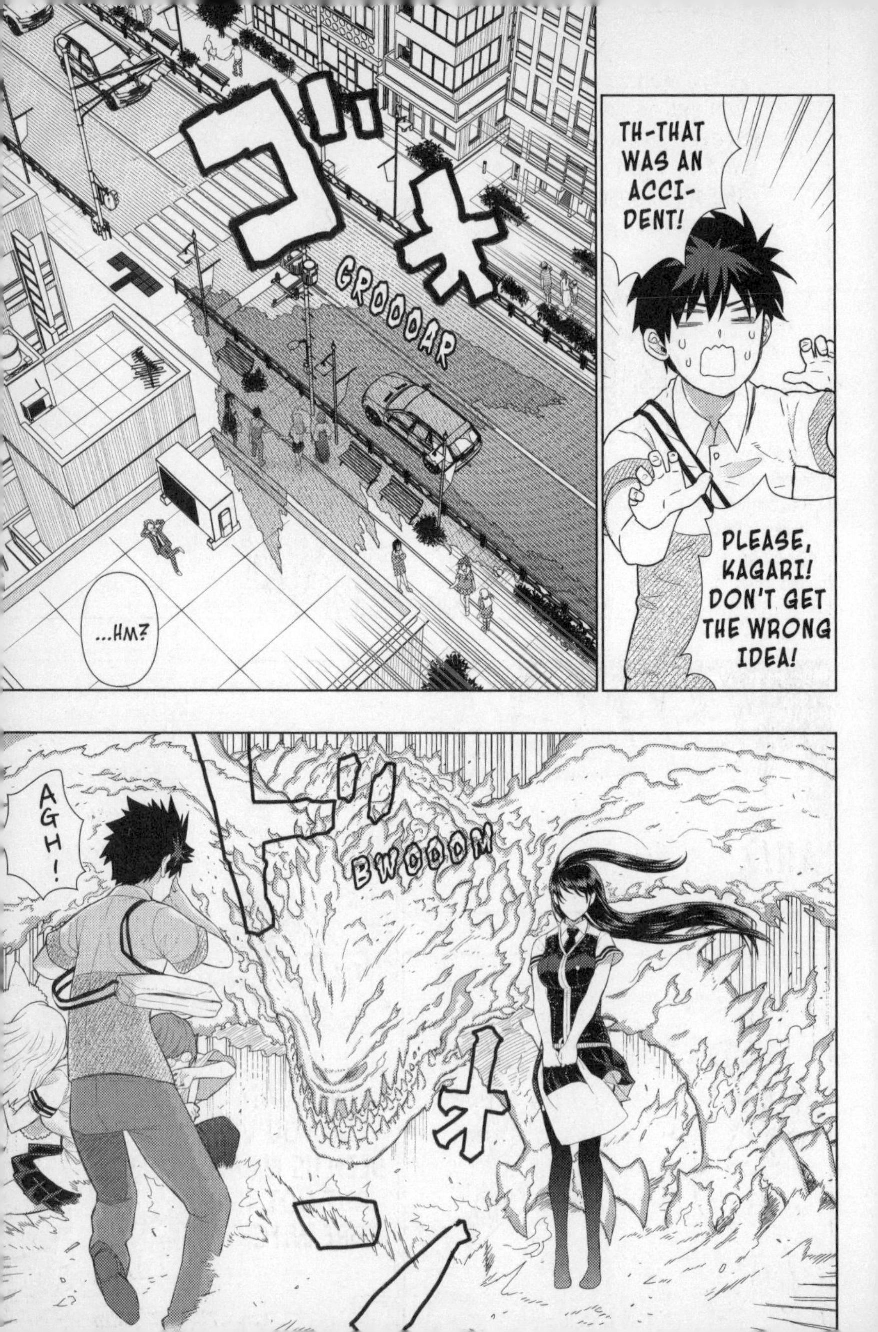
TH-THAT WAS AN ACCI-DENT!
PLEASE, KAGARI! DON'T GET THE WRONG IDEA!
GROOOOAR
...HM?
BWOOOOM
AGH!

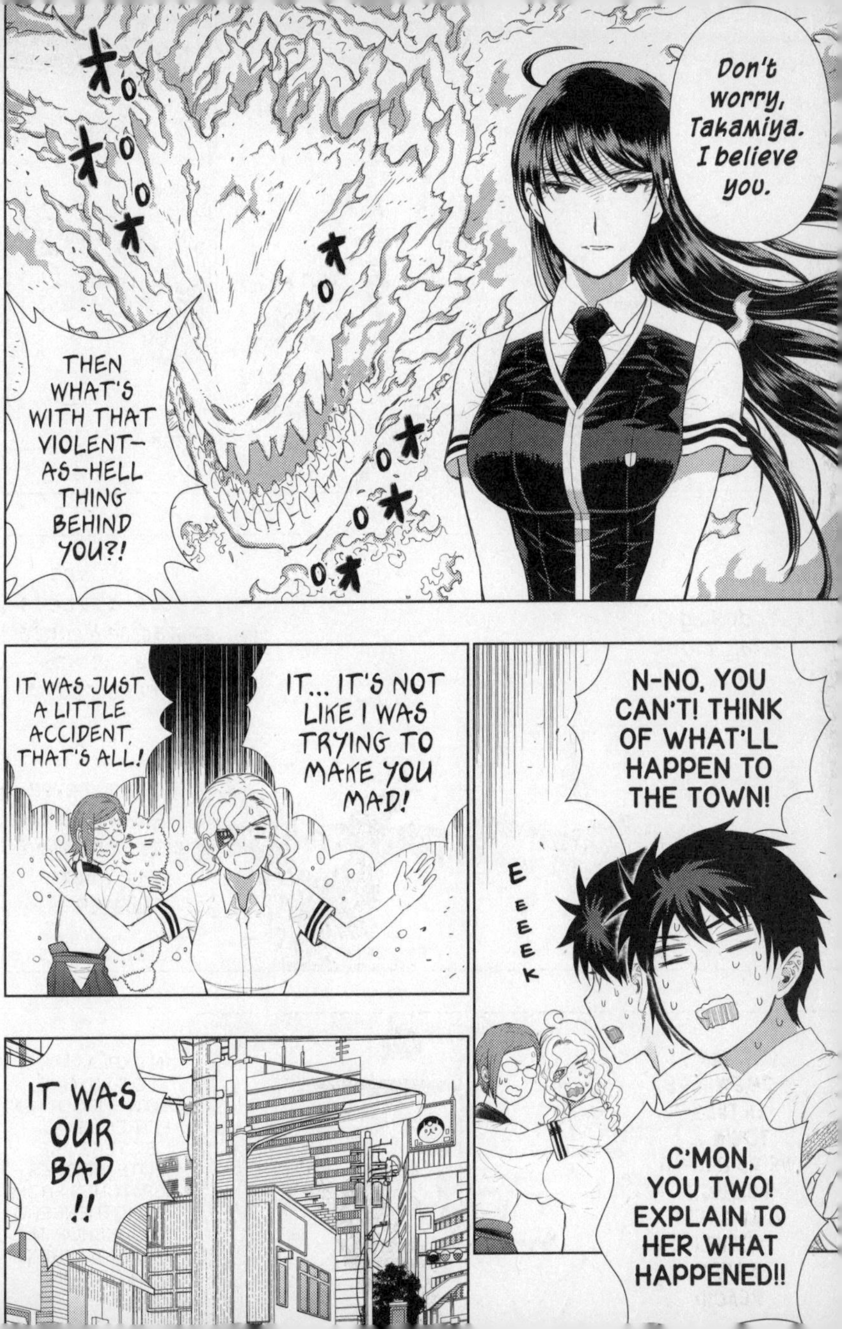
Don't worry, Takamiya. I believe you.
THEN WHAT'S WITH THAT VIOLENT-AS-HELL THING BEHIND YOU?!
N-NO, YOU CAN'T! THINK OF WHAT'LL HAPPEN TO THE TOWN!
EEEEK
C'MON, YOU TWO! EXPLAIN TO HER WHAT HAPPENED!!
IT... IT'S NOT LIKE I WAS TRYING TO MAKE YOU MAD!
IT WAS JUST A LITTLE ACCIDENT, THAT'S ALL!
IT WAS OUR BAD!!

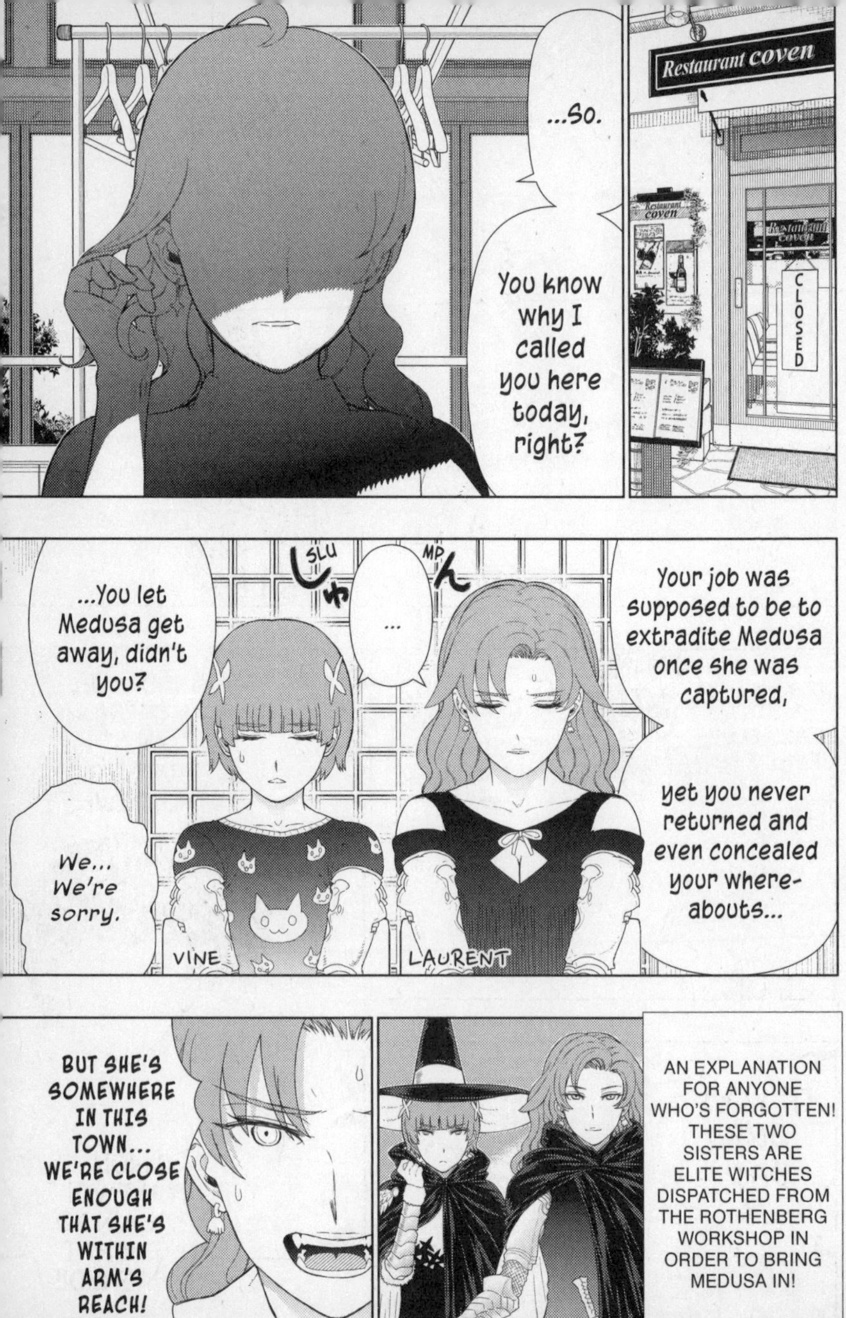
Restaurant coven
Restaurant coven
Restaurant coven
CLOSED
...So.
You know why I called you here today, right?
Your job was supposed to be to extradite Medusa once she was captured,
yet you never returned and even concealed your where-abouts...
MP ん
...
SLU しゅ
...You let Medusa get away, didn't you?
We... We're sorry.
LAURENT
VINE
AN EXPLANATION FOR ANYONE WHO'S FORGOTTEN! THESE TWO SISTERS ARE ELITE WITCHES DISPATCHED FROM THE ROTHENBERG WORKSHOP IN ORDER TO BRING MEDUSA IN!
BUT SHE'S SOMEWHERE IN THIS TOWN... WE'RE CLOSE ENOUGH THAT SHE'S WITHIN ARM'S REACH!

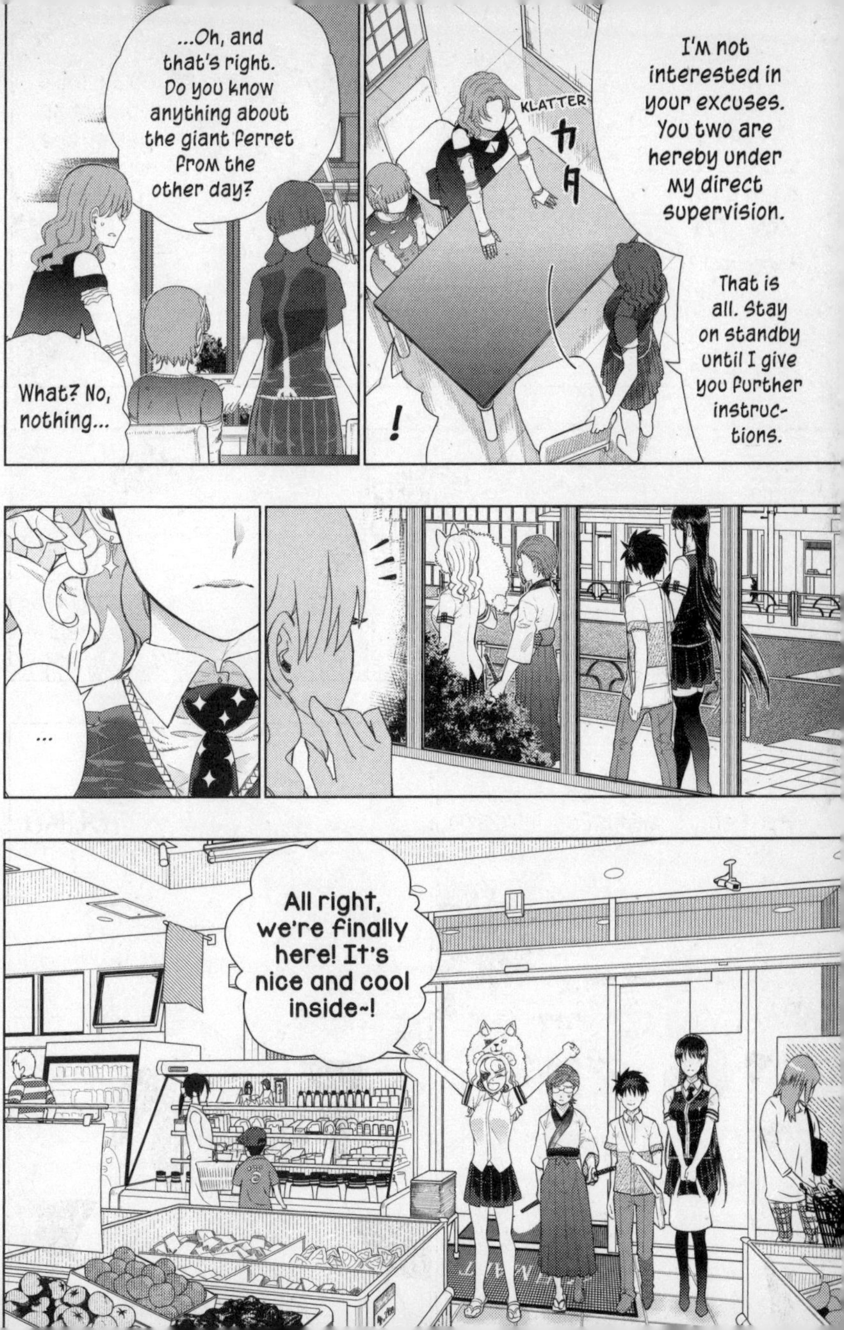
I'm not interested in your excuses. You two are hereby under my direct supervision.
KLATTER
カタ
That is all. Stay on standby until I give you further instructions.
!
...Oh, and that's right. Do you know anything about the giant ferret from the other day?
What? No, nothing...
...
All right, we're finally here! It's nice and cool inside~!

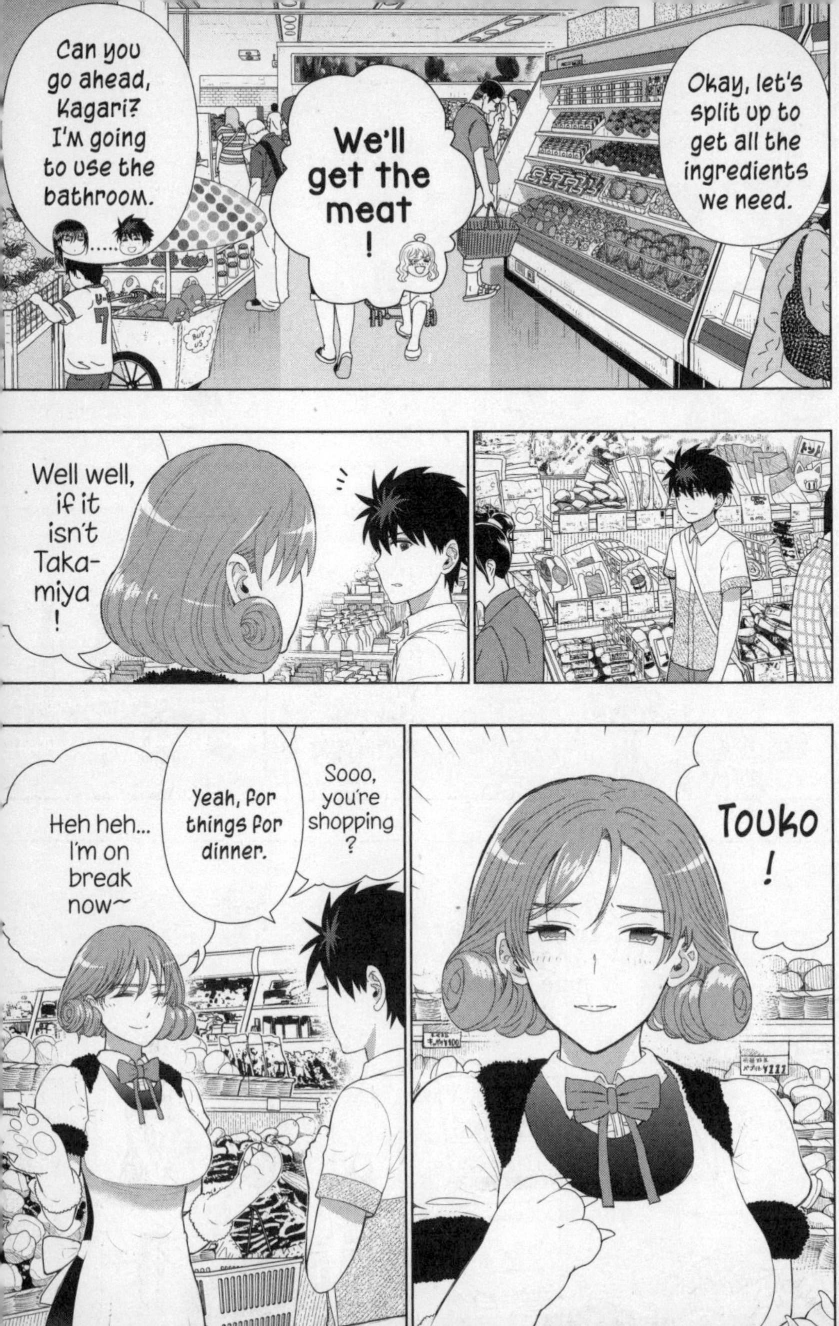
Okay, let's split up to get all the ingredients we need.
We'll get the meat!
Can you go ahead, Kagari? I'm going to use the bathroom.
.....
BUY US
Well well, if it isn't Takamiya!
TOUKO!
Sooo, you're shopping?
Yeah, for things for dinner.
Heh heh... I'm on break now~

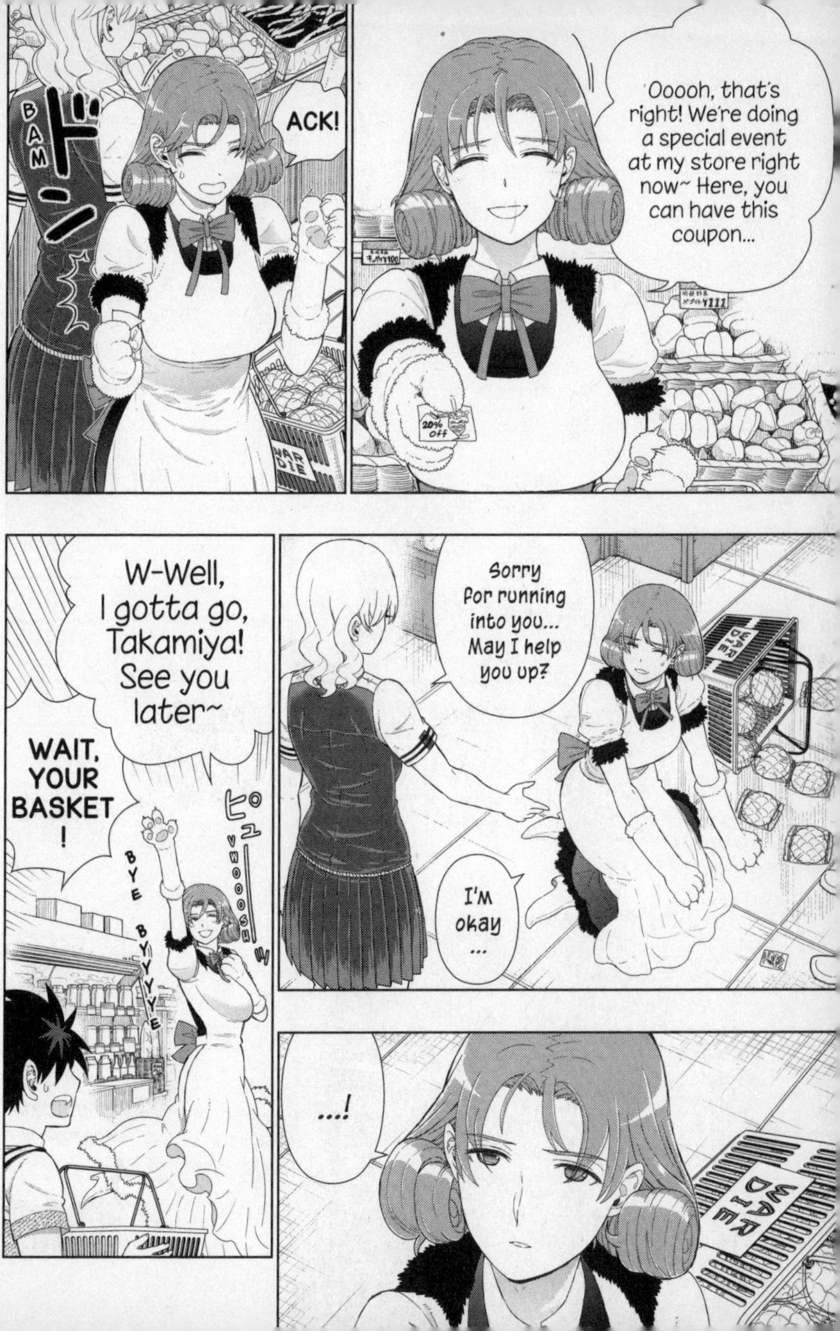
Ooooh, that's right! We're doing a special event at my store right now~ Here, you can have this coupon...
20% Off
BAM
ACK!
Sorry for running into you... May I help you up?
I'm okay ...
WAR DIE
...!
WAR DIE
W-Well, I gotta go, Takamiya! See you later~
WAIT, YOUR BASKET!
VWOOOSH
BYE BYYYYE

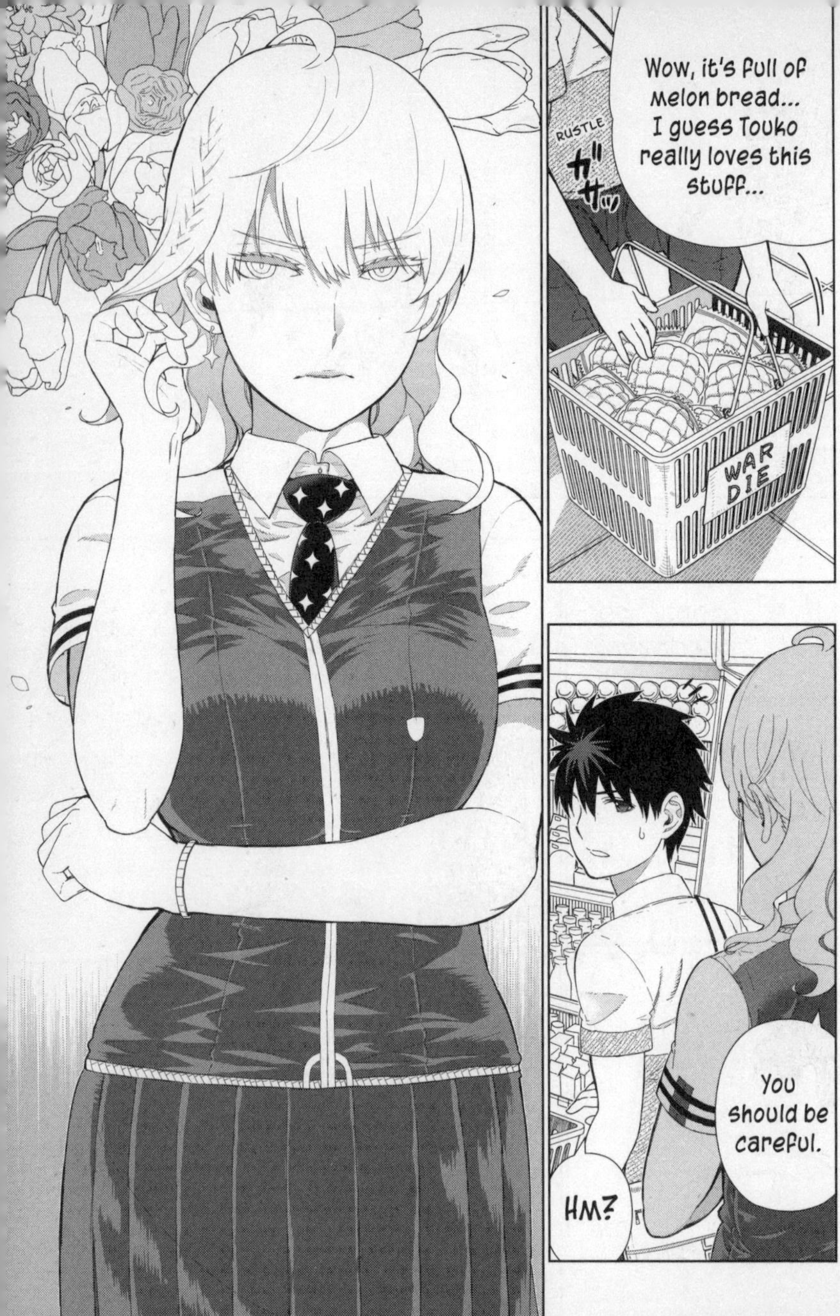

RUSTLE
Wow, it's full of melon bread... I guess Touko really loves this stuff...
WAR DIE
You should be careful.
HM?

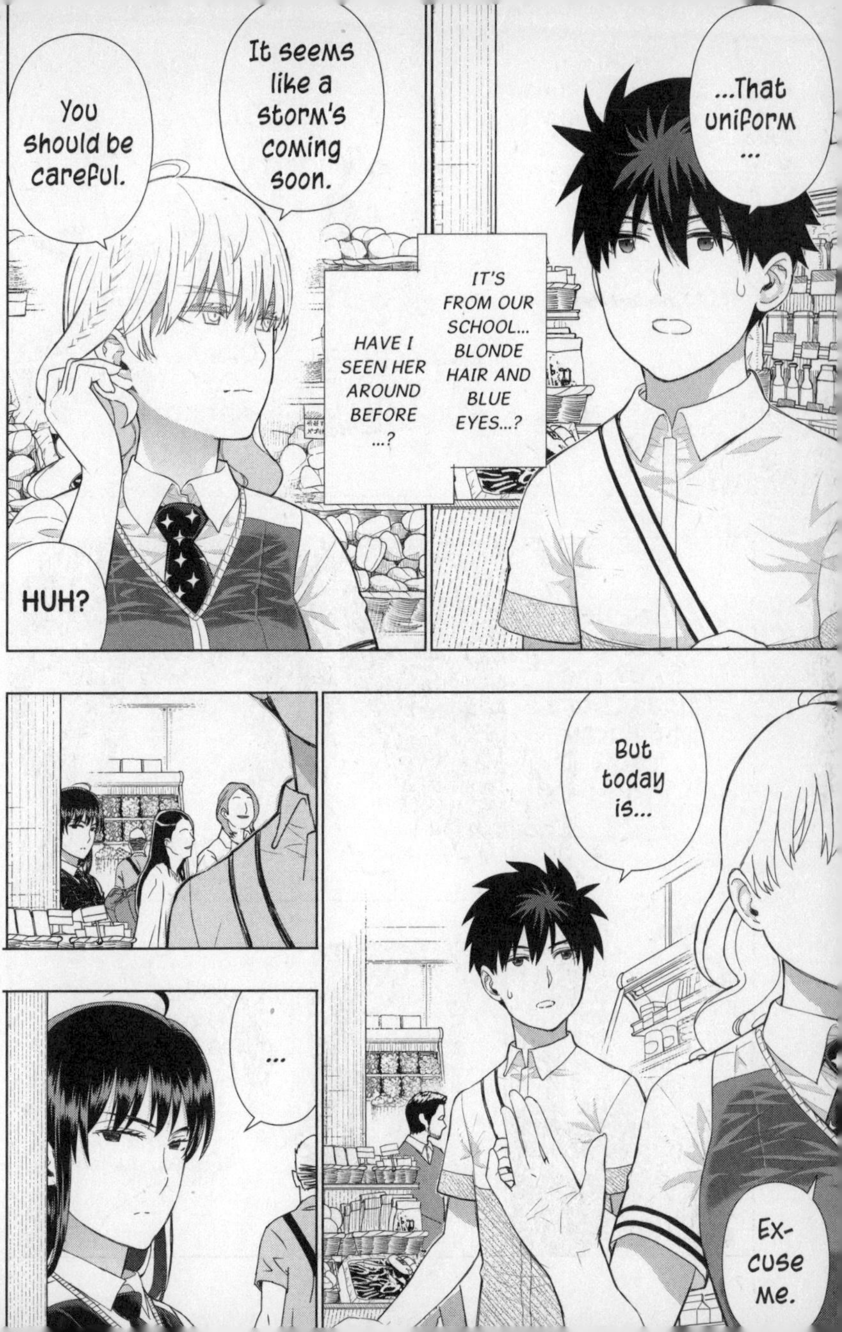
...That uniform ...
IT'S FROM OUR SCHOOL... BLONDE HAIR AND BLUE EYES...?
HAVE I SEEN HER AROUND BEFORE ...?
It seems like a storm's coming soon.
You should be careful.
HUH?
But today is...
Ex-cuse me.
...

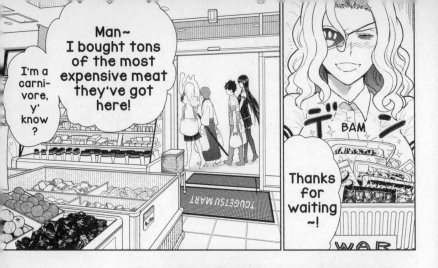

BAM
Thanks for waiting ~!
WAR
Man~ I bought tons of the most expensive meat they've got here!
I'm a carni-vore, y' know ?
TOUGETSU MART
じ
STARE...
Wh- What's wrong?
...No. It's nothing.
And of course I got the nicest cans of Furry chow, too~!
Ah ha ha...
COMIC NET

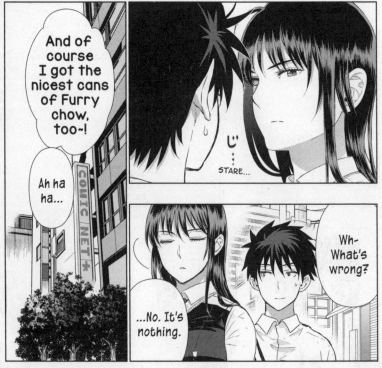

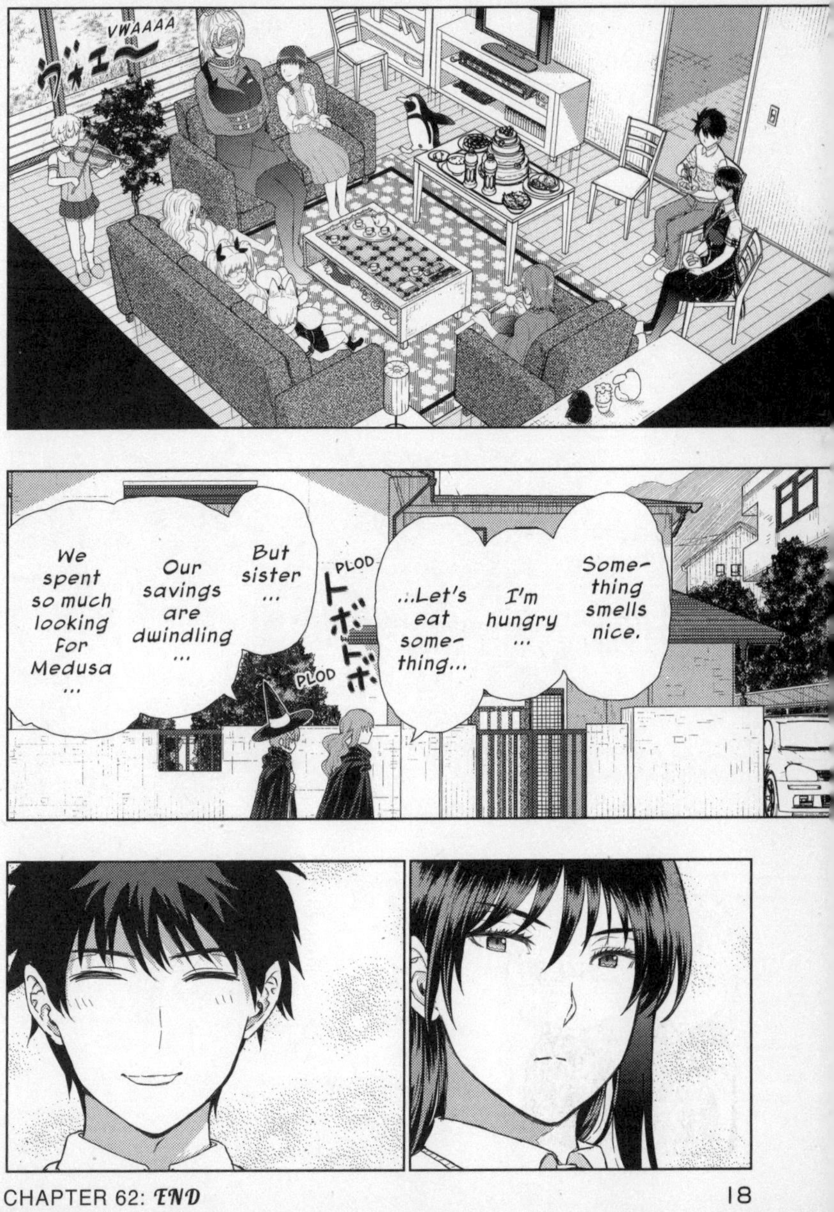
VWAAAA
ヴォエ〜
Something smells nice.
I'm hungry...
...Let's eat something...
PLOD
トボトボ
PLOD
But sister...
Our savings are dwindling...
We spent so much looking for Medusa...

CHAPTER 62: END

Witchcraft Works

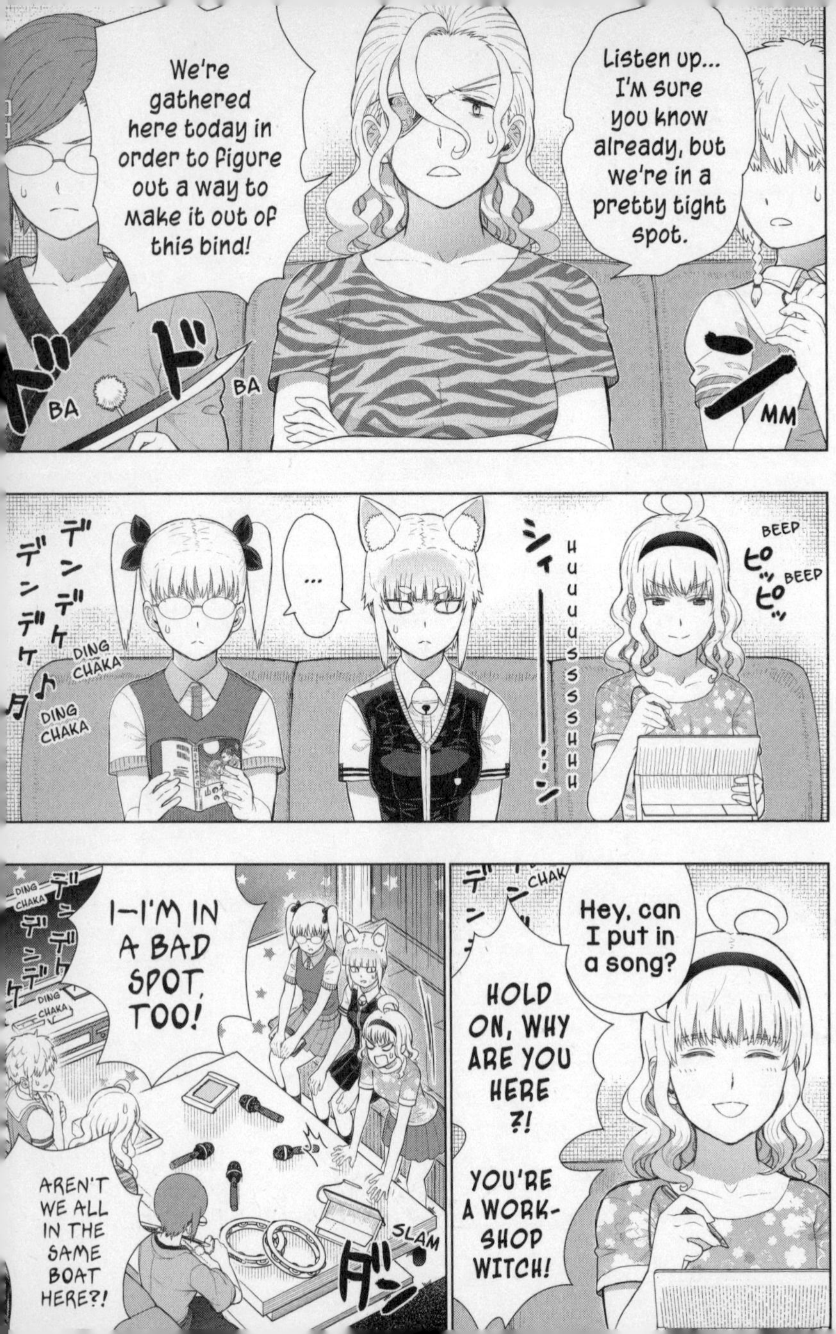
Listen up... I'm sure you know already, but we're in a pretty tight spot.
We're gathered here today in order to figure out a way to make it out of this bind!
MM
BA
BA
BEEP
BEEP
HUUUUSSSSHHHH
...
DING CHAKA
DING CHAKA
Hey, can I put in a song?
HOLD ON, WHY ARE YOU HERE ?!
YOU'RE A WORK-SHOP WITCH!
CHAK
I-I'M IN A BAD SPOT, TOO!
DING CHAKA
DING CHAKA
SLAM
AREN'T WE ALL IN THE SAME BOAT HERE?!

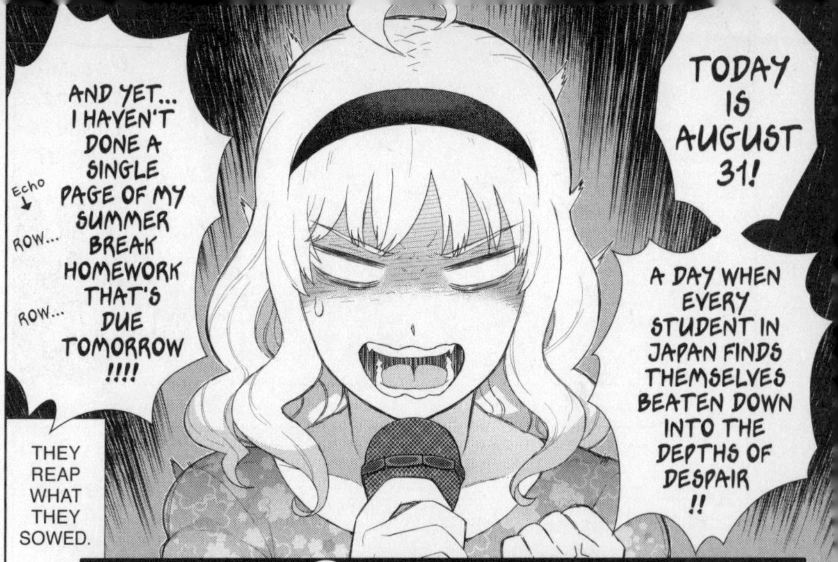
TODAY IS AUGUST 31!
A DAY WHEN EVERY STUDENT IN JAPAN FINDS THEMSELVES BEATEN DOWN INTO THE DEPTHS OF DESPAIR !!
AND YET... I HAVEN'T DONE A SINGLE PAGE OF MY SUMMER BREAK HOMEWORK THAT'S DUE TOMORROW !!!!
Echo
ROW...
ROW...
THEY REAP WHAT THEY SOWED.

CHAPTER 63 Takamiya and the Last Day of Summer Break

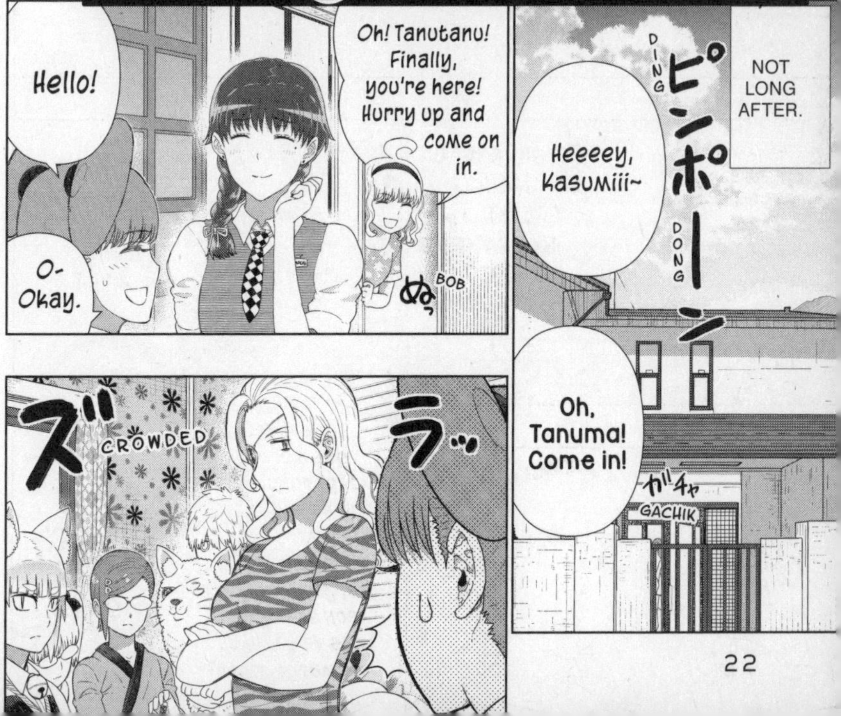
NOT LONG AFTER.
DING
ピンポーン
DONG
Heeeey, Kasumiii~
Oh, Tanuma! Come in!
ガチャ
GACHIK
Oh! Tanutanu! Finally, you're here! Hurry up and come on in.
Hello!
O-Okay.
ぬっ
BOB
ズラッ
CROWDED

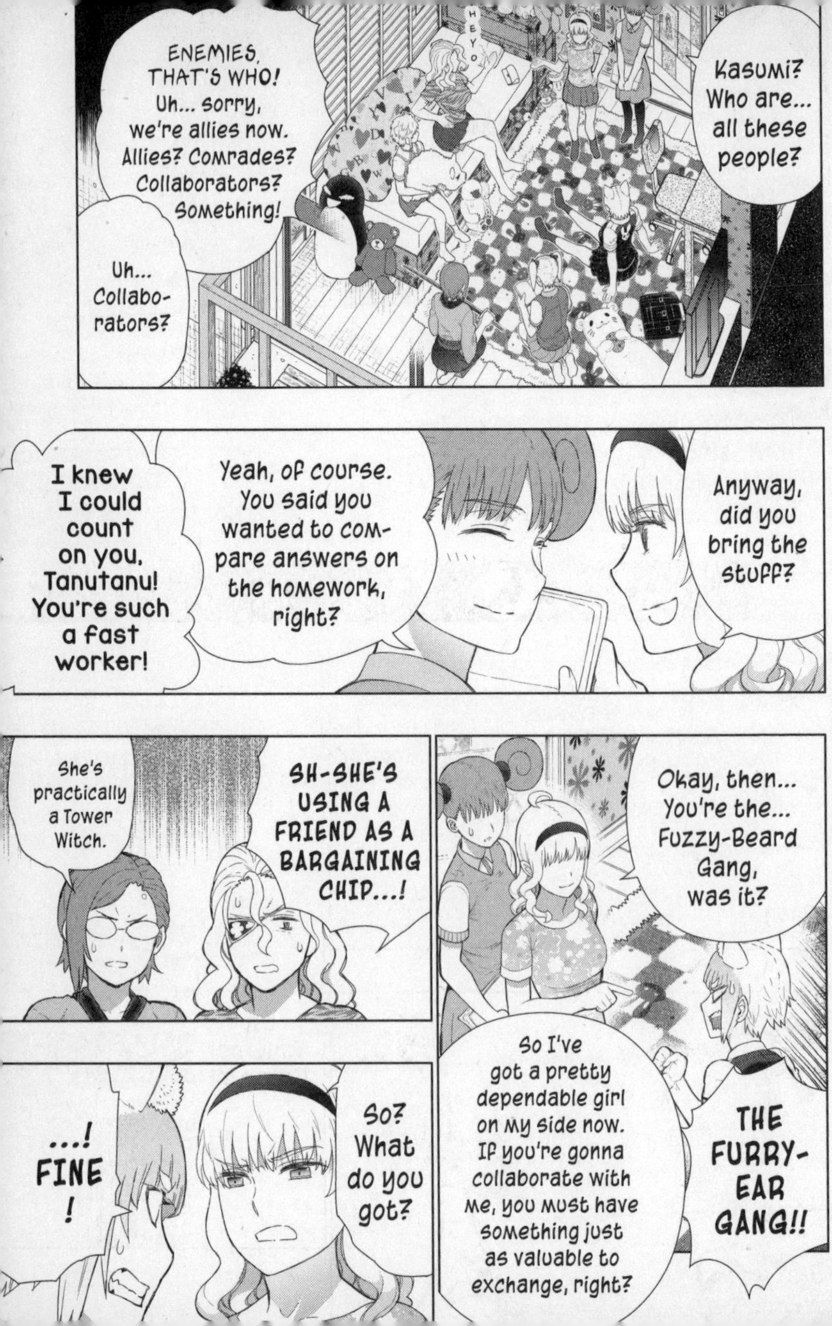

Kasumi? Who are... all these people?
HEYO
ENEMIES, THAT'S WHO! Uh... sorry, we're allies now. Allies? Comrades? Collaborators? Something!
Uh... Collabo-rators?
Anyway, did you bring the stuff?
Yeah, of course. You said you wanted to com-pare answers on the homework, right?
I knew I could count on you, Tanutanu! You're such a fast worker!
Okay, then... You're the... Fuzzy-Beard Gang, was it?
THE FURRY-EAR GANG!!
So I've got a pretty dependable girl on my side now. If you're gonna collaborate with me, you must have something just as valuable to exchange, right?
SH-SHE'S USING A FRIEND AS A BARGAINING CHIP...!
She's practically a Tower Witch.
So? What do you got?
...! FINE!

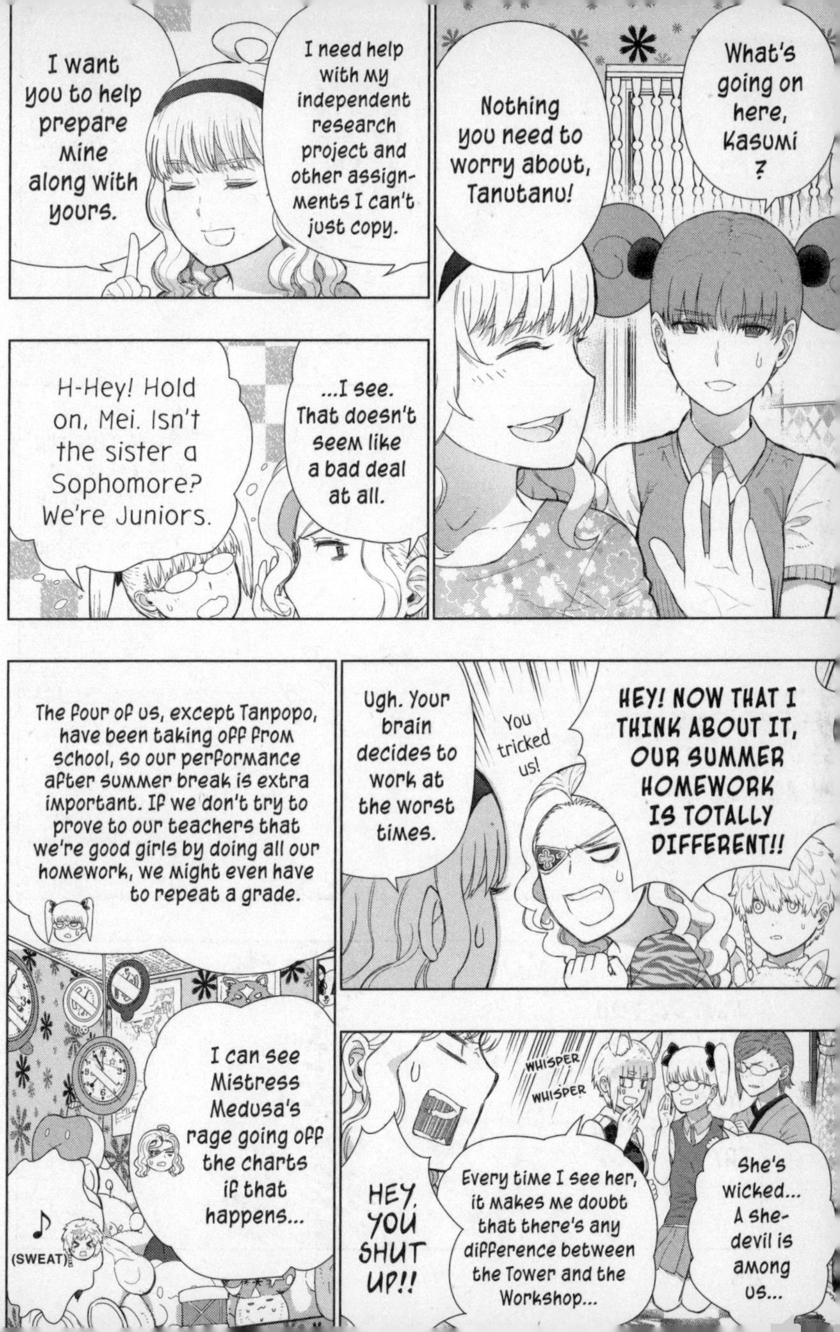
What's going on here, Kasumi?
Nothing you need to worry about, Tanutanu!
I need help with my independent research project and other assignments I can't just copy.
I want you to help prepare mine along with yours.
...I see. That doesn't seem like a bad deal at all.
H-Hey! Hold on, Mei. Isn't the sister a Sophomore? We're Juniors.
HEY! NOW THAT I THINK ABOUT IT, OUR SUMMER HOMEWORK IS TOTALLY DIFFERENT!!
You tricked us!
Ugh. Your brain decides to work at the worst times.
WHISPER
WHISPER
She's wicked... A she-devil is among us...
Every time I see her, it makes me doubt that there's any difference between the Tower and the Workshop...
HEY, YOU SHUT UP!!
The four of us, except Tanpopo, have been taking off from school, so our performance after summer break is extra important. If we don't try to prove to our teachers that we're good girls by doing all our homework, we might even have to repeat a grade.
I can see Mistress Medusa's rage going off the charts if that happens...
♪
(SWEAT)

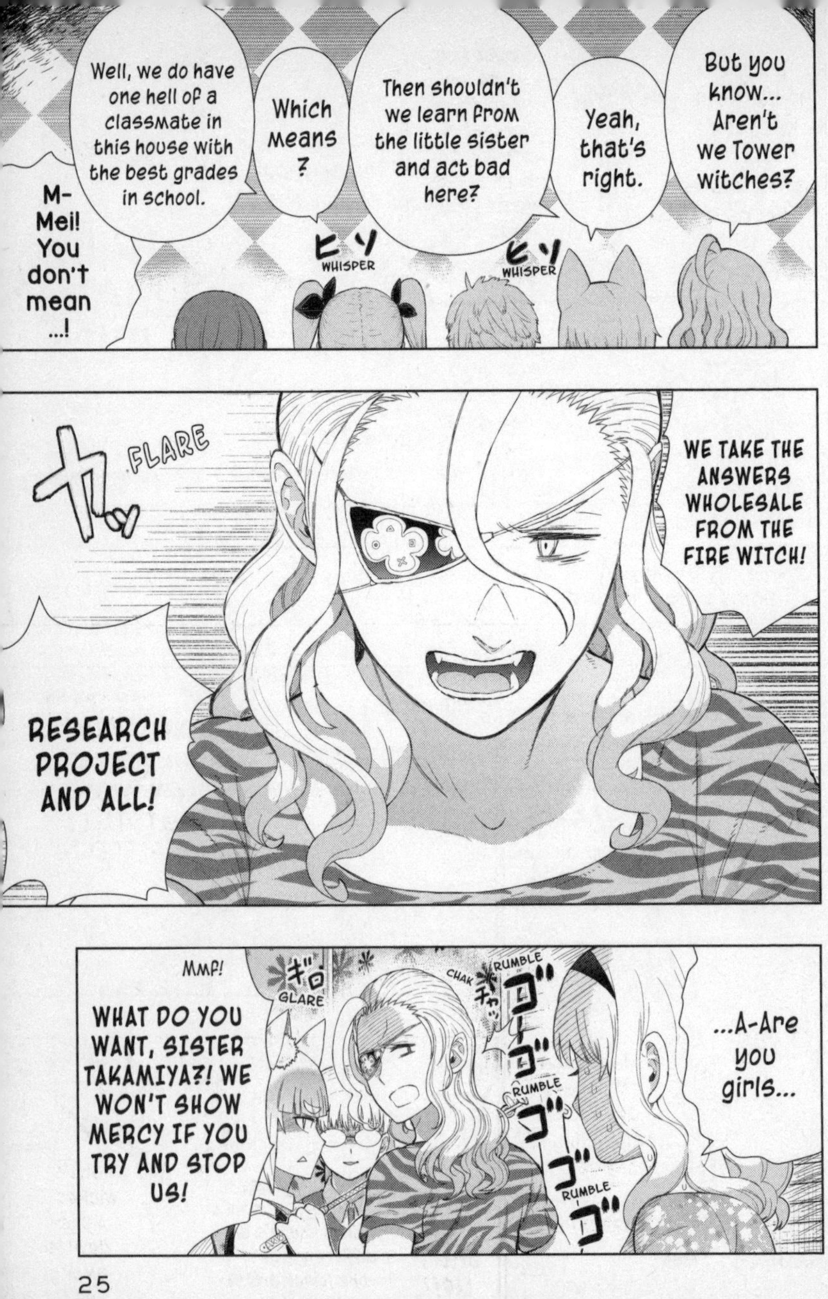
But you know... Aren't we Tower witches?
Yeah, that's right.
ヒソ
WHISPER
Then shouldn't we learn from the little sister and act bad here?
Which means?
ヒソ
WHISPER
Well, we do have one hell of a classmate in this house with the best grades in school.
M-Mei! You don't mean ...!
WE TAKE THE ANSWERS WHOLESALE FROM THE FIRE WITCH!
カッ
FLARE
RESEARCH PROJECT AND ALL!
...A-Are you girls...
ゴゴゴゴ
RUMBLE
RUMBLE
RUMBLE
チャッ
CHAK
ギロ
GLARE
WHAT DO YOU WANT, SISTER TAKAMIYA?! WE WON'T SHOW MERCY IF YOU TRY AND STOP US!
Mmf!

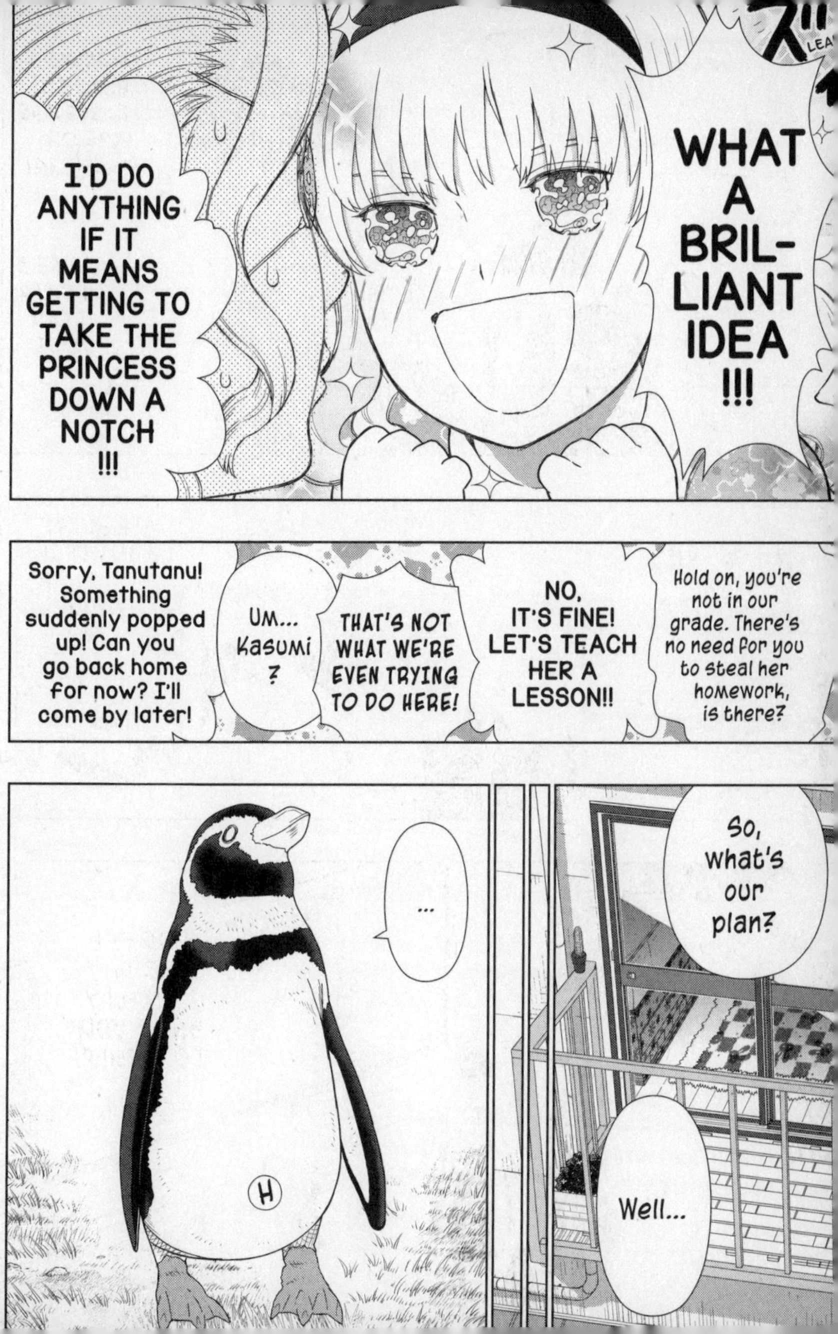
WHAT A BRIL-LIANT IDEA!!!
I'D DO ANYTHING IF IT MEANS GETTING TO TAKE THE PRINCESS DOWN A NOTCH!!!
Hold on, you're not in our grade. There's no need for you to steal her homework, is there?
NO, IT'S FINE! LET'S TEACH HER A LESSON!!
THAT'S NOT WHAT WE'RE EVEN TRYING TO DO HERE!
UM... Kasumi?
Sorry, Tanutanu! Something suddenly popped up! Can you go back home for now? I'll come by later!
So, what's our plan?
Well...
...

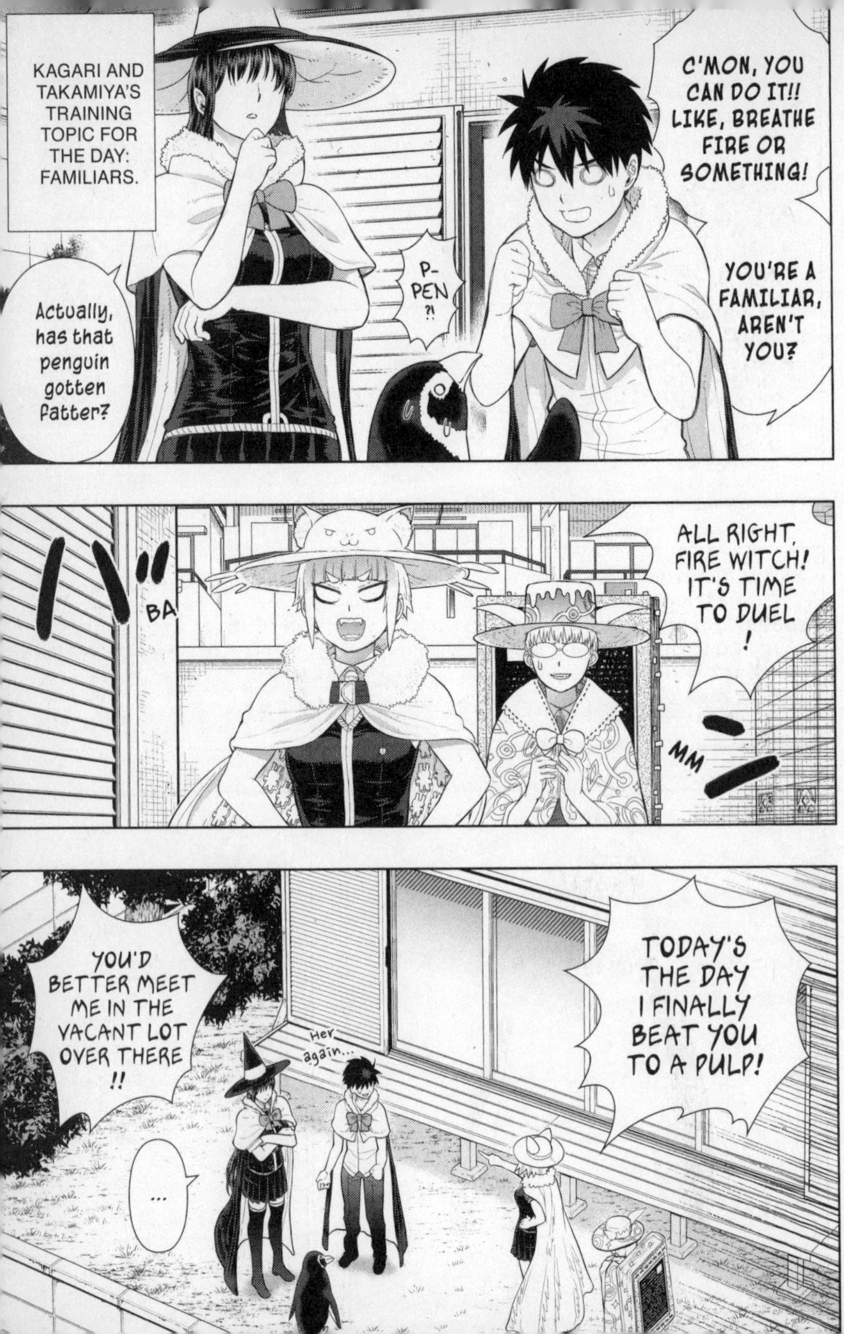
C'MON, YOU CAN DO IT!! LIKE, BREATHE FIRE OR SOMETHING!
YOU'RE A FAMILIAR, AREN'T YOU?
P-PEN?!
KAGARI AND TAKAMIYA'S TRAINING TOPIC FOR THE DAY: FAMILIARS.
Actually, has that penguin gotten fatter?
ALL RIGHT, FIRE WITCH! IT'S TIME TO DUEL!
MM
BA
TODAY'S THE DAY I FINALLY BEAT YOU TO A PULP!
Her again...
YOU'D BETTER MEET ME IN THE VACANT LOT OVER THERE!!
...

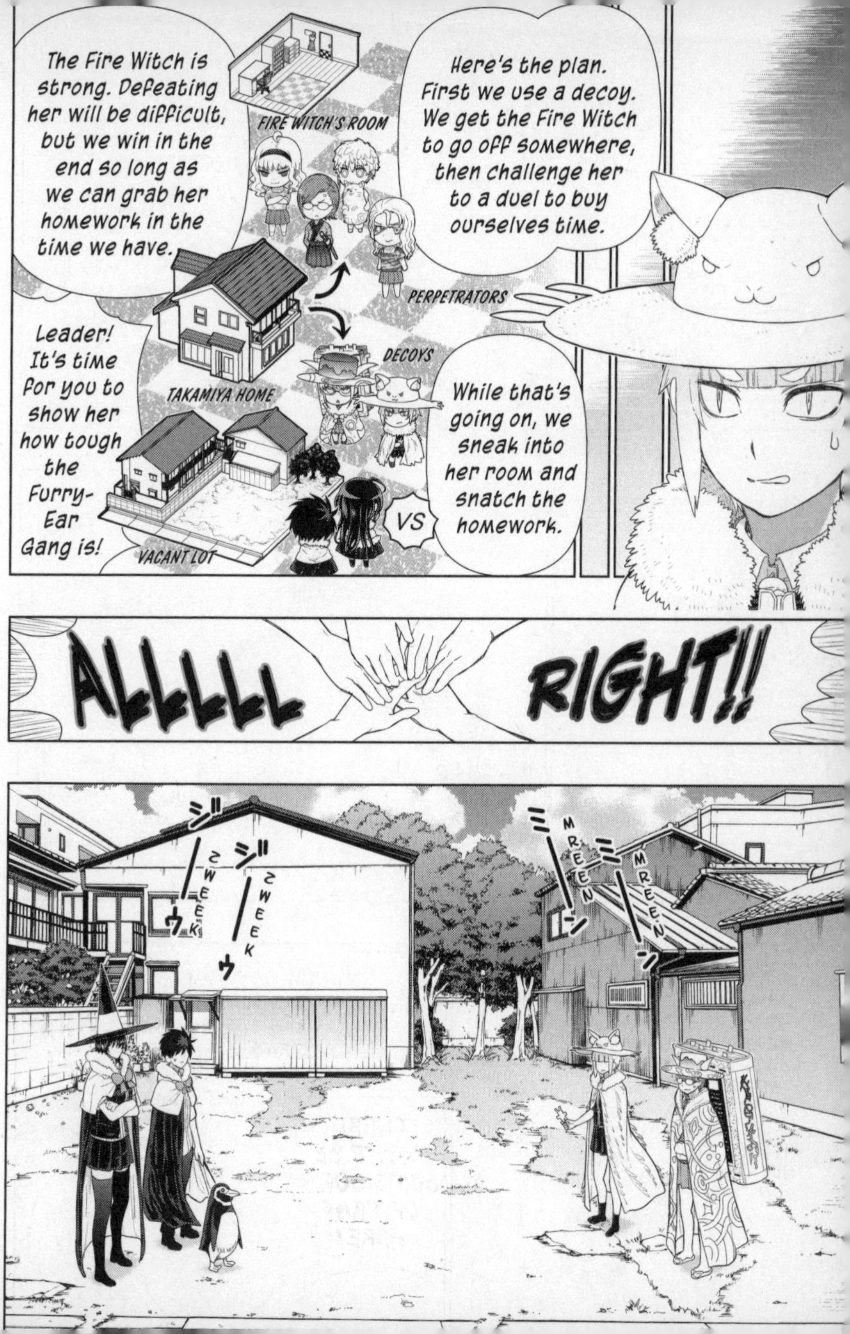
Here's the plan. First we use a decoy. We get the Fire Witch to go off somewhere, then challenge her to a duel to buy ourselves time.
The Fire Witch is strong. Defeating her will be difficult, but we win in the end so long as we can grab her homework in the time we have.
FIRE WITCH'S ROOM
PERPETRATORS
DECOYS
While that's going on, we sneak into her room and snatch the homework.
TAKAMIYA HOME
Leader! It's time for you to show her how tough the Furry-Ear Gang is!
VS
VACANT LOT
ALLLLL RIGHT!!
MREEN
MREEN
ZWEEK
ZWEEK

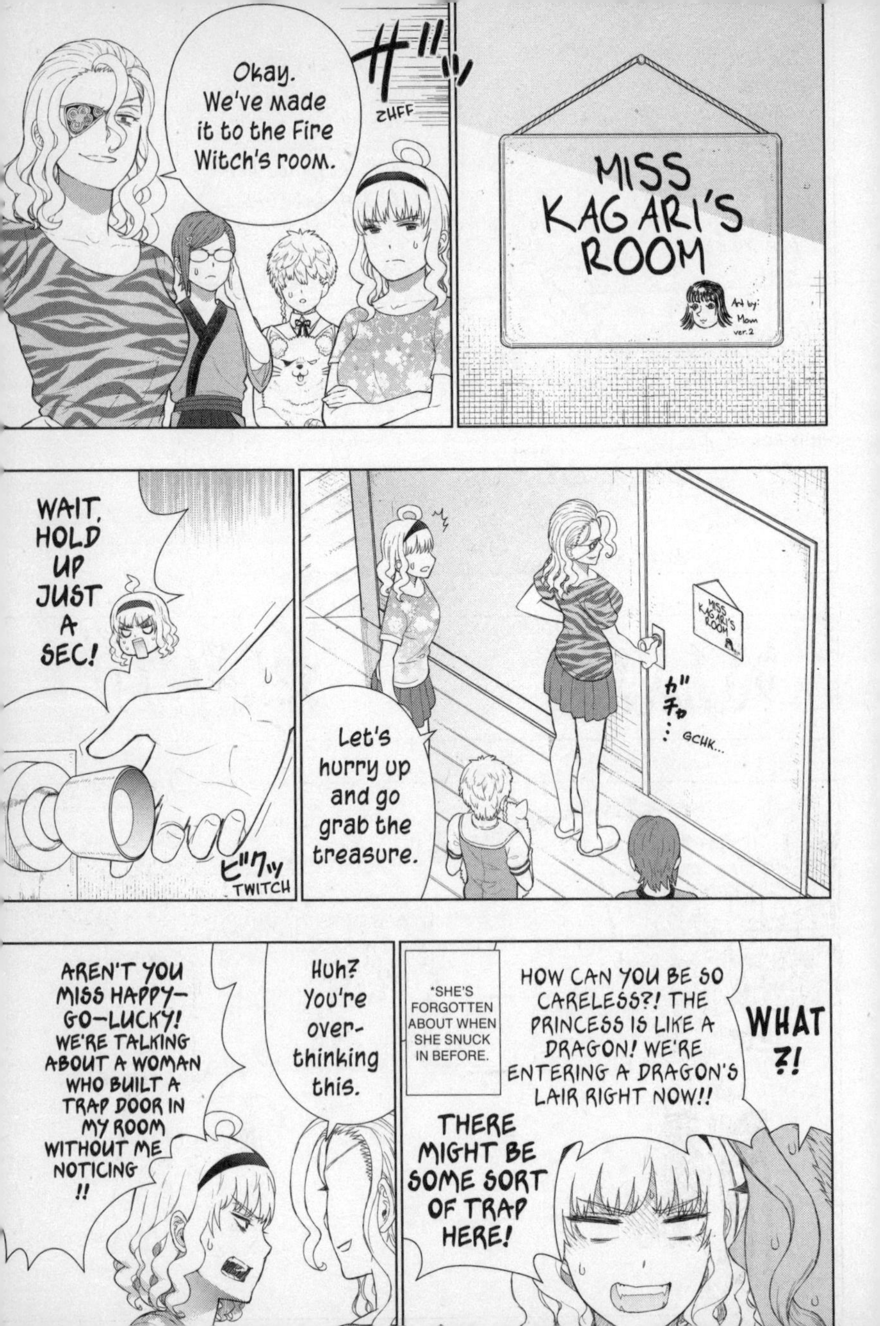
MISS KAGARI'S ROOM
Art by: Mom ver.2
ZHFF
Okay. We've made it to the Fire Witch's room.
MISS KAGARI'S ROOM
GCHK...
Let's hurry up and go grab the treasure.
WAIT, HOLD UP JUST A SEC!
TWITCH
WHAT?!
HOW CAN YOU BE SO CARELESS?! THE PRINCESS IS LIKE A DRAGON! WE'RE ENTERING A DRAGON'S LAIR RIGHT NOW!!
*SHE'S FORGOTTEN ABOUT WHEN SHE SNUCK IN BEFORE.
THERE MIGHT BE SOME SORT OF TRAP HERE!
Huh? You're over-thinking this.
AREN'T YOU MISS HAPPY-GO-LUCKY! WE'RE TALKING ABOUT A WOMAN WHO BUILT A TRAP DOOR IN MY ROOM WITHOUT ME NOTICING!!

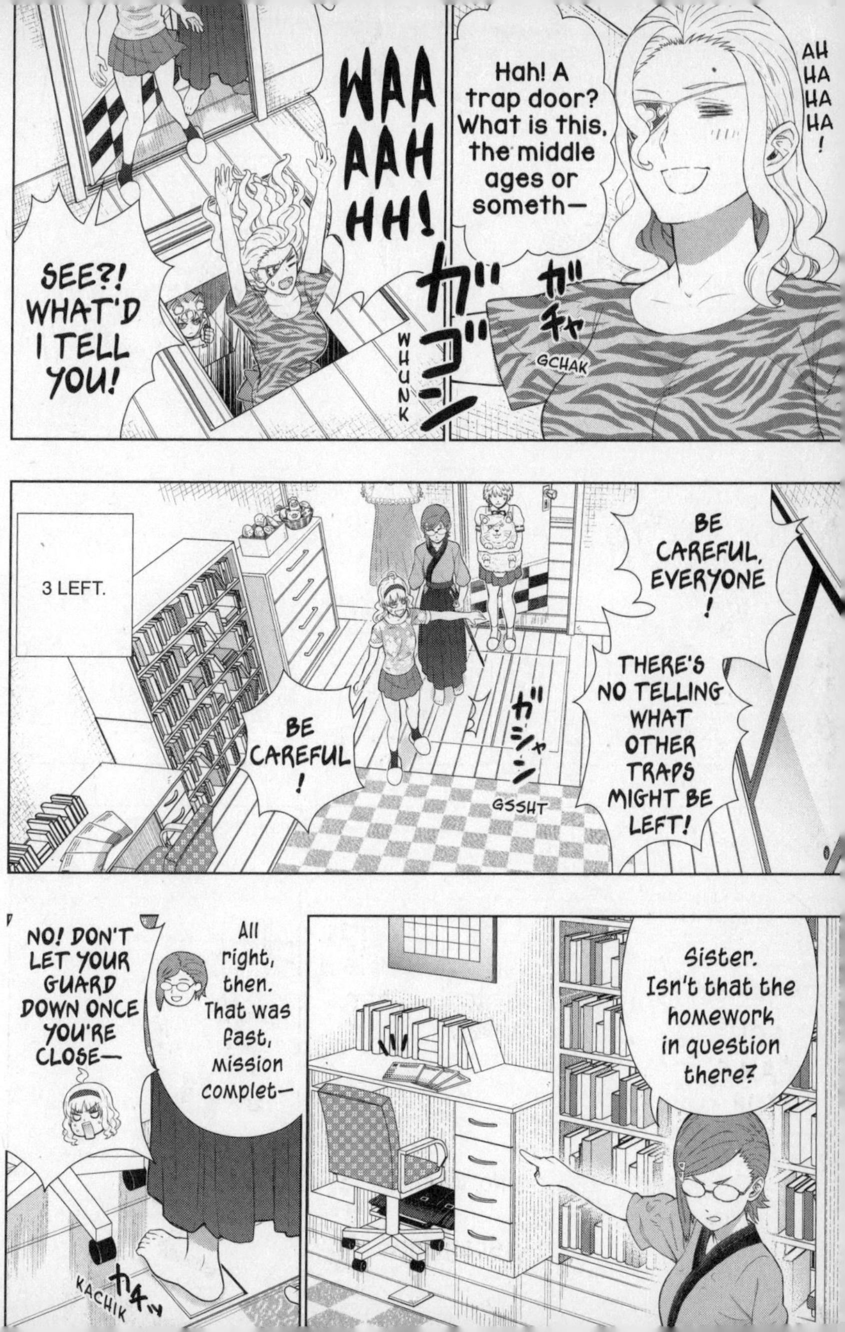

Hah! A trap door? What is this, the middle ages or someth—
AH HA HA HA!
ガチャ
GCHAK
WAAAAHHH!
ガゴン
WHUNK
SEE?! WHAT'D I TELL YOU!
BE CAREFUL, EVERYONE!
THERE'S NO TELLING WHAT OTHER TRAPS MIGHT BE LEFT!
ガシャン
GSSHT
BE CAREFUL!
3 LEFT.
Sister. Isn't that the homework in question there?
All right, then. That was fast, mission complet—
NO! DON'T LET YOUR GUARD DOWN ONCE YOU'RE CLOSE—
カチッ
KACHIK

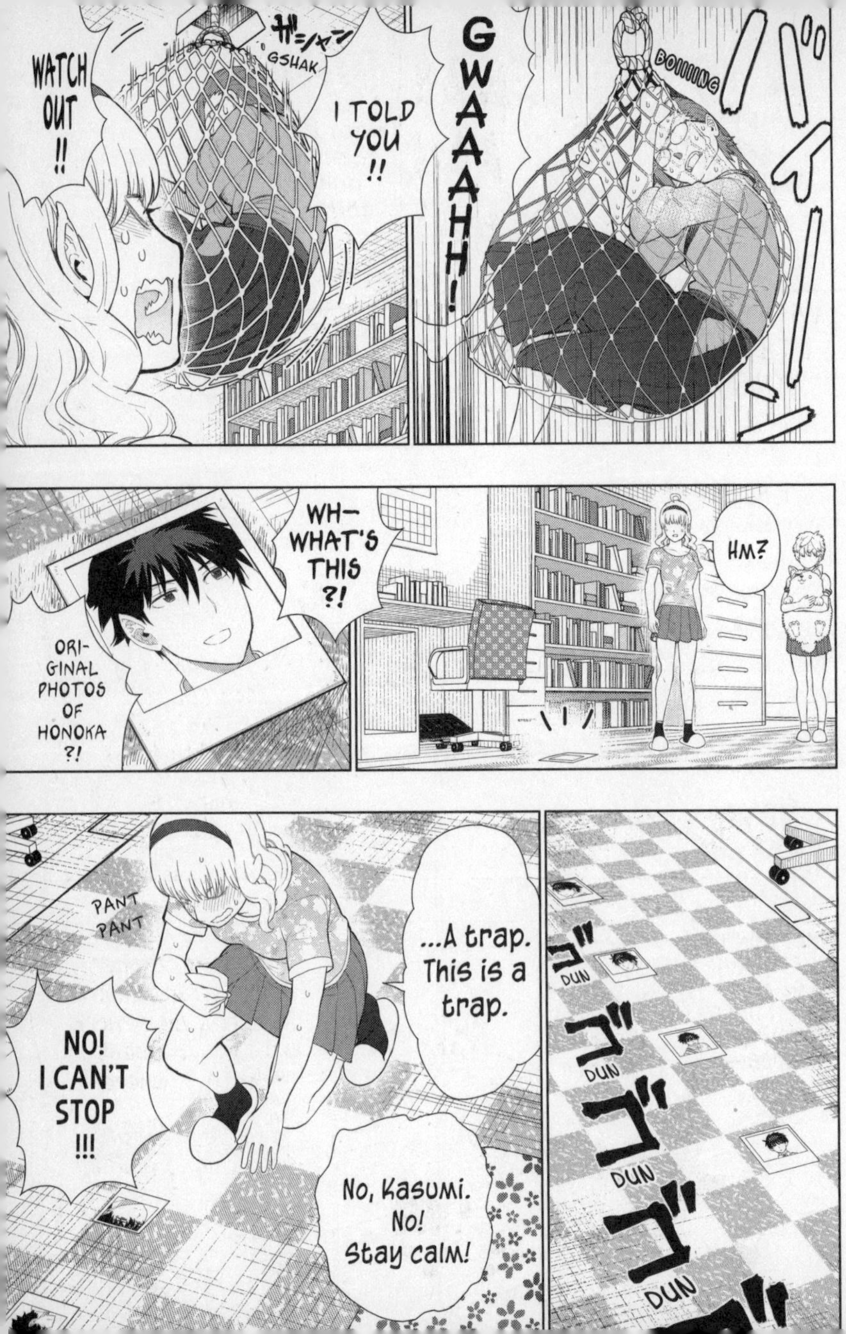

BOIIIING
GWAAAHH!
I TOLD YOU!!
GSHAK
WATCH OUT!!
HM?
WH-WHAT'S THIS?!
ORIGINAL PHOTOS OF HONOKA?!
DUN
DUN
DUN
DUN
...A trap. This is a trap.
PANT PANT
NO! I CAN'T STOP!!!
No, Kasumi. No! Stay calm!

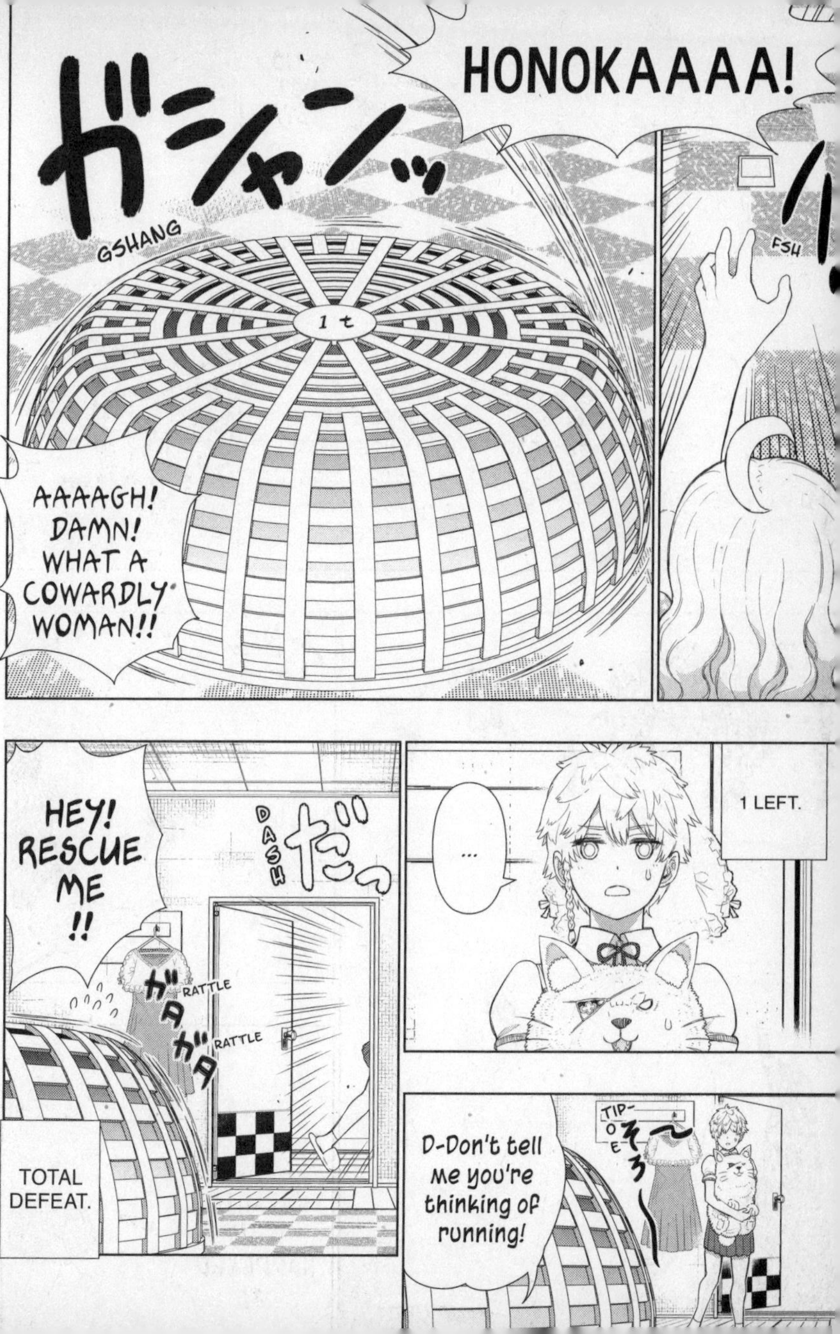
HONOKAAAA!
FSH
ガシャンッ
GSHANG
AAAAGH! DAMN! WHAT A COWARDLY WOMAN!!
1 LEFT.
...
TIP-TOE
D-Don't tell me you're thinking of running!
HEY! RESCUE ME !!
DASH
RATTLE
RATTLE
TOTAL DEFEAT.

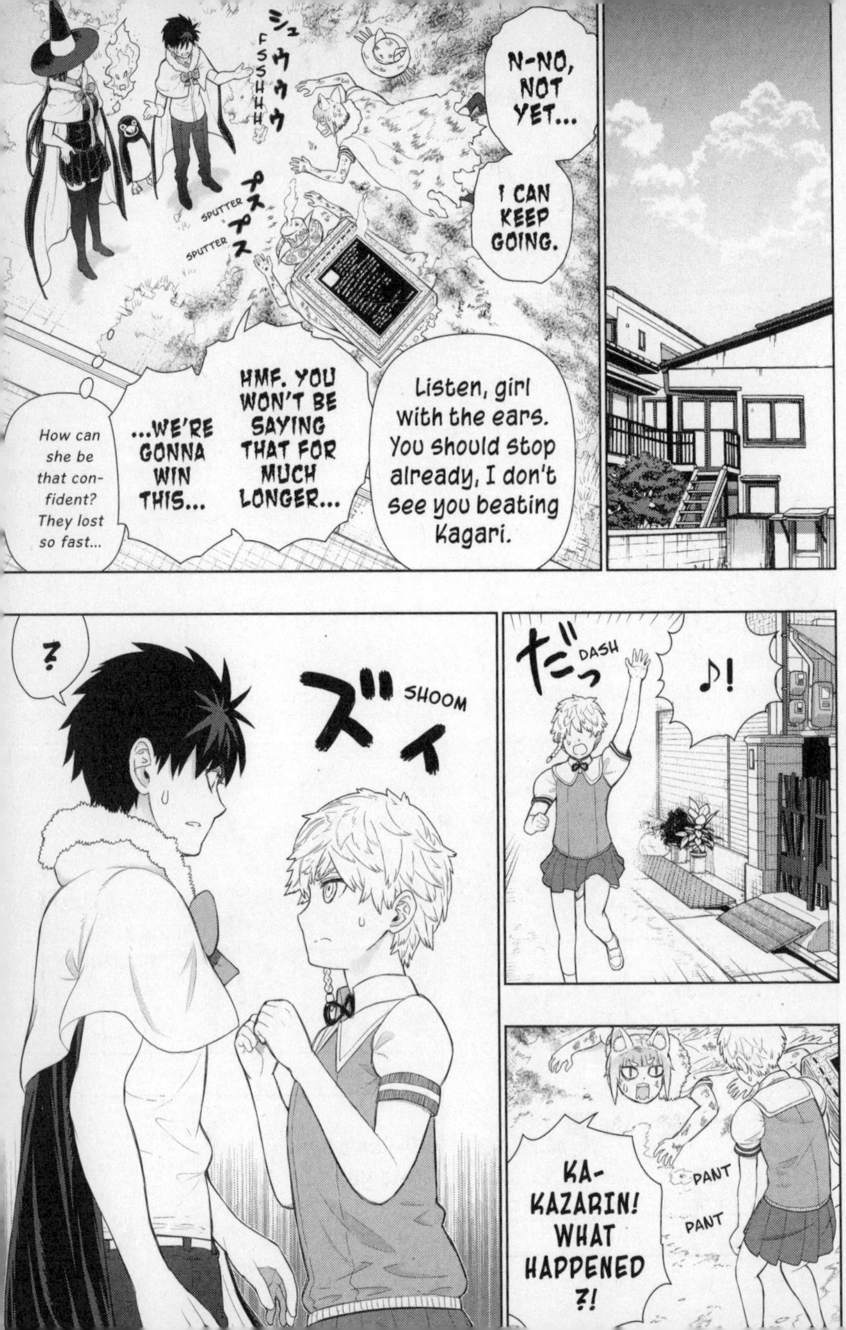

N-NO, NOT YET...
I CAN KEEP GOING.
シュウウウ FSSHHH
プスプス SPUTTER SPUTTER
Listen, girl with the ears. You should stop already, I don't see you beating Kagari.
HMF. YOU WON'T BE SAYING THAT FOR MUCH LONGER...
...WE'RE GONNA WIN THIS...
How can she be that con-fident? They lost so fast...
だっ DASH
♪!
KA-KAZARIN! WHAT HAPPENED?!
PANT
PANT
?
ズイ SHOOM

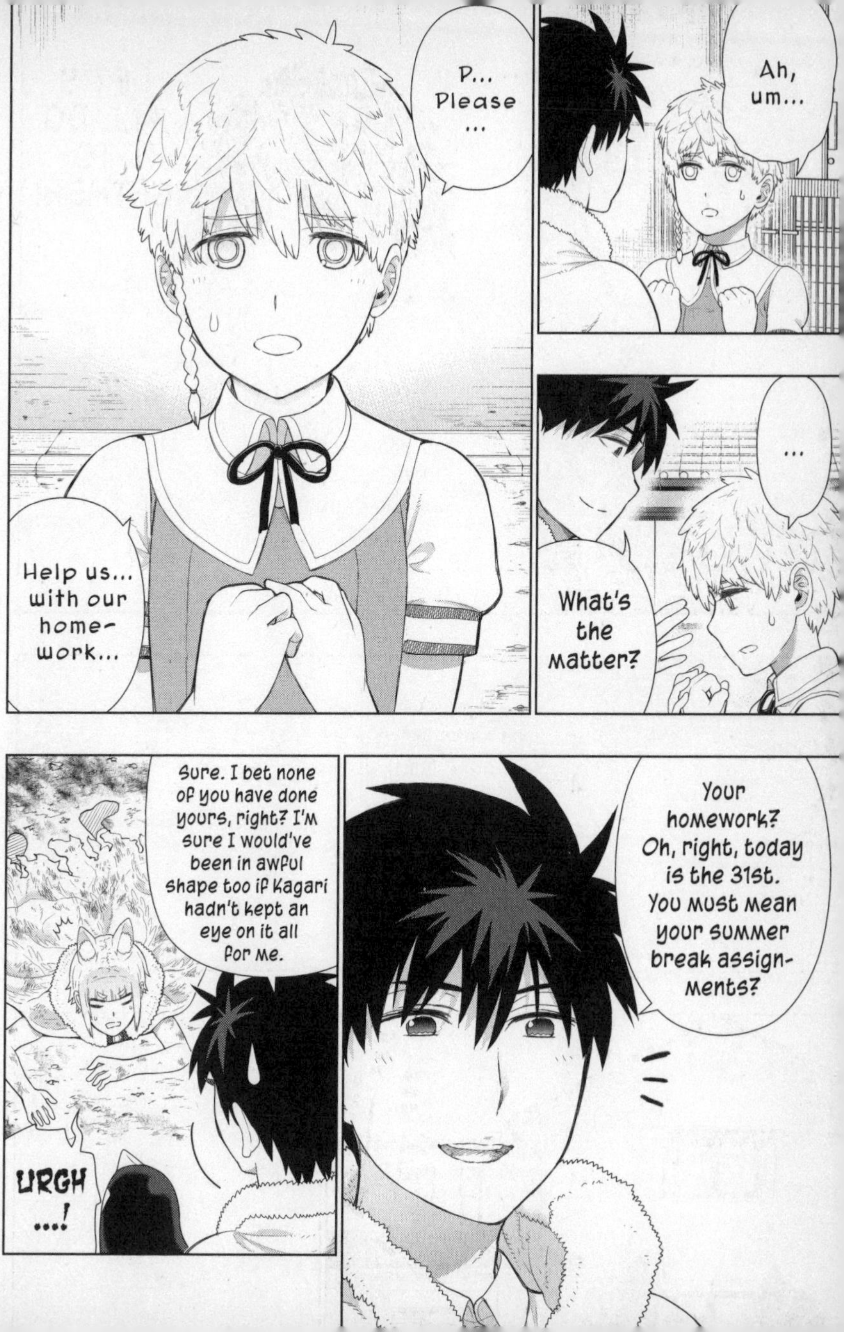
Ah, um...
...
What's the matter?
P... Please ...
Help us... with our home-work...
Your homework? Oh, right, today is the 31st. You must mean your summer break assign-ments?
Sure. I bet none of you have done yours, right? I'm sure I would've been in awful shape too if Kagari hadn't kept an eye on it all for me.
URGH ...!

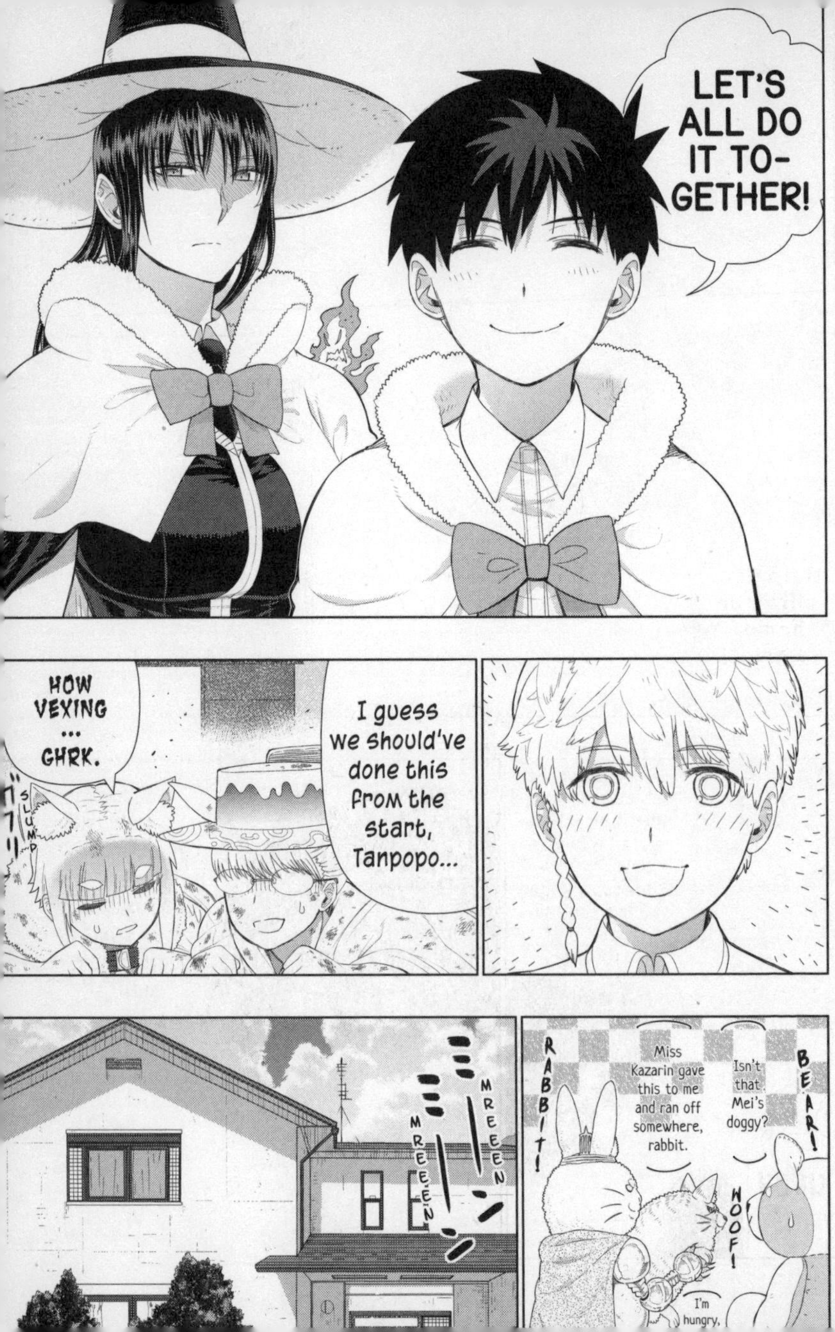
LET'S ALL DO IT TO-GETHER!
I guess we should've done this from the start, Tanpopo...
HOW VEXING ... GHRK.
SLUMP
BEAR!
Isn't that Mei's doggy?
Miss Kazarin gave this to me and ran off somewhere, rabbit.
RABBIT!
WOOF!
I'm hungry,
MREEEN
MREEEN

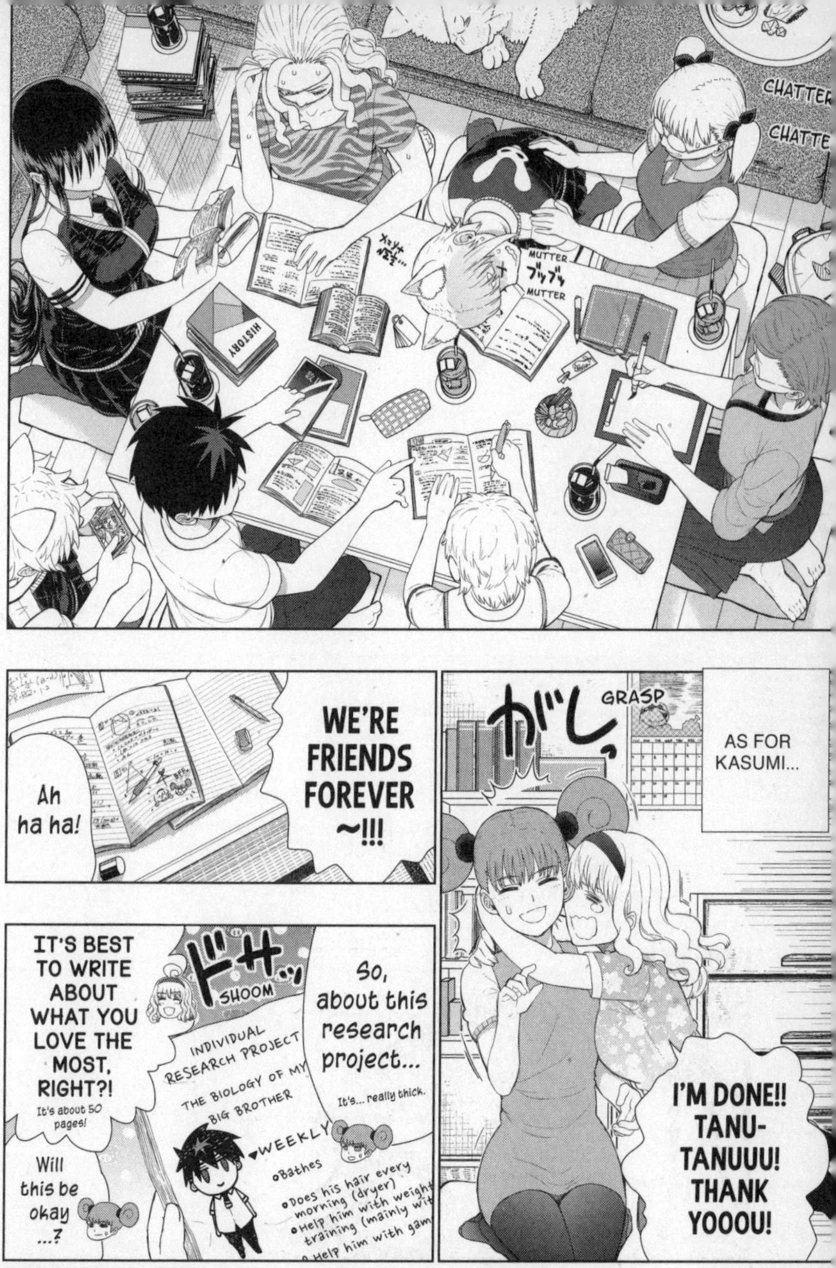

CHATTER
CHATTE
MUTTER
ブツブツ
MUTTER
HISTORY
AS FOR KASUMI...
がし
GRASP
I'M DONE!! TANU-TANUUU! THANK YOOOU!
WE'RE FRIENDS FOREVER ~!!!
Ah ha ha!
ドサッ
SHOOM
So, about this research project...
It's... really thick.
IT'S BEST TO WRITE ABOUT WHAT YOU LOVE THE MOST, RIGHT?!
It's about 50 pages!
INDIVIDUAL RESEARCH PROJECT
THE BIOLOGY OF MY BIG BROTHER
▼WEEKLY
○Bathes
○Does his hair every morning (dryer)
○Help him with weight training (mainly wit
○Help him with gam
Will this be okay ...?

CHAPTER 63: END

Atori's Presentation

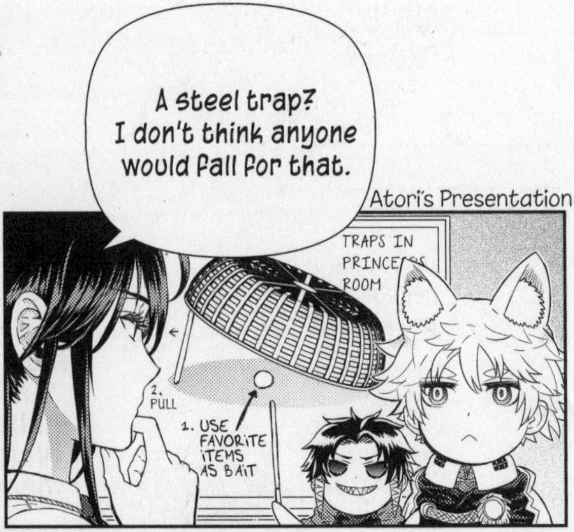
A steel trap? I don't think anyone would fall for that.
TRAPS IN
PRINCE
ROOM
2. PULL
1. USE FAVORITE ITEMS AS BAIT

Witchcraft Works

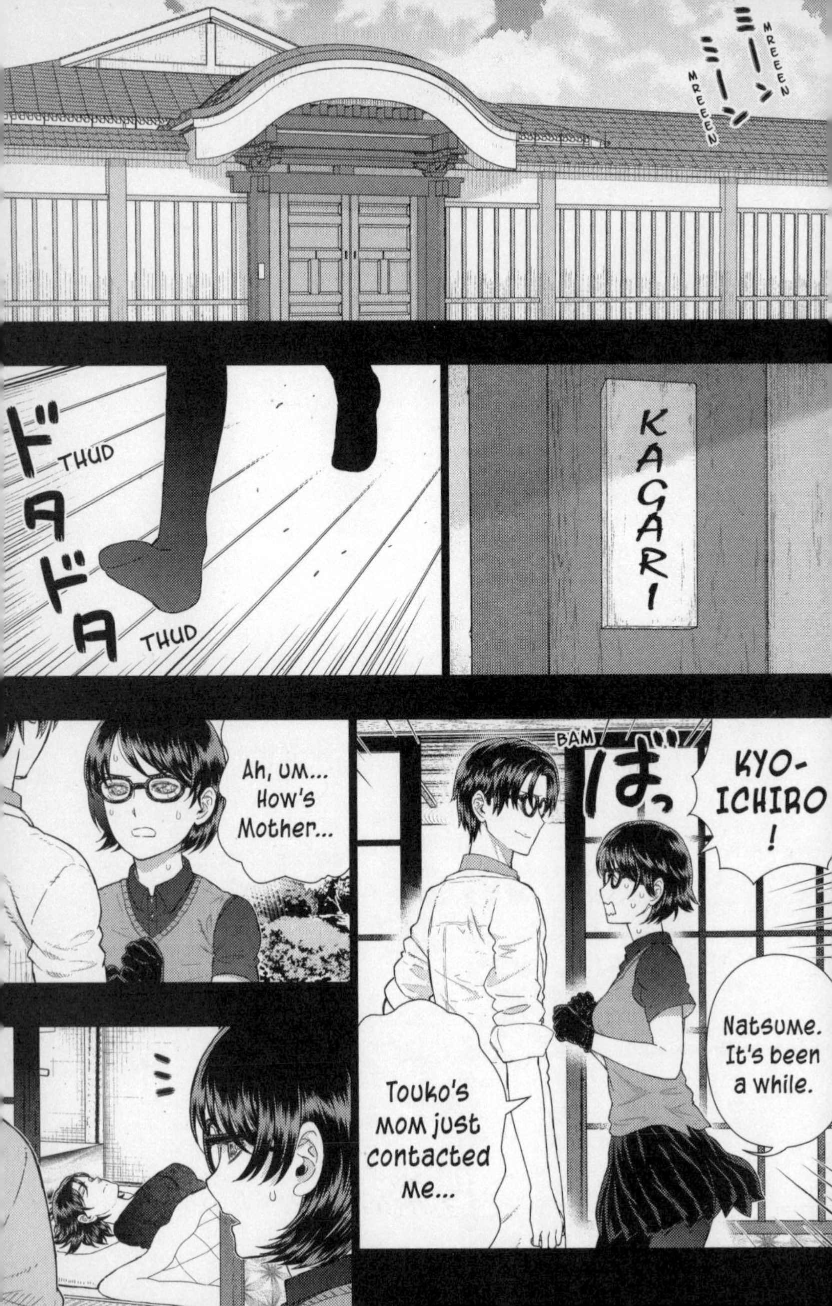
ミーン
MREEEN
ミーン
MREEEN
KAGARI
ドタドタ
THUD
THUD
ばっ
BAM
KYO-ICHIRO!
Natsume. It's been a while.
Touko's MOM just contacted me...
Ah, um... How's Mother...
ミ

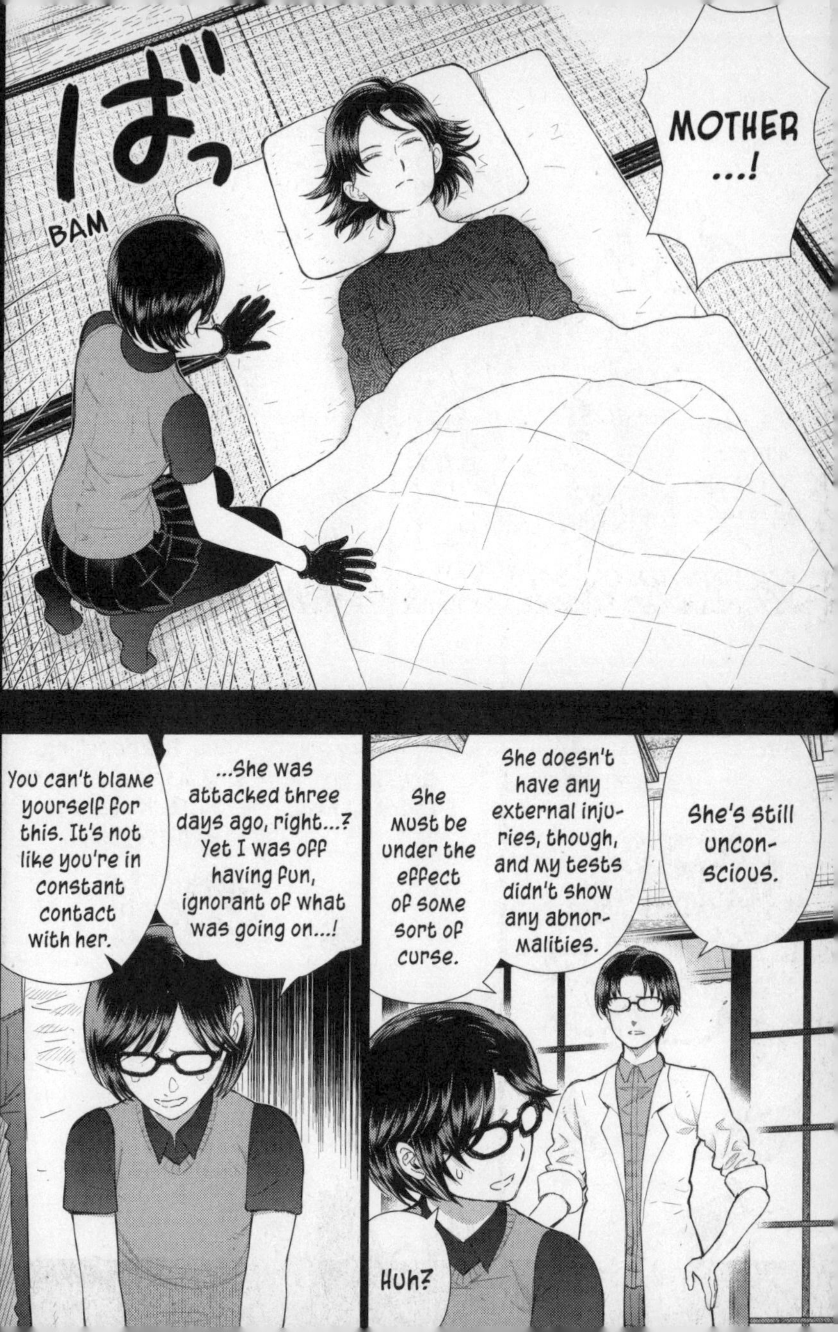
MOTHER ...!
ばっ
BAM
She's still uncon-scious.
She doesn't have any external inju-ries, though, and my tests didn't show any abnor-malities.
She must be under the effect of some sort of curse.
Huh?
...She was attacked three days ago, right...? Yet I was off having fun, ignorant of what was going on...!
You can't blame yourself for this. It's not like you're in constant contact with her.

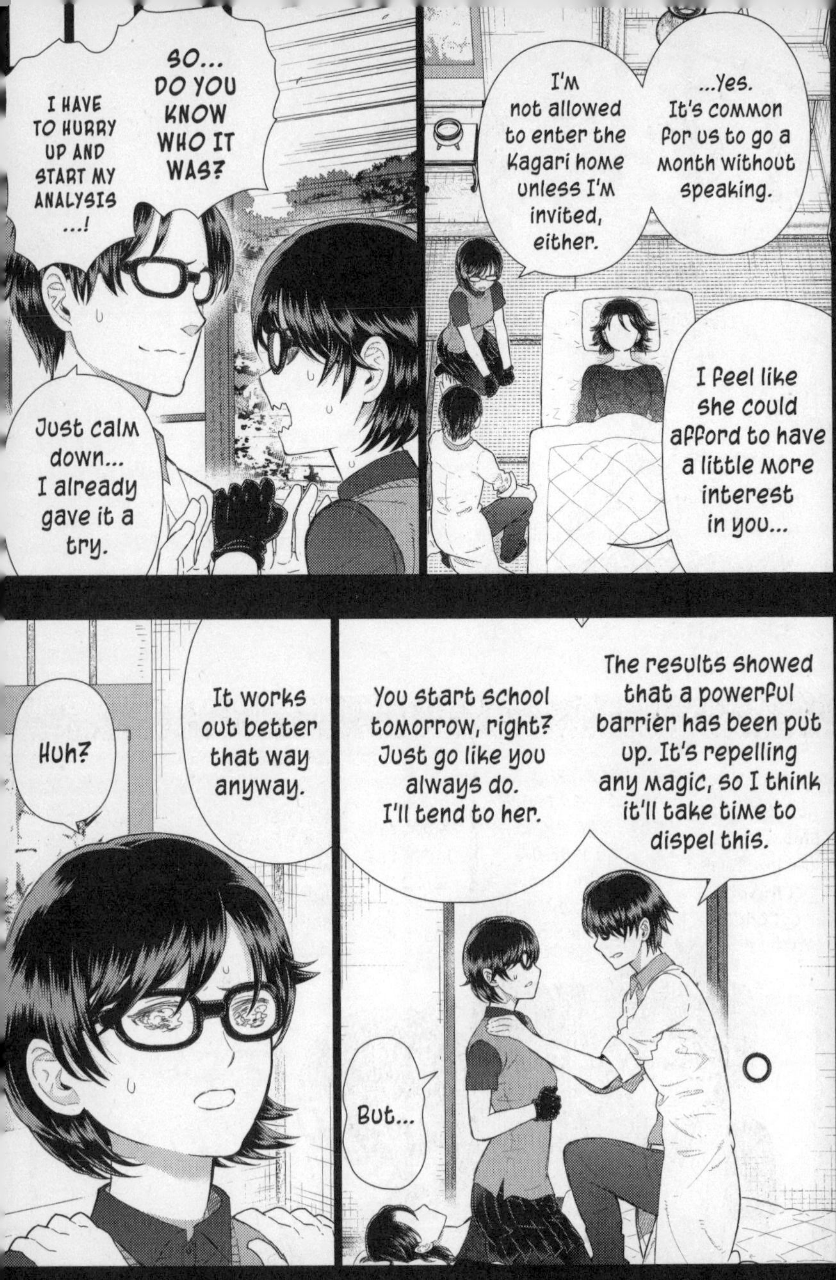
...Yes. It's common for us to go a month without speaking.
I'm not allowed to enter the Kagari home unless I'm invited, either.
I feel like she could afford to have a little more interest in you...
SO... DO YOU KNOW WHO IT WAS?
I HAVE TO HURRY UP AND START MY ANALYSIS ...!
Just calm down... I already gave it a try.
The results showed that a powerful barrier has been put up. It's repelling any magic, so I think it'll take time to dispel this.
You start school tomorrow, right? Just go like you always do. I'll tend to her.
But...
It works out better that way anyway.
Huh?

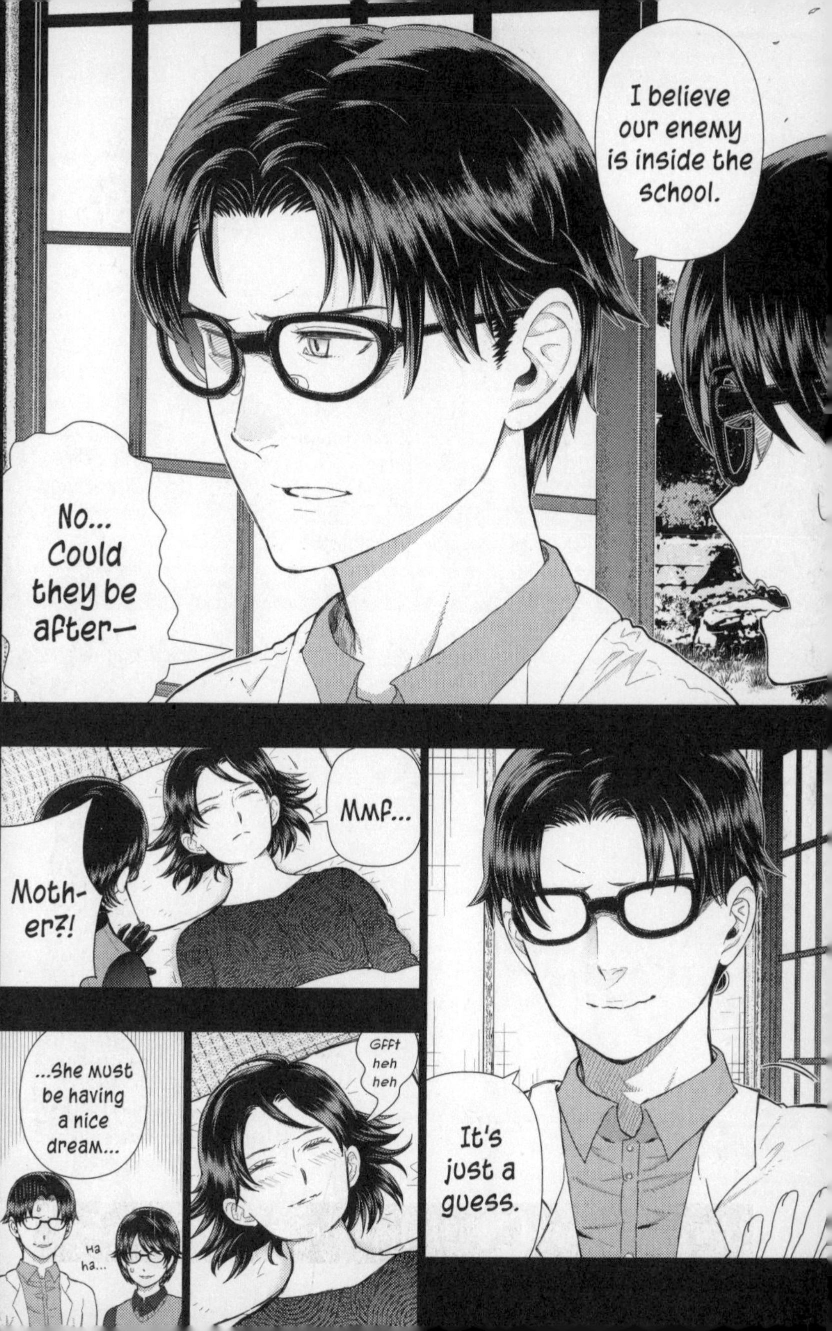
I believe our enemy is inside the school.
No... Could they be after—
It's just a guess.
Mmf...
Moth- er?!
Gfft heh heh
...She must be having a nice dream...
Ha ha...

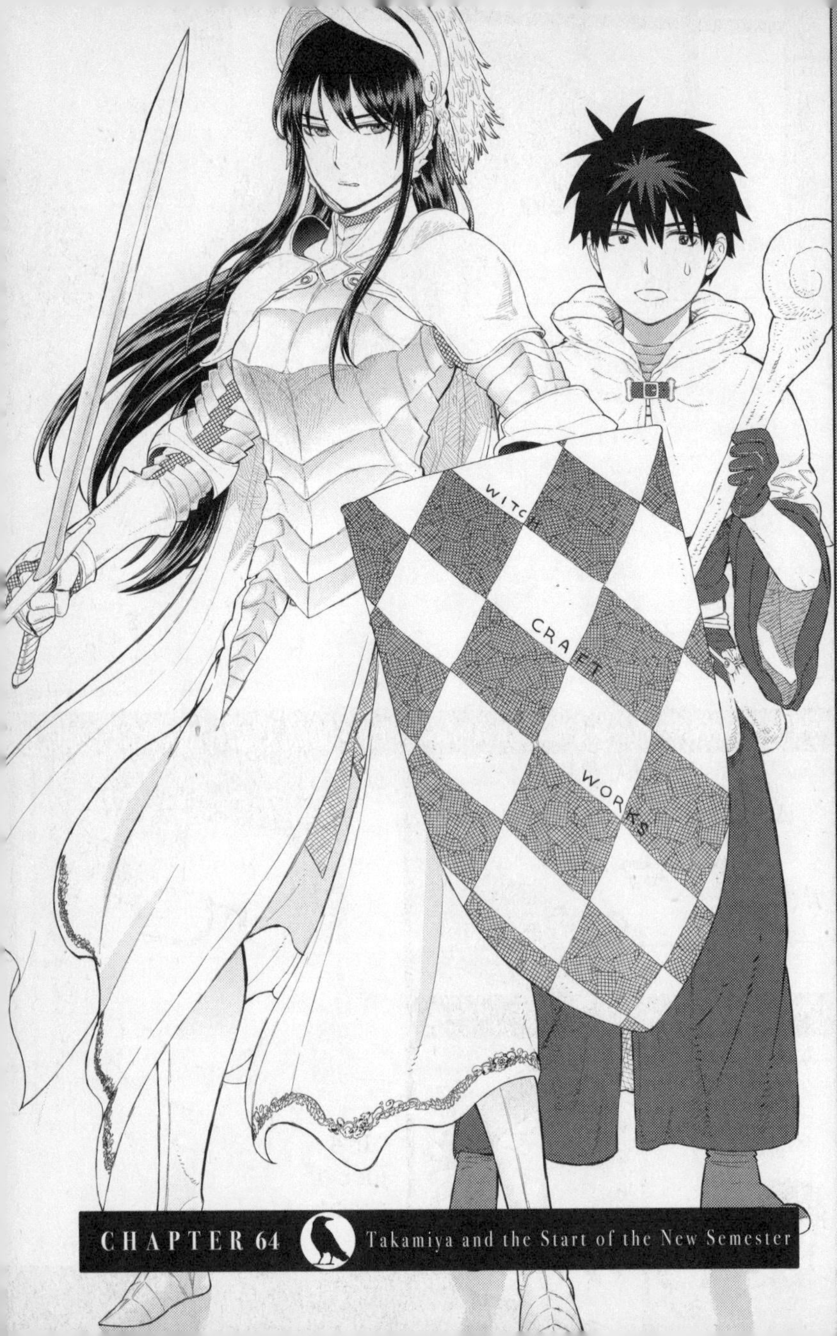
WITCH
CRAFT
WORKS

CHAPTER 64 Takamiya and the Start of the New Semester

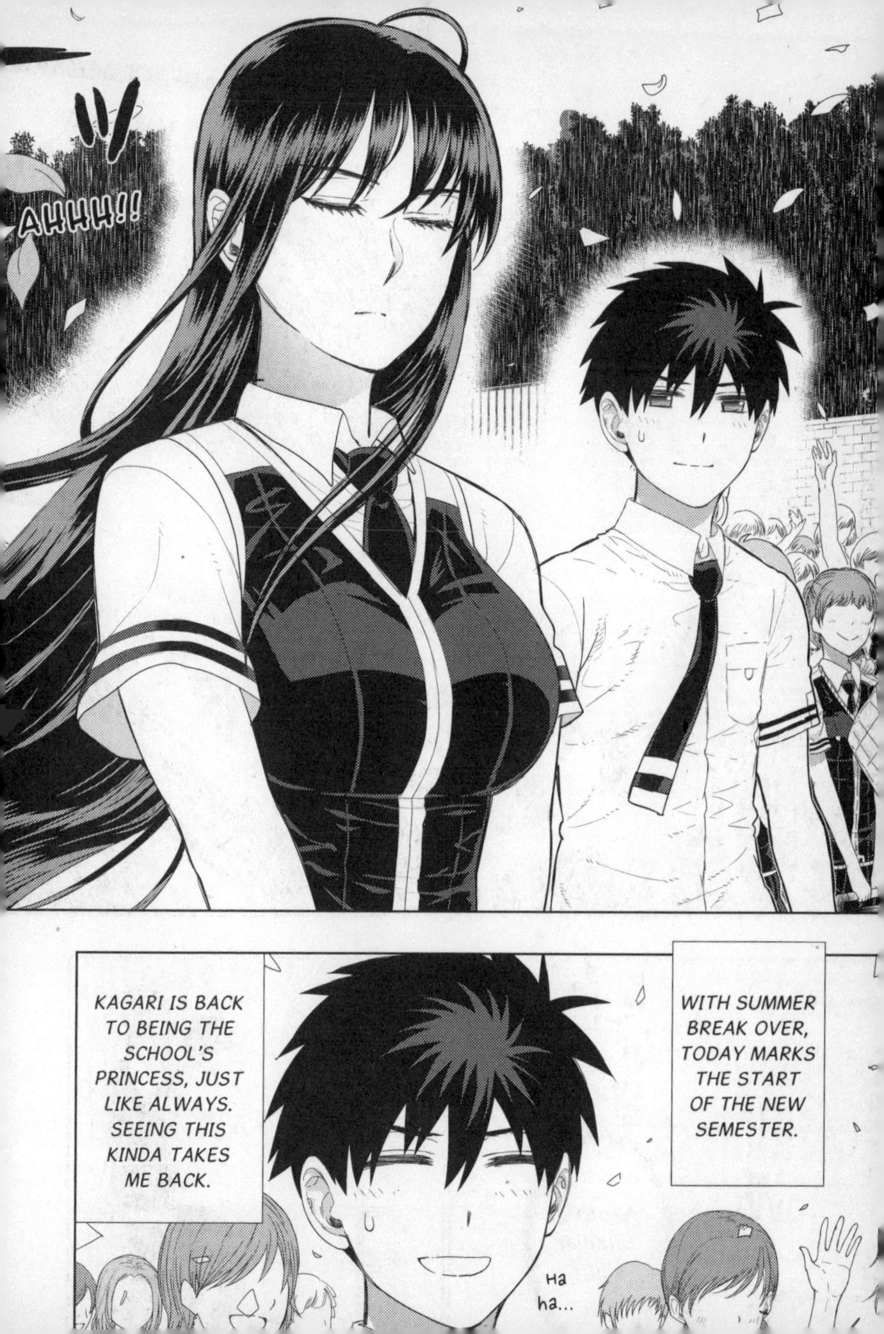

AHHH!!
WITH SUMMER BREAK OVER, TODAY MARKS THE START OF THE NEW SEMESTER.
KAGARI IS BACK TO BEING THE SCHOOL'S PRINCESS, JUST LIKE ALWAYS. SEEING THIS KINDA TAKES ME BACK.
Ha ha...

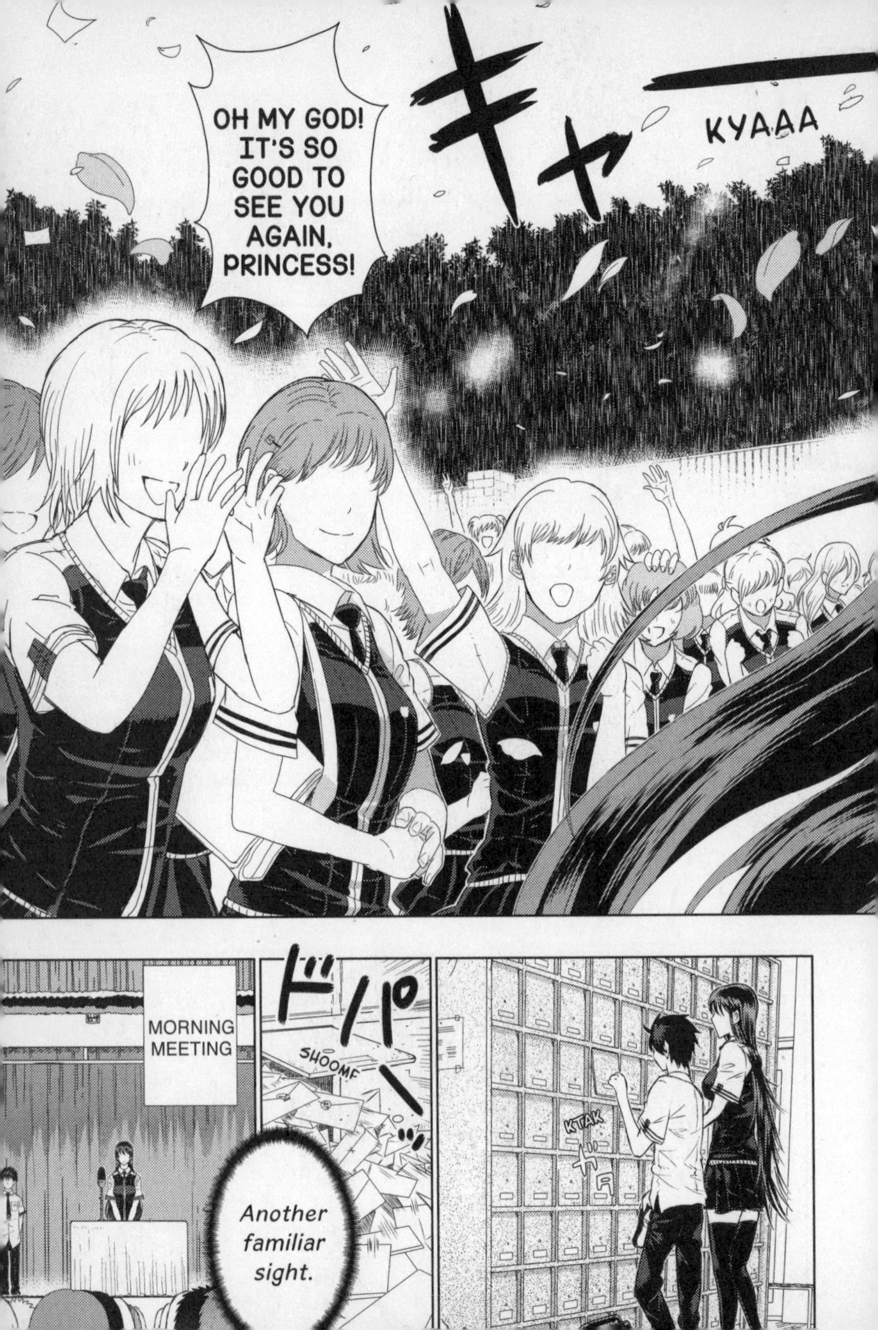
キャー
KYAAA
OH MY GOD! IT'S SO GOOD TO SEE YOU AGAIN, PRINCESS!
ガタ
KTAK
ドパッ
SHOOMF
Another familiar sight.
MORNING MEETING

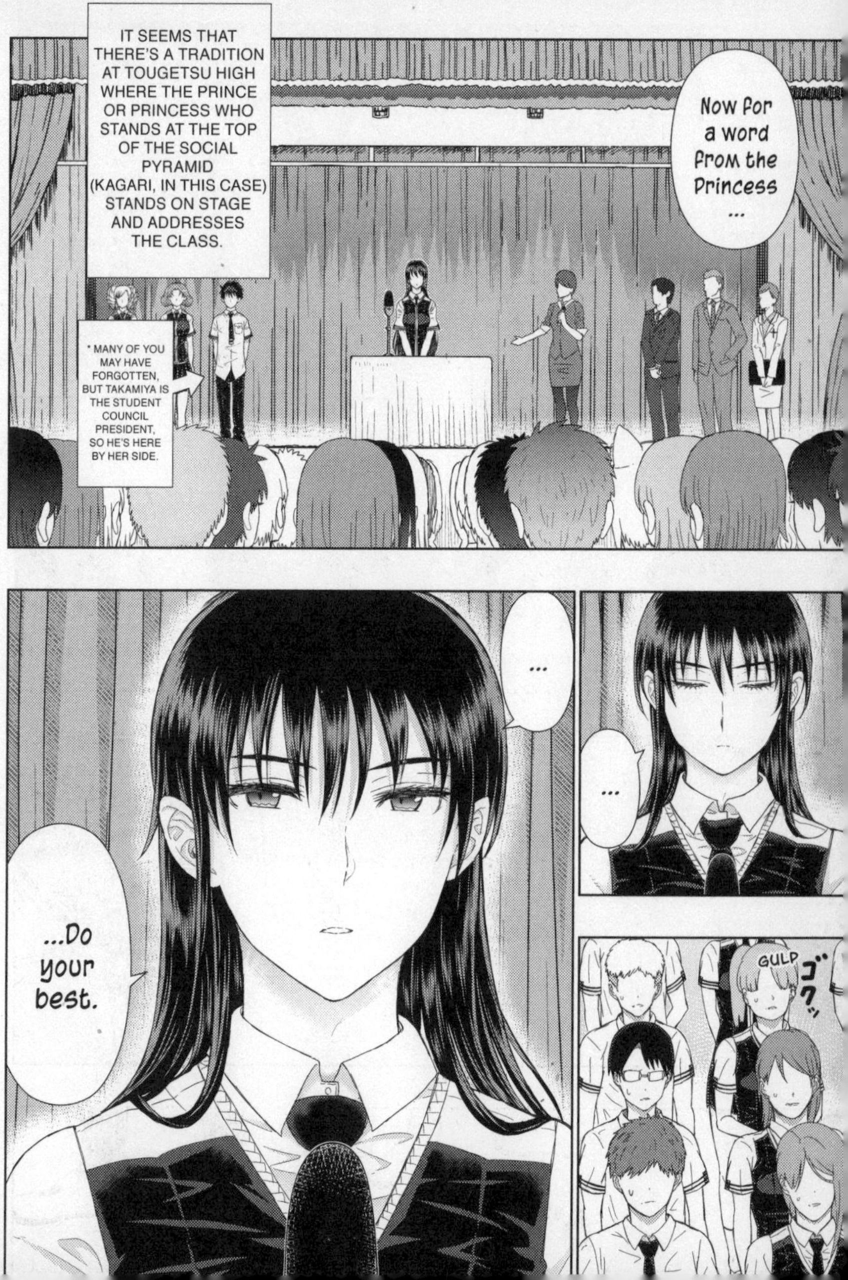
Now for a word from the Princess ...
IT SEEMS THAT THERE'S A TRADITION AT TOUGETSU HIGH WHERE THE PRINCE OR PRINCESS WHO STANDS AT THE TOP OF THE SOCIAL PYRAMID (KAGARI, IN THIS CASE) STANDS ON STAGE AND ADDRESSES THE CLASS.
* MANY OF YOU MAY HAVE FORGOTTEN, BUT TAKAMIYA IS THE STUDENT COUNCIL PRESIDENT, SO HE'S HERE BY HER SIDE.
...
GULP
...
...Do your best.

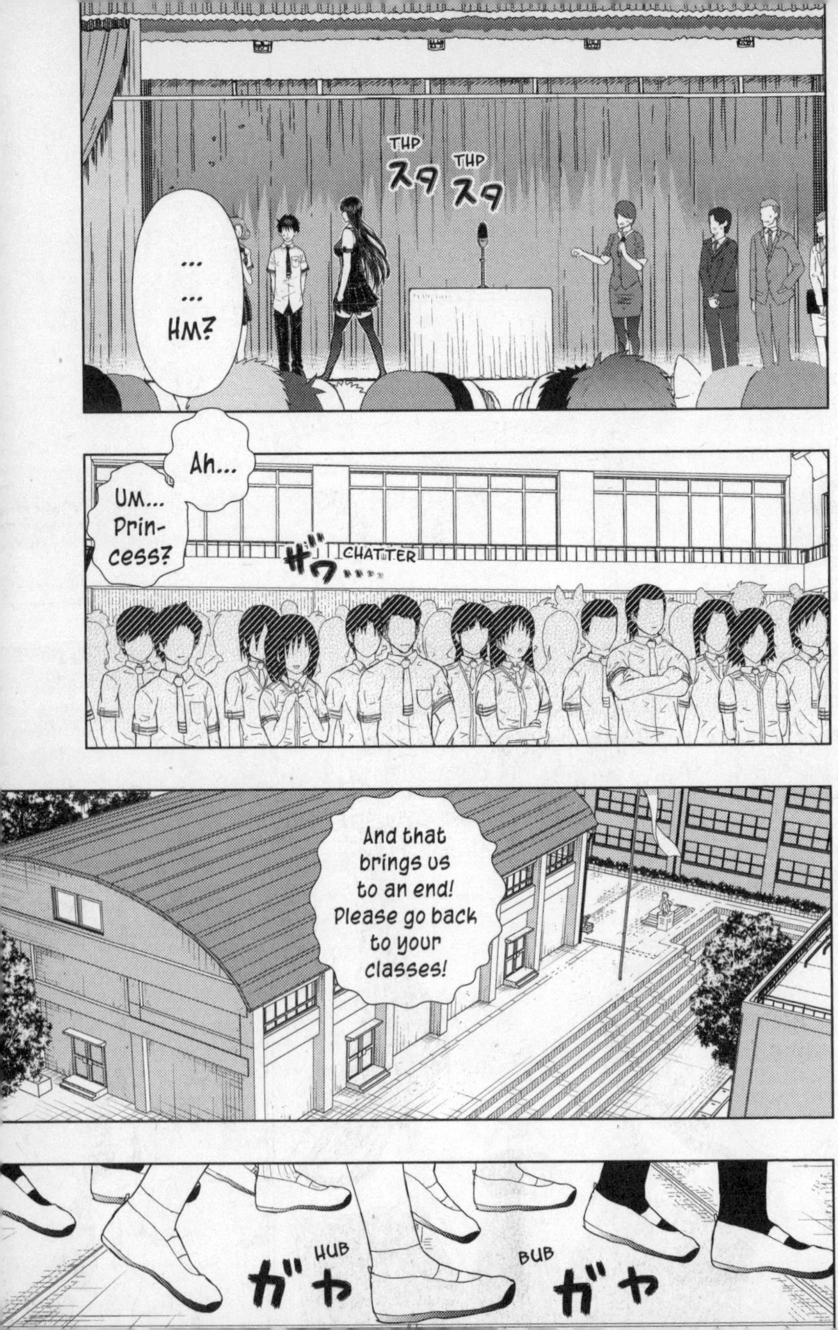
THP スタ THP スタ
... ... HM?
Ah...
Um... Prin-cess?
ザワ CHATTER
And that brings us to an end! Please go back to your classes!
HUB ガヤ BUB ガヤ

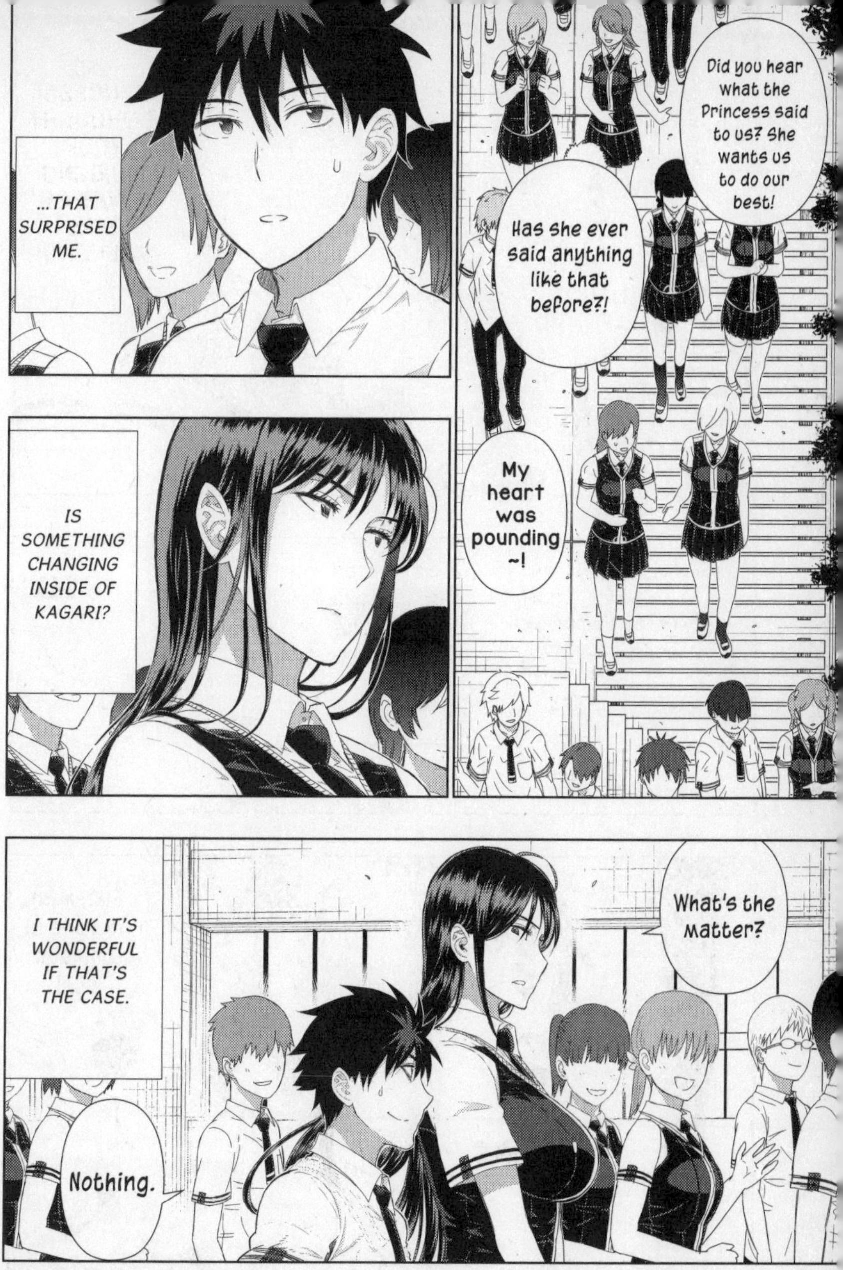
Did you hear what the Princess said to us? She wants us to do our best!
Has she ever said anything like that before?!
My heart was pounding ~!
...THAT SURPRISED ME.
IS SOMETHING CHANGING INSIDE OF KAGARI?
What's the Matter?
I THINK IT'S WONDERFUL IF THAT'S THE CASE.
Nothing.

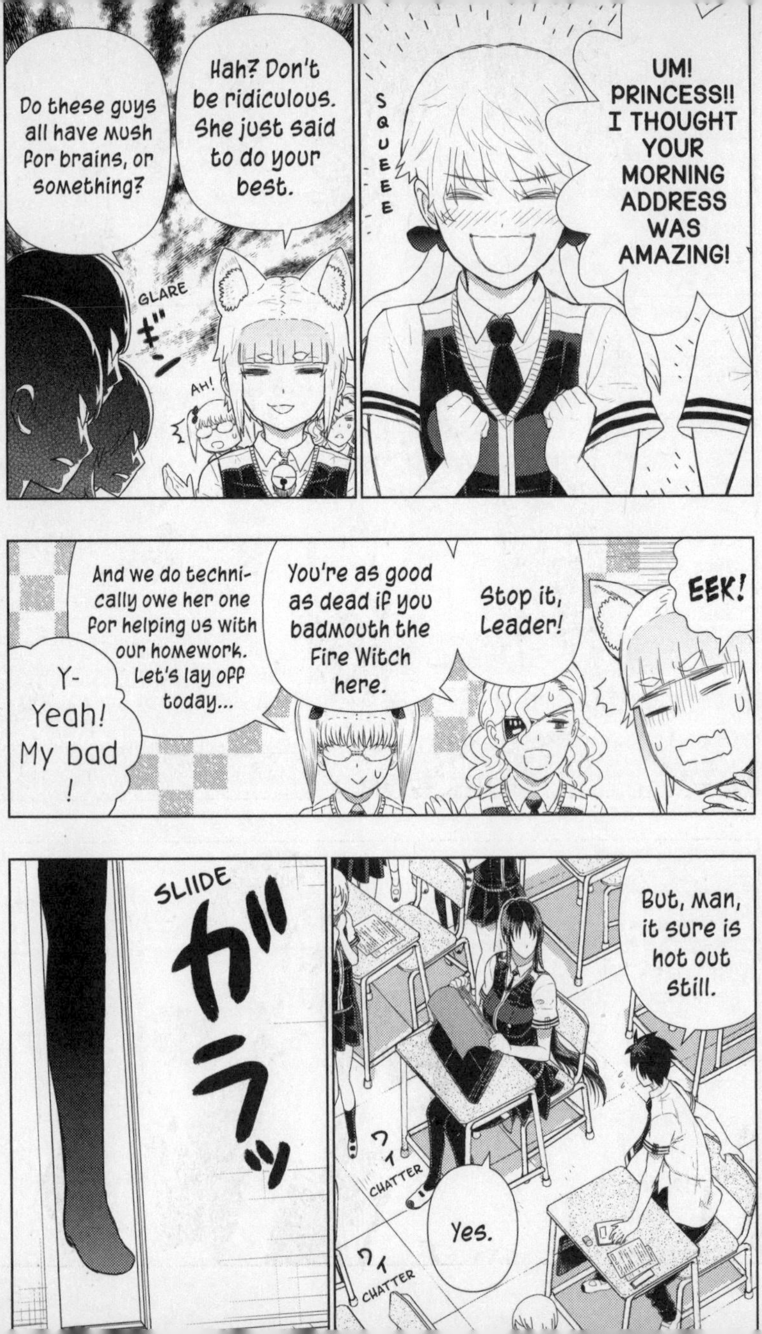
SQUEEEE
UM! PRINCESS!! I THOUGHT YOUR MORNING ADDRESS WAS AMAZING!
Hah? Don't be ridiculous. She just said to do your best.
Do these guys all have mush for brains, or something?
GLARE
ギン
AH!
EEK!
Stop it, Leader!
You're as good as dead if you badmouth the Fire Witch here.
And we do technically owe her one for helping us with our homework. Let's lay off today...
Y- Yeah! My bad!
But, man, it sure is hot out still.
ワイ
CHATTER
Yes.
ワイ
CHATTER
SLIIDE
ガラッ

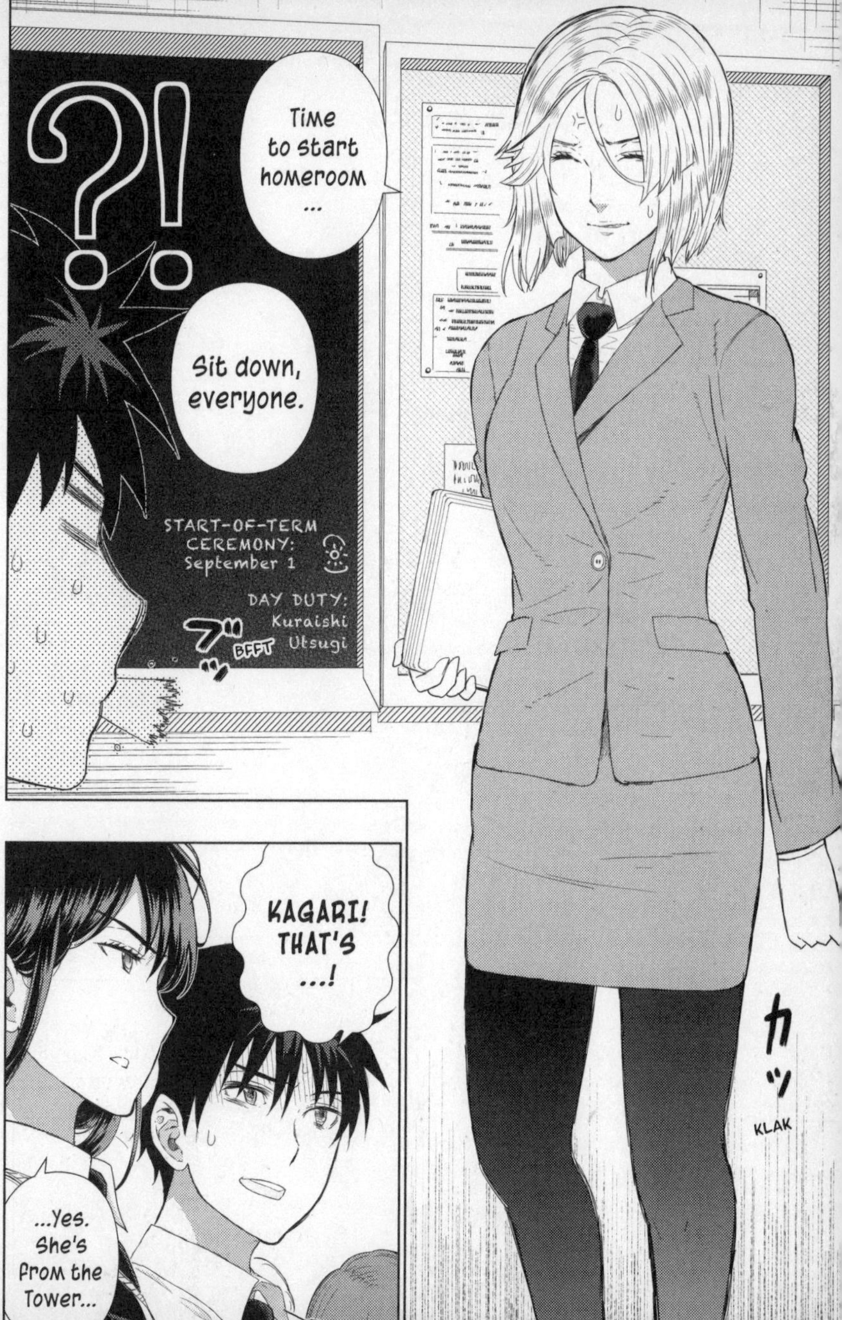
カッ
KLAK
?!
Time to start homeroom ...
Sit down, everyone.
START-OF-TERM CEREMONY: September 1
DAY DUTY: Kuraishi Utsugi
BFFT
KAGARI! THAT'S ...!
...Yes. She's from the Tower...

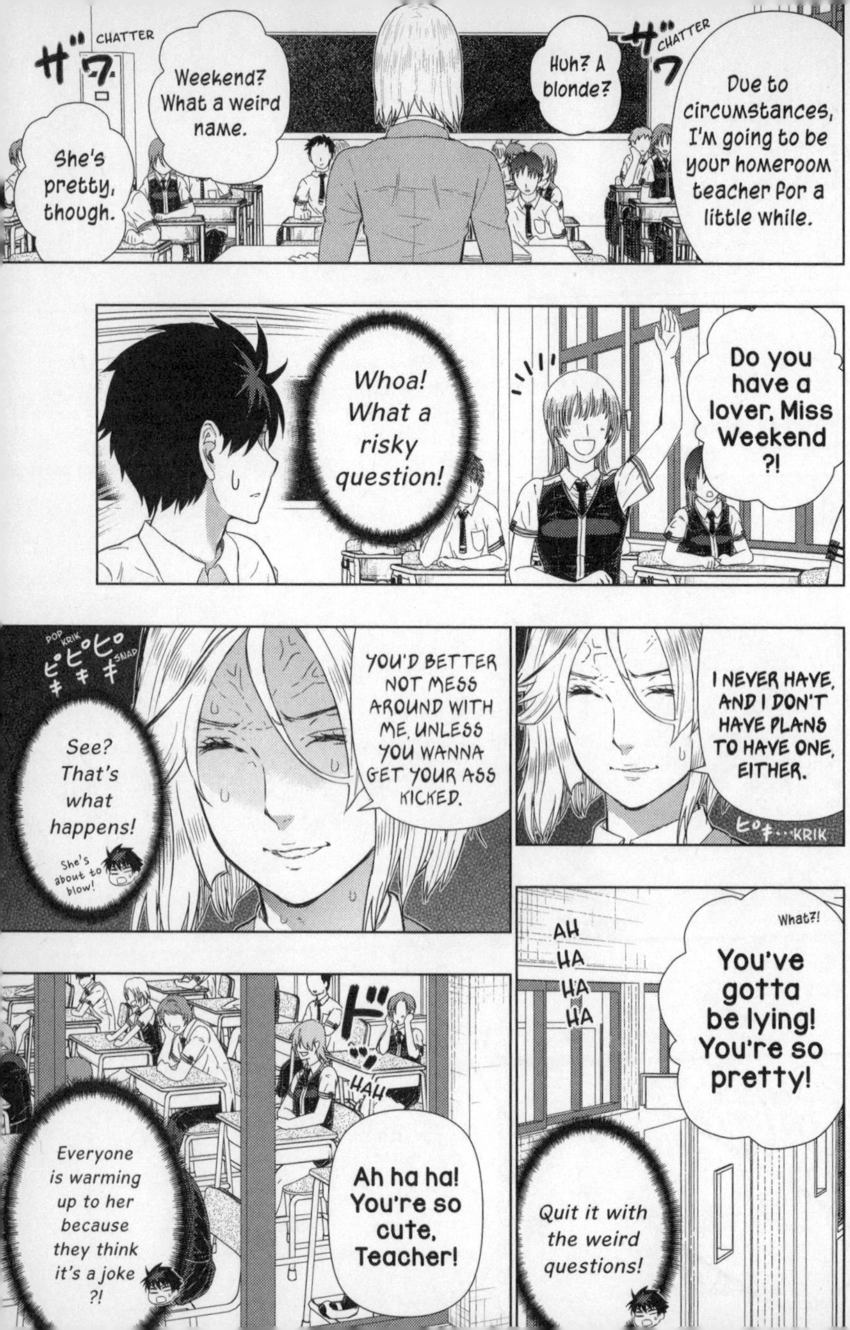
ザワ CHATTER
Due to circumstances, I'm going to be your homeroom teacher for a little while.
Huh? A blonde?
Weekend? What a weird name.
ザワ CHATTER
She's pretty, though.
Do you have a lover, Miss Weekend?!
Whoa! What a risky question!
I NEVER HAVE, AND I DON'T HAVE PLANS TO HAVE ONE, EITHER.
ピキ… KRIK
YOU'D BETTER NOT MESS AROUND WITH ME, UNLESS YOU WANNA GET YOUR ASS KICKED.
ピキピキピキ POP KRIK SNAP
See? That's what happens!
She's about to blow!
What?!
You've gotta be lying! You're so pretty!
AH HA HA HA
Quit it with the weird questions!
ド
HAH
Ah ha ha! You're so cute, Teacher!
Everyone is warming up to her because they think it's a joke?!

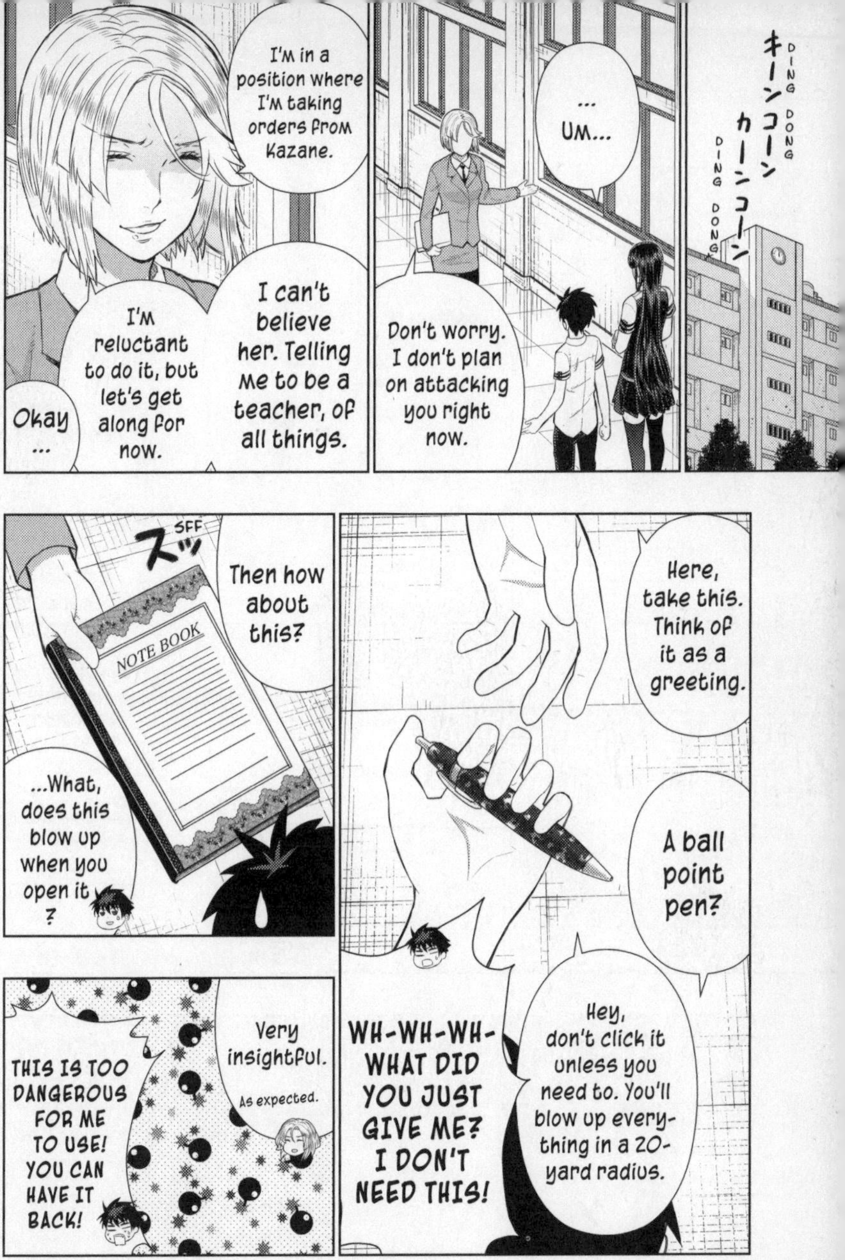
キーンコーン
DING DONG
カーンコーン
DING DONG
... UM...
Don't worry. I don't plan on attacking you right now.
I'm in a position where I'm taking orders from Kazane.
I can't believe her. Telling me to be a teacher, of all things.
I'm reluctant to do it, but let's get along for now.
Okay ...
Here, take this. Think of it as a greeting.
A ball point pen?
Hey, don't click it unless you need to. You'll blow up every-thing in a 20-yard radius.
WH-WH-WH-WHAT DID YOU JUST GIVE ME? I DON'T NEED THIS!
ズッ
SFF
Then how about this?
NOTE BOOK
...What, does this blow up when you open it ?
Very insightful.
As expected.
THIS IS TOO DANGEROUS FOR ME TO USE! YOU CAN HAVE IT BACK!

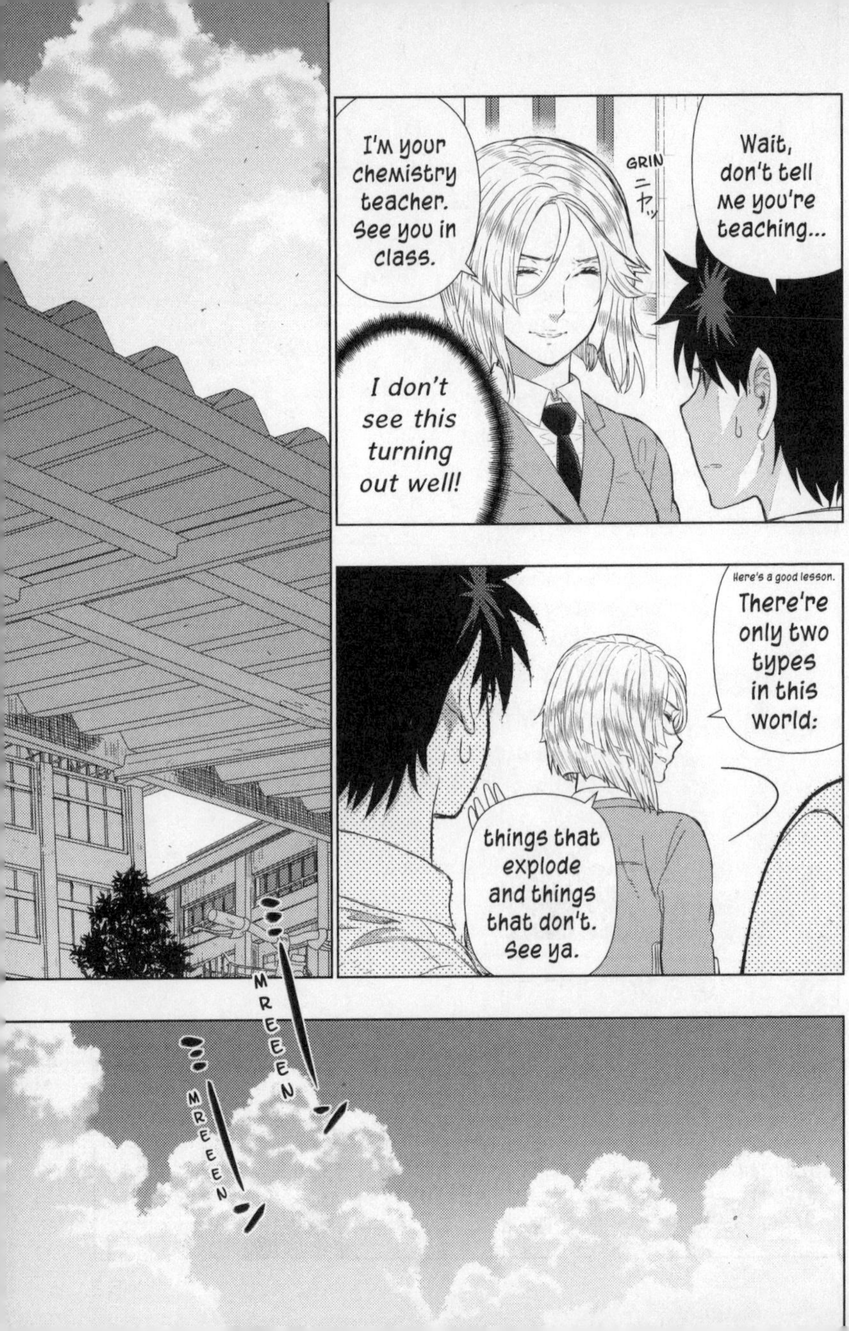
Wait, don't tell me you're teaching...
GRIN
I'm your chemistry teacher. See you in class.
I don't see this turning out well!
Here's a good lesson.
There're only two types in this world:
things that explode and things that don't. See ya.
MREEEN
MREEEN

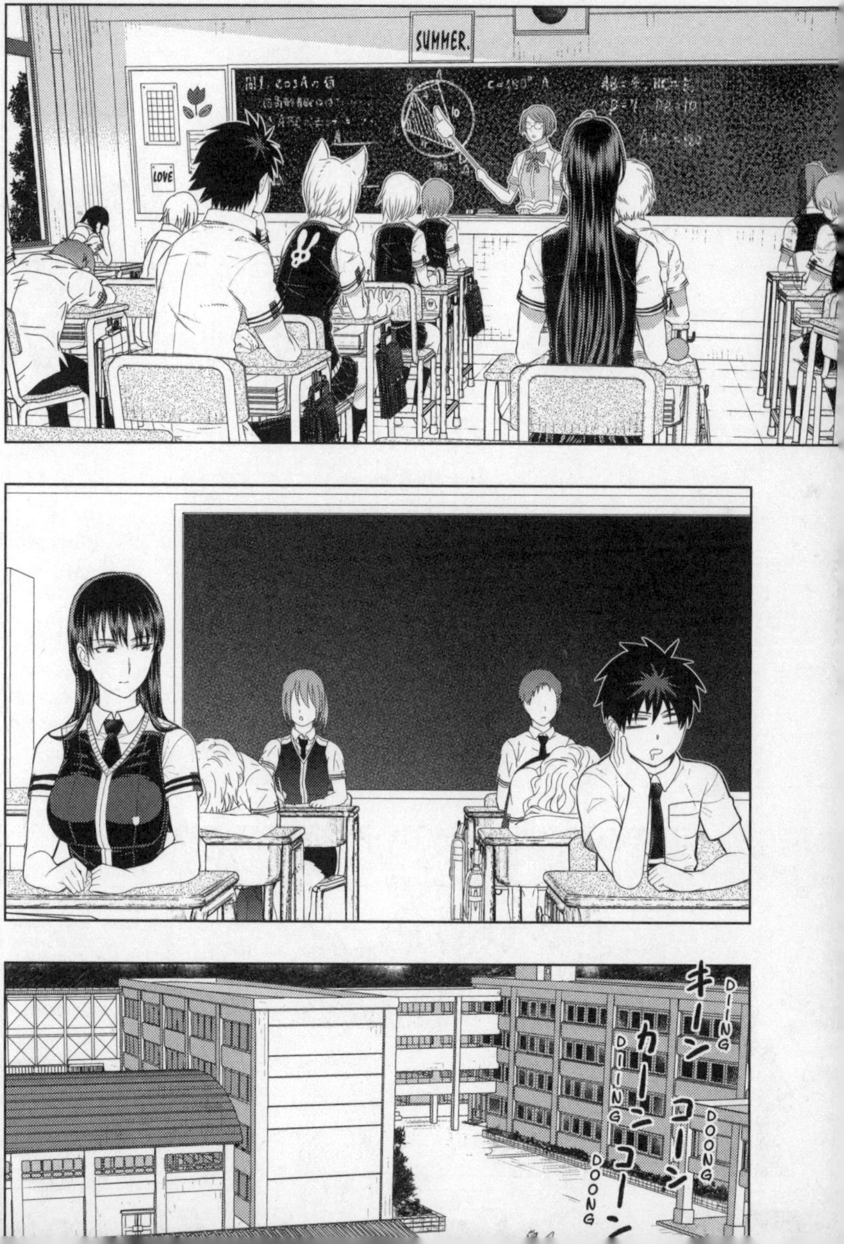
SUMMER.
LOVE
キーン
DING
コーン
DOONG
カーン
DING
コーン
DOONG

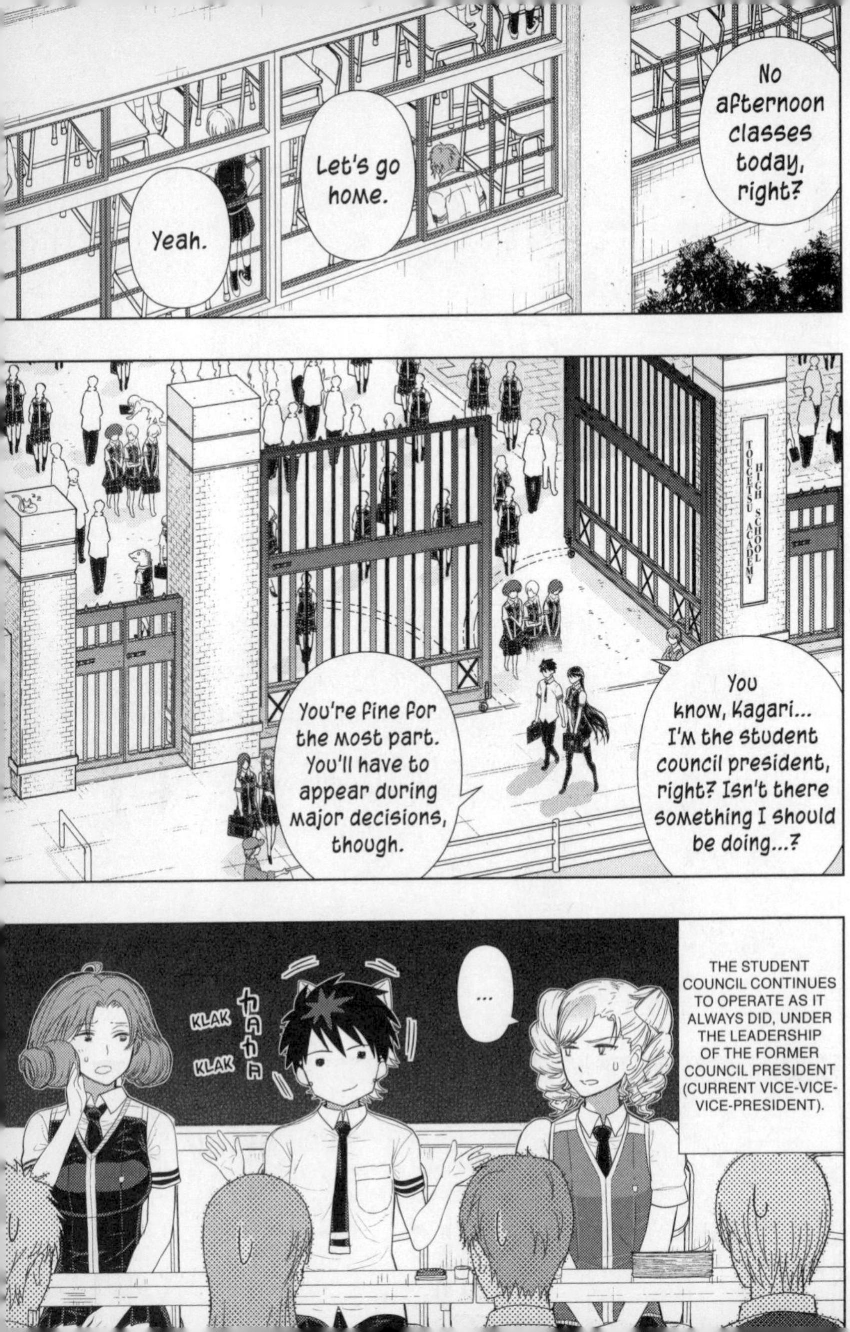
No afternoon classes today, right?
Let's go home.
Yeah.
TOUGETSU ACADEMY HIGH SCHOOL
You know, Kagari... I'm the student council president, right? Isn't there something I should be doing...?
You're fine for the most part. You'll have to appear during major decisions, though.
THE STUDENT COUNCIL CONTINUES TO OPERATE AS IT ALWAYS DID, UNDER THE LEADERSHIP OF THE FORMER COUNCIL PRESIDENT (CURRENT VICE-VICE-VICE-PRESIDENT).
...
KLAK
KLAK

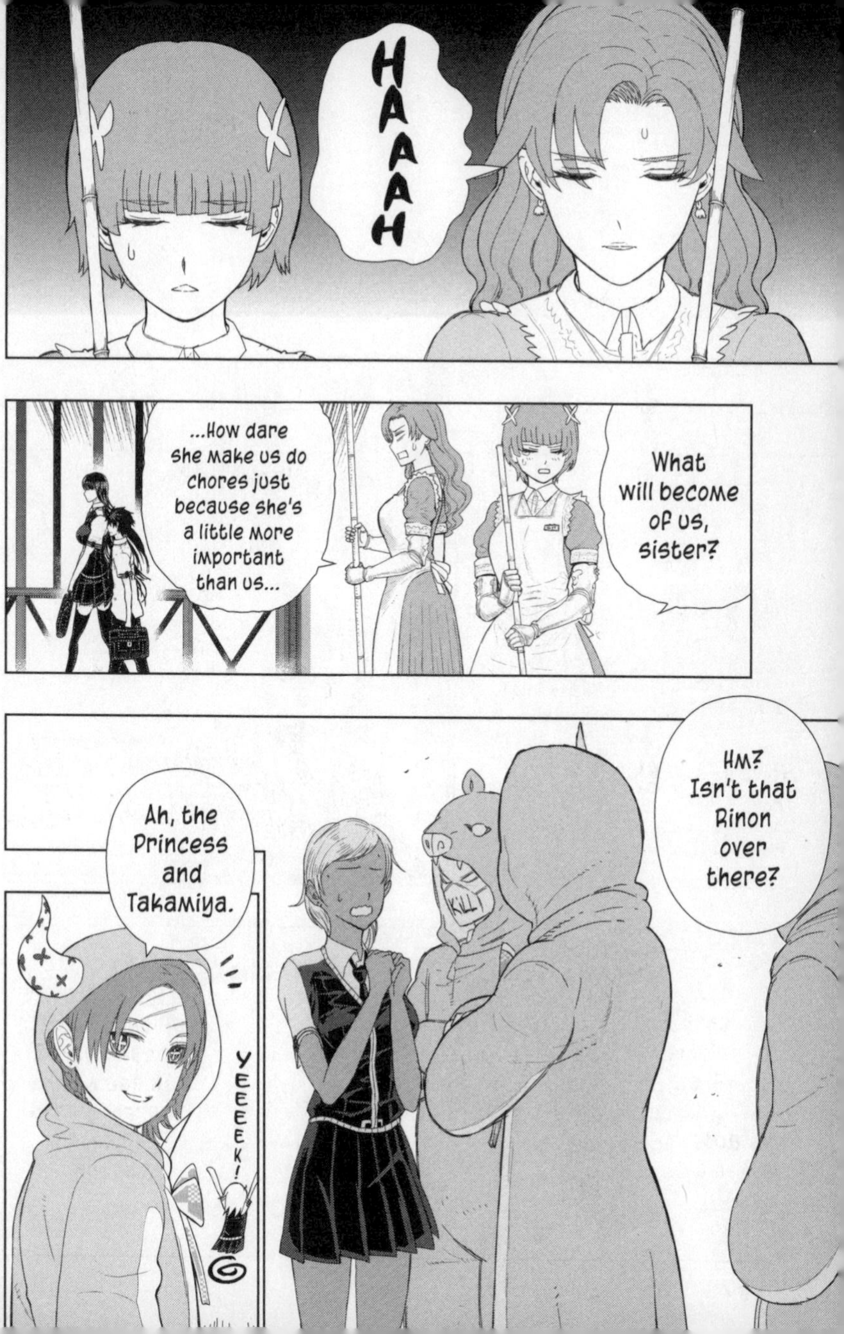
HAAAH
What will become of us, sister?
...How dare she make us do chores just because she's a little more important than us...
Hm? Isn't that Rinon over there?
KILL
Ah, the Princess and Takamiya.
YEEEEEK!

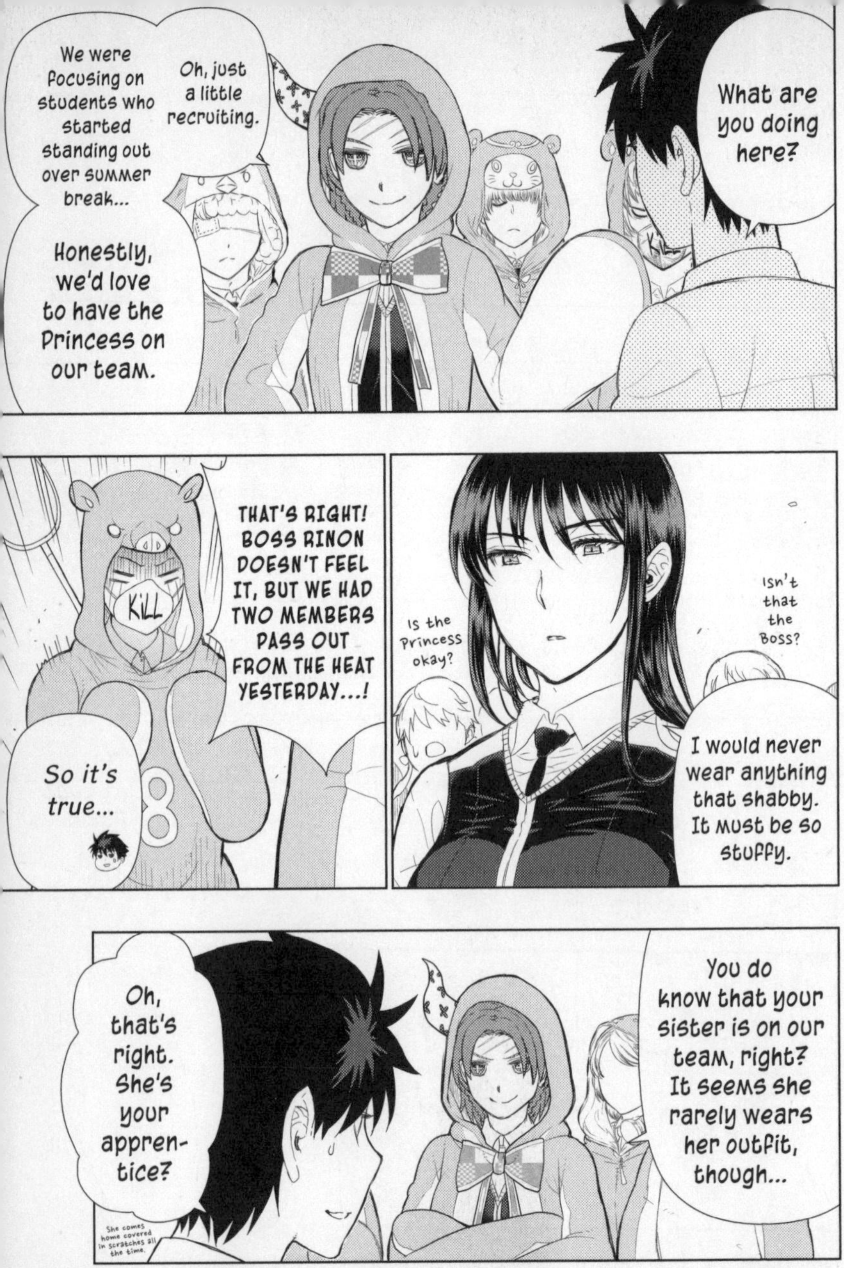
What are you doing here?
Oh, just a little recruiting.
We were focusing on students who started standing out over summer break...
Honestly, we'd love to have the Princess on our team.
Isn't that the Boss?
Is the Princess okay?
I would never wear anything that shabby. It must be so stuffy.
THAT'S RIGHT! BOSS RINON DOESN'T FEEL IT, BUT WE HAD TWO MEMBERS PASS OUT FROM THE HEAT YESTERDAY...!
KILL
So it's true...
You do know that your sister is on our team, right? It seems she rarely wears her outfit, though...
Oh, that's right. She's your apprentice?
She comes home covered in scratches all the time.

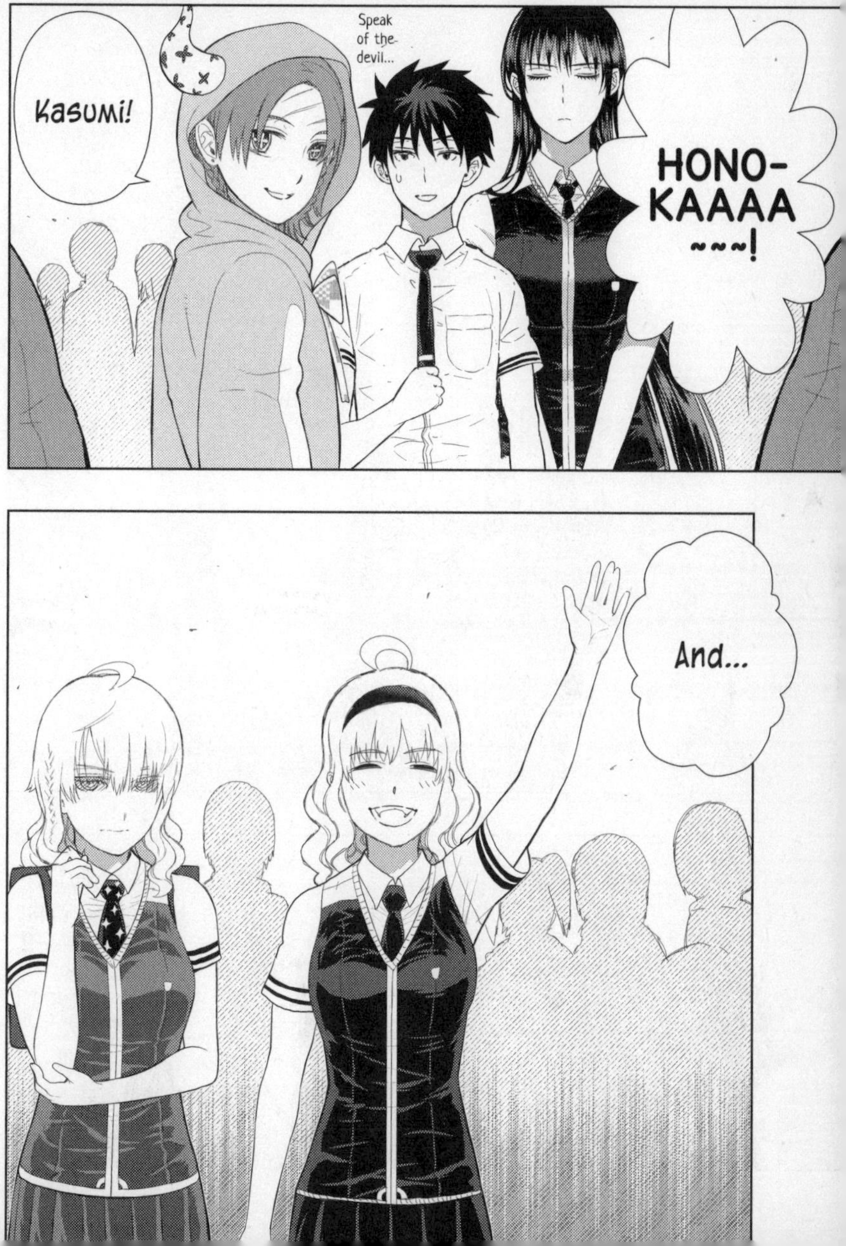
HONO-KAAAA ~~~!
Speak of the devil...
Kasumi!
And...

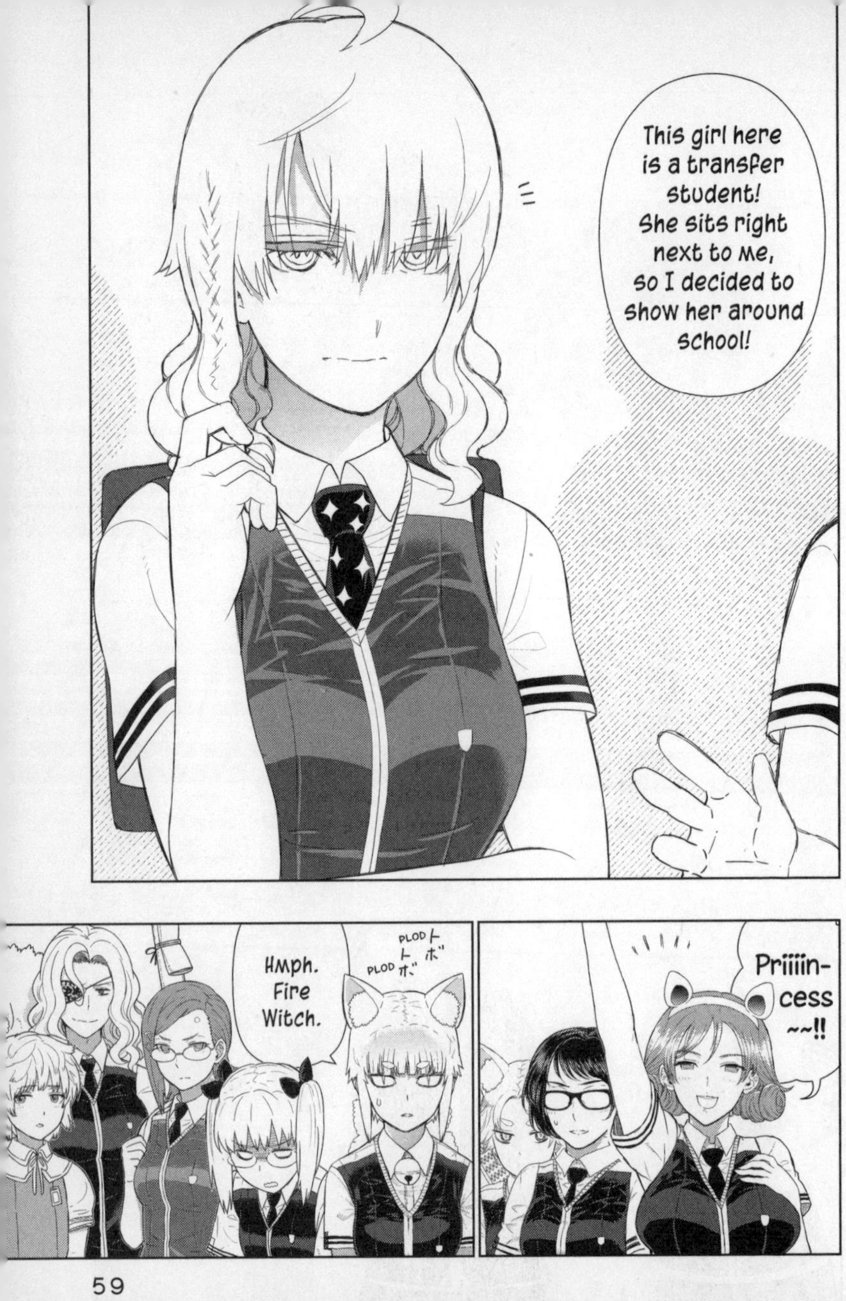
This girl here is a transfer student! She sits right next to me, so I decided to show her around school!
Priiiin-cess~~!!
PLOD トボ
PLOD トボ
Hmph. Fire Witch.

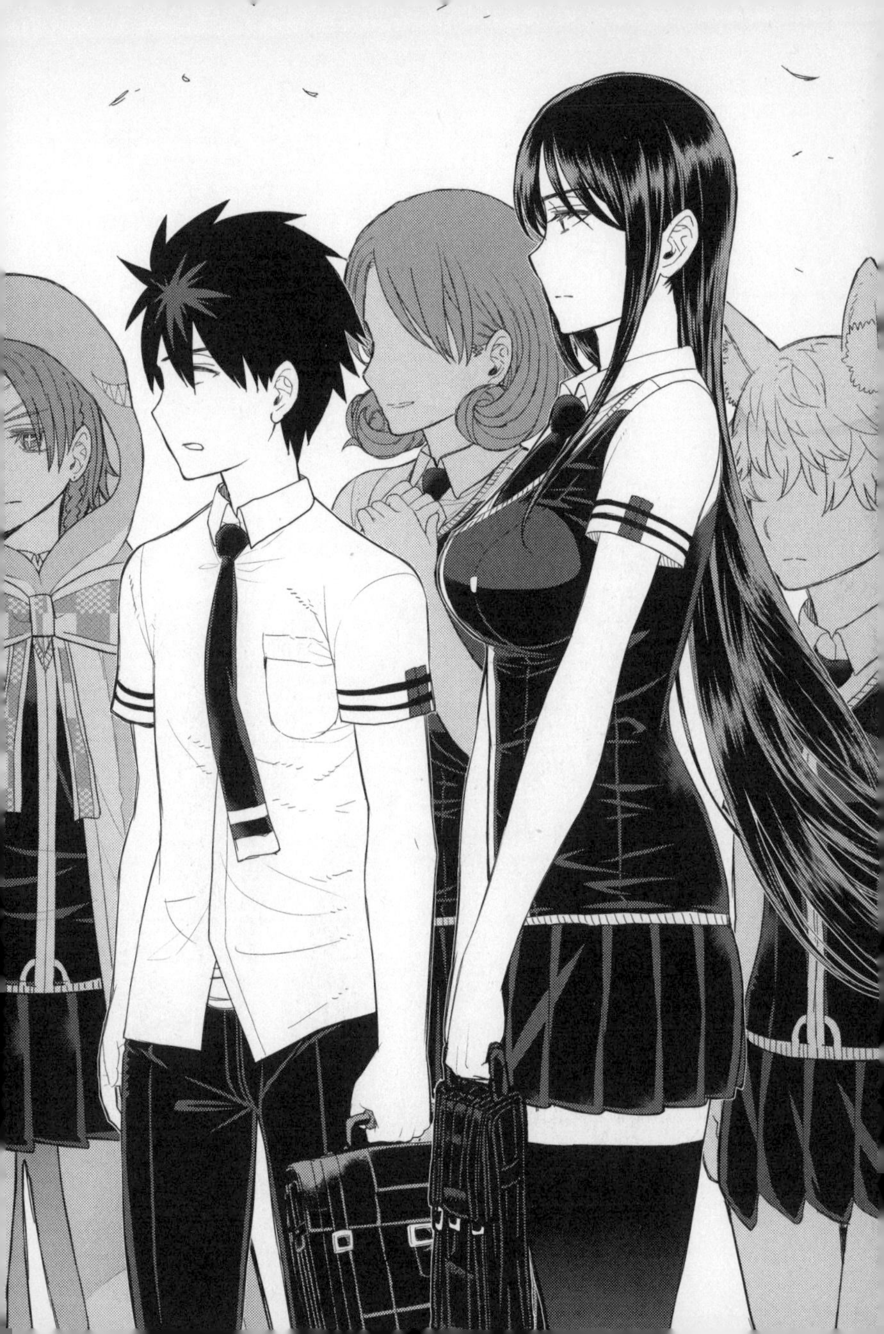

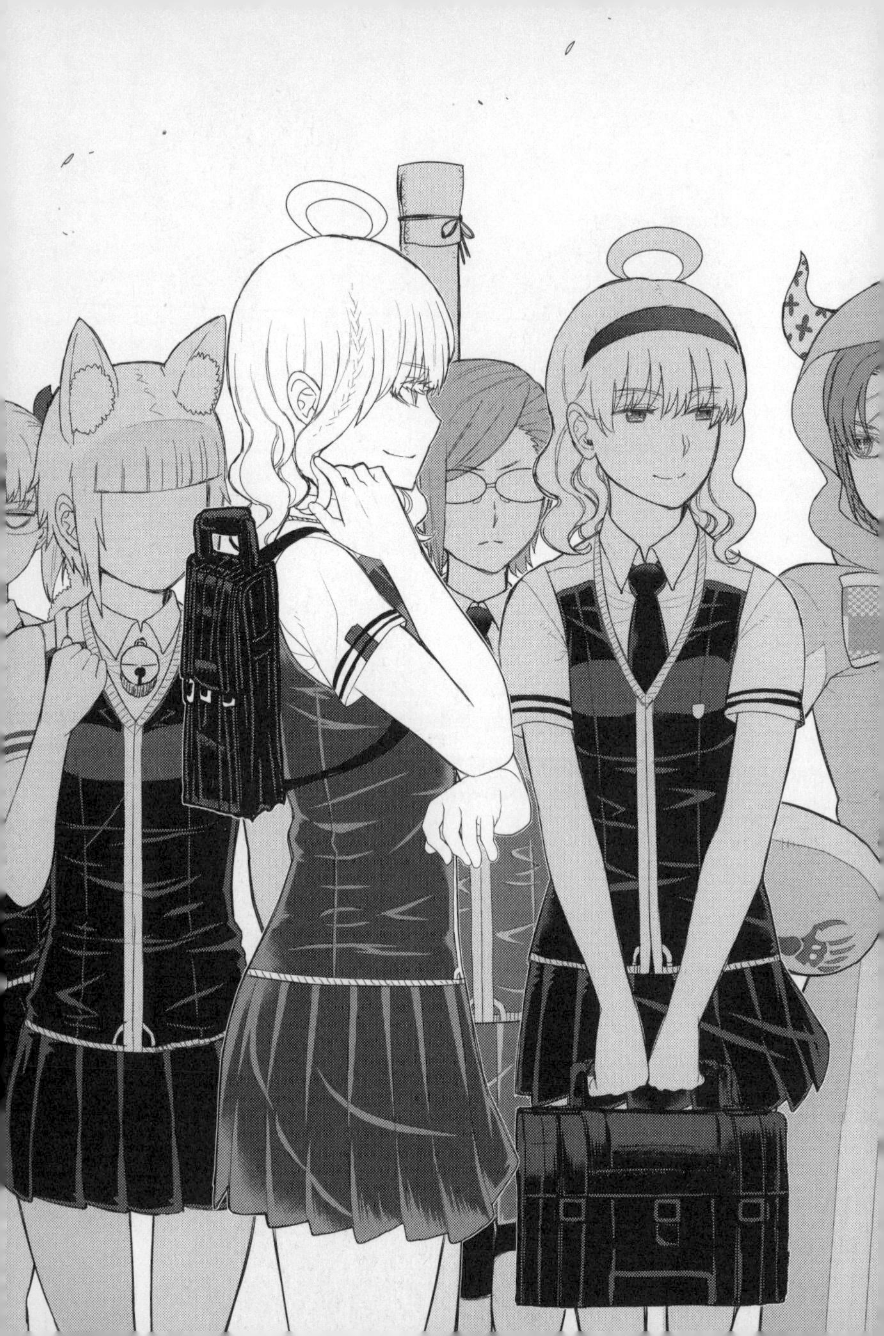

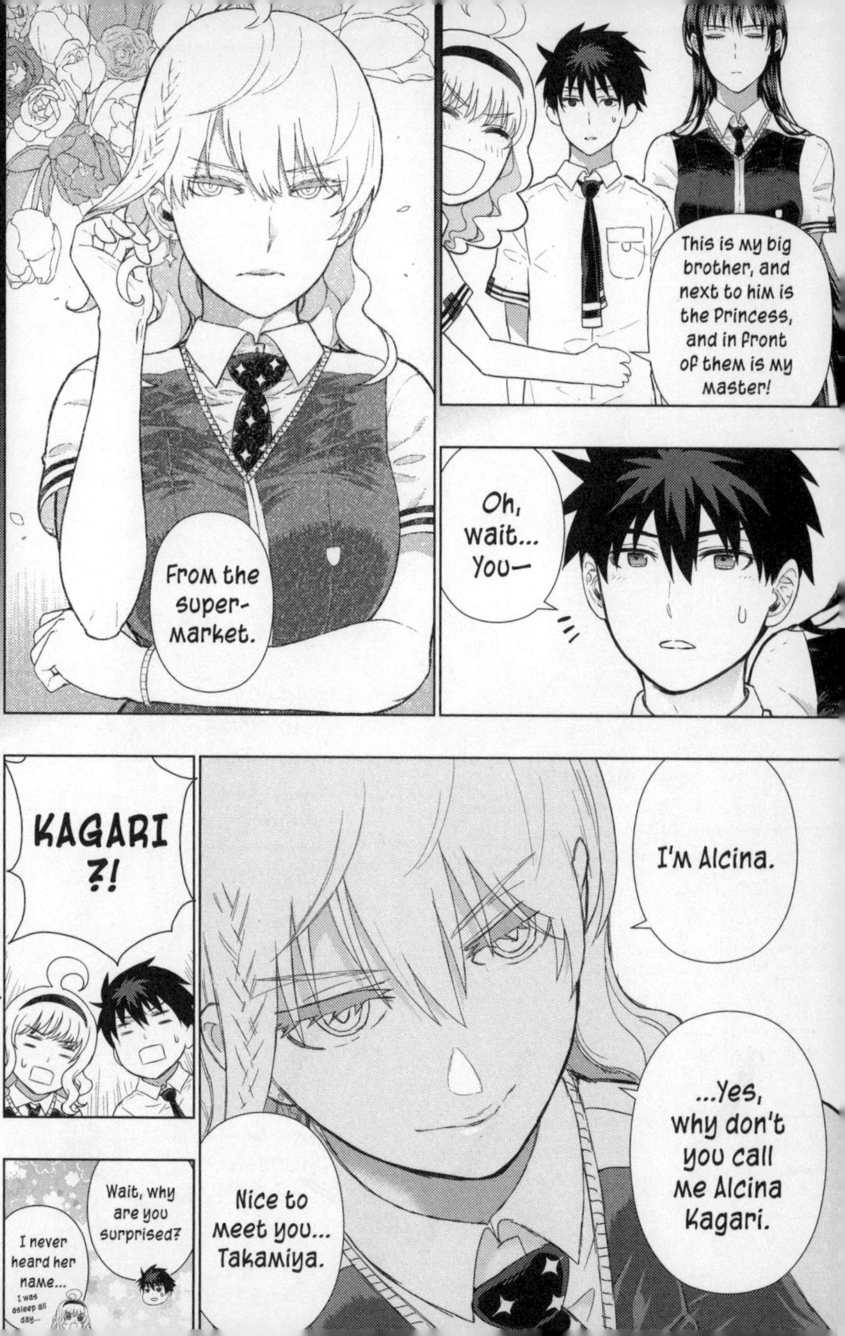
This is my big brother, and next to him is the Princess, and in front of them is my master!
Oh, wait... You—
From the super-market.
I'm Alcina.
...Yes, why don't you call me Alcina Kagari.
Nice to meet you... Takamiya.
KAGARI ?!
Wait, why are you surprised?
I never heard her name...
I was asleep all day...

CHAPTER 64 END

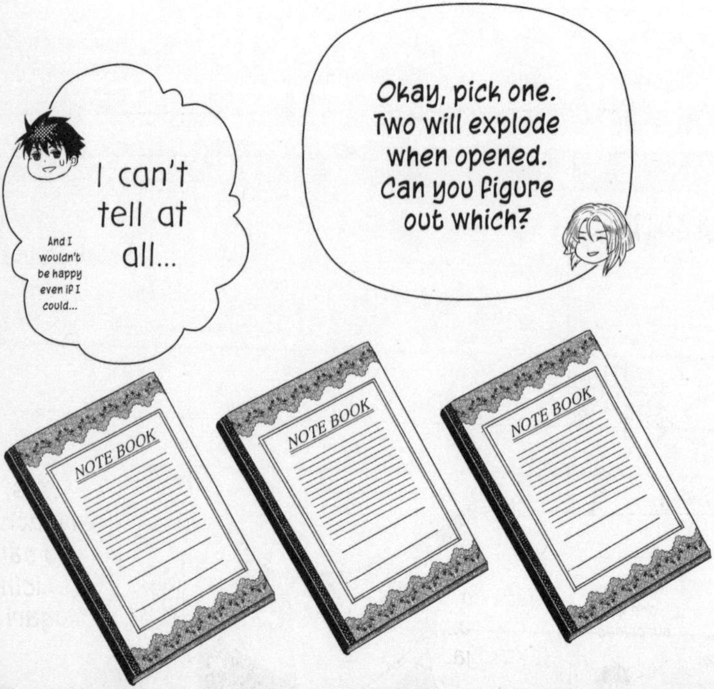
Okay, pick one. Two will explode when opened. Can you figure out which?
I can't tell at all...
And I wouldn't be happy even if I could...
NOTE BOOK
NOTE BOOK
NOTE BOOK

Witchcraft Works

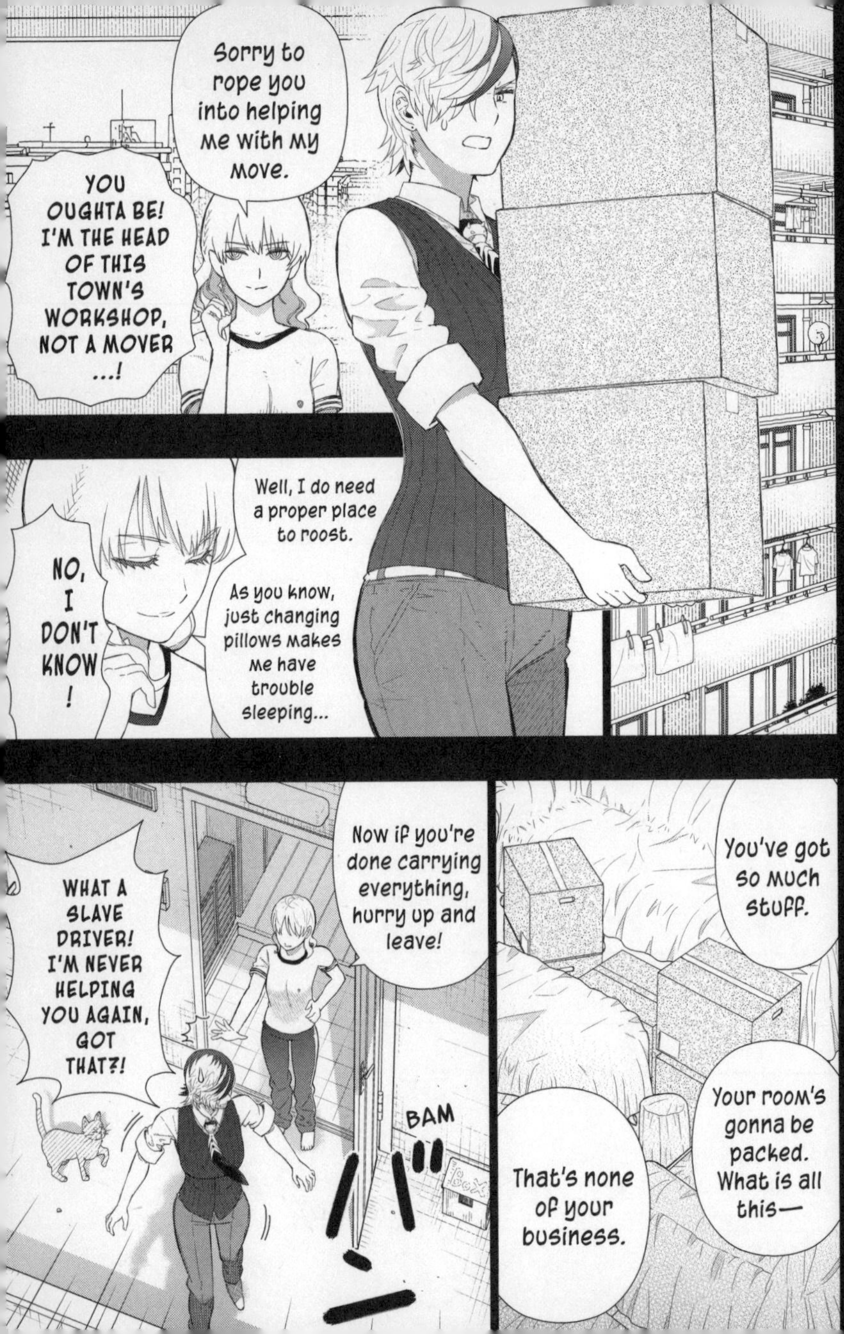
Sorry to rope you into helping me with my move.
YOU OUGHTA BE! I'M THE HEAD OF THIS TOWN'S WORKSHOP, NOT A MOVER ...!
Well, I do need a proper place to roost.
As you know, just changing pillows makes me have trouble sleeping...
NO, I DON'T KNOW!
You've got so much stuff.
Your room's gonna be packed. What is all this—
That's none of your business.
Now if you're done carrying everything, hurry up and leave!
BAM
WHAT A SLAVE DRIVER! I'M NEVER HELPING YOU AGAIN, GOT THAT?!

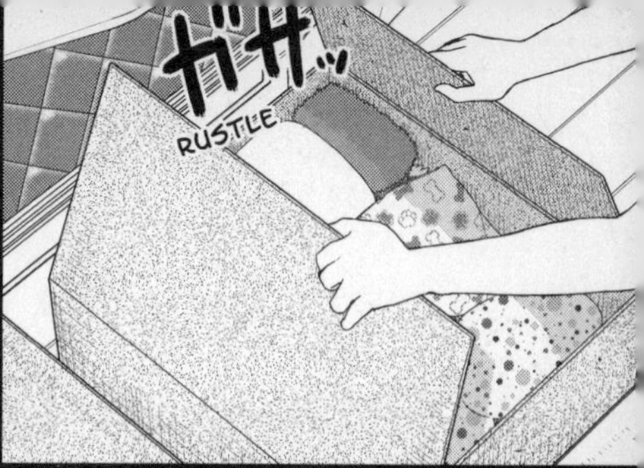
RUSTLE

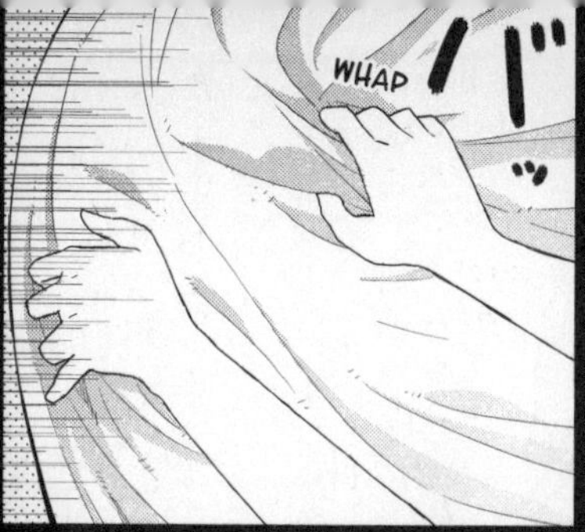
WHAP

CHAPTER 65 Takamiya and the Mysterious Transfer Student

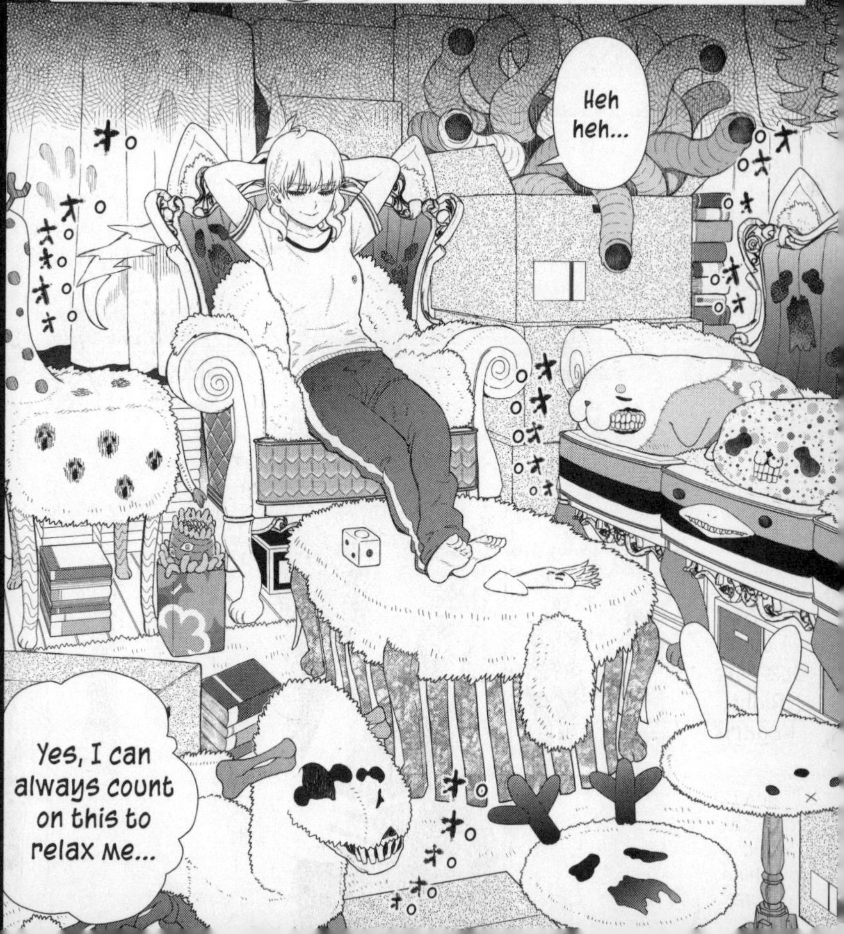
Heh heh...
Yes, I can always count on this to relax me...

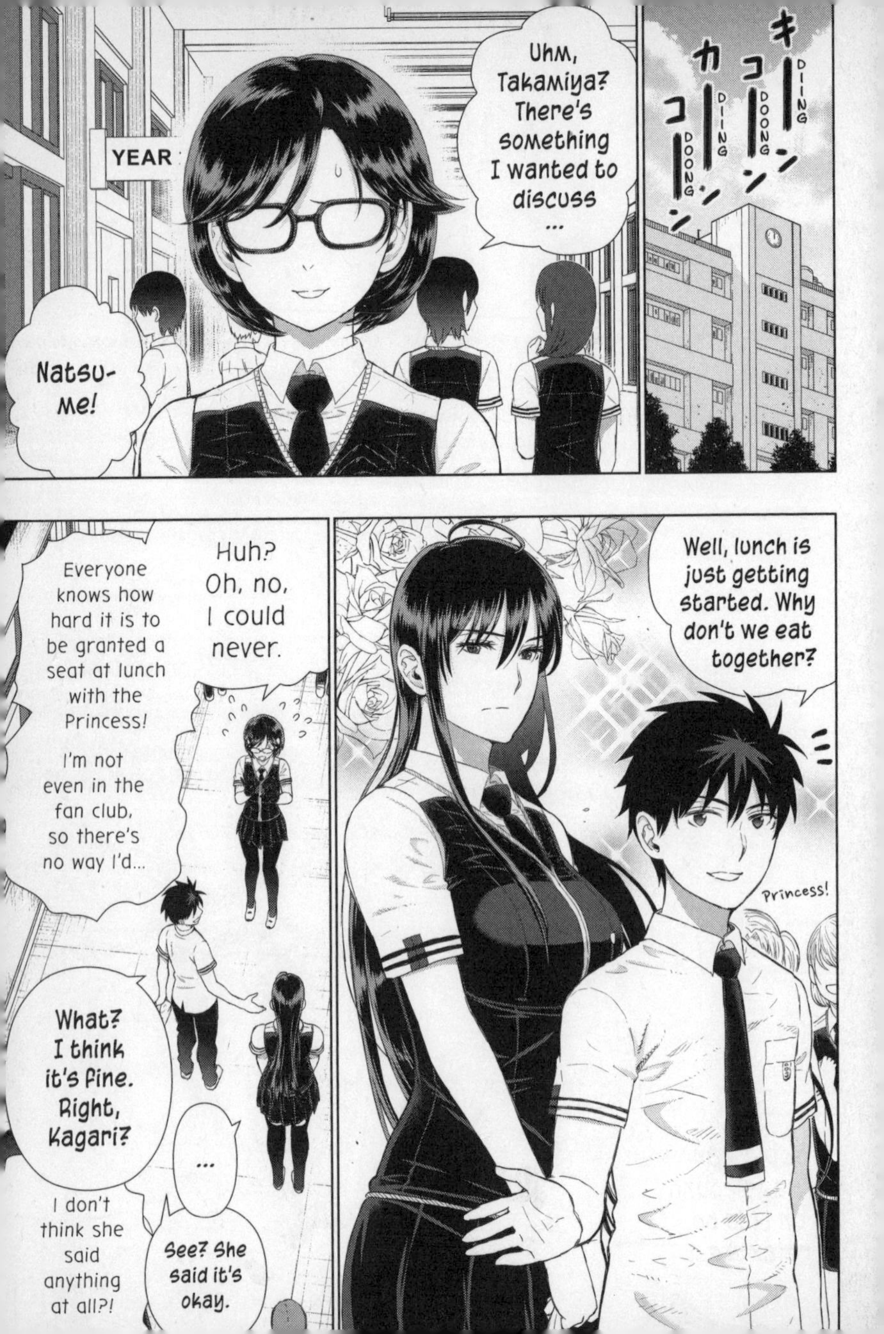
キーンコーン
DIING DOONG
カーンコーン
DIING DOONG
Uhm, Takamiya? There's something I wanted to discuss ...
YEAR
Natsume!
Well, lunch is just getting started. Why don't we eat together?
Princess!
Huh? Oh, no, I could never.
Everyone knows how hard it is to be granted a seat at lunch with the Princess!
I'm not even in the fan club, so there's no way I'd...
What? I think it's fine. Right, Kagari?
...
See? She said it's okay.
I don't think she said anything at all?!

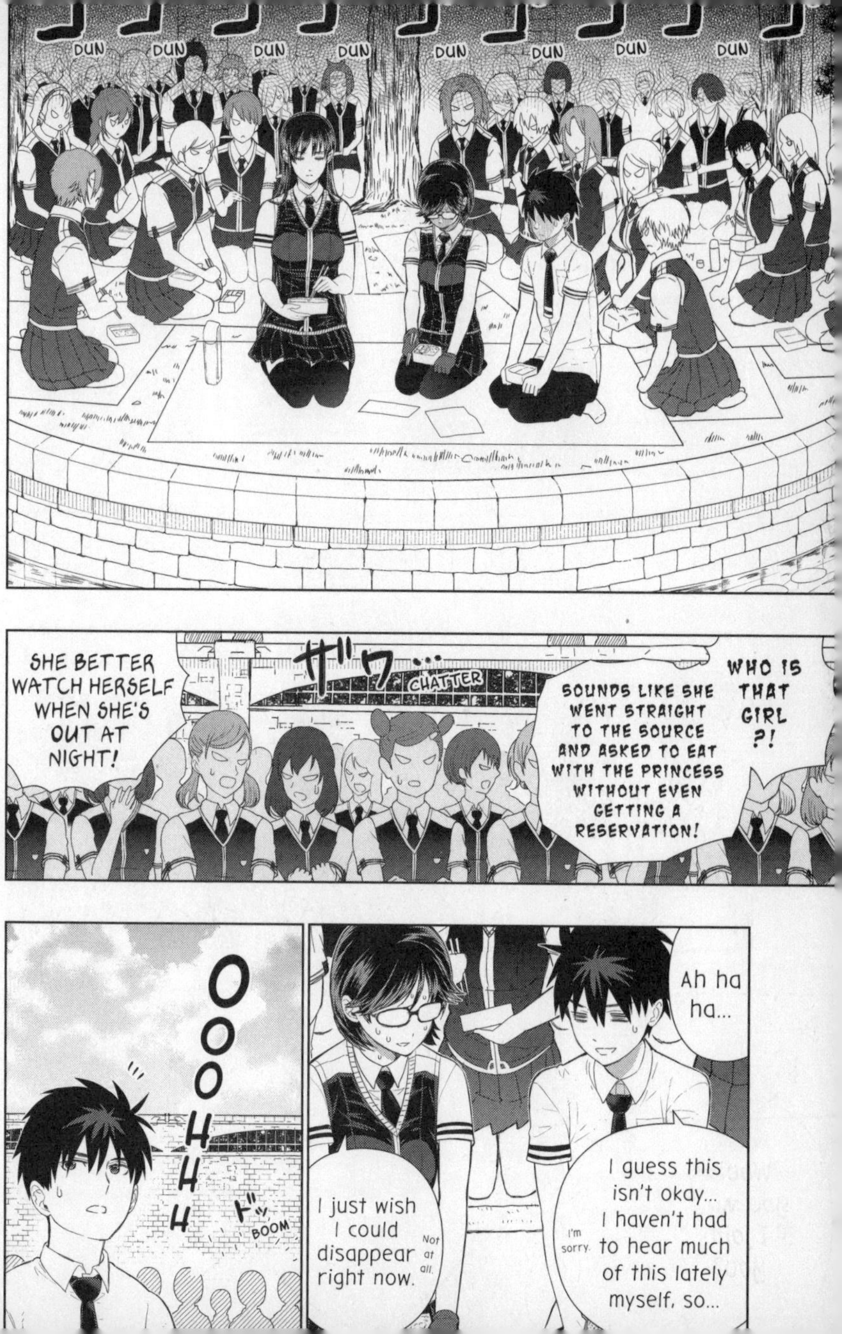
DUN DUN DUN DUN DUN DUN DUN DUN
WHO IS THAT GIRL?!
SOUNDS LIKE SHE WENT STRAIGHT TO THE SOURCE AND ASKED TO EAT WITH THE PRINCESS WITHOUT EVEN GETTING A RESERVATION!
CHATTER
SHE BETTER WATCH HERSELF WHEN SHE'S OUT AT NIGHT!
Ah ha ha...
I guess this isn't okay... I haven't had to hear much of this lately myself, so...
I'm sorry.
Not at all.
I just wish I could disappear right now.
OOOHHHH
BOOM

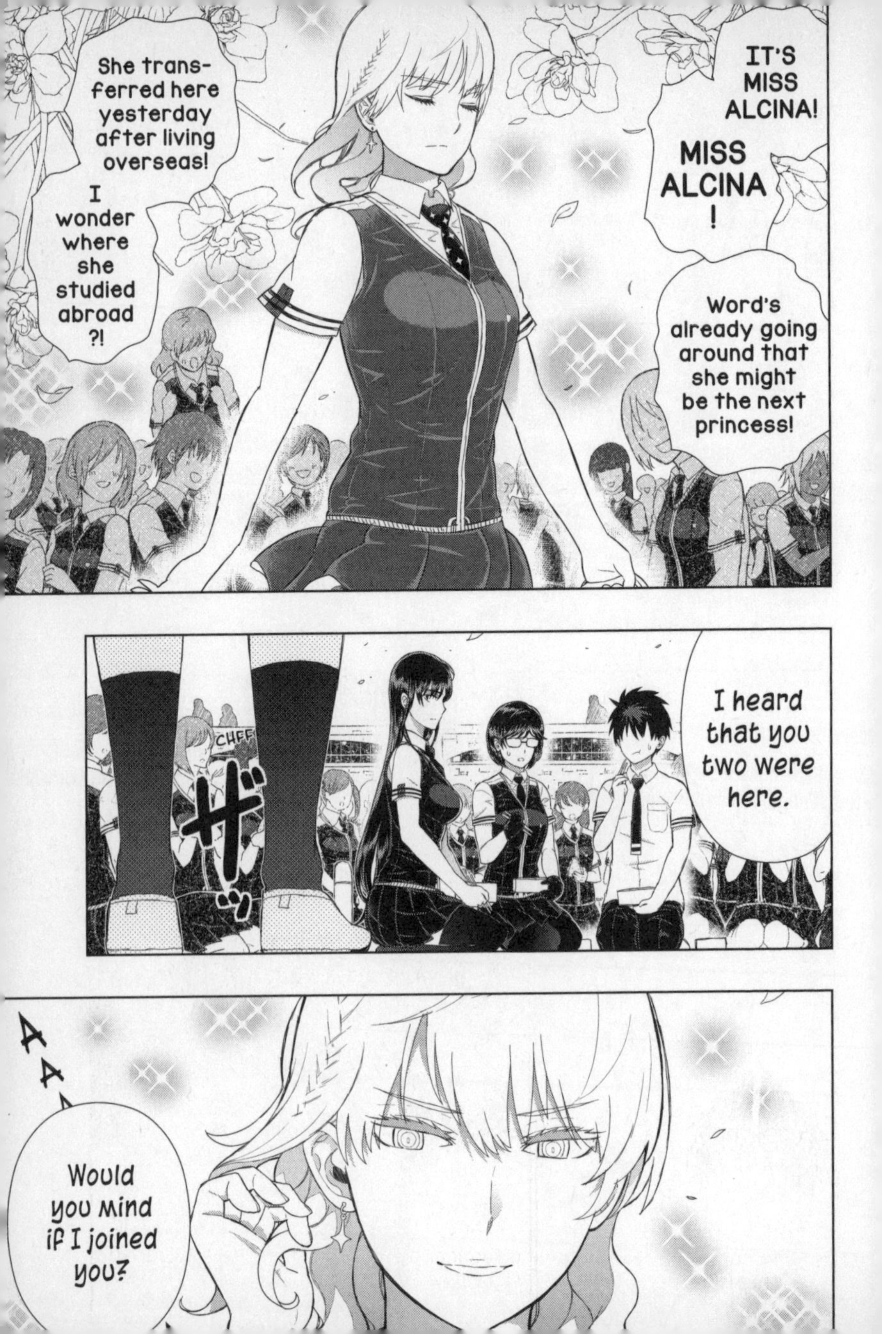
IT'S MISS ALCINA!
MISS ALCINA!
Word's already going around that she might be the next princess!
She trans-ferred here yesterday after living overseas!
I wonder where she studied abroad?!
I heard that you two were here.
CHFF
ザッ
Would you mind if I joined you?

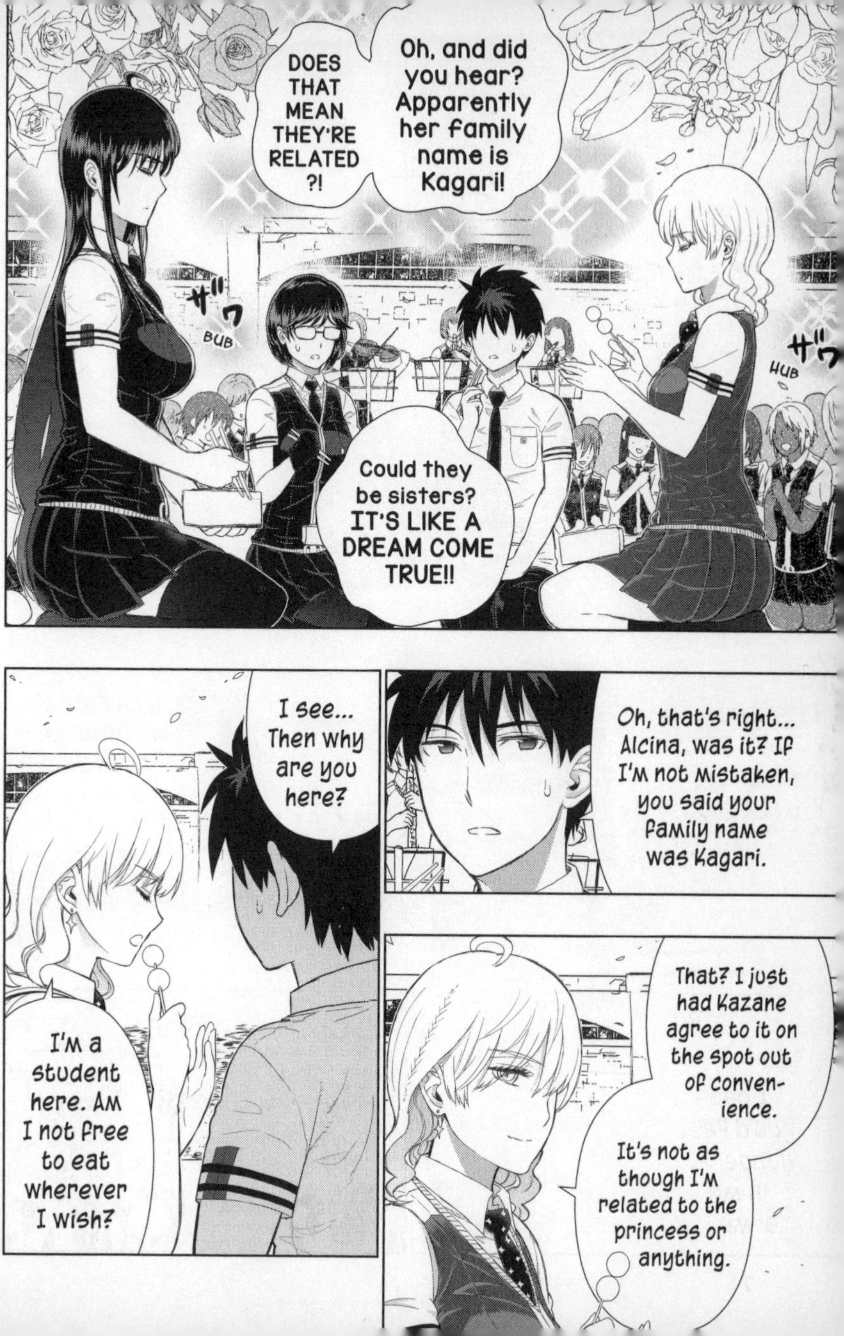
ザワ
HUB
Oh, and did you hear? Apparently her family name is Kagari!
DOES THAT MEAN THEY'RE RELATED ?!
ザワ
BUB
Could they be sisters? IT'S LIKE A DREAM COME TRUE!!
Oh, that's right... Alcina, was it? If I'm not mistaken, you said your family name was Kagari.
That? I just had Kazane agree to it on the spot out of conven-ience.
It's not as though I'm related to the princess or anything.
I see... Then why are you here?
I'm a student here. Am I not free to eat wherever I wish?

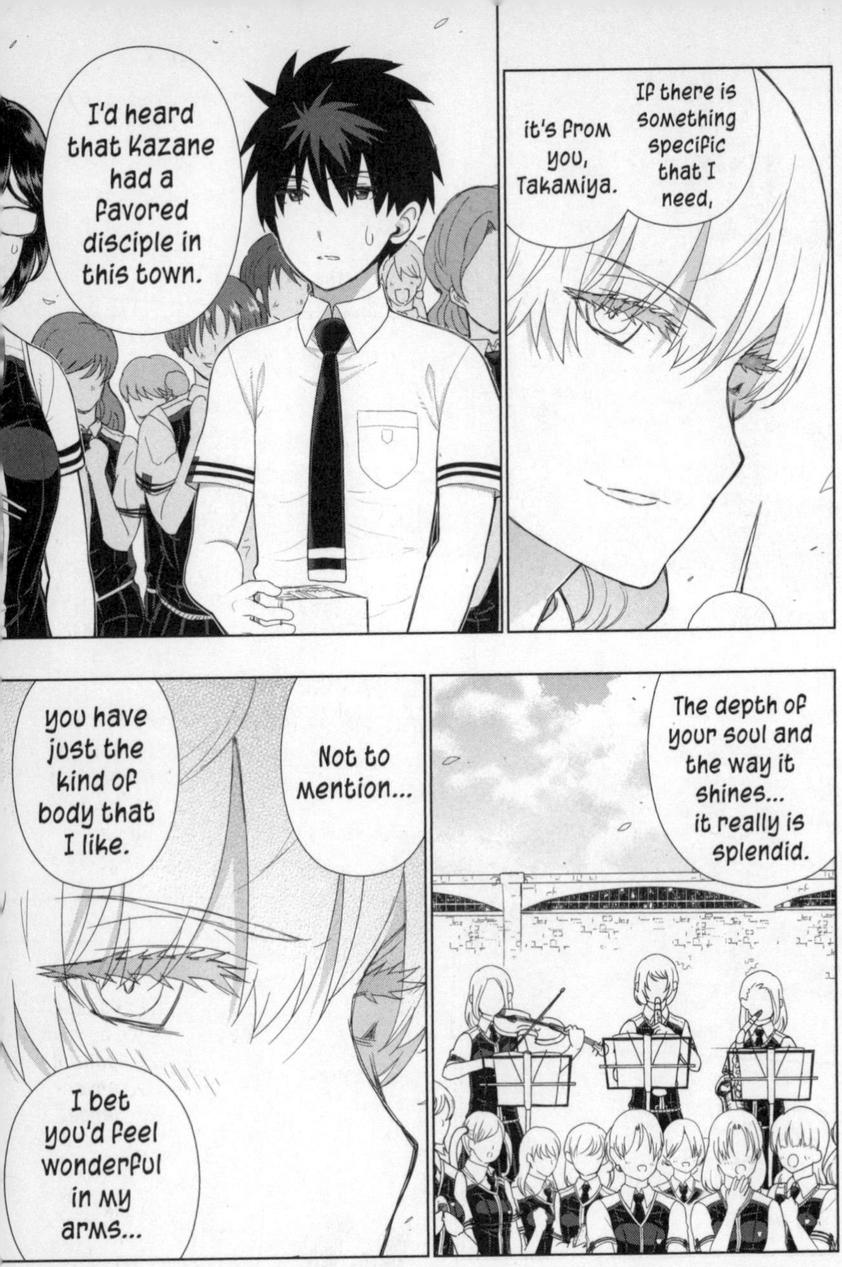
If there is something specific that I need,
it's from you, Takamiya.
I'd heard that Kazane had a favored disciple in this town.
The depth of your soul and the way it shines... it really is splendid.
Not to mention...
you have just the kind of body that I like.
I bet you'd feel wonderful in my arms...

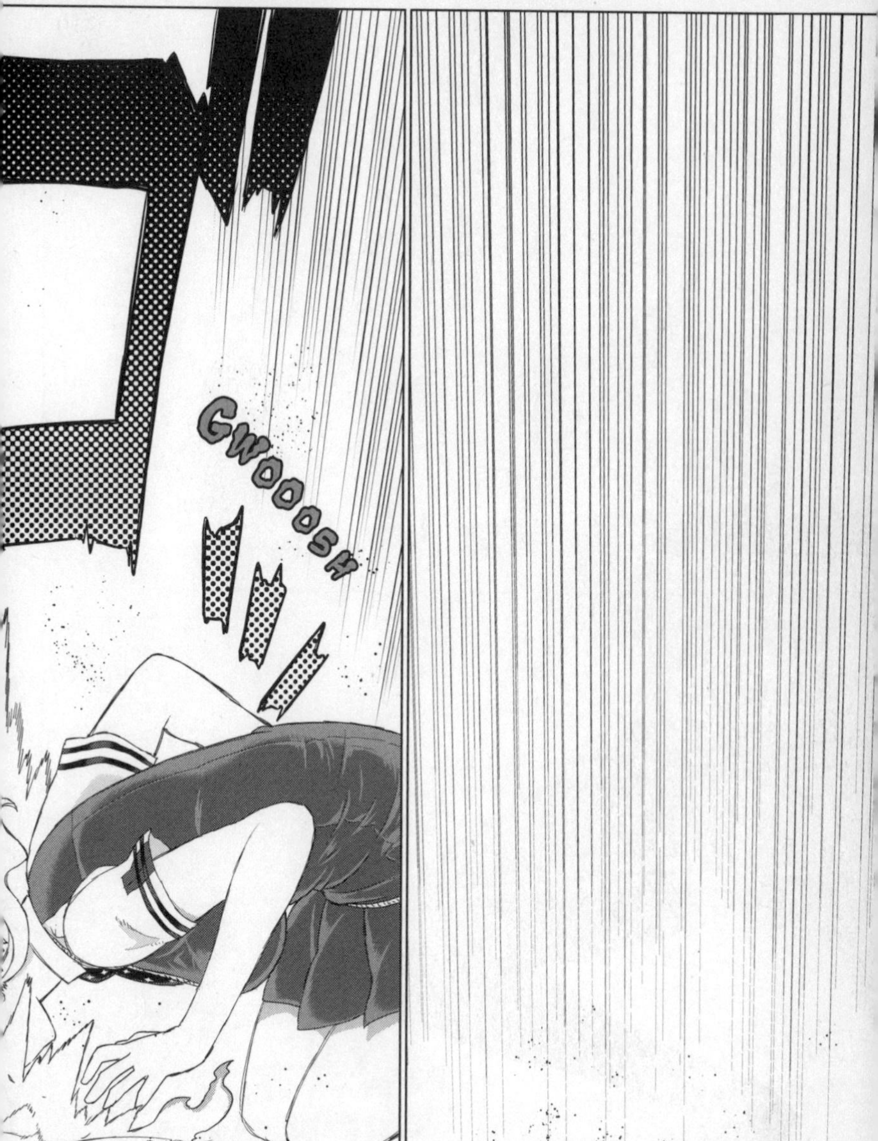
GWOOOSH

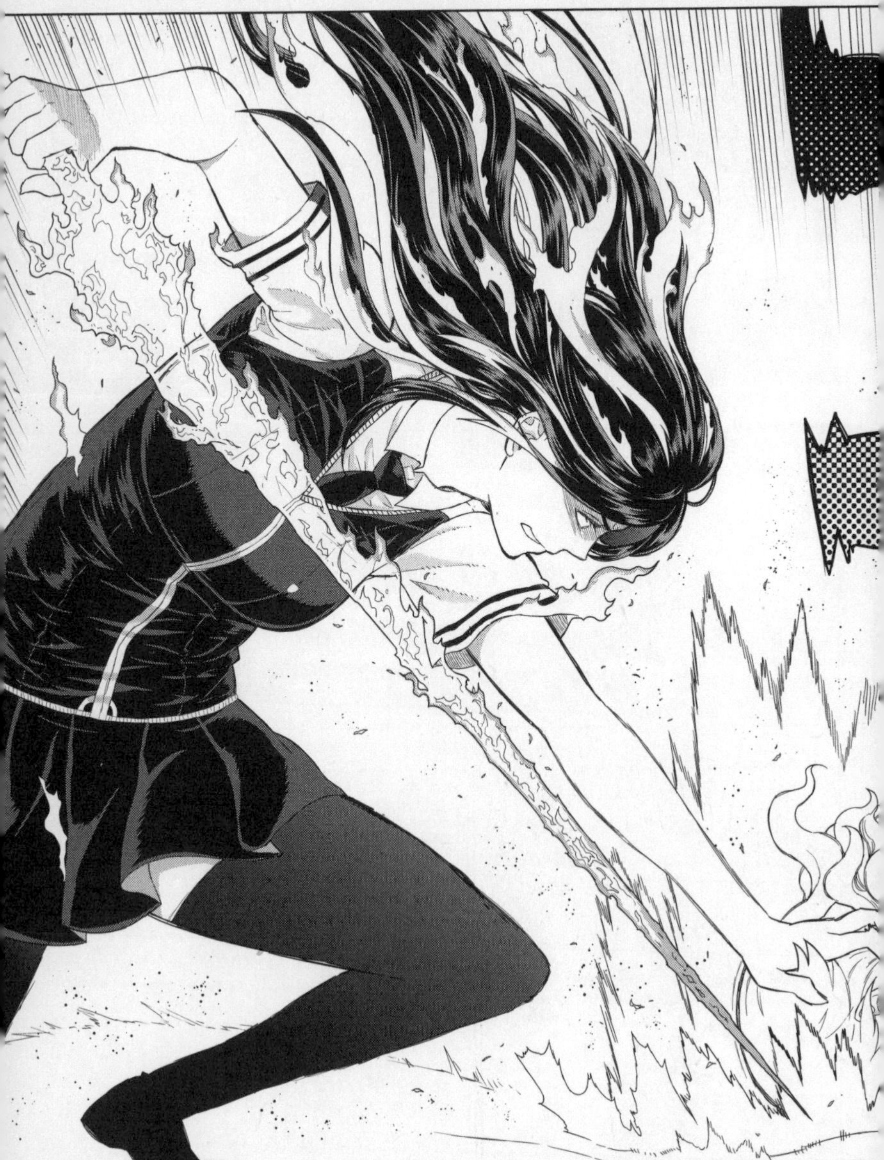

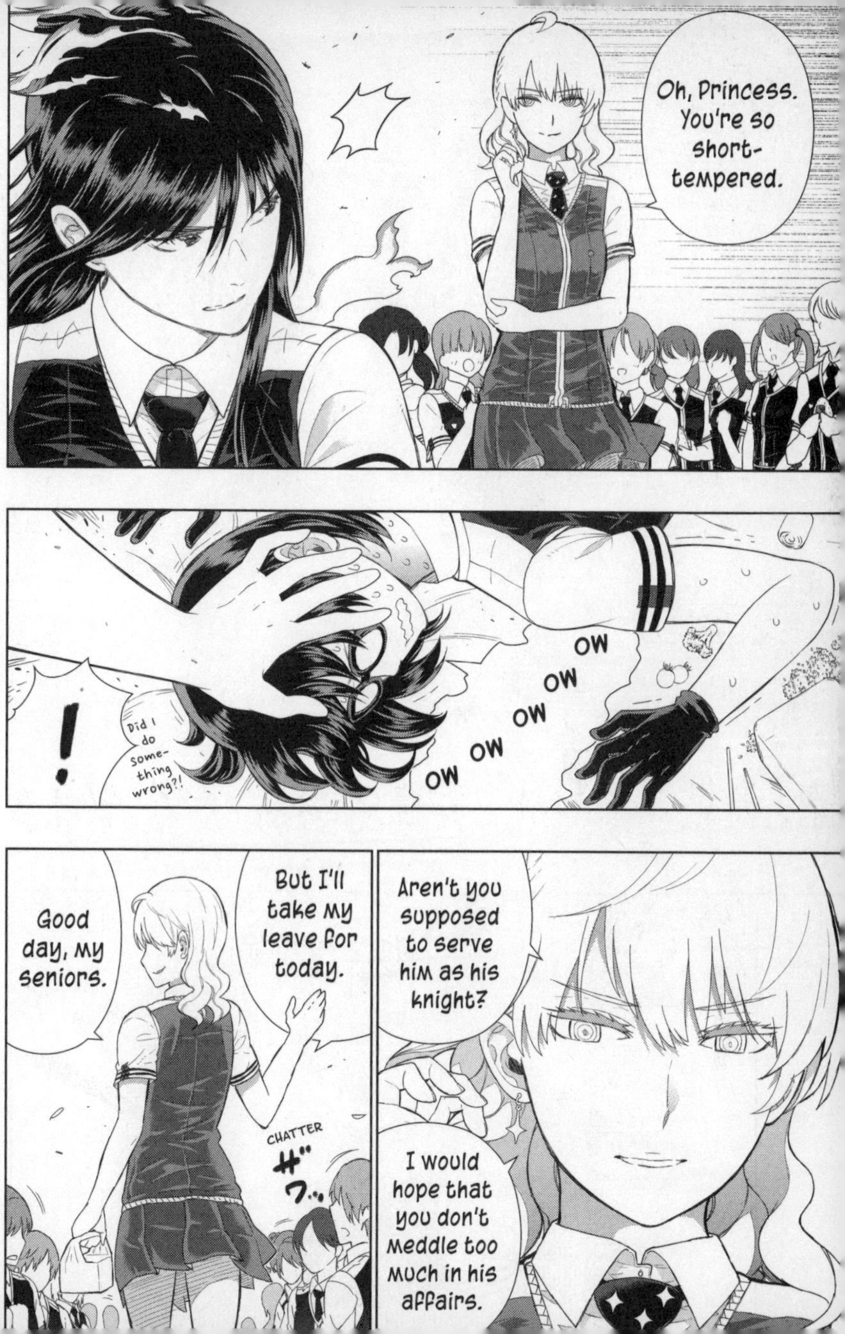
Oh, Princess. You're so short-tempered.
OW OW OW OW OW
Did I do something wrong?!
Aren't you supposed to serve him as his knight?
I would hope that you don't meddle too much in his affairs.
But I'll take my leave for today.
Good day, my seniors.
CHATTER

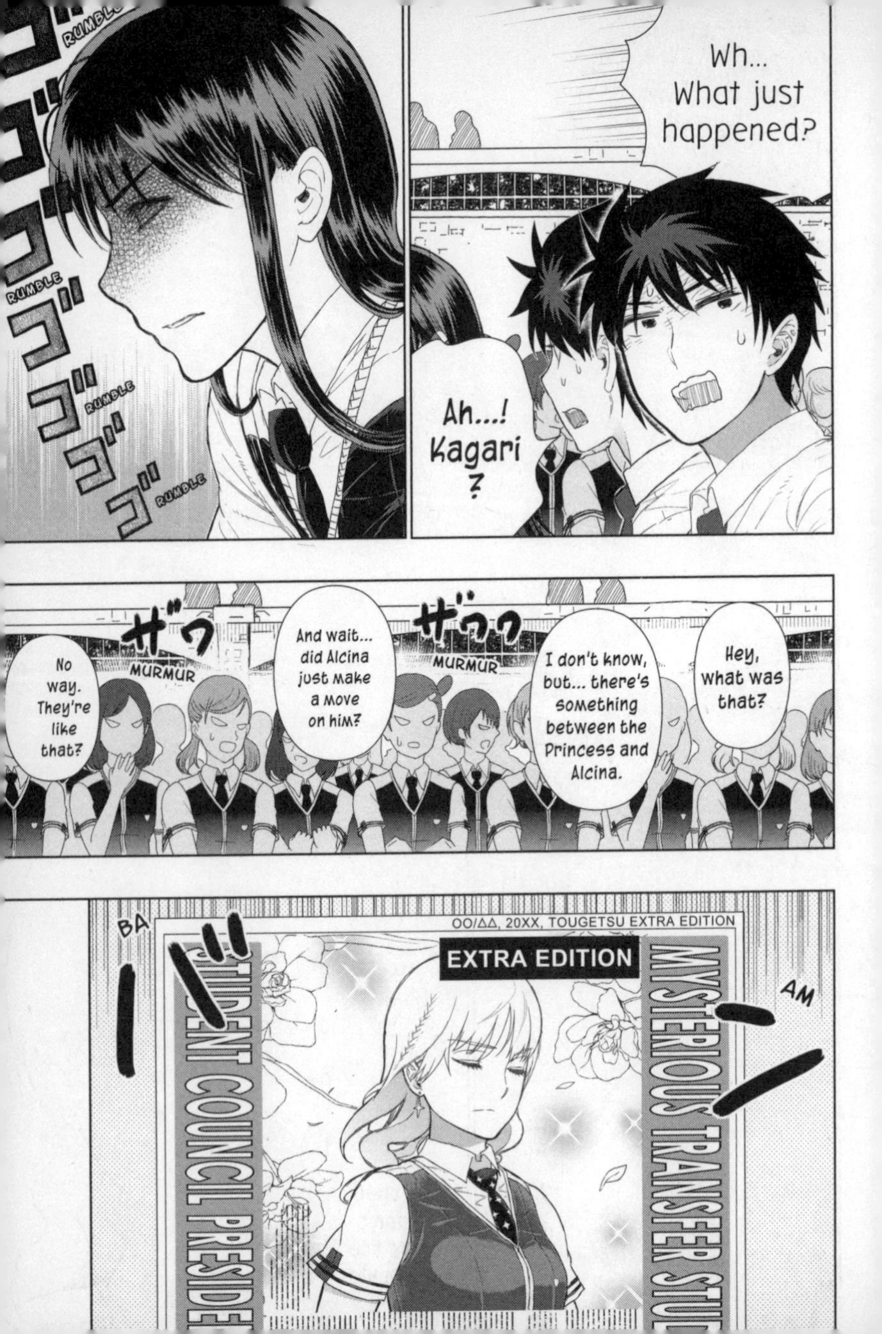
Wh... What just happened?
Ah...! Kagari?
RUMBLE
RUMBLE
RUMBLE
RUMBLE
Hey, what was that?
I don't know, but... there's something between the Princess and Alcina.
MURMUR
And wait... did Alcina just make a move on him?
MURMUR
No way. They're like that?
BA
AM
OO/ΔΔ, 20XX, TOUGETSU EXTRA EDITION
EXTRA EDITION
MYSTERIOUS TRANSFER STUD
STUDENT COUNCIL PRESIDE

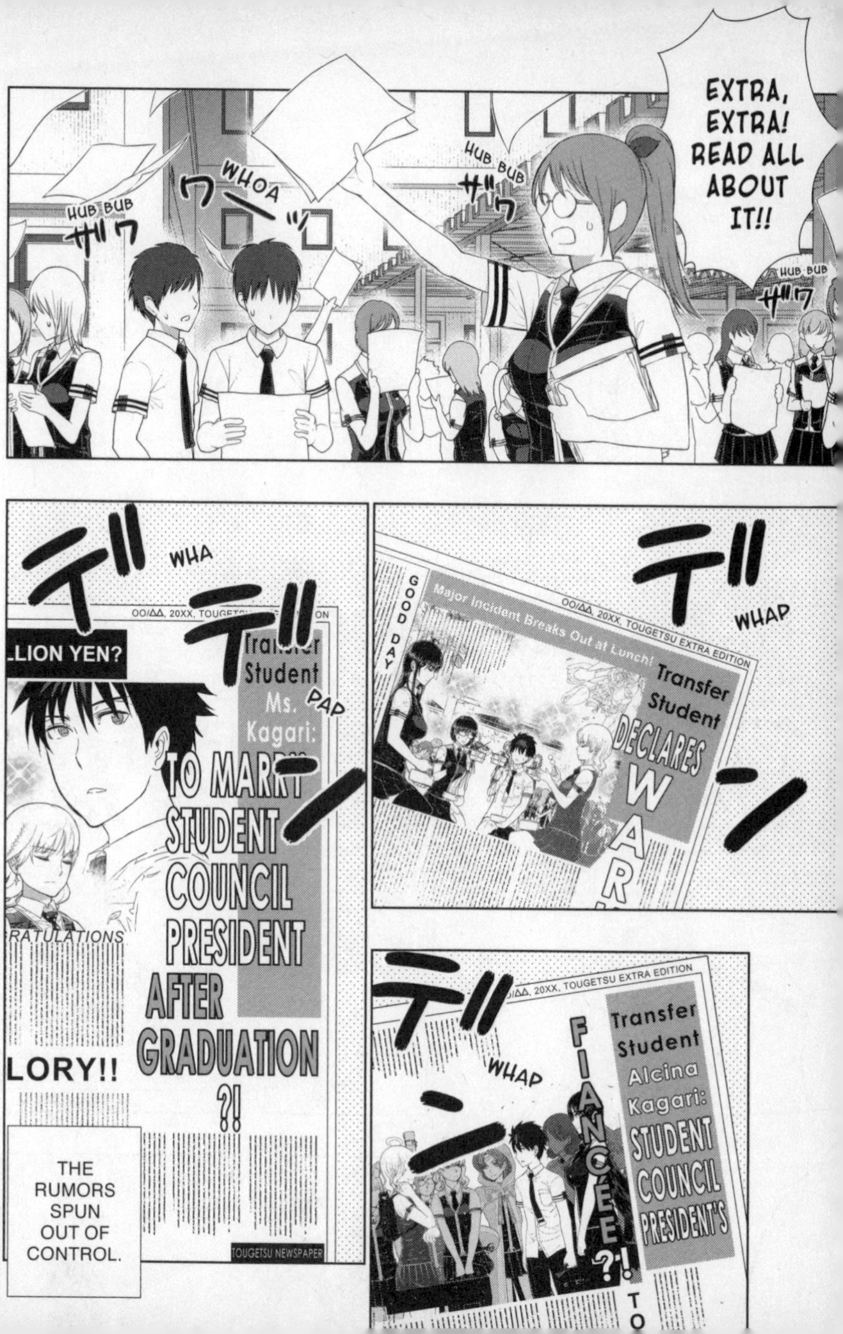
EXTRA, EXTRA! READ ALL ABOUT IT!!
HUB BUB ザワ
HUB BUB ザワ
WHOA ワーッ
HUB BUB ザワ
デデーン
WHAP
OO/ΔΔ, 20XX, TOUGETSU EXTRA EDITION
GOOD DAY
Major Incident Breaks Out at Lunch!
Transfer Student DECLARES WAR
デデーン
WHAP
/ΔΔ, 20XX, TOUGETSU EXTRA EDITION
Transfer Student Alcina Kagari: STUDENT COUNCIL PRESIDENT'S FIANCÉE?!
TO
デデーン
WHA
PAP
OO/ΔΔ, 20XX, TOUGETSU
LLION YEN?
Transfer Student Ms. Kagari: TO MARRY STUDENT COUNCIL PRESIDENT AFTER GRADUATION ?!
RATULATIONS
LORY!!
TOUGETSU NEWSPAPER
THE RUMORS SPUN OUT OF CONTROL.

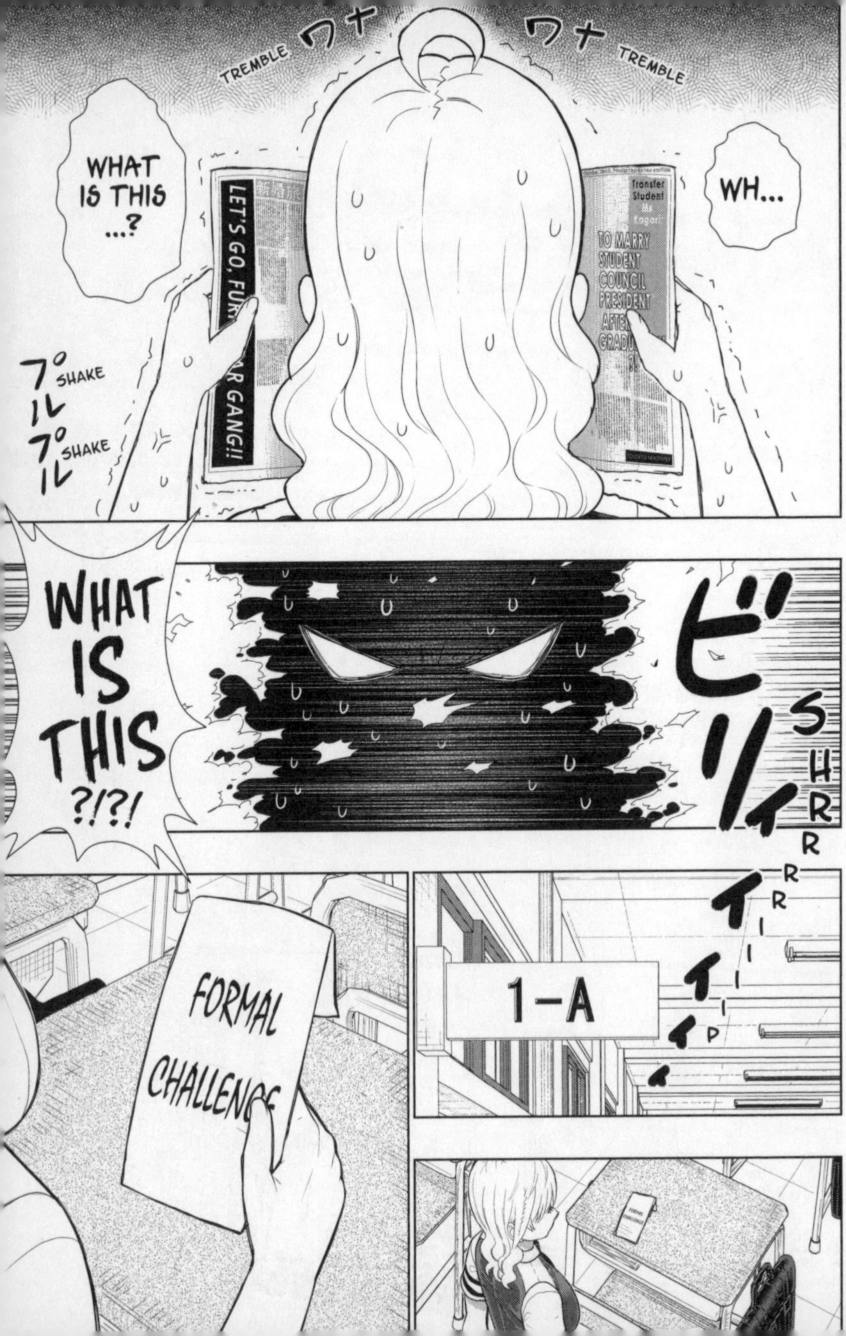

ワナ TREMBLE
ワナ TREMBLE
WH...
TO MARRY STUDENT COUNCIL PRESIDENT AFTER
LET'S GO, FUR
AR GANG!!
WHAT IS THIS ...?
プルプル SHAKE SHAKE
ビリイイイ SHRRRRIIIIP
WHAT IS THIS ?!?!
1-A
FORMAL CHALLENGE

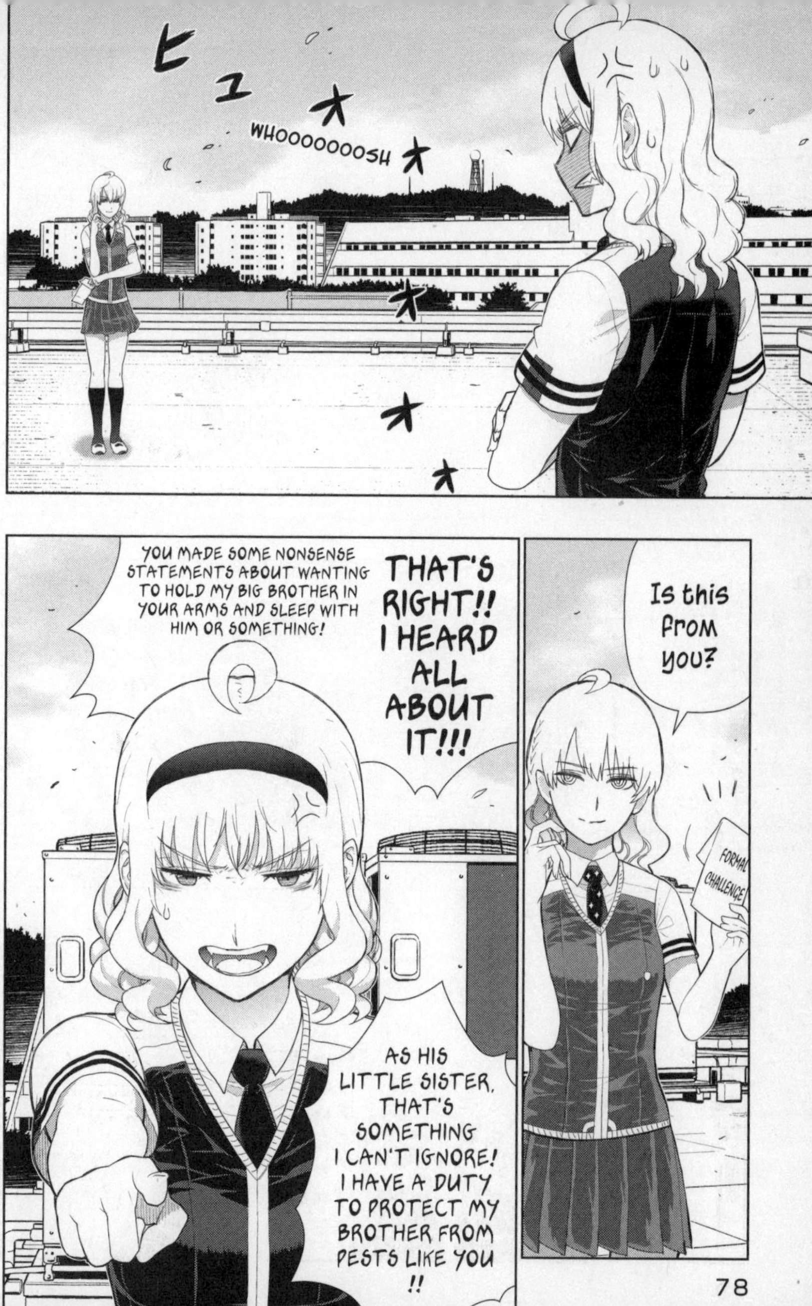
ヒュオ
WHOOOOOOOOSH
Is this from you?
FORMAL CHALLENGE
THAT'S RIGHT!! I HEARD ALL ABOUT IT!!!
YOU MADE SOME NONSENSE STATEMENTS ABOUT WANTING TO HOLD MY BIG BROTHER IN YOUR ARMS AND SLEEP WITH HIM OR SOMETHING!
AS HIS LITTLE SISTER, THAT'S SOMETHING I CAN'T IGNORE! I HAVE A DUTY TO PROTECT MY BROTHER FROM PESTS LIKE YOU !!

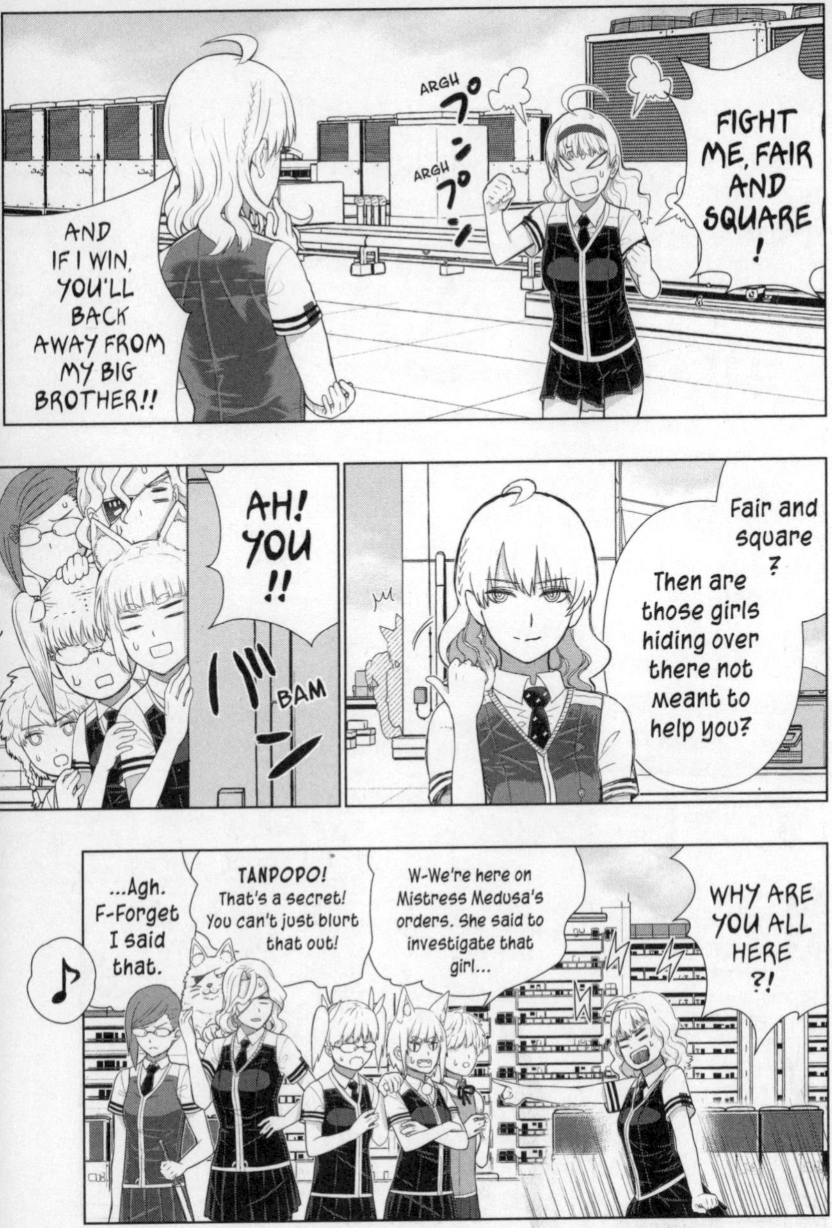
FIGHT ME, FAIR AND SQUARE!
ARGH
ARGH
AND IF I WIN, YOU'LL BACK AWAY FROM MY BIG BROTHER!!
Fair and square? Then are those girls hiding over there not meant to help you?
AH! YOU!!
BAM
WHY ARE YOU ALL HERE?!
W-We're here on Mistress Medusa's orders. She said to investigate that girl...
TANPOPO! That's a secret! You can't just blurt that out!
...Agh. F-Forget I said that.
♪

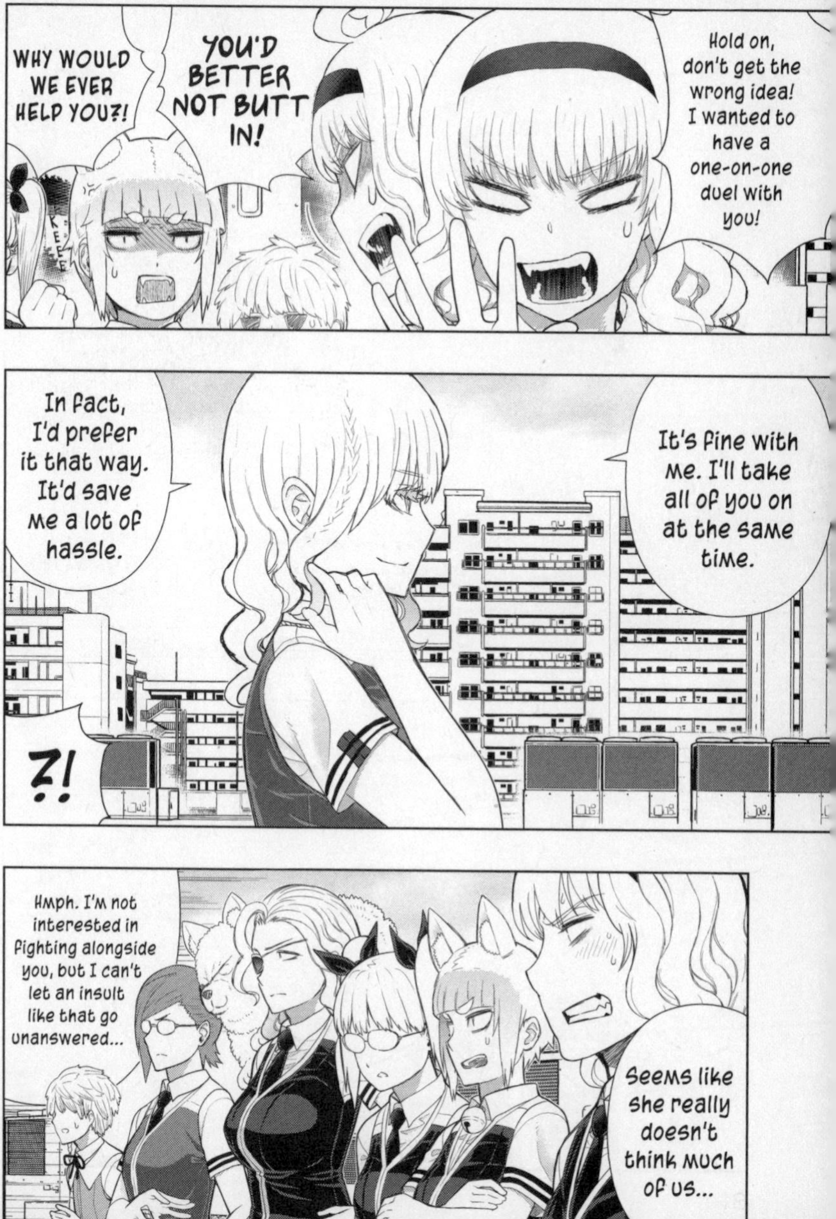
Hold on, don't get the wrong idea! I wanted to have a one-on-one duel with you!
YOU'D BETTER NOT BUTT IN!
WHY WOULD WE EVER HELP YOU?!
It's fine with me. I'll take all of you on at the same time.
In fact, I'd prefer it that way. It'd save me a lot of hassle.
?!
Seems like she really doesn't think much of us...
Hmph. I'm not interested in fighting alongside you, but I can't let an insult like that go unanswered...

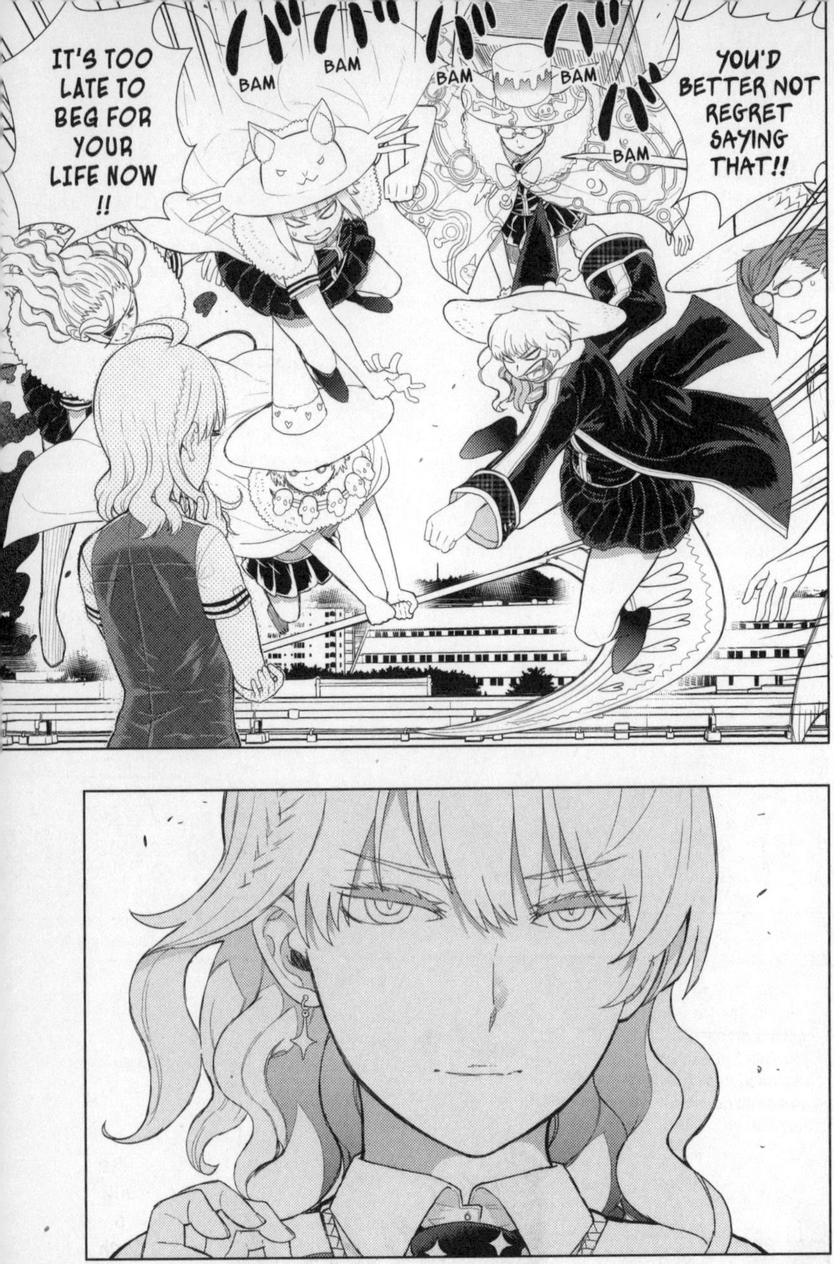
YOU'D BETTER NOT REGRET SAYING THAT!!
BAM
BAM
BAM
BAM
BAM
IT'S TOO LATE TO BEG FOR YOUR LIFE NOW !!

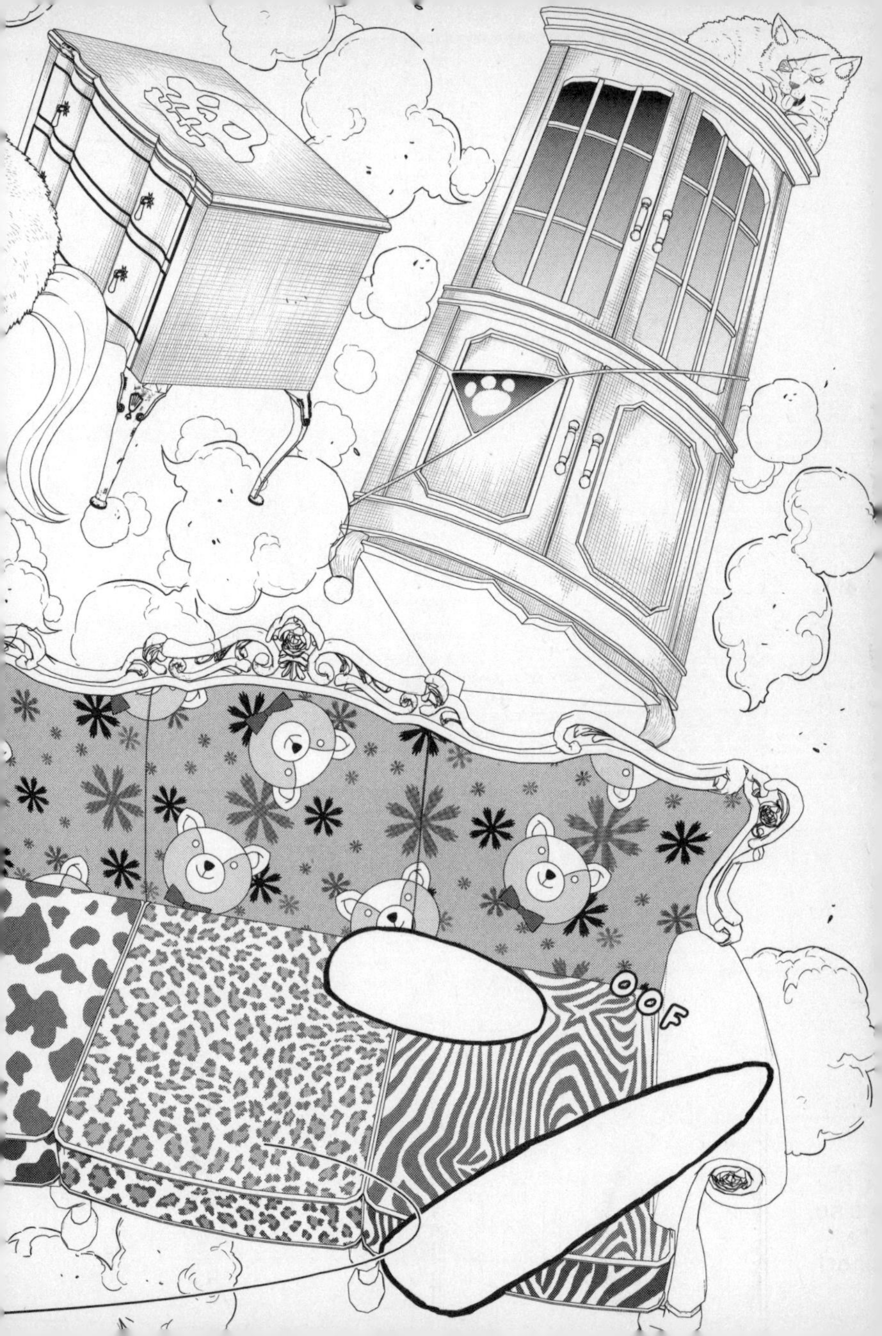
OOF

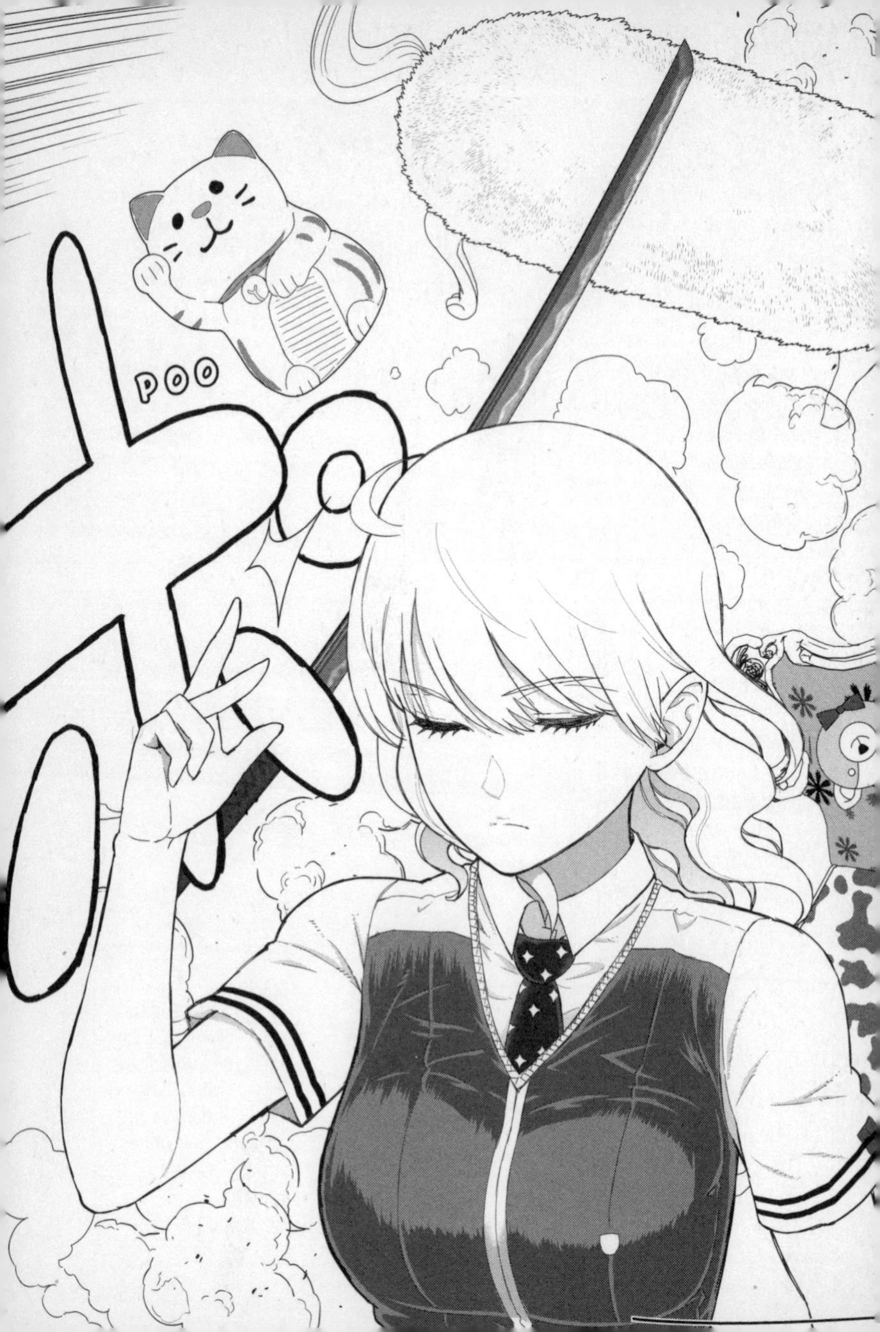
POO

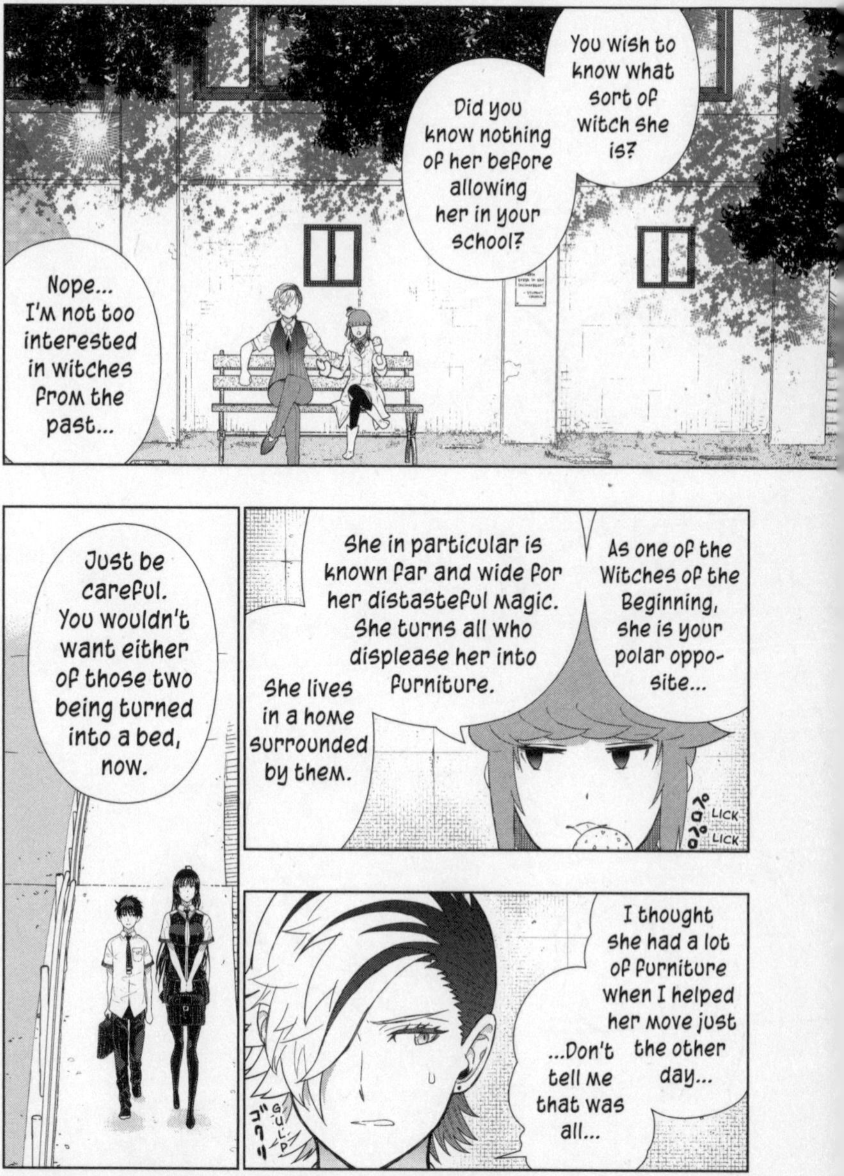
You wish to know what sort of witch she is?
Did you know nothing of her before allowing her in your school?
Nope... I'm not too interested in witches from the past...
As one of the Witches of the Beginning, she is your polar opposite...
She in particular is known far and wide for her distasteful magic. She turns all who displease her into furniture.
She lives in a home surrounded by them.
LICK LICK
I thought she had a lot of furniture when I helped her move just the other day...
...Don't tell me that was all...
GULP
Just be careful. You wouldn't want either of those two being turned into a bed, now.

Witchcraft Works

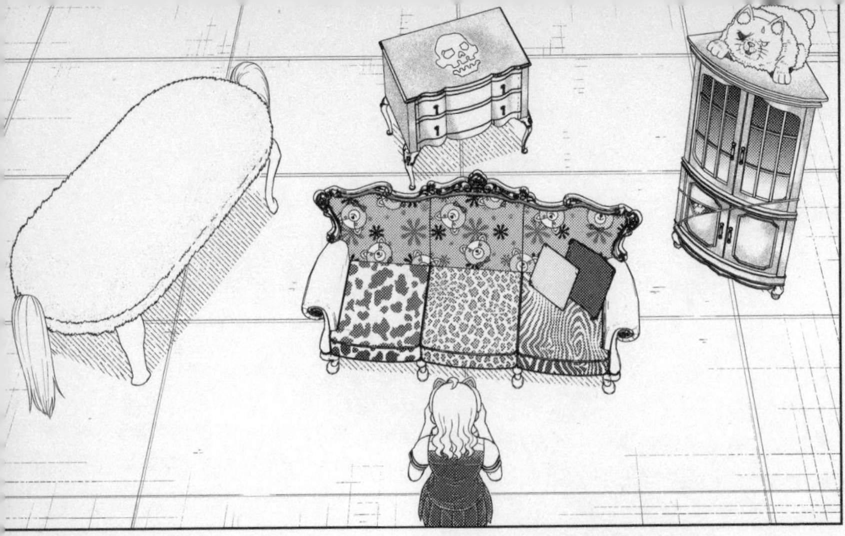

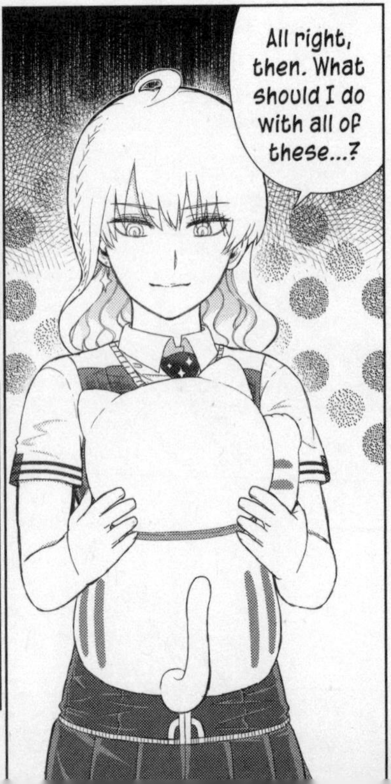
All right, then. What should I do with all of these...?

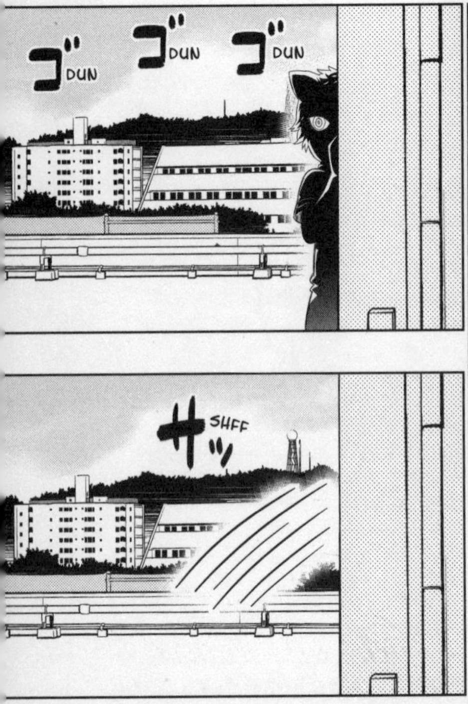
ゴ DUN
ゴ DUN
ゴ DUN
サッ SHFF

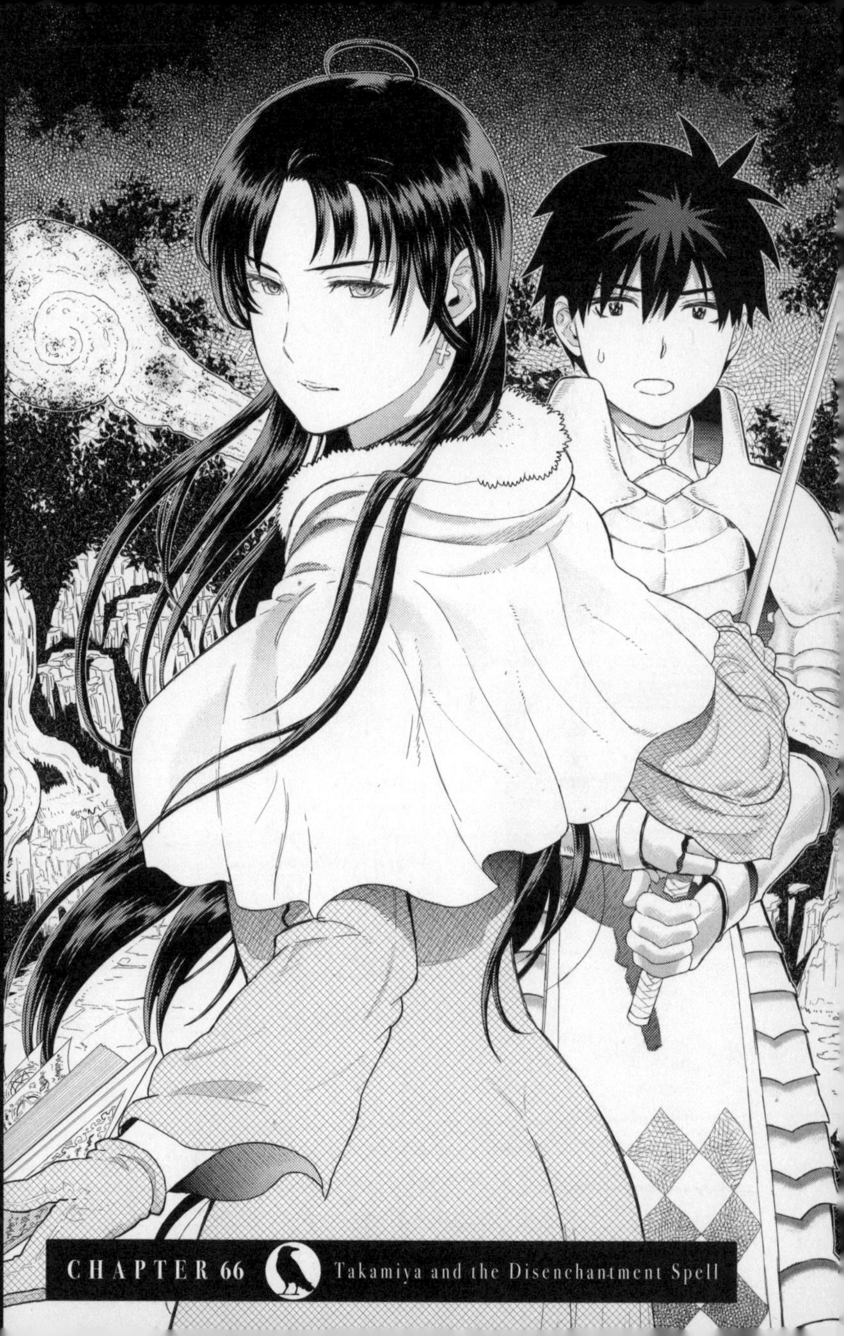

CHAPTER 66 Takamiya and the Disenchantment Spell

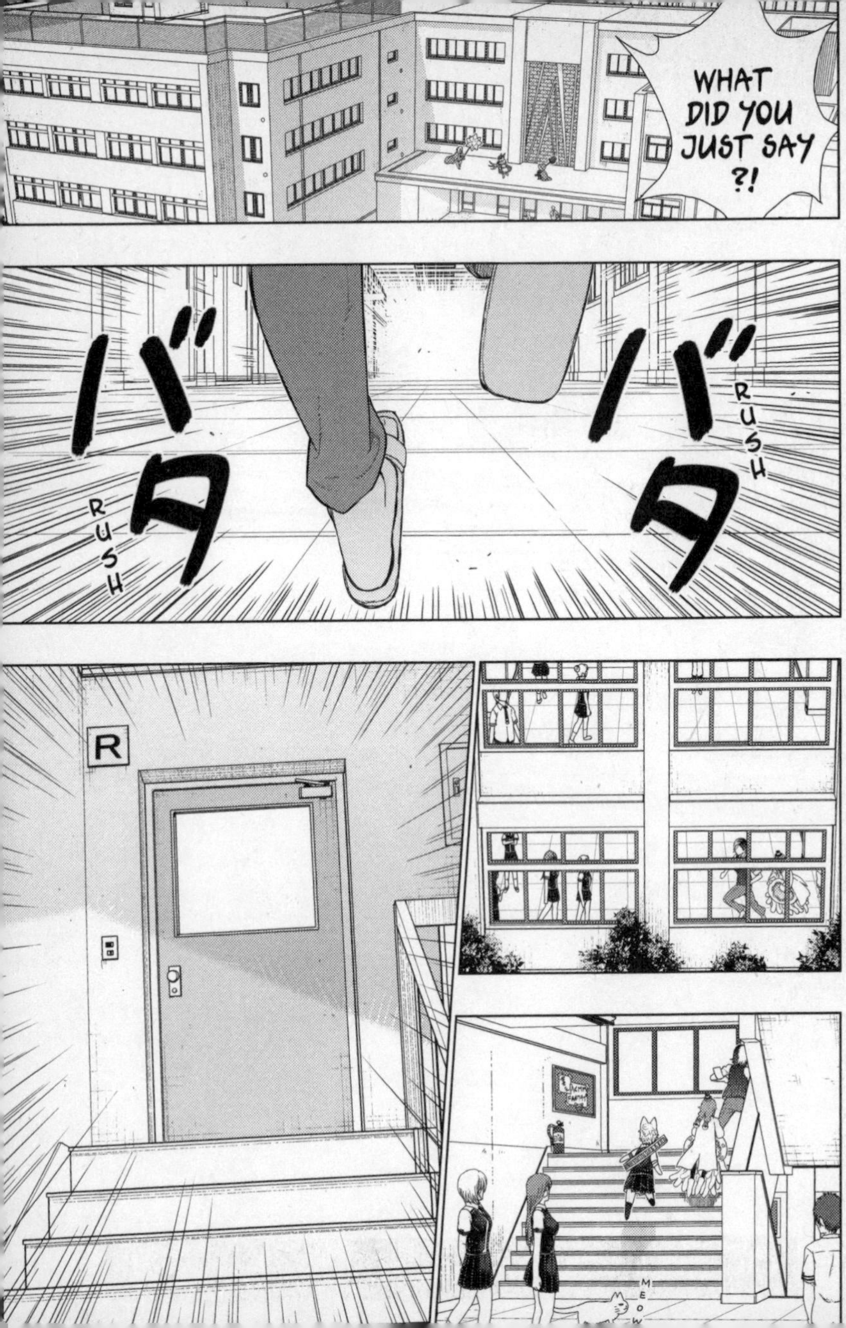
WHAT DID YOU JUST SAY ?!
バタ
RUSH
バタ
RUSH
MEOW
R

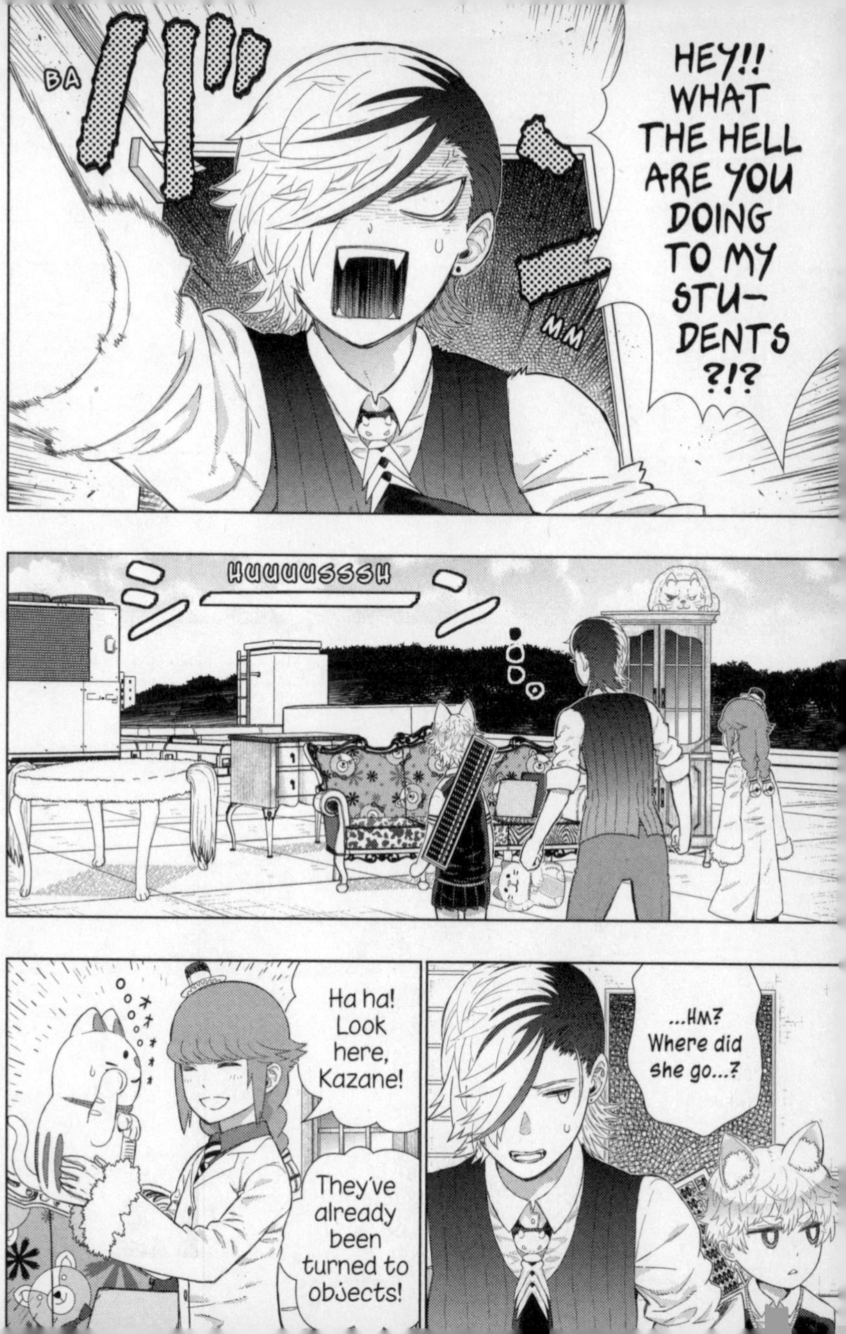

BA
MM
HEY!! WHAT THE HELL ARE YOU DOING TO MY STU-DENTS ?!?
HUUUUSSSH
...HM? Where did she go...?
Ha ha! Look here, Kazane!
They've already been turned to objects!

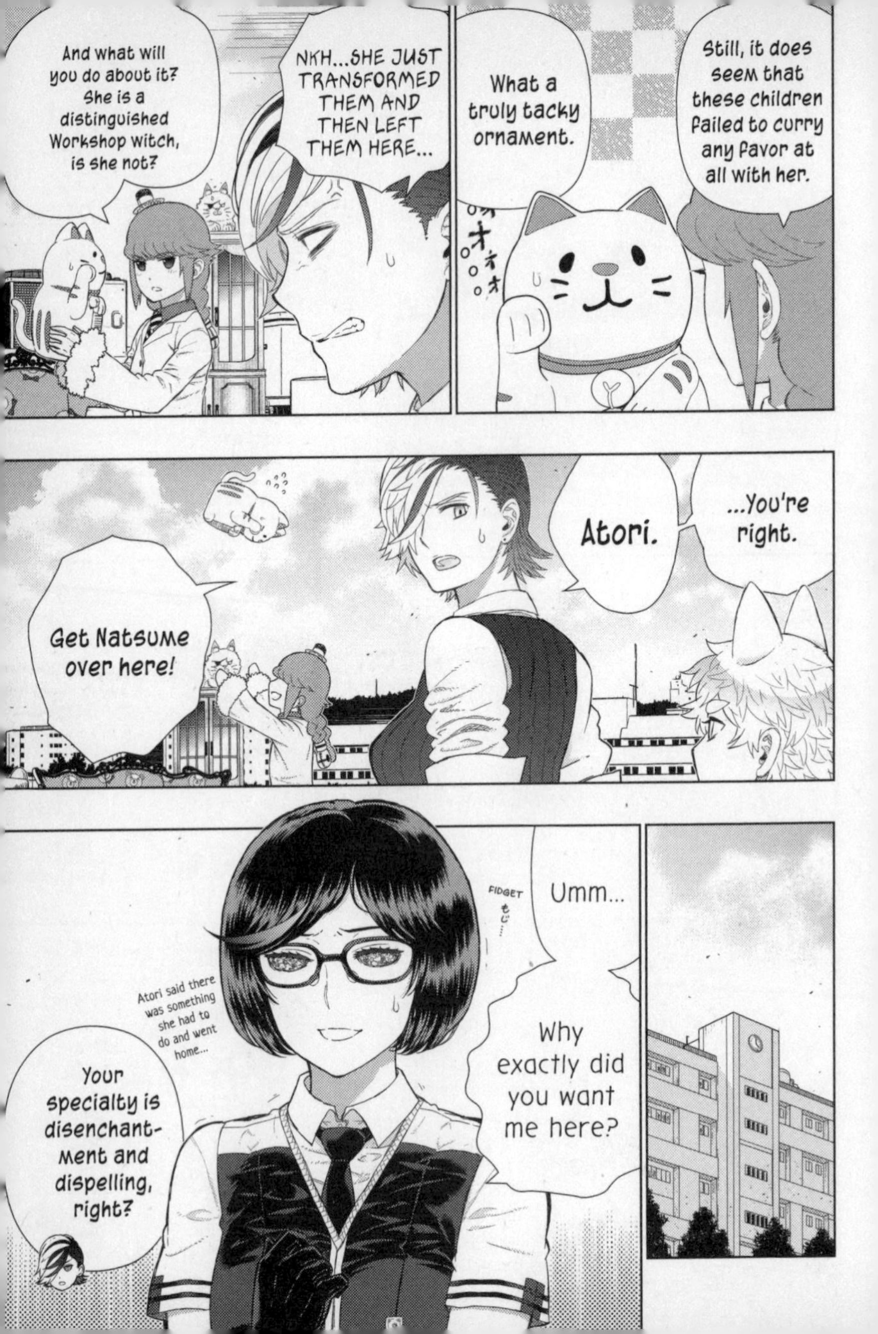
Still, it does seem that these children failed to curry any favor at all with her.
What a truly tacky ornament.
NKH...SHE JUST TRANSFORMED THEM AND THEN LEFT THEM HERE...
And what will you do about it? She is a distinguished Workshop witch, is she not?
...You're right.
Atori.
Get Natsume over here!
Umm...
FIDGET
もじ…
Why exactly did you want me here?
Atori said there was something she had to do and went home...
Your specialty is disenchant-ment and dispelling, right?

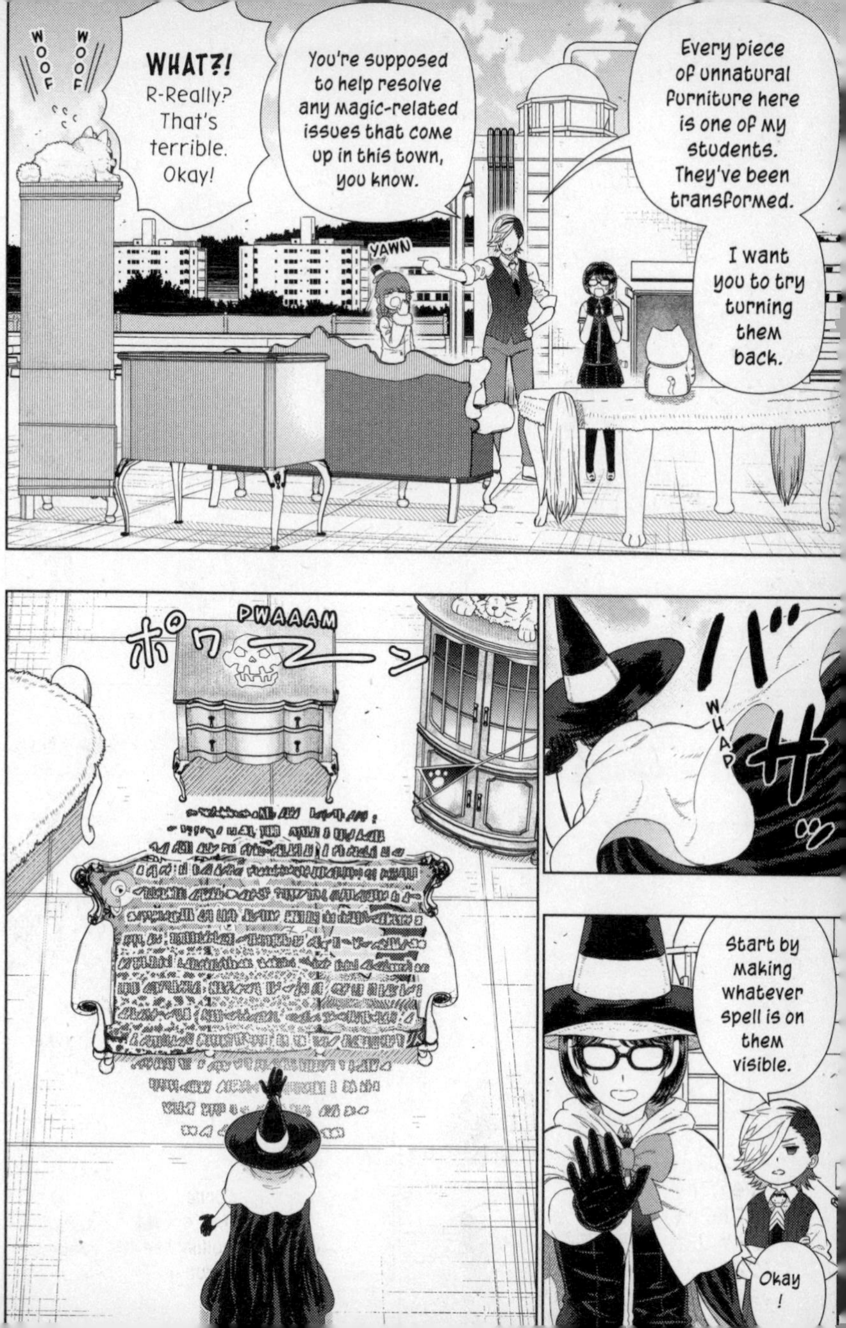

Every piece of unnatural furniture here is one of my students. They've been transformed.
I want you to try turning them back.
You're supposed to help resolve any magic-related issues that come up in this town, you know.
YAWN
WHAT?! R-Really? That's terrible. Okay!
WOOF WOOF
バサッ
WHAP
Start by making whatever spell is on them visible.
Okay!
ポワーン
PWAAAM

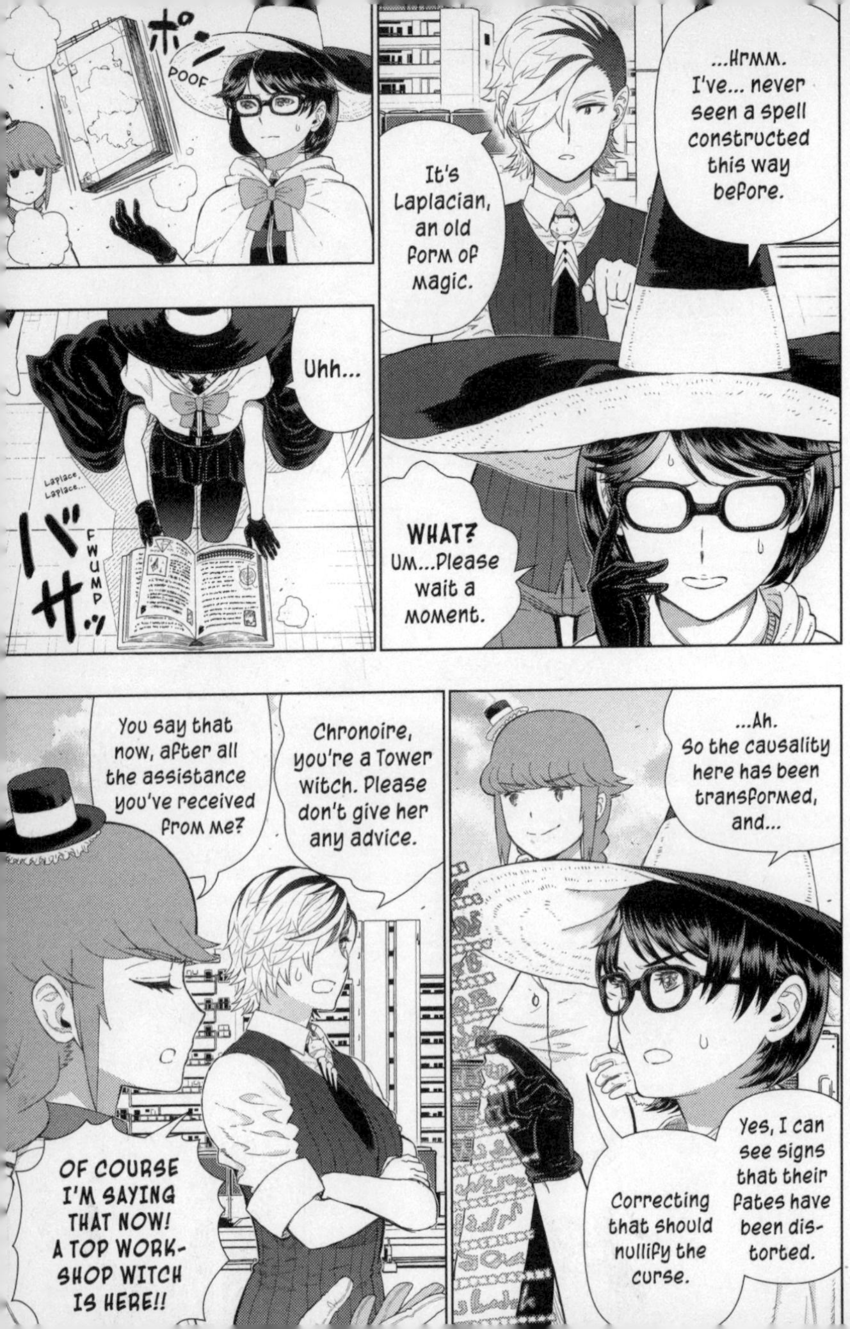
...Hrmm. I've... never seen a spell constructed this way before.
It's Laplacian, an old form of magic.
ポン
POOF
WHAT? Um...Please wait a moment.
Uhh...
Laplace, Laplace...
バサッ
FWUMP
...Ah. So the causality here has been transformed, and...
Yes, I can see signs that their fates have been dis-torted.
Correcting that should nullify the curse.
Chronoire, you're a Tower witch. Please don't give her any advice.
You say that now, after all the assistance you've received from me?
OF COURSE I'M SAYING THAT NOW! A TOP WORK-SHOP WITCH IS HERE!!

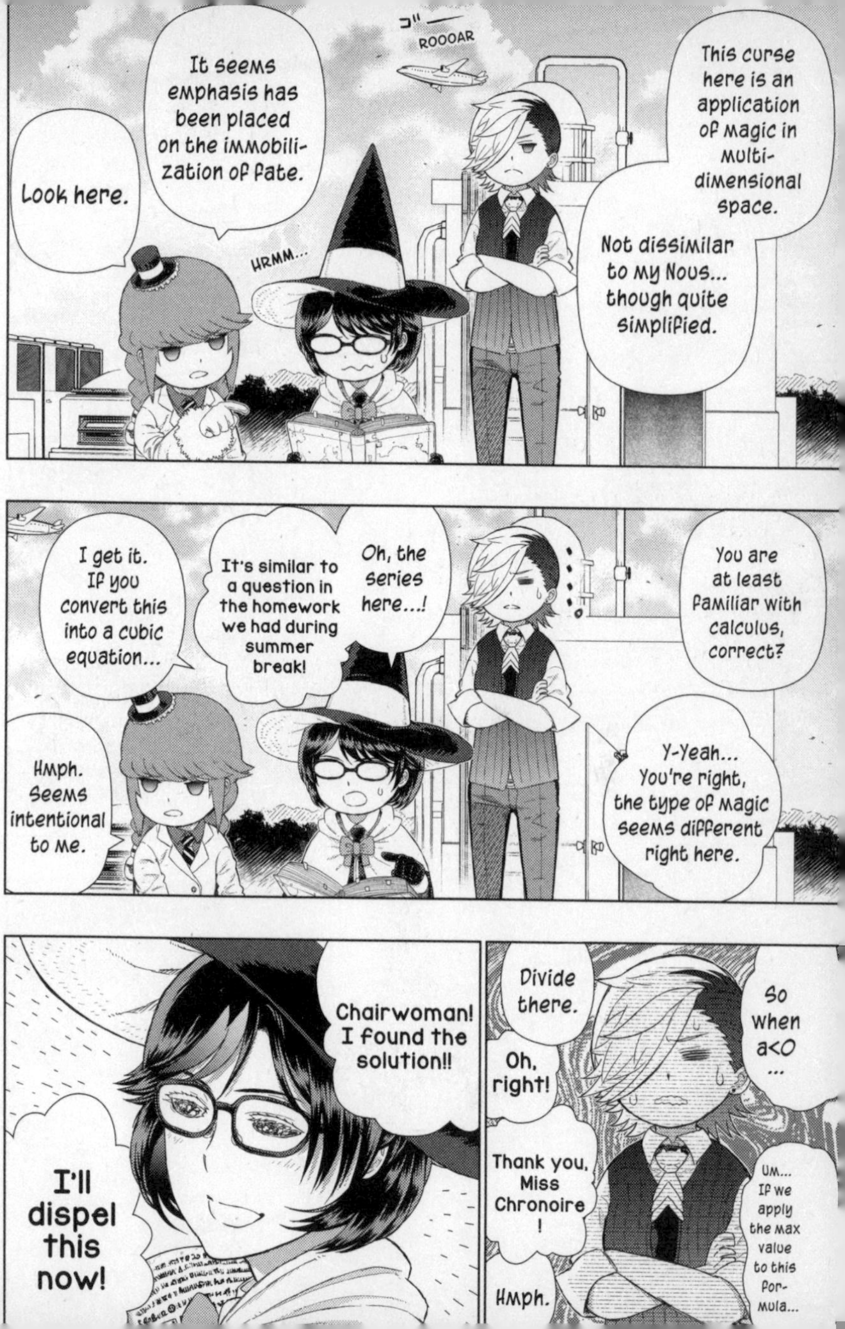
This curse here is an application of magic in multi-dimensional space.
Not dissimilar to my Nous... though quite simplified.
ゴー
ROOOAR
It seems emphasis has been placed on the immobilization of fate.
HRMM...
Look here.
You are at least familiar with calculus, correct?
Y-Yeah... You're right, the type of magic seems different right here.
Oh, the series here...!
It's similar to a question in the homework we had during summer break!
I get it. If you convert this into a cubic equation...
Hmph. Seems intentional to me.
So when a<0 ...
Um... If we apply the max value to this formula...
Divide there.
Oh, right!
Thank you, Miss Chronoire!
Hmph.
Chairwoman! I found the solution!!
I'll dispel this now!

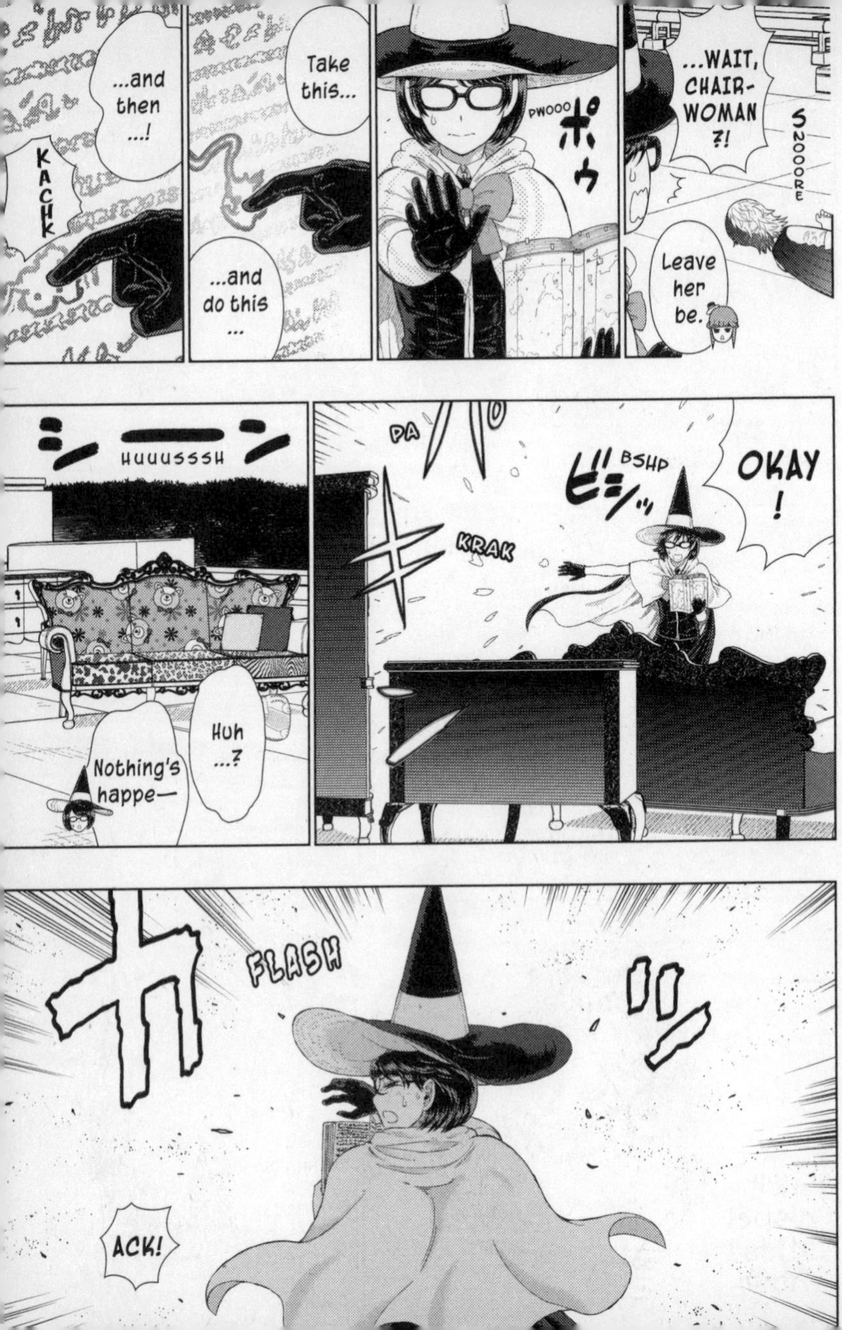
...WAIT, CHAIR-WOMAN?!
SNOOOORE
Leave her be.
PWOOO ポウ
Take this...
...and do this ...
...and then ...!
KACHK
OKAY!
PA
BSHP ビシッ
KRAK
シーン
HUUUSSSH
Huh ...?
Nothing's happe—
カッ
FLASH
ACK!

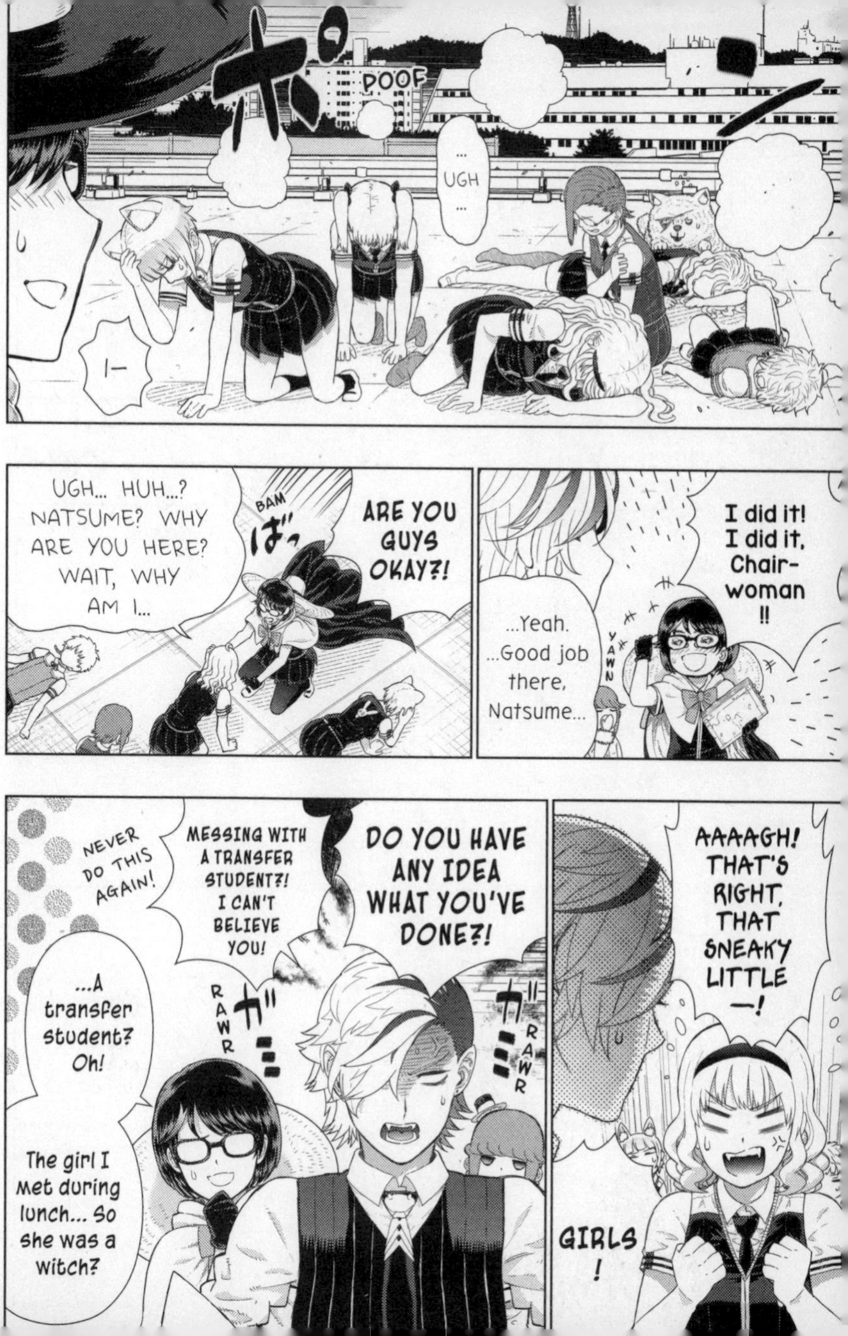
POOF
...
UGH
...
I—
I did it! I did it, Chair-woman!!
YAWN
...Yeah. ...Good job there, Natsume...
ARE YOU GUYS OKAY?!
BAM
UGH... HUH...? NATSUME? WHY ARE YOU HERE? WAIT, WHY AM I...
AAAAGH! THAT'S RIGHT, THAT SNEAKY LITTLE—!
GIRLS!
DO YOU HAVE ANY IDEA WHAT YOU'VE DONE?!
RAWR
MESSING WITH A TRANSFER STUDENT?! I CAN'T BELIEVE YOU!
NEVER DO THIS AGAIN!
RAWR
...A transfer student? Oh!
The girl I met during lunch... So she was a witch?

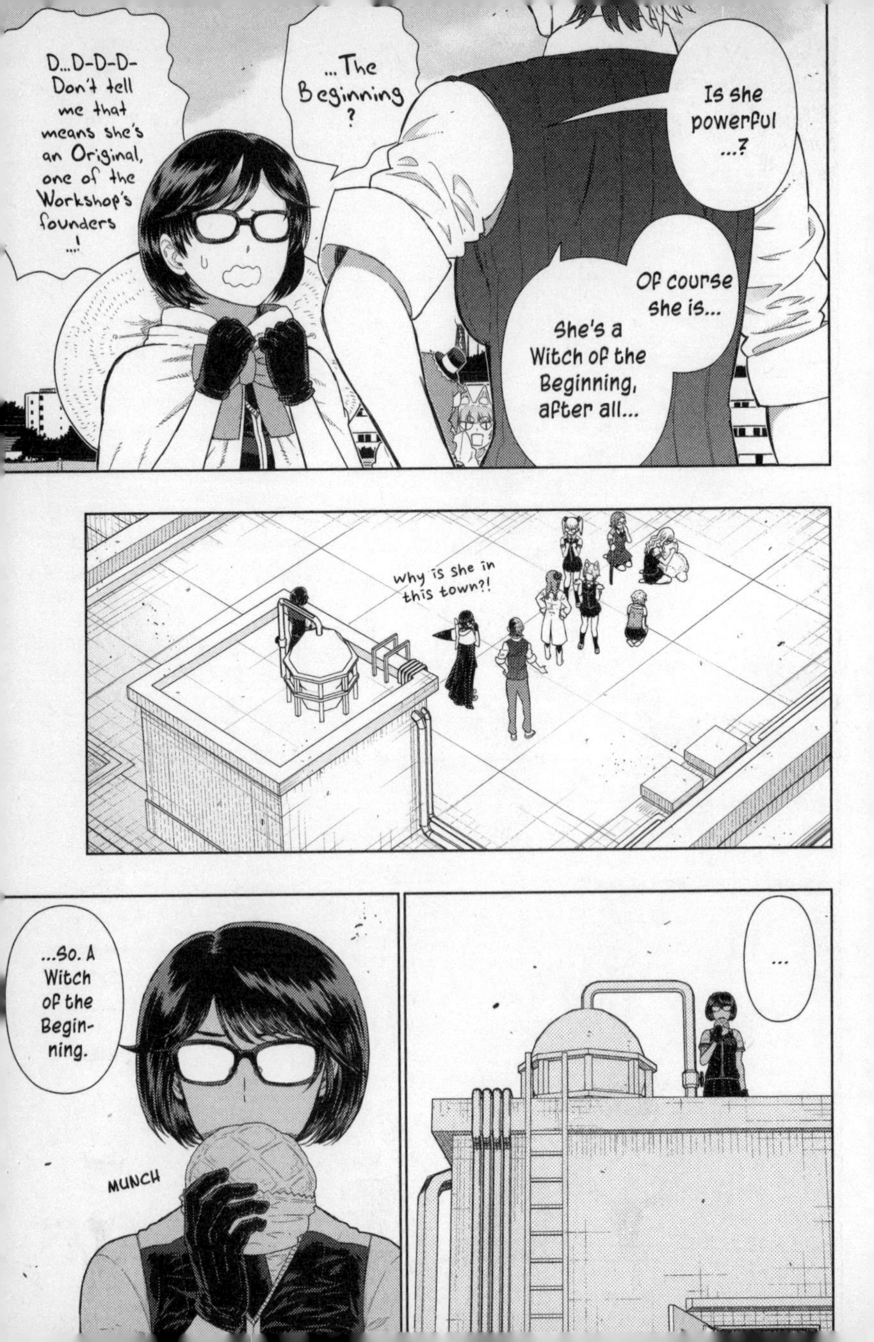

Is she powerful ...?
Of course she is... She's a Witch of the Beginning, after all...
...The Beginning?
D...D-D-D- Don't tell me that means she's an Original, one of the Workshop's founders ...!
Why is she in this town?!
...
...So. A Witch of the Beginning.
MUNCH

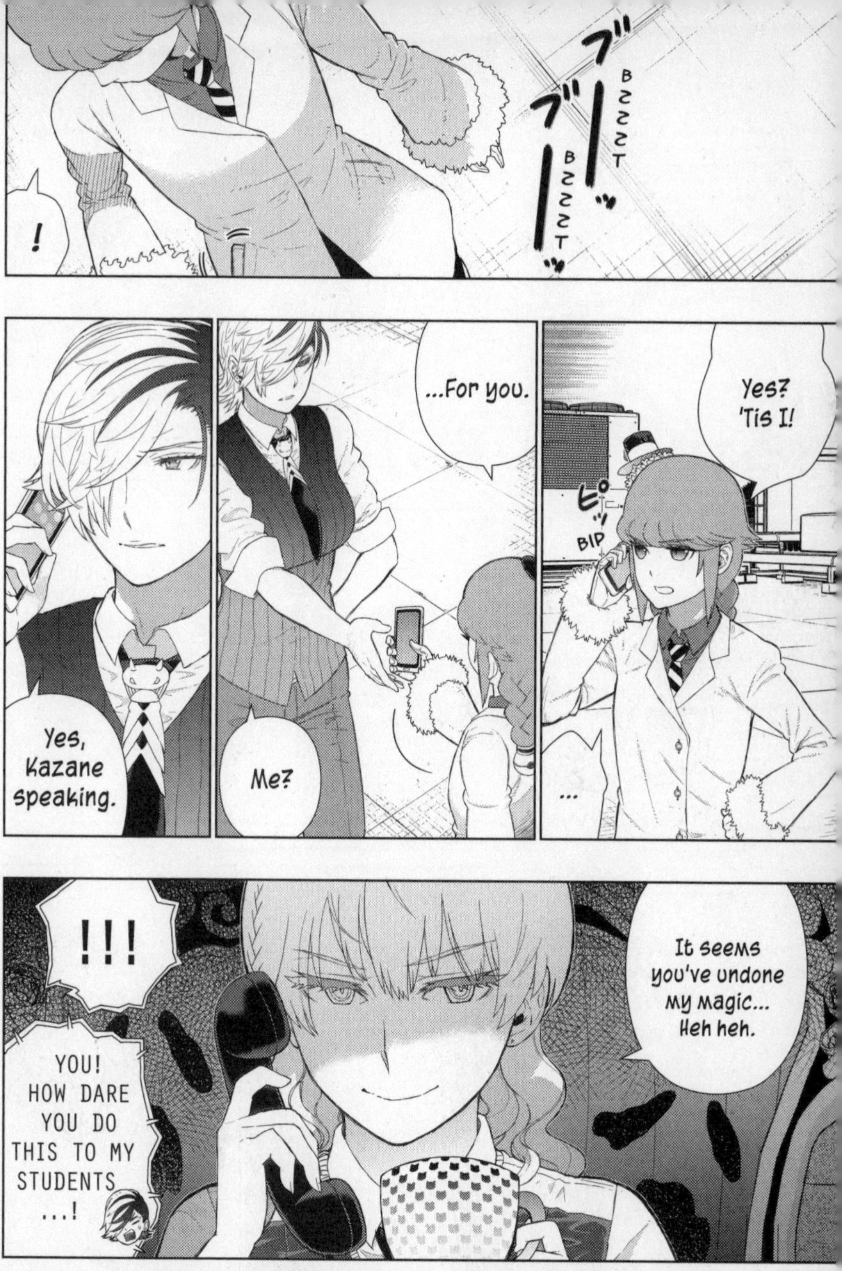
ブー
BZZZT
ブー
BZZZT
!
Yes? 'Tis I!
ピッ
BIP
...
...For you.
Me?
Yes, Kazane speaking.
It seems you've undone my magic... Heh heh.
!!!
YOU! HOW DARE YOU DO THIS TO MY STUDENTS ...!

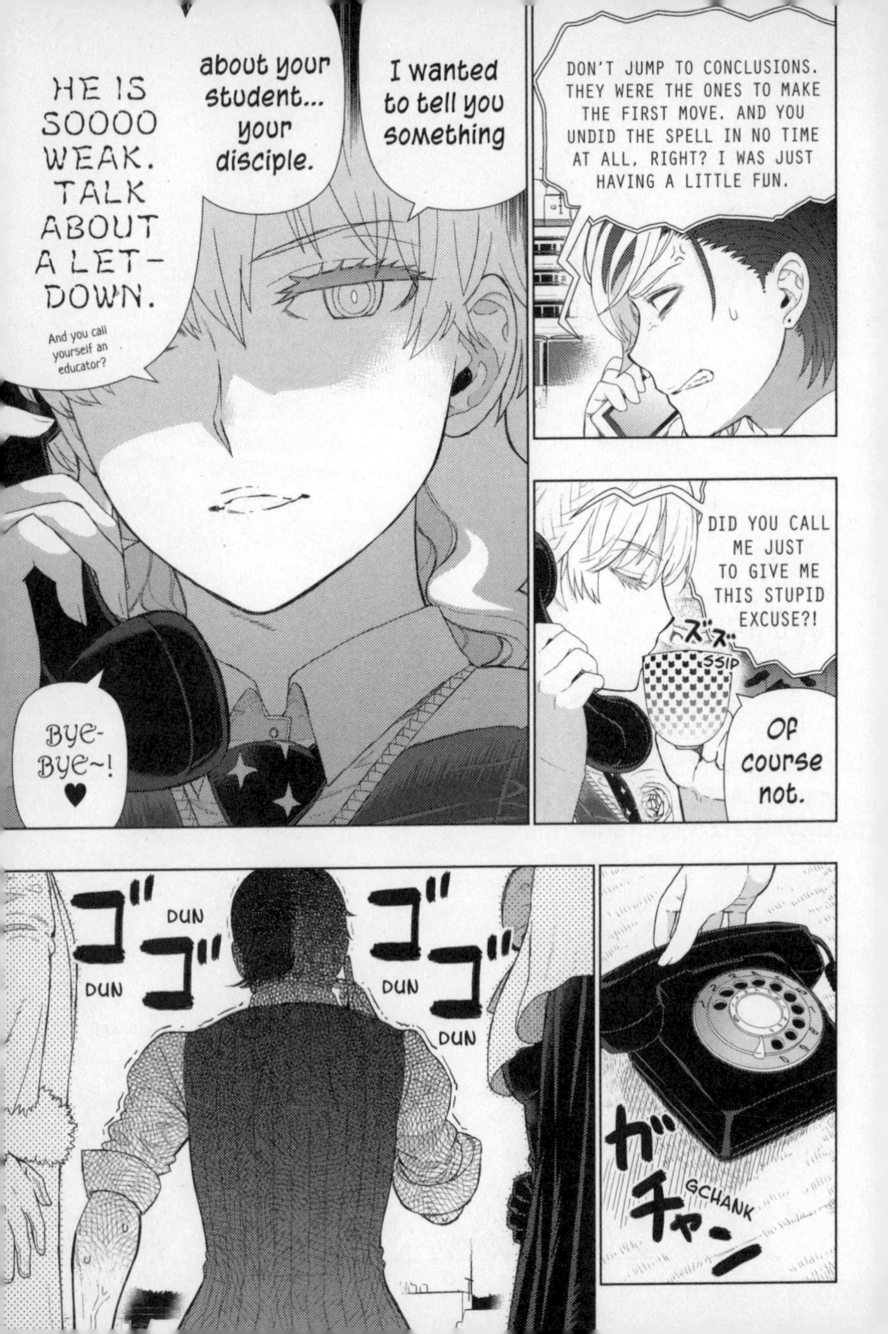
DON'T JUMP TO CONCLUSIONS. THEY WERE THE ONES TO MAKE THE FIRST MOVE. AND YOU UNDID THE SPELL IN NO TIME AT ALL, RIGHT? I WAS JUST HAVING A LITTLE FUN.
DID YOU CALL ME JUST TO GIVE ME THIS STUPID EXCUSE?!
ズズ
SSIP
Of course not.
I wanted to tell you something
about your student... your disciple.
HE IS SOOOO WEAK. TALK ABOUT A LET-DOWN.
And you call yourself an educator?
BYE-BYE~! ♥
ガチャー
GCHANK
ゴゴゴゴ
DUN DUN DUN DUN

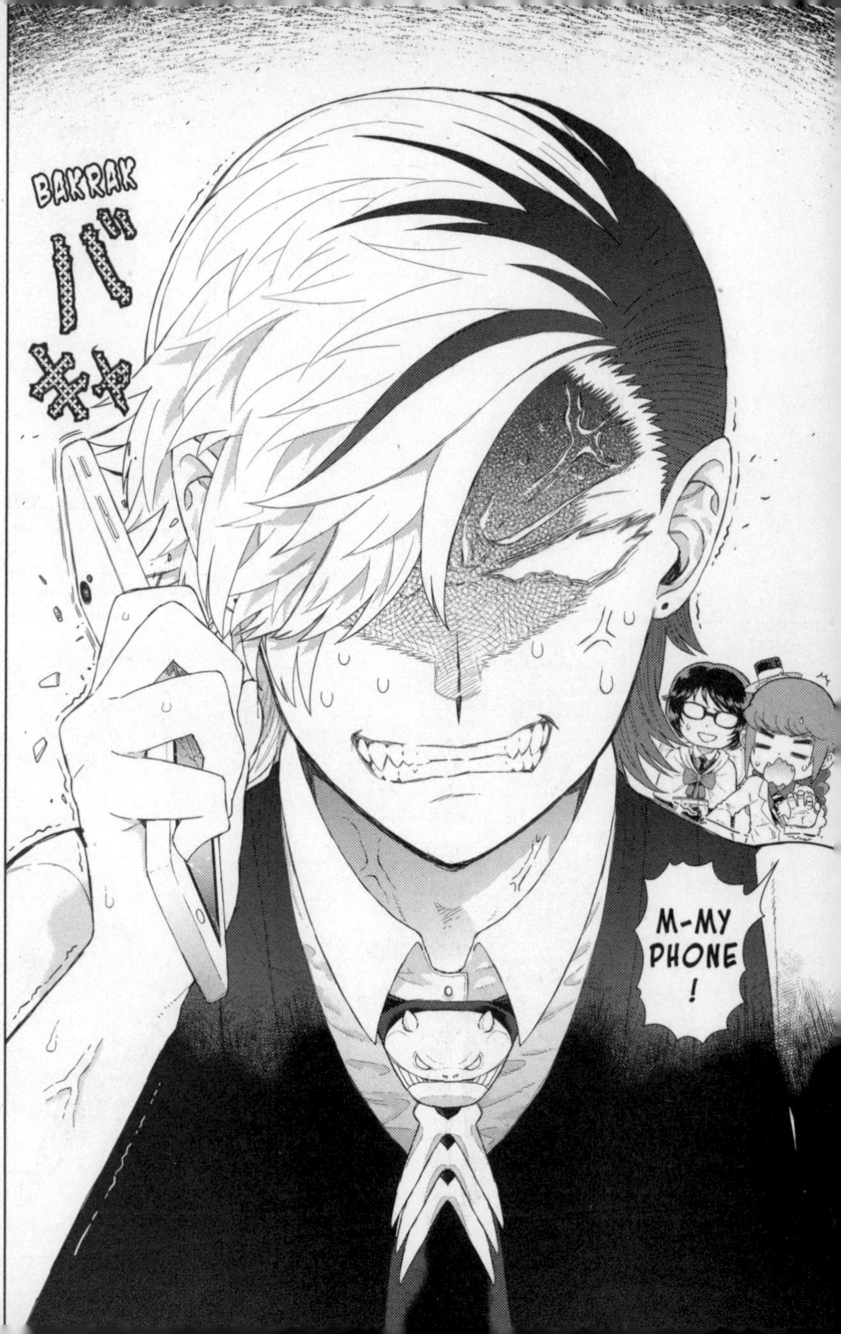
BAKRAK
バキ
M-MY PHONE!

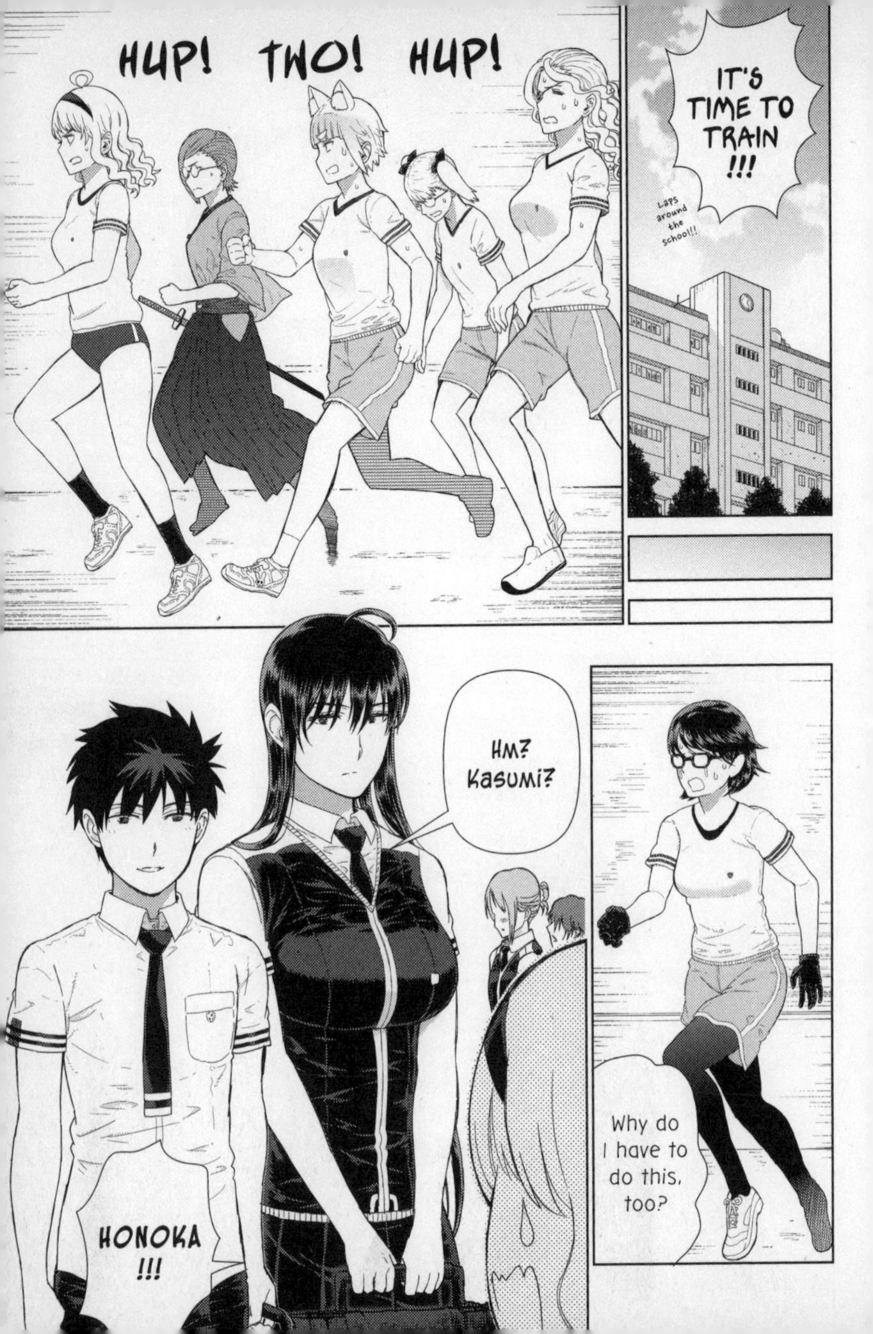

IT'S TIME TO TRAIN !!!
Laps around the school!!!
HUP! TWO! HUP!
Why do I have to do this, too?
Hm? Kasumi?
HONOKA !!!

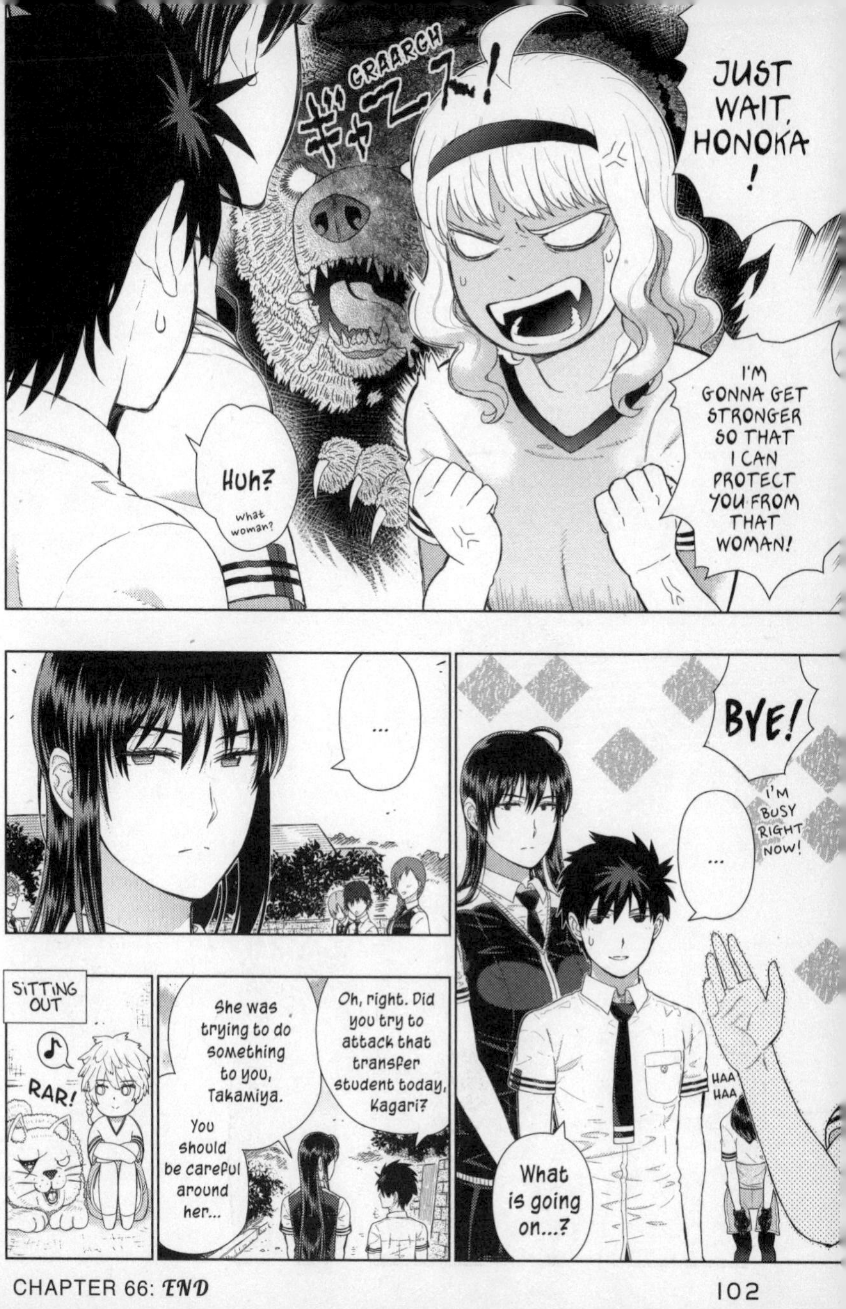
JUST WAIT, HONOKA!
I'M GONNA GET STRONGER SO THAT I CAN PROTECT YOU FROM THAT WOMAN!
ギャース!
GRAARCH
Huh?
what woman?
BYE!
I'M BUSY RIGHT NOW!
...
HAA HAA
What is going on...?
...
Oh, right. Did you try to attack that transfer student today, Kagari?
She was trying to do something to you, Takamiya.
You should be careful around her...
SITTING OUT
♪
RAR!

Chronoire seems like she might actually make a good teacher...

Witchcraft Works

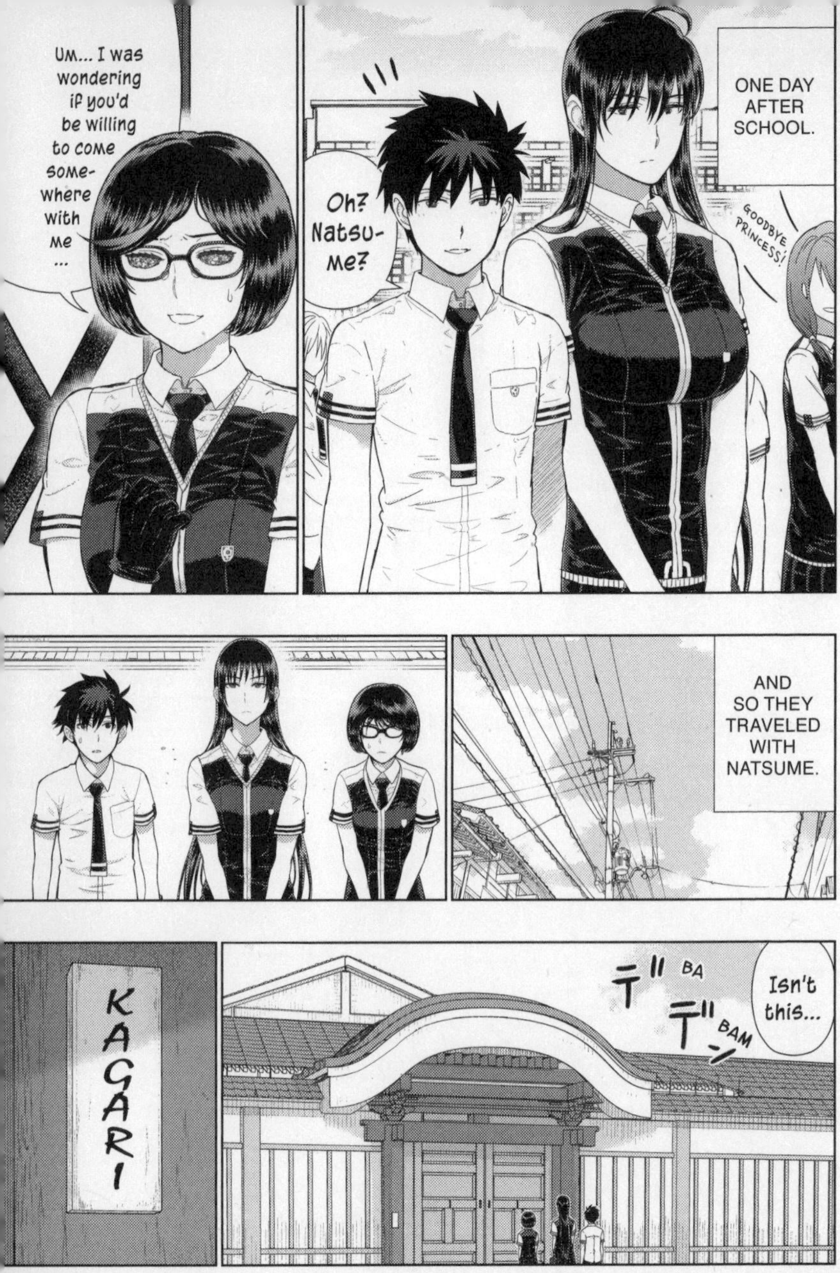
ONE DAY AFTER SCHOOL.
GOODBYE PRINCESS!
Oh? Natsume?
Um... I was wondering if you'd be willing to come some-where with me ...
AND SO THEY TRAVELED WITH NATSUME.
Isn't this...
BA
BAM
KAGARI

CHAPTER 67 Takamiya and the Mikage Family's Circumstances

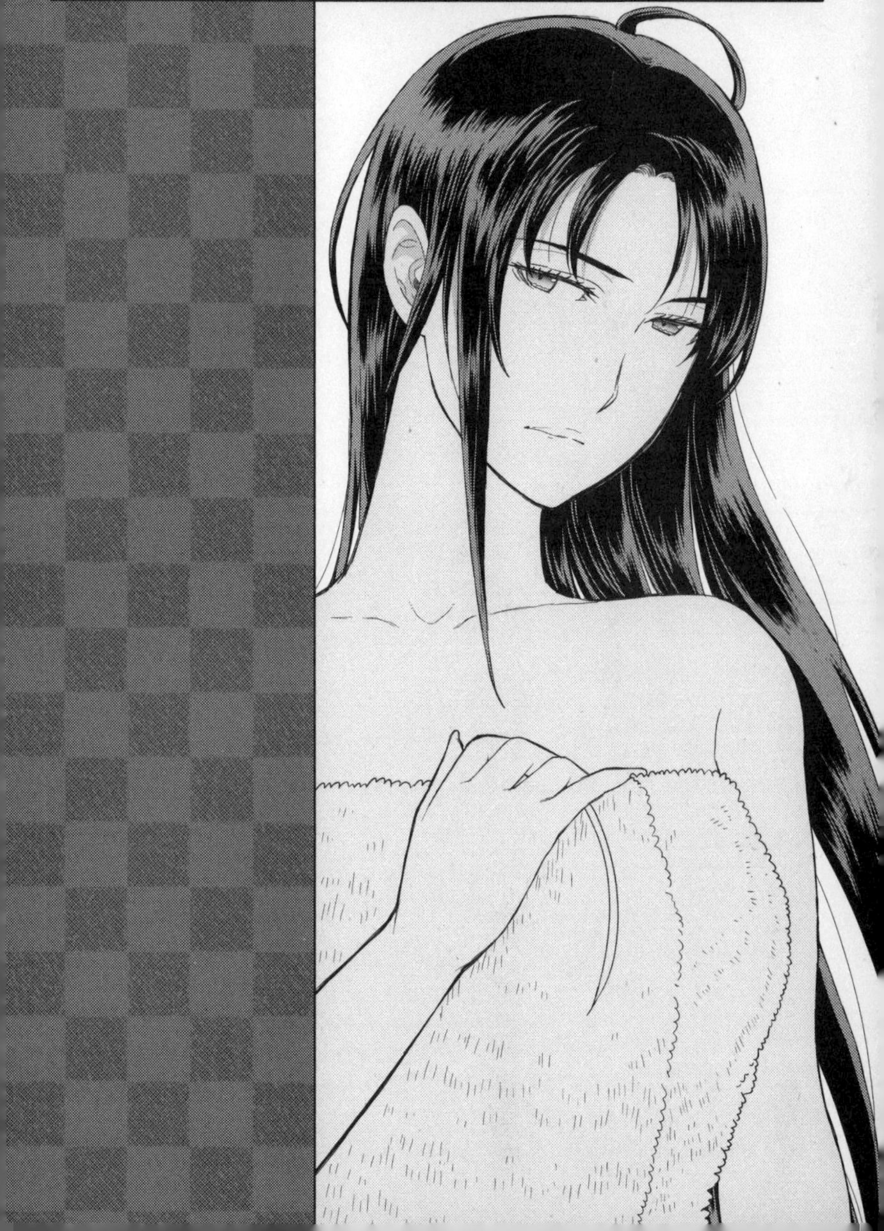

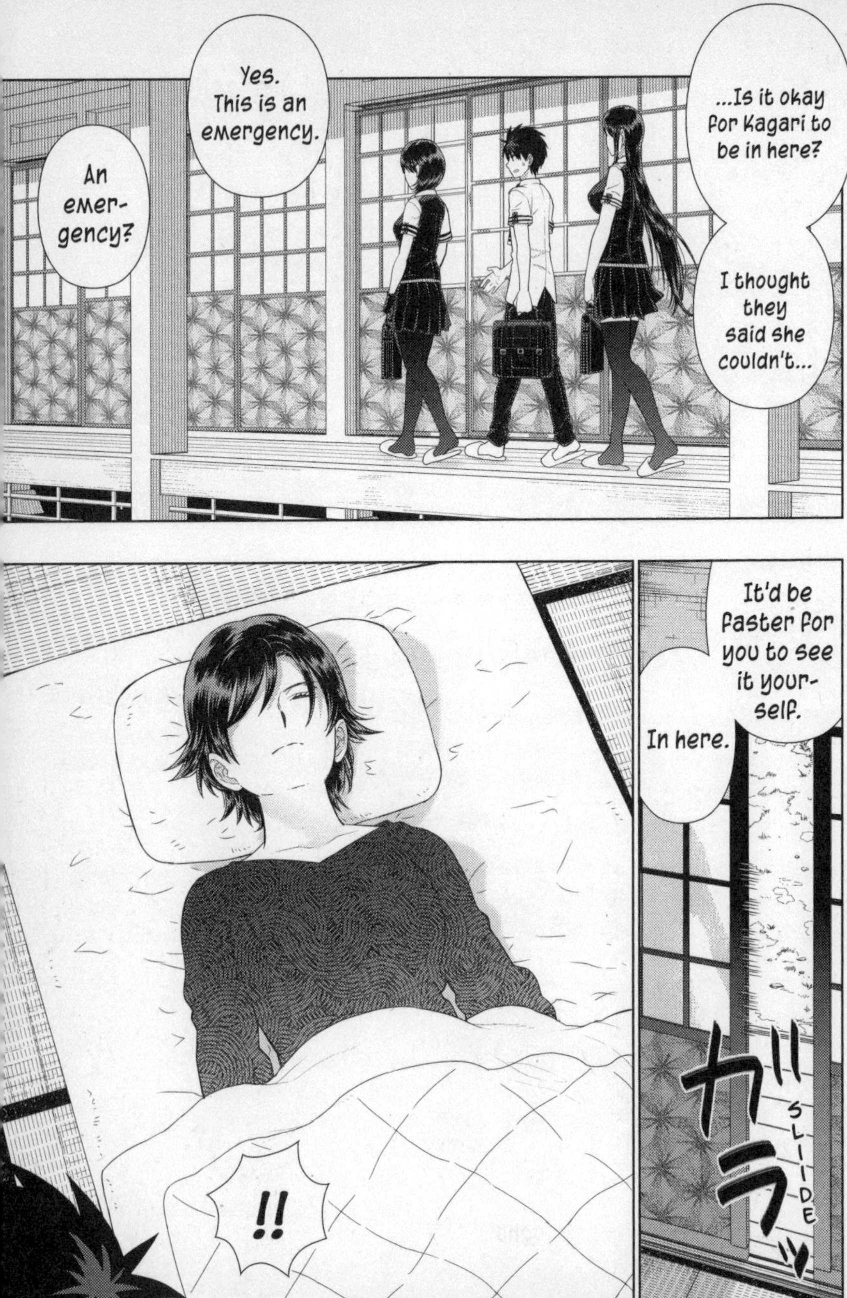
...Is it okay for Kagari to be in here?
I thought they said she couldn't...
Yes. This is an emergency.
An emer-gency?
It'd be faster for you to see it your-self.
In here.
SLIIDE
!!

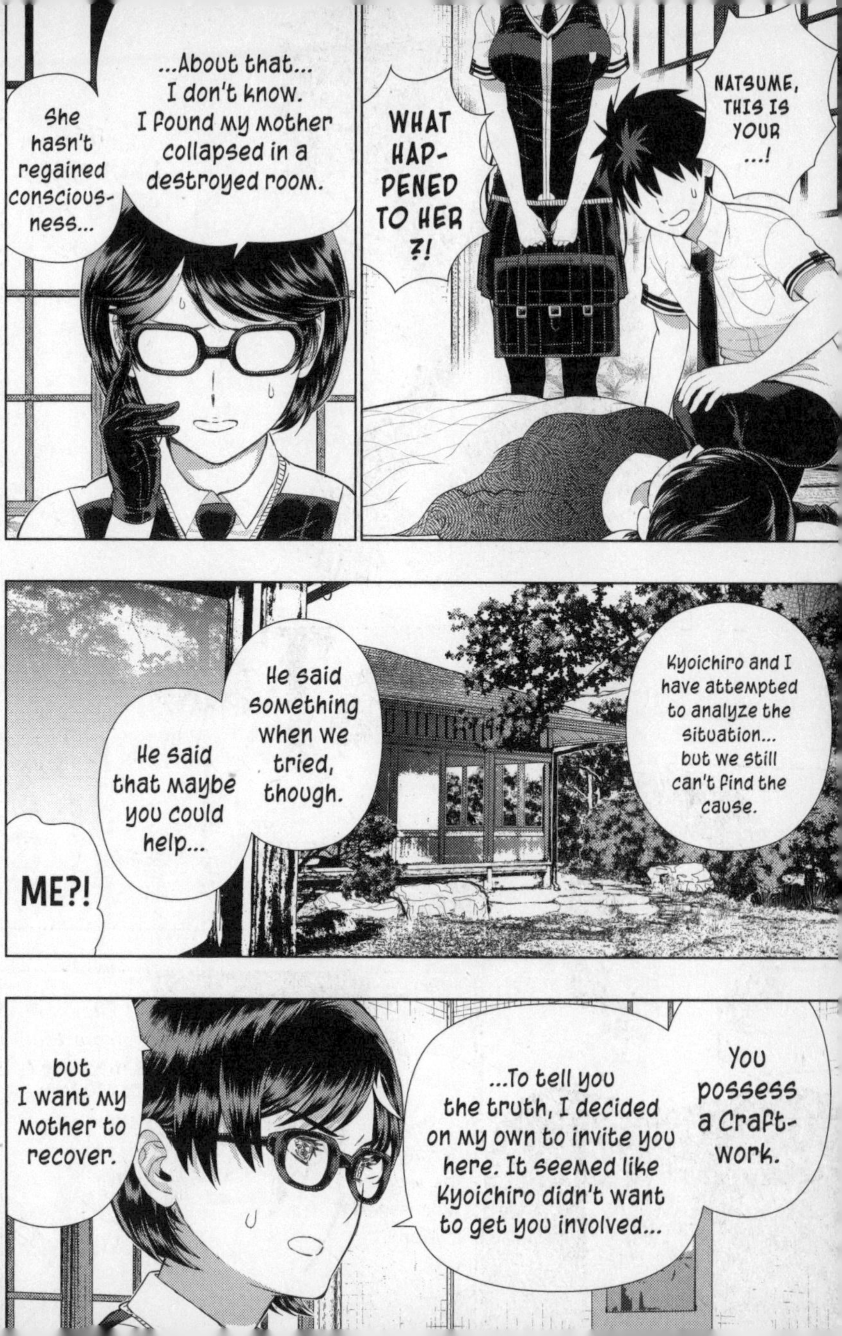
NATSUME, THIS IS YOUR ...!
WHAT HAPPENED TO HER ?!
...About that... I don't know. I found my mother collapsed in a destroyed room.
She hasn't regained consciousness...
Kyoichiro and I have attempted to analyze the situation... but we still can't find the cause.
He said something when we tried, though.
He said that maybe you could help...
ME?!
You possess a Craftwork.
...To tell you the truth, I decided on my own to invite you here. It seemed like Kyoichiro didn't want to get you involved...
but I want my mother to recover.

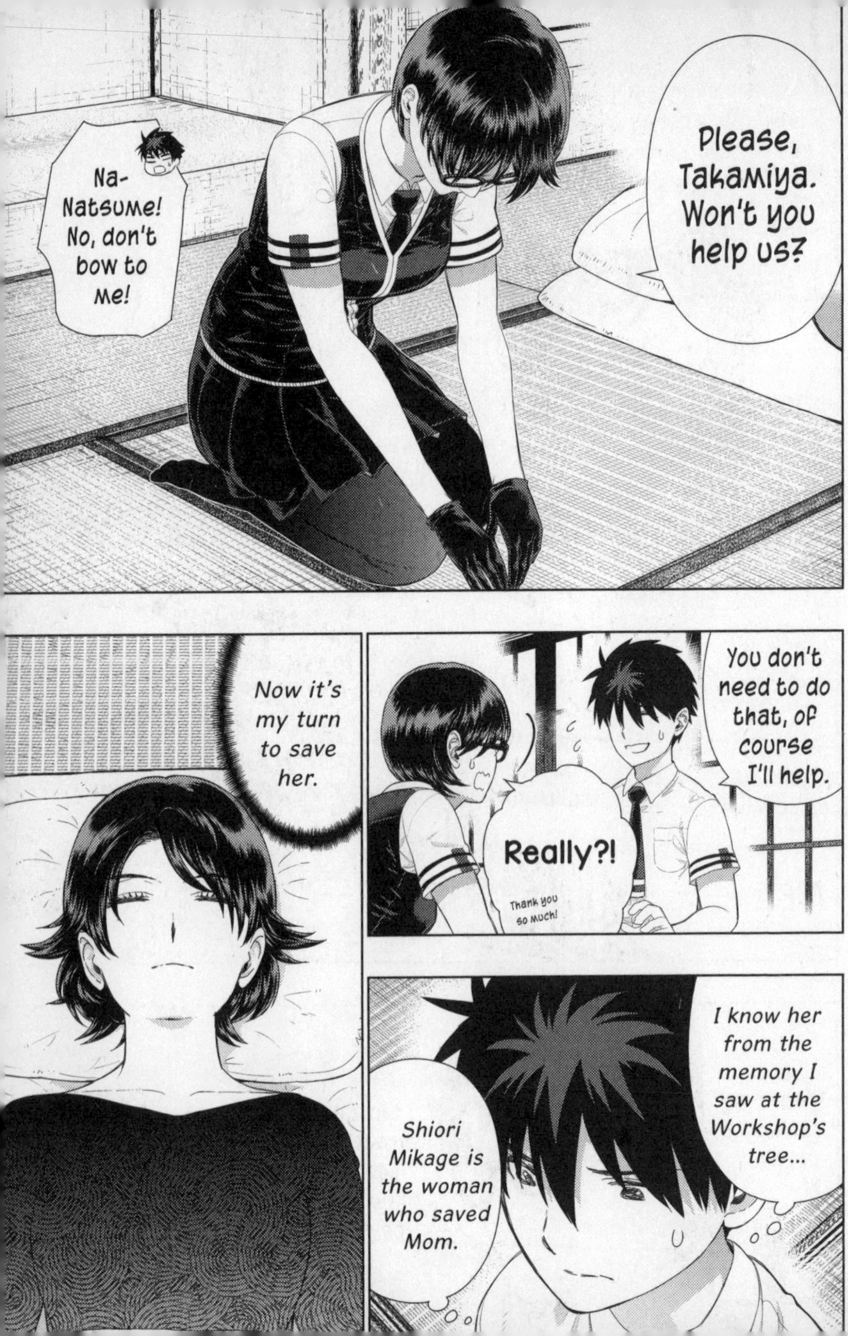
Please, Takamiya. Won't you help us?
Na-Natsume! No, don't bow to me!
You don't need to do that, of course I'll help.
Really?!
Thank you so much!
I know her from the memory I saw at the Workshop's tree...
Shiori Mikage is the woman who saved Mom.
Now it's my turn to save her.

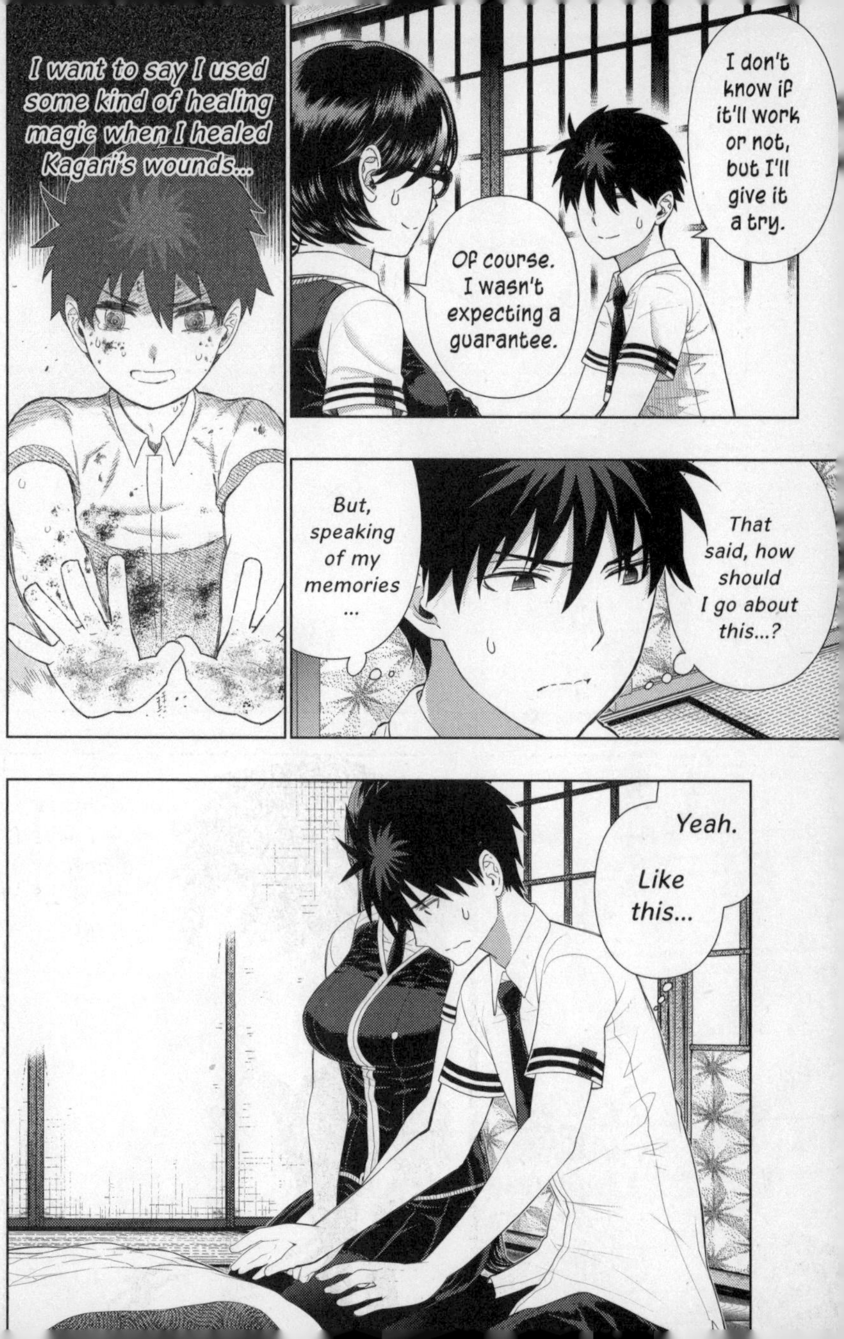
I don't know if it'll work or not, but I'll give it a try.
Of course. I wasn't expecting a guarantee.
That said, how should I go about this...?
But, speaking of my memories ...
I want to say I used some kind of healing magic when I healed Kagari's wounds...
Yeah.
Like this...

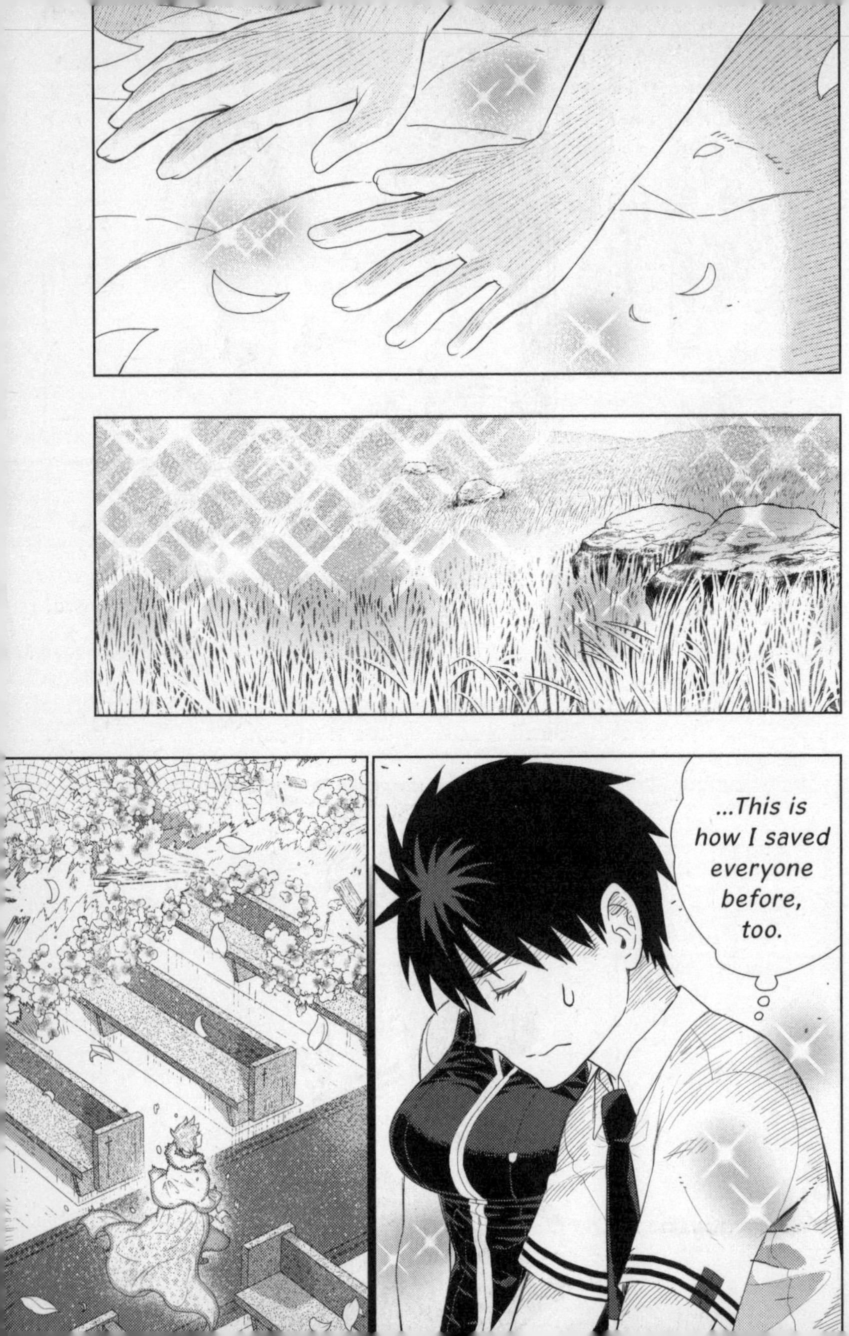
...This is how I saved everyone before, too.

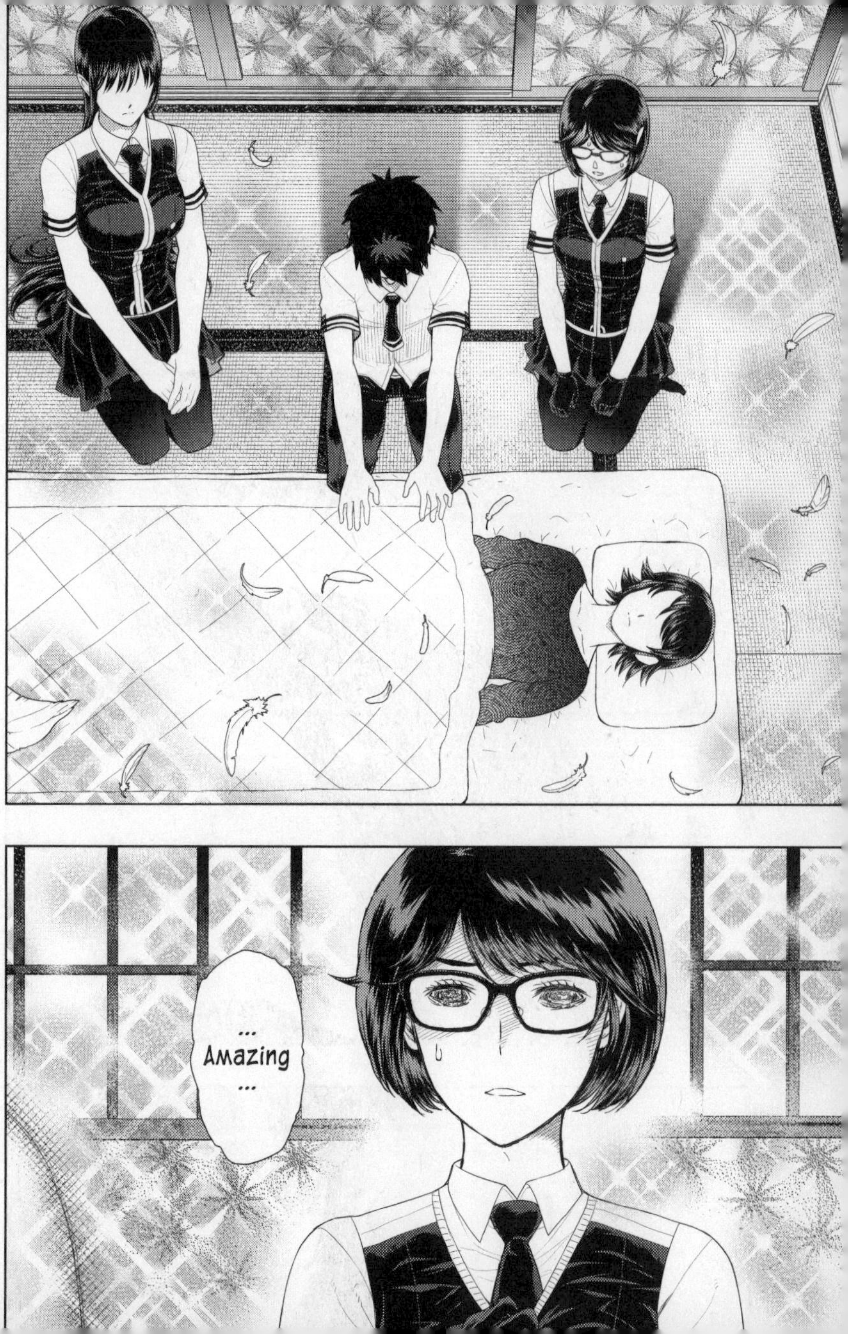
...Amazing...

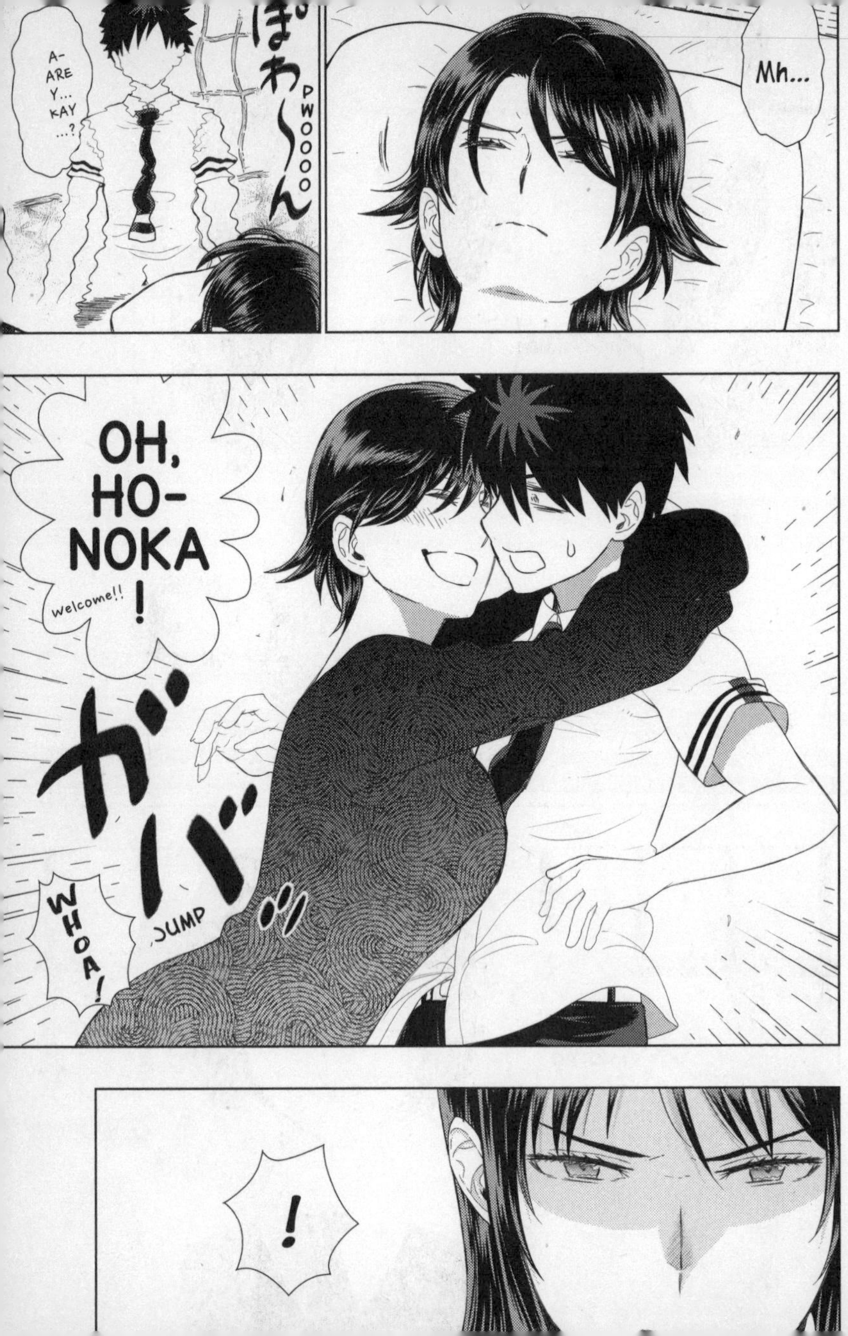
Mh...
ぽわ〜ん
PWOOOO
A- ARE Y... KAY ...?
OH, HO-NOKA!
welcome!!
ガバッ
JUMP
WHOA!
!

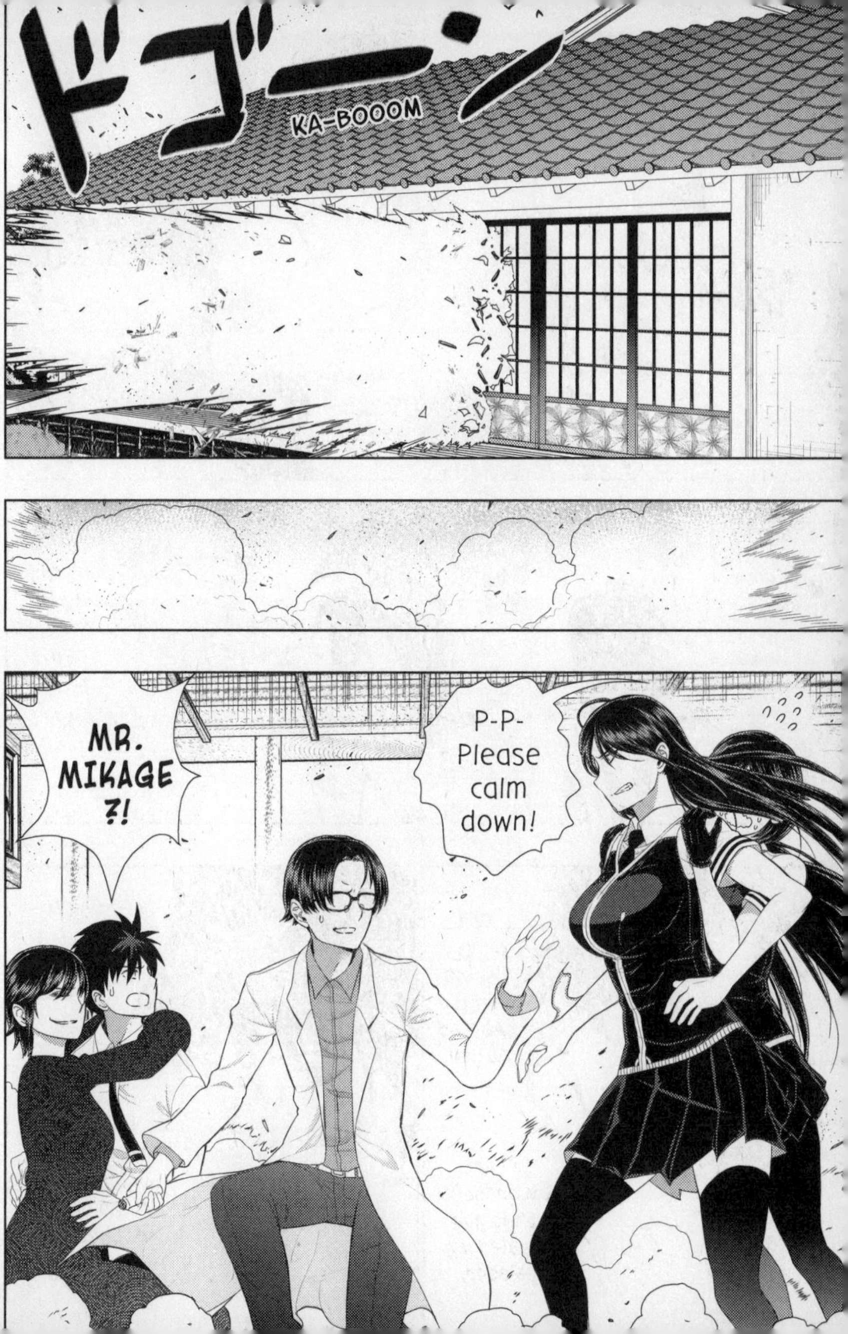
ドゴーン
KA-BOOOM
P-P-Please calm down!
MR. MIKAGE ?!

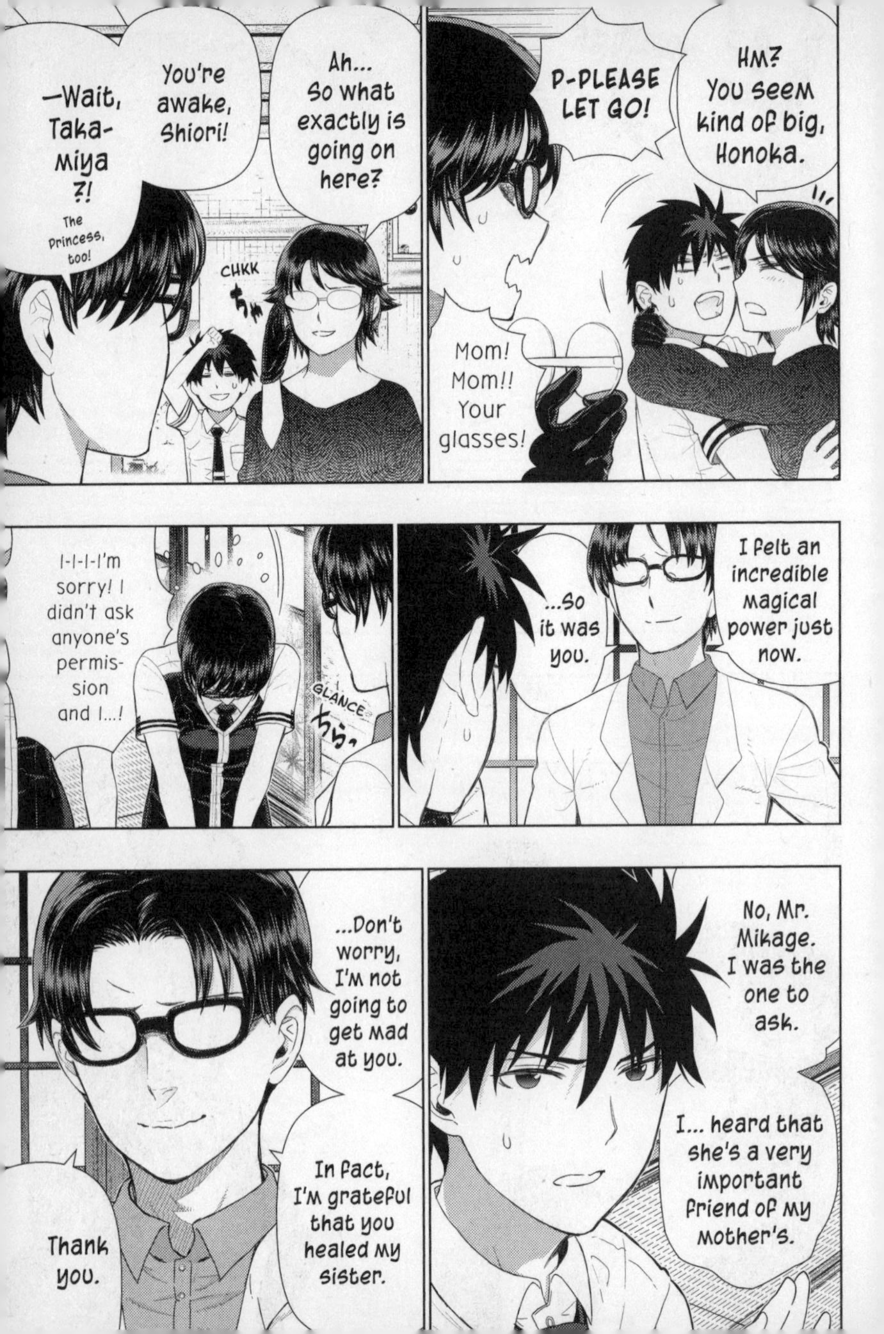
HM? You seem kind of big, Honoka.
P-PLEASE LET GO!
Mom! Mom!! Your glasses!
Ah... So what exactly is going on here?
You're awake, Shiori!
—Wait, Taka-miya?!
The Princess, too!
CHKK
ちゃ
I felt an incredible magical power just now.
...So it was you.
I-I-I-I'm sorry! I didn't ask anyone's permis-sion and I...!
GLANCE
ちら
No, Mr. Mikage. I was the one to ask.
I... heard that she's a very important friend of my mother's.
...Don't worry, I'm not going to get mad at you.
In fact, I'm grateful that you healed my sister.
Thank you.

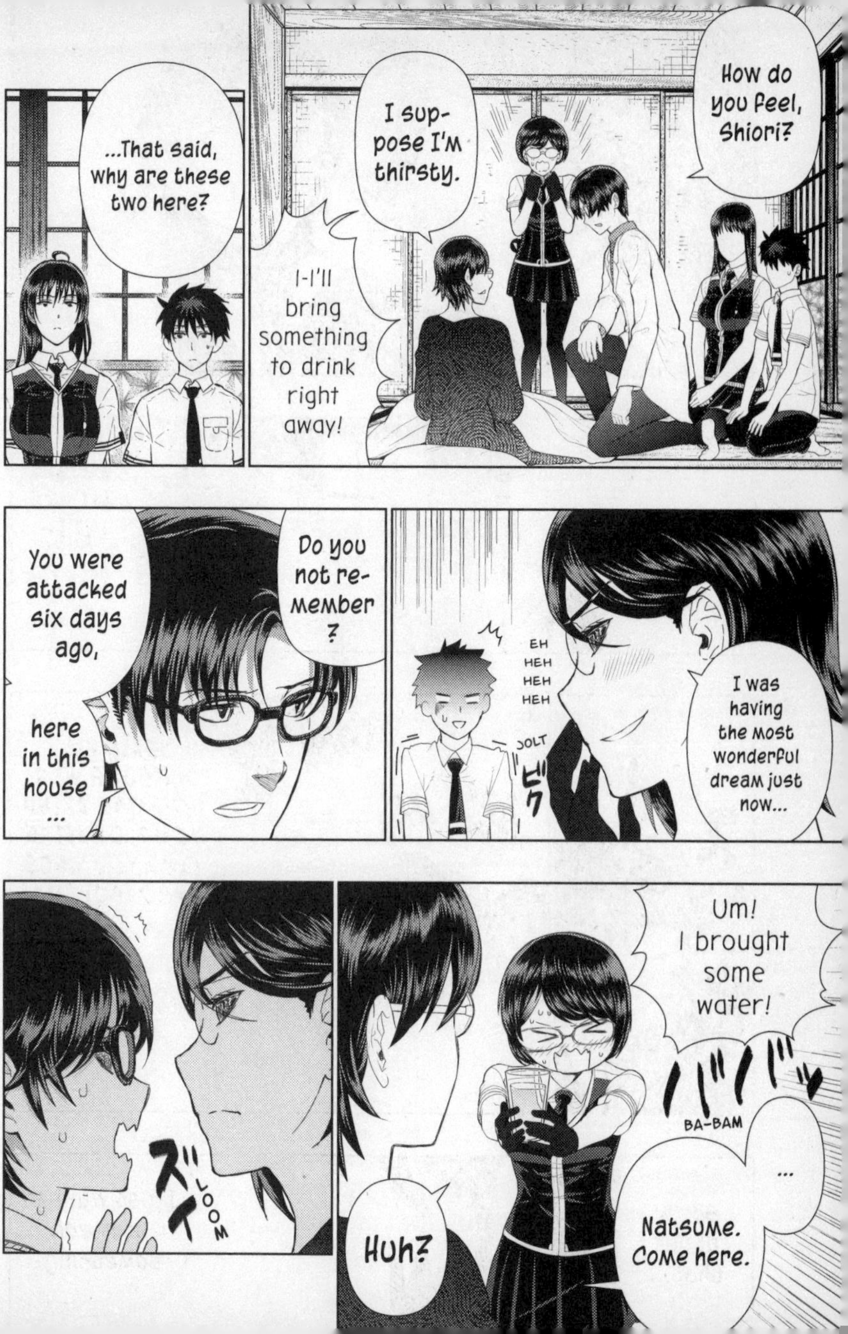
How do you feel, Shiori?
I sup-pose I'm thirsty.
I-I'll bring something to drink right away!
...That said, why are these two here?
I was having the most wonderful dream just now...
EH HEH HEH HEH
JOLT
ビク
Do you not re-member?
You were attacked six days ago,
here in this house...
Um! I brought some water!
バババッ
BA-BAM
...
Natsume. Come here.
Huh?
ズイ
LOOM

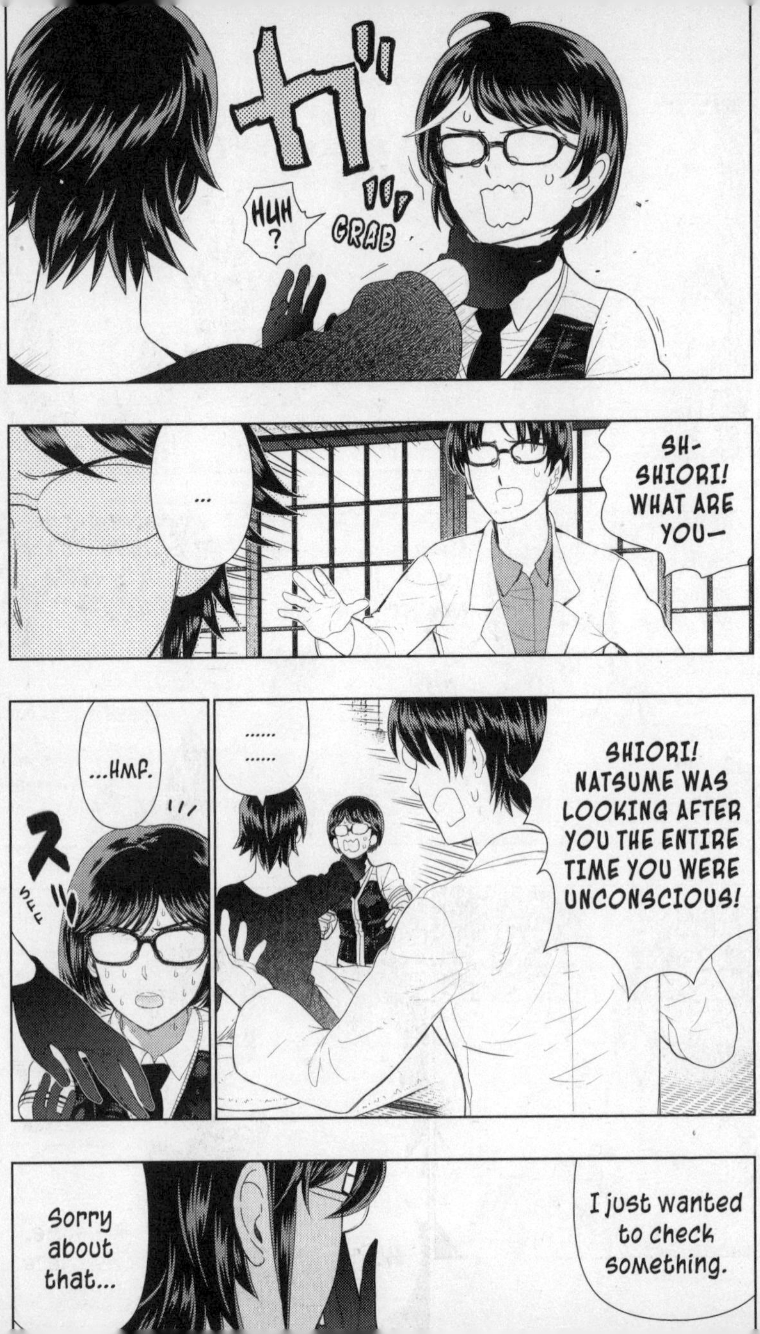
ガ
GRAB
HUH?
SH-SHIORI! WHAT ARE YOU—
...
SHIORI! NATSUME WAS LOOKING AFTER YOU THE ENTIRE TIME YOU WERE UNCONSCIOUS!
....
...HMF.
ス
I just wanted to check something.
Sorry about that...

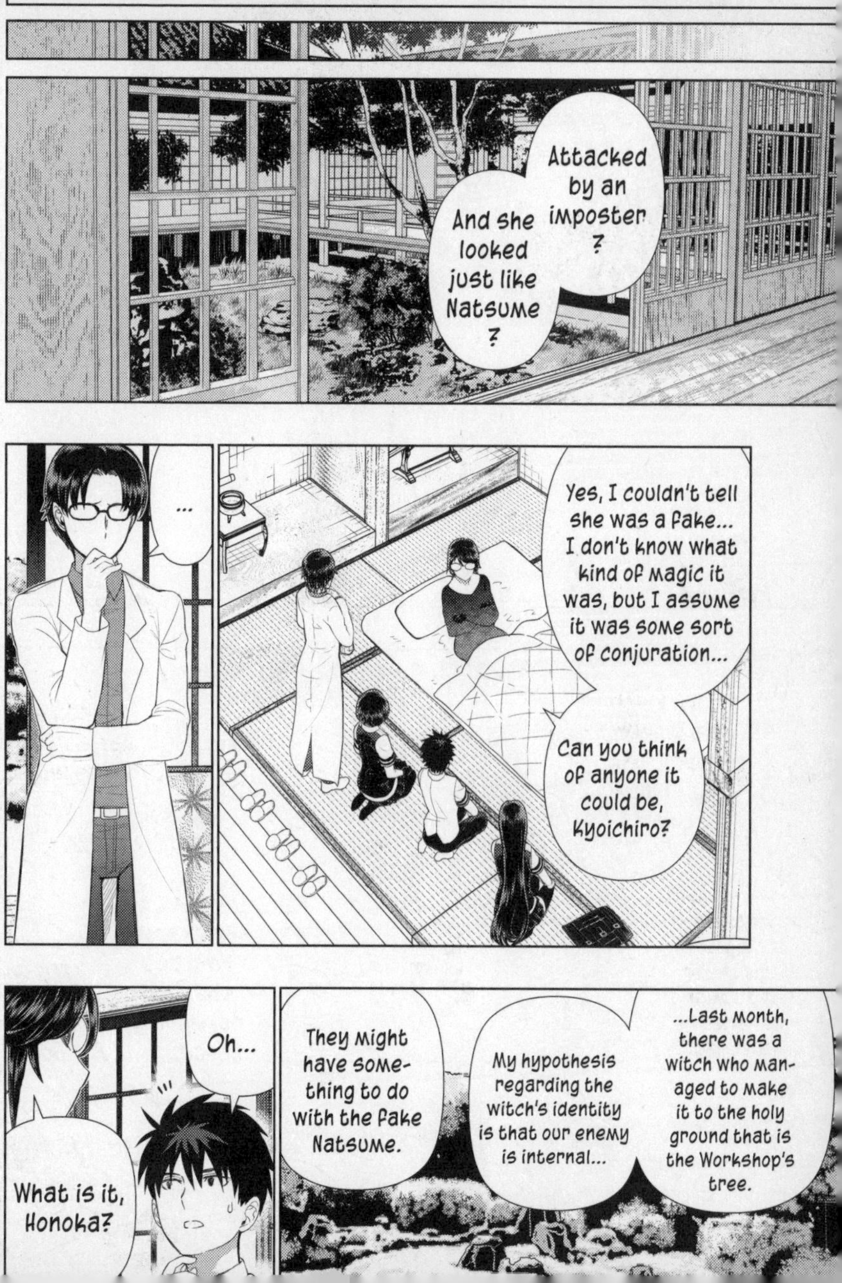

Attacked by an imposter?
And she looked just like Natsume?
Yes, I couldn't tell she was a fake... I don't know what kind of magic it was, but I assume it was some sort of conjuration...
Can you think of anyone it could be, Kyoichiro?
...
...Last month, there was a witch who managed to make it to the holy ground that is the Workshop's tree.
My hypothesis regarding the witch's identity is that our enemy is internal...
They might have something to do with the fake Natsume.
Oh...
What is it, Honoka?

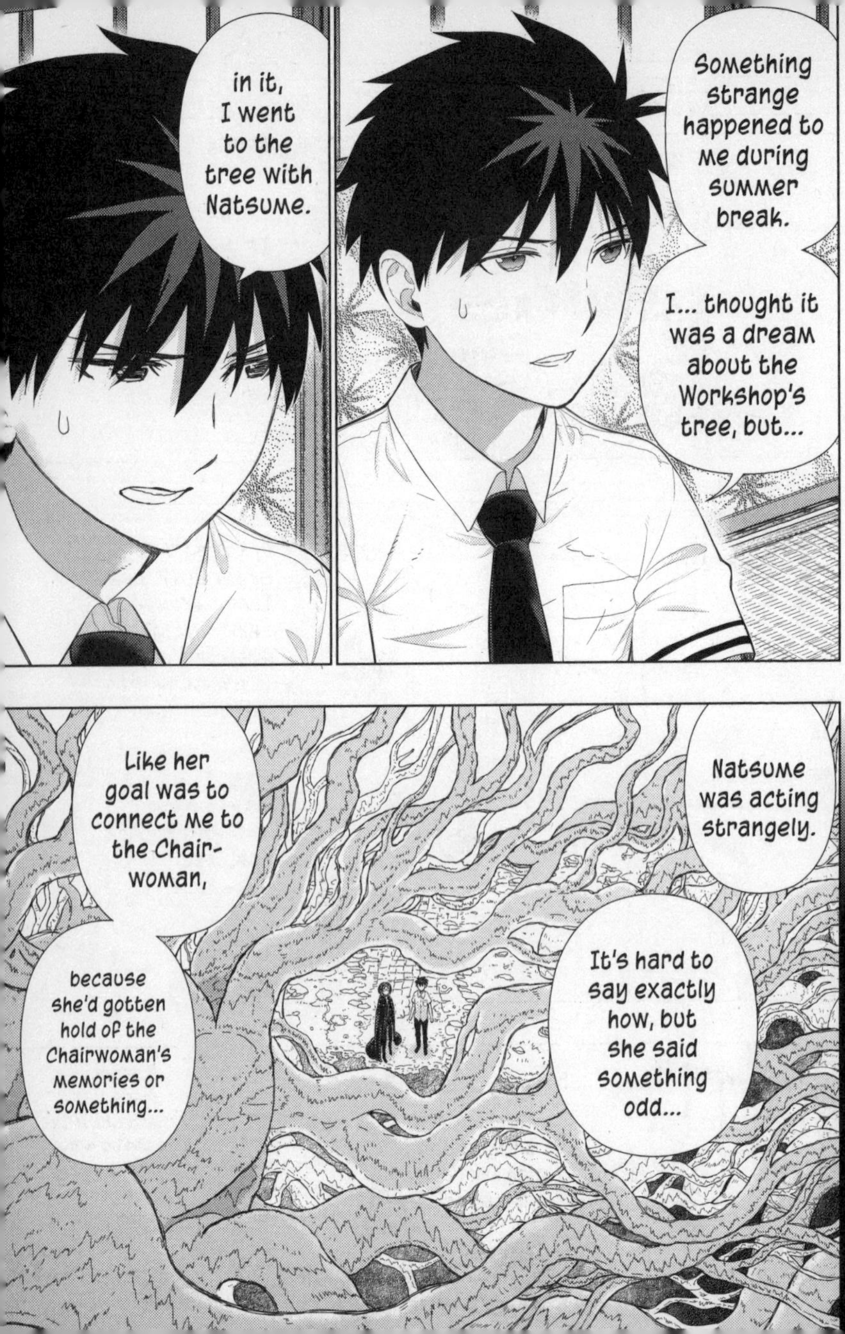
Something strange happened to me during summer break.
I... thought it was a dream about the Workshop's tree, but...
in it, I went to the tree with Natsume.
Natsume was acting strangely.
It's hard to say exactly how, but she said something odd...
Like her goal was to connect me to the Chair-woman,
because she'd gotten hold of the Chairwoman's memories or something...

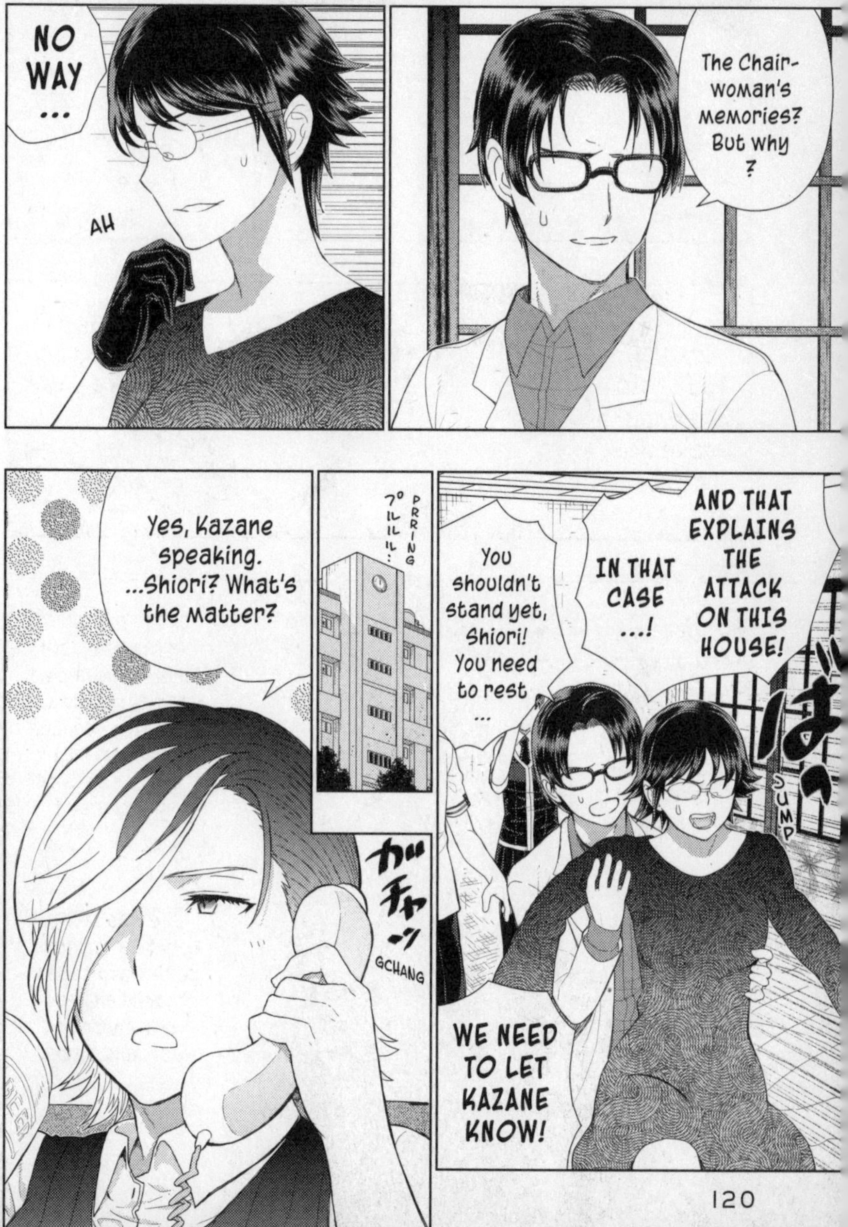

The Chair-woman's memories? But why ?
NO WAY ...
AH
AND THAT EXPLAINS THE ATTACK ON THIS HOUSE!
IN THAT CASE ...!
You shouldn't stand yet, Shiori! You need to rest ...
ばっ
JUMP
WE NEED TO LET KAZANE KNOW!
プルルル
PRRING
Yes, Kazane speaking. ...Shiori? What's the matter?
ガチャッ
GCHANG

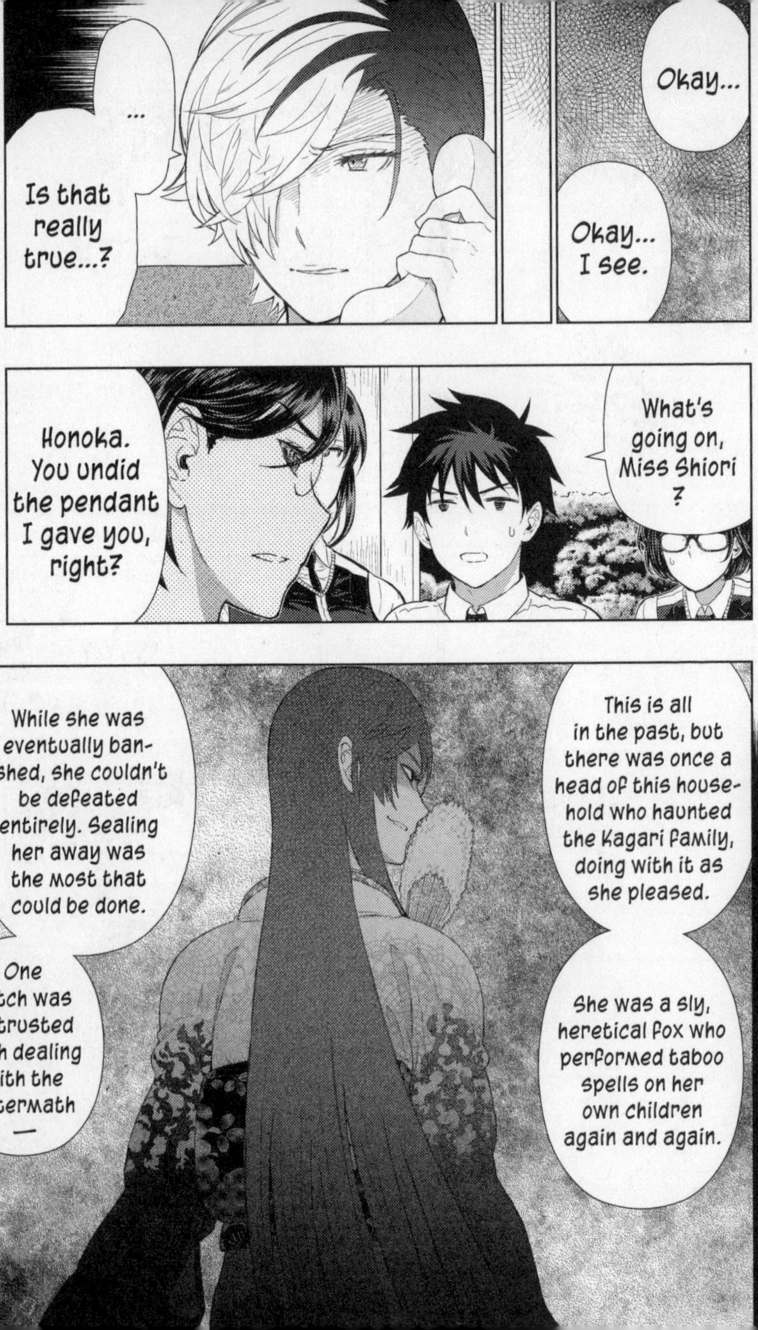
Okay...
Okay... I see.
...
Is that really true...?
What's going on, Miss Shiori?
Honoka. You undid the pendant I gave you, right?
This is all in the past, but there was once a head of this household who haunted the Kagari family, doing with it as she pleased.
She was a sly, heretical fox who performed taboo spells on her own children again and again.
While she was eventually banished, she couldn't be defeated entirely. Sealing her away was the most that could be done.
One witch was entrusted with dealing with the aftermath—

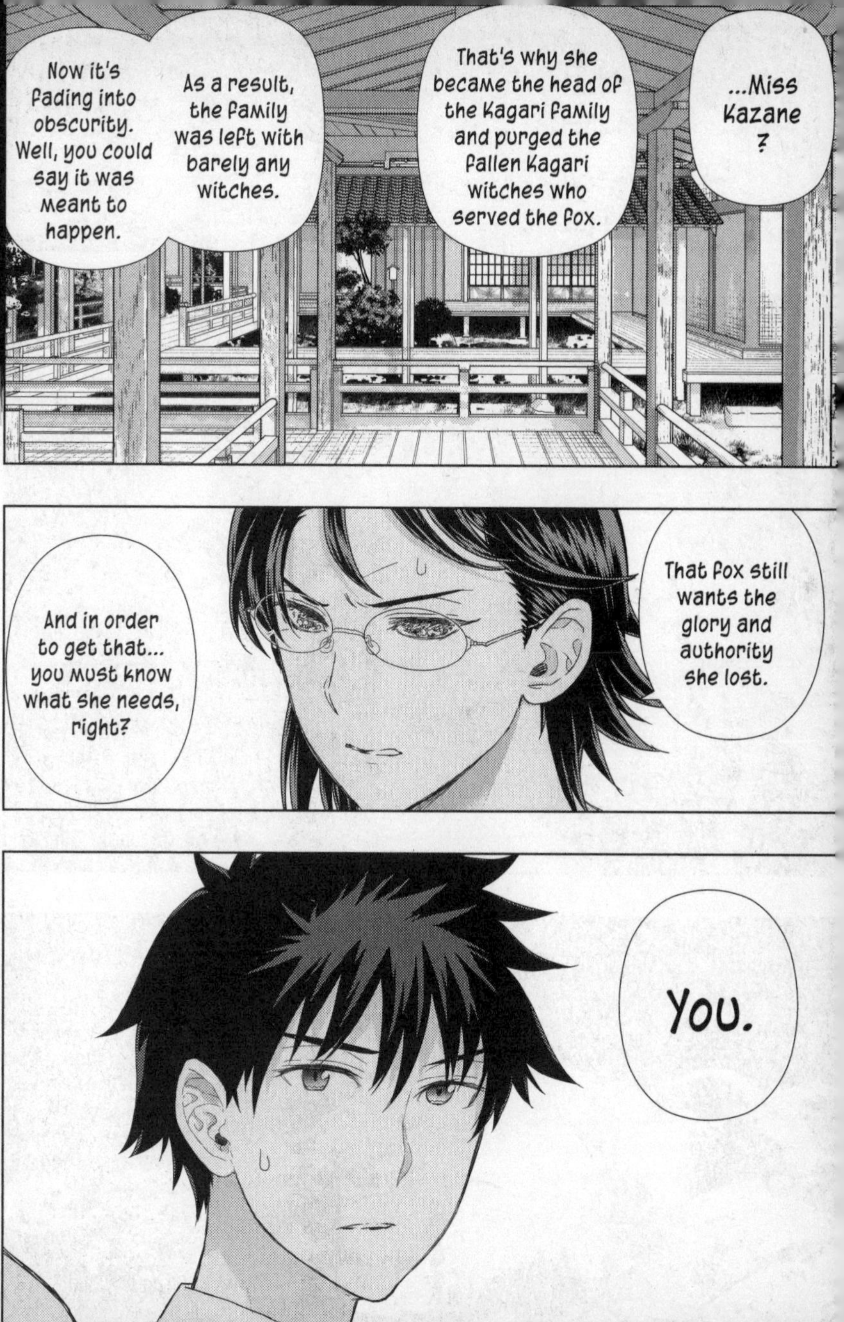
...Miss Kazane?
That's why she became the head of the Kagari family and purged the fallen Kagari witches who served the fox.
As a result, the family was left with barely any witches.
Now it's fading into obscurity. Well, you could say it was meant to happen.
That fox still wants the glory and authority she lost.
And in order to get that... you must know what she needs, right?
YOU.

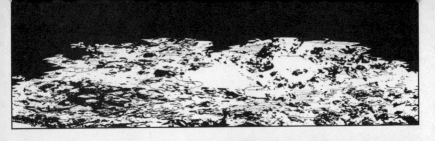

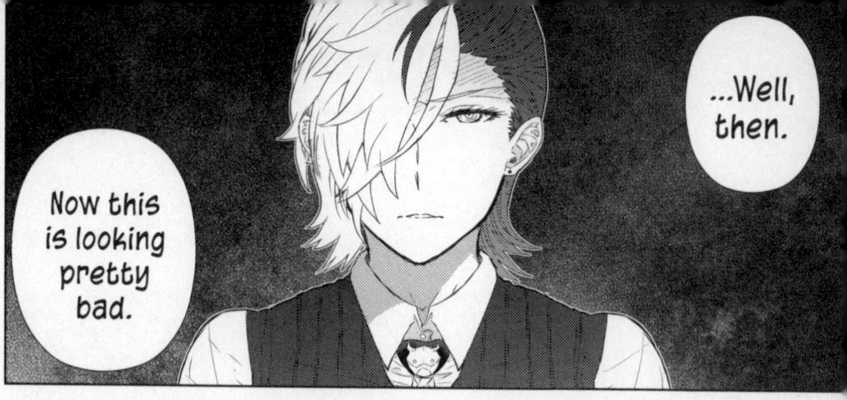
...Well, then.
Now this is looking pretty bad.
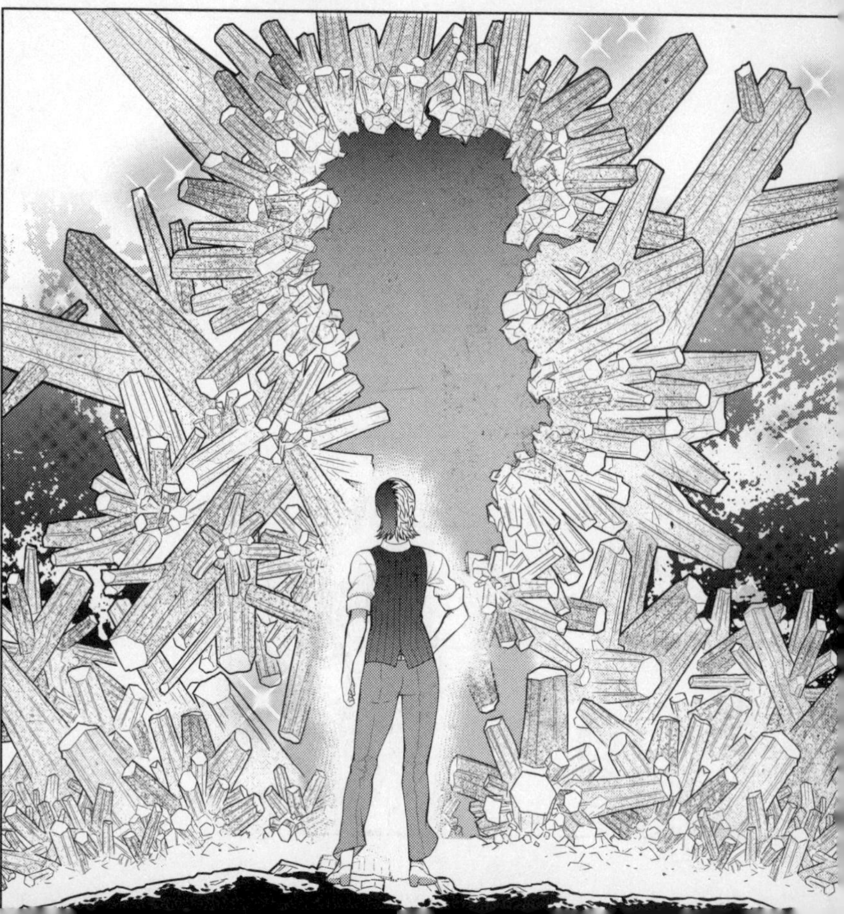

CHAPTER 67 END

Shiori's Dream

It's nice to meet you, my mother-in-law! I'm here to-day to ask for Miss Natsume's hand in marriage—

Oh my! heh heh...

Witchcraft Works

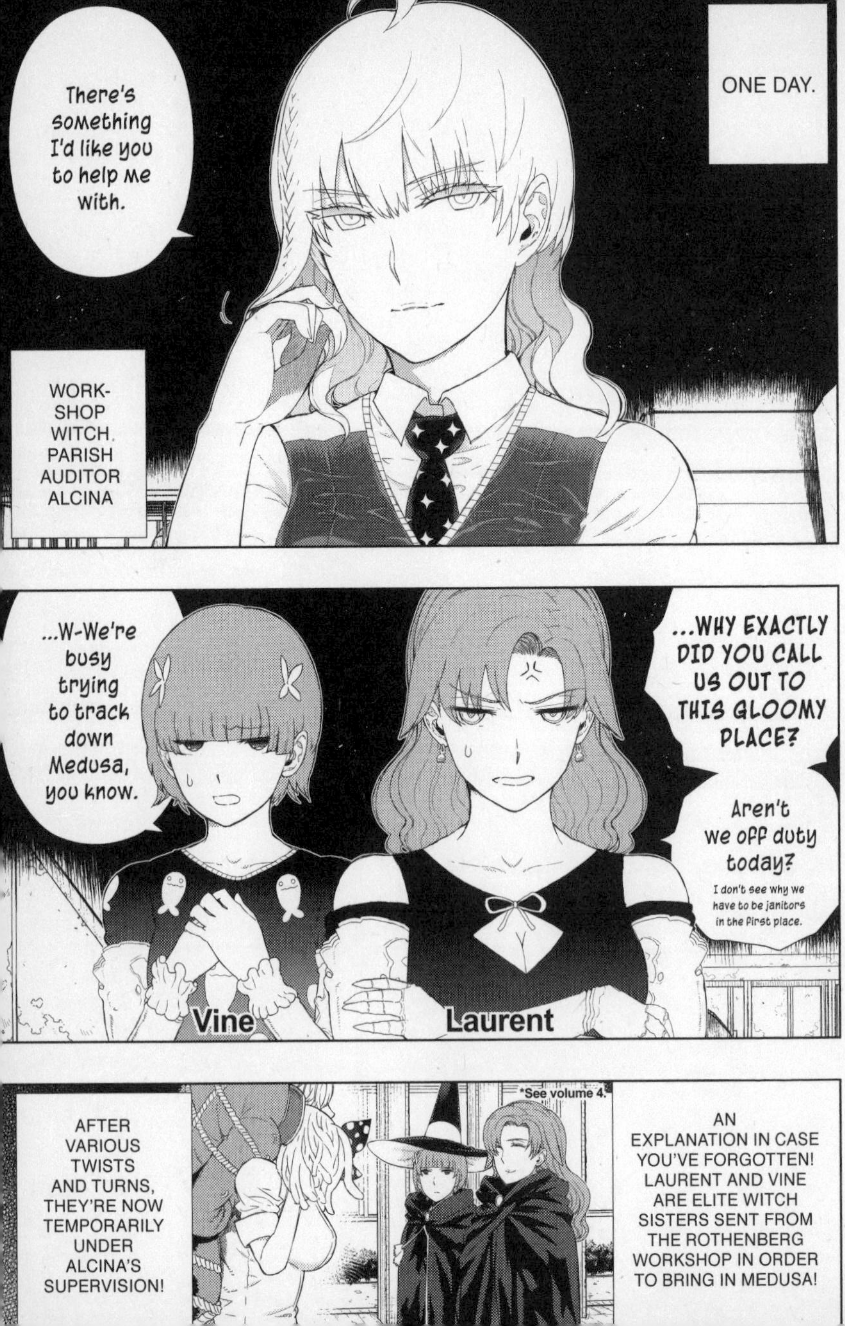
ONE DAY.
There's something I'd like you to help me with.
WORK-SHOP WITCH PARISH AUDITOR ALCINA
...WHY EXACTLY DID YOU CALL US OUT TO THIS GLOOMY PLACE?
Aren't we off duty today?
I don't see why we have to be janitors in the first place.
...W-We're busy trying to track down Medusa, you know.
Laurent
Vine
AN EXPLANATION IN CASE YOU'VE FORGOTTEN! LAURENT AND VINE ARE ELITE WITCH SISTERS SENT FROM THE ROTHENBERG WORKSHOP IN ORDER TO BRING IN MEDUSA!
*See volume 4.
AFTER VARIOUS TWISTS AND TURNS, THEY'RE NOW TEMPORARILY UNDER ALCINA'S SUPERVISION!

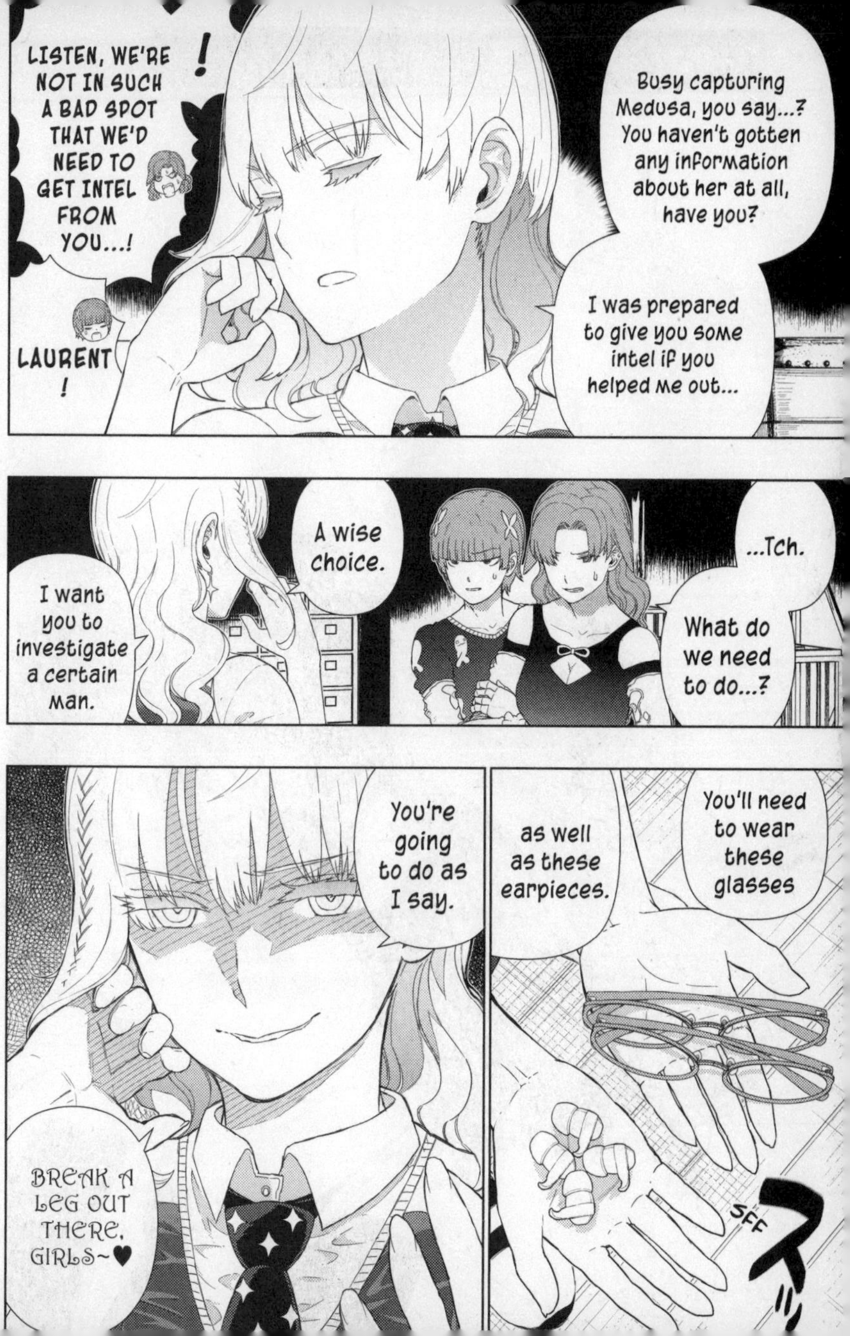
Busy capturing Medusa, you say...? You haven't gotten any information about her at all, have you?
I was prepared to give you some intel if you helped me out...
LISTEN, WE'RE NOT IN SUCH A BAD SPOT THAT WE'D NEED TO GET INTEL FROM YOU...!
LAURENT!
...Tch.
What do we need to do...?
A wise choice.
I want you to investigate a certain man.
You'll need to wear these glasses
as well as these earpieces.
SFF
You're going to do as I say.
BREAK A LEG OUT THERE, GIRLS~♥

CHAPTER 68 Takamiya and Alcina's Scenario

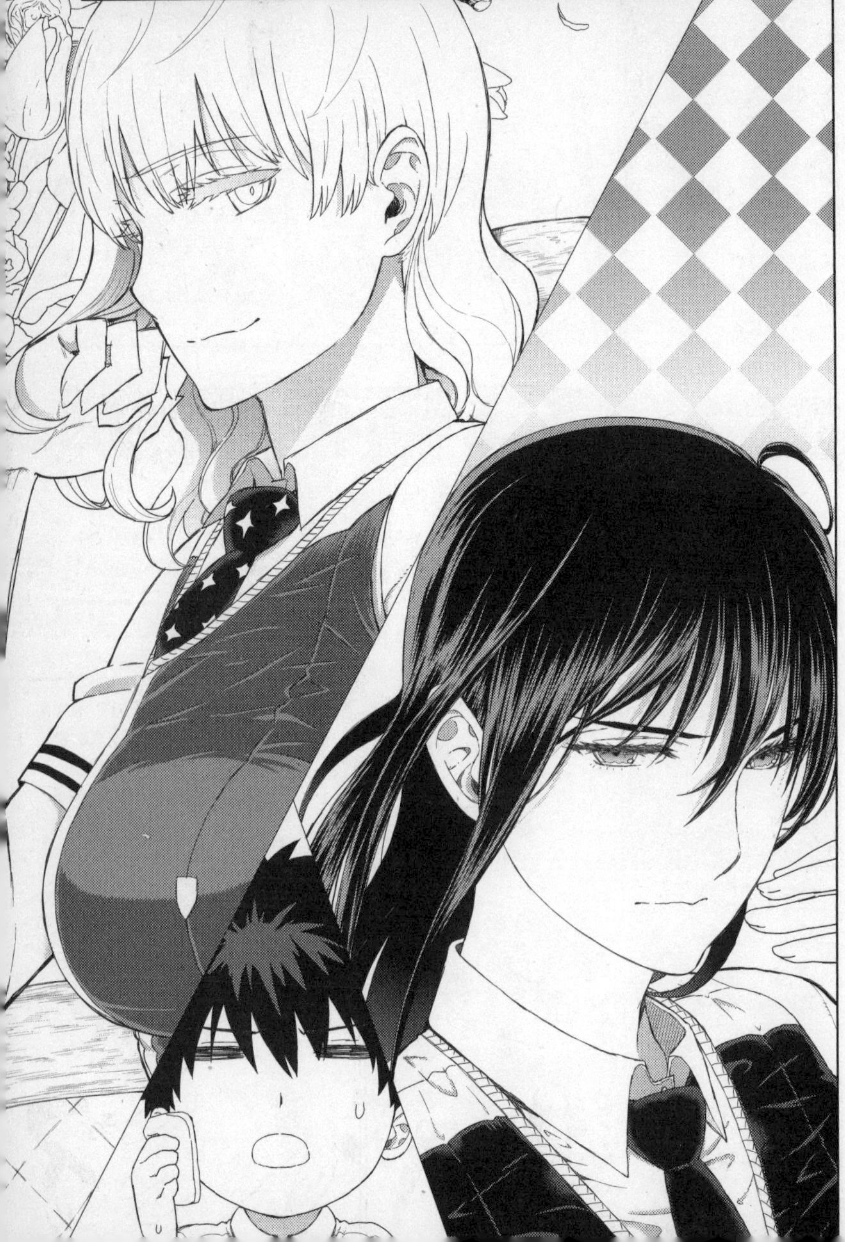

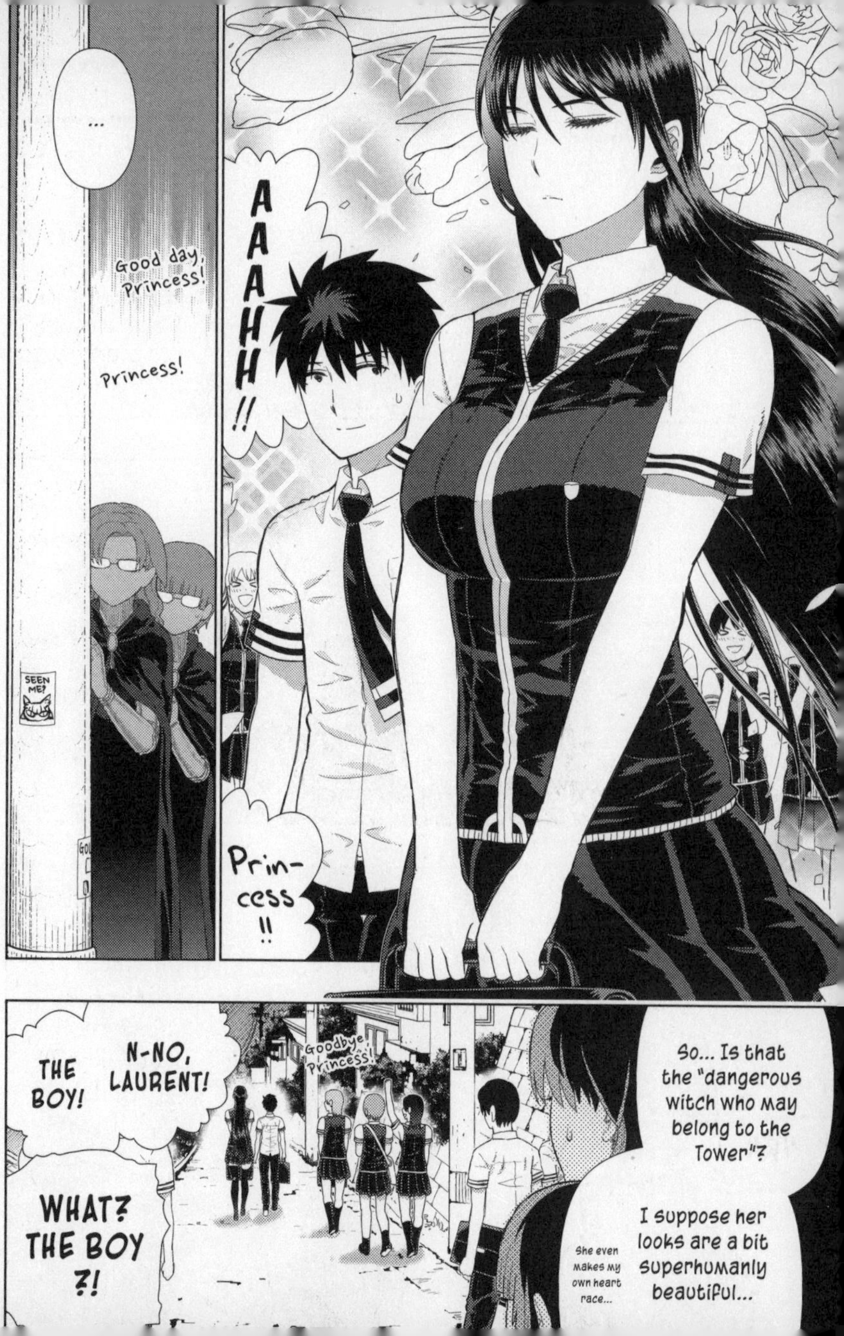
AAAAHH!!
Good day, Princess!
Princess!
SEEN ME?
Prin-cess!!
...
So... Is that the "dangerous witch who may belong to the Tower"?
I suppose her looks are a bit superhumanly beautiful...
She even makes my own heart race...
Goodbye Princess!
N-NO, LAURENT!
THE BOY!
WHAT? THE BOY?!

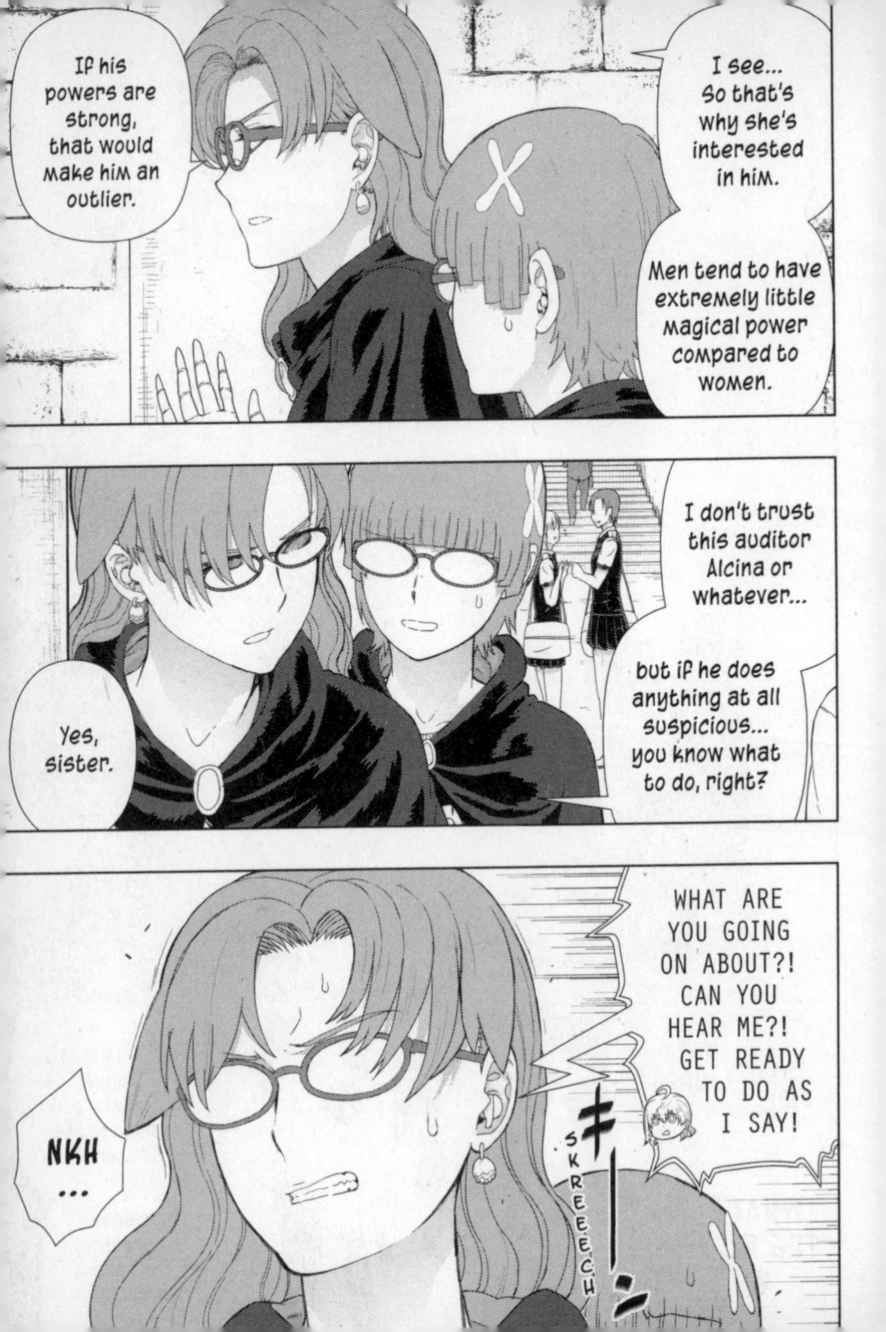
I see... So that's why she's interested in him.
Men tend to have extremely little magical power compared to women.
If his powers are strong, that would make him an outlier.
I don't trust this auditor Alcina or whatever...
but if he does anything at all suspicious... you know what to do, right?
Yes, sister.
WHAT ARE YOU GOING ON ABOUT?! CAN YOU HEAR ME?! GET READY TO DO AS I SAY!
SKREEECH
NKH ...

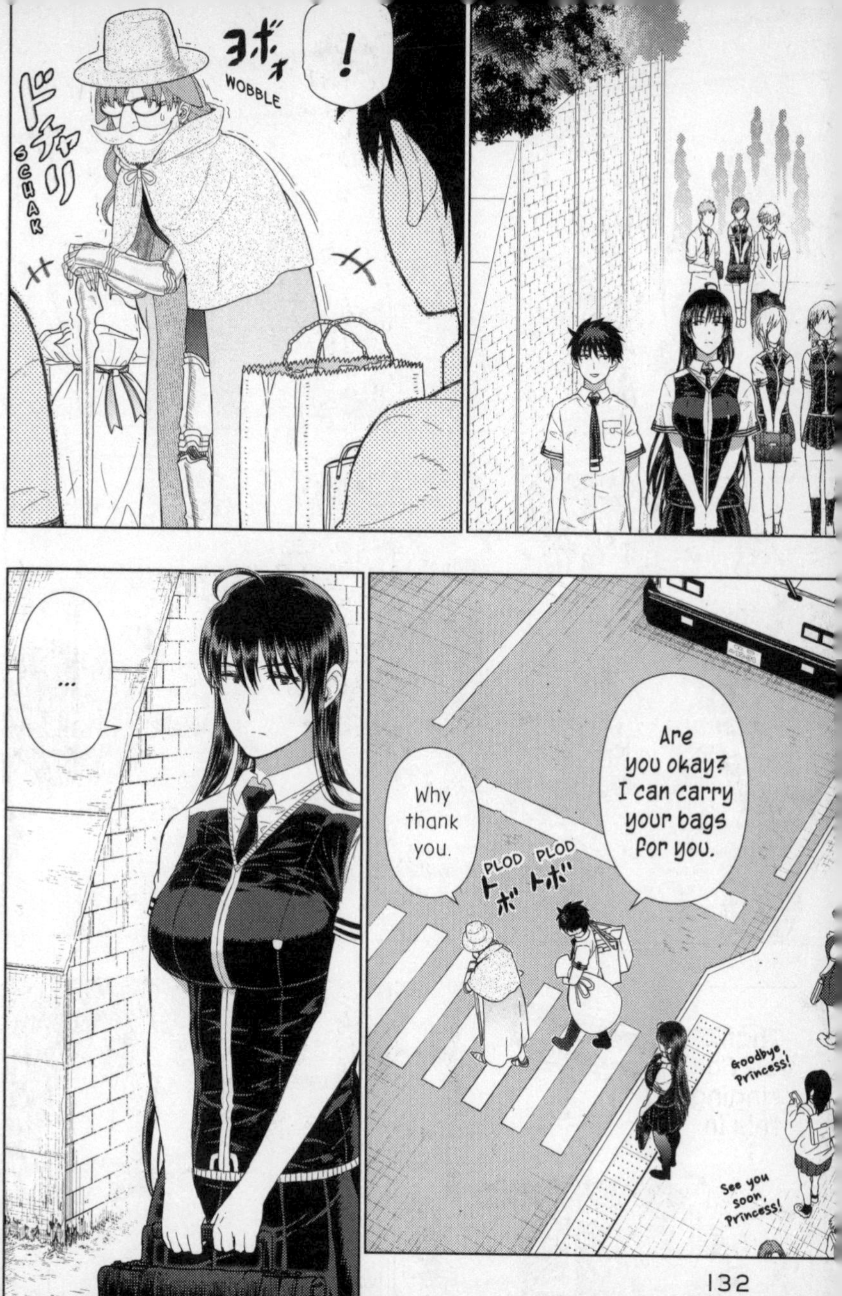
!
ヨボォ
WOBBLE
ドチャリ
SCHAK
Are you okay? I can carry your bags for you.
Why thank you.
トボトボ
PLOD PLOD
Goodbye, Princess!
See you soon, Princess!
...

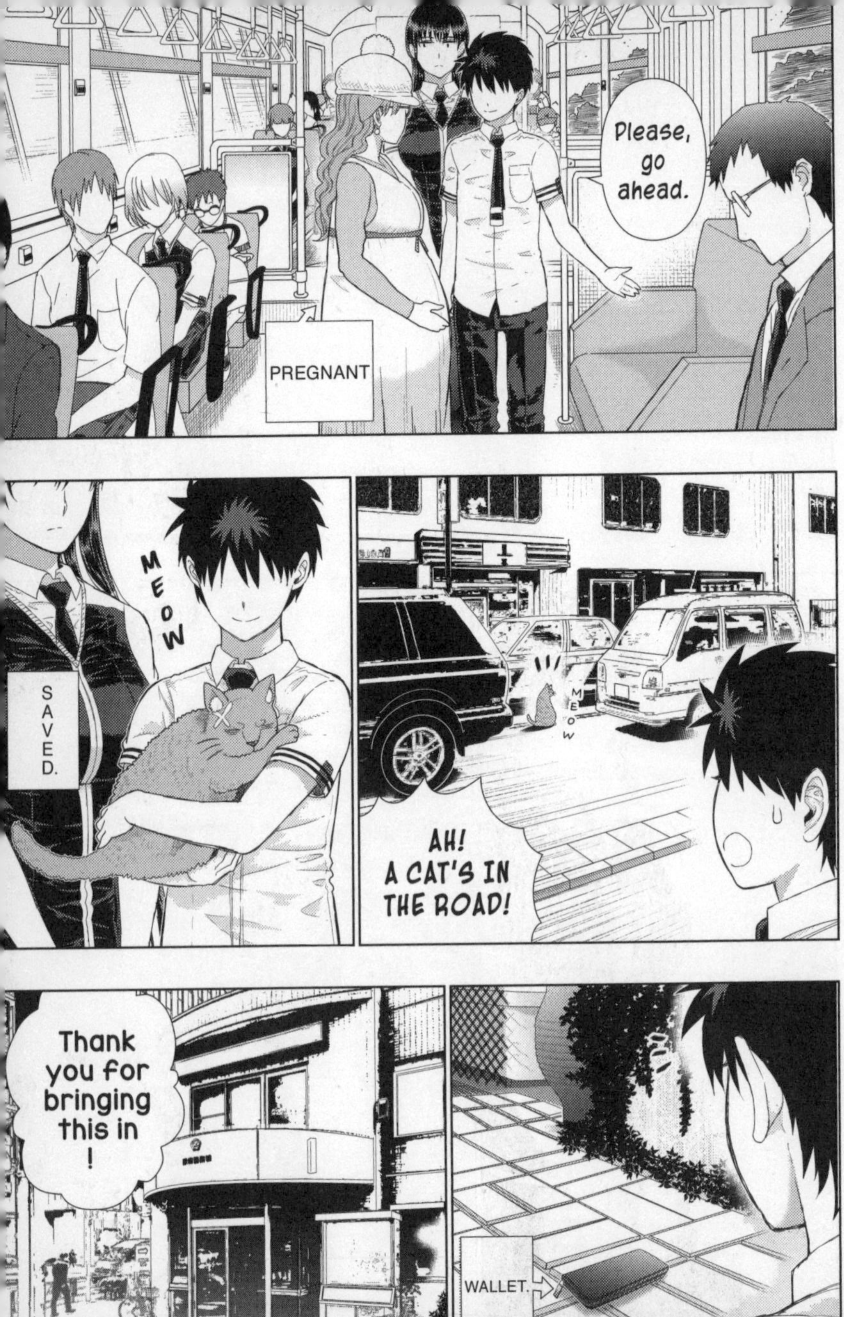
Please, go ahead.
PREGNANT
MEOW
AH! A CAT'S IN THE ROAD!
MEOW
SAVED.
WALLET.
Thank you for bringing this in !

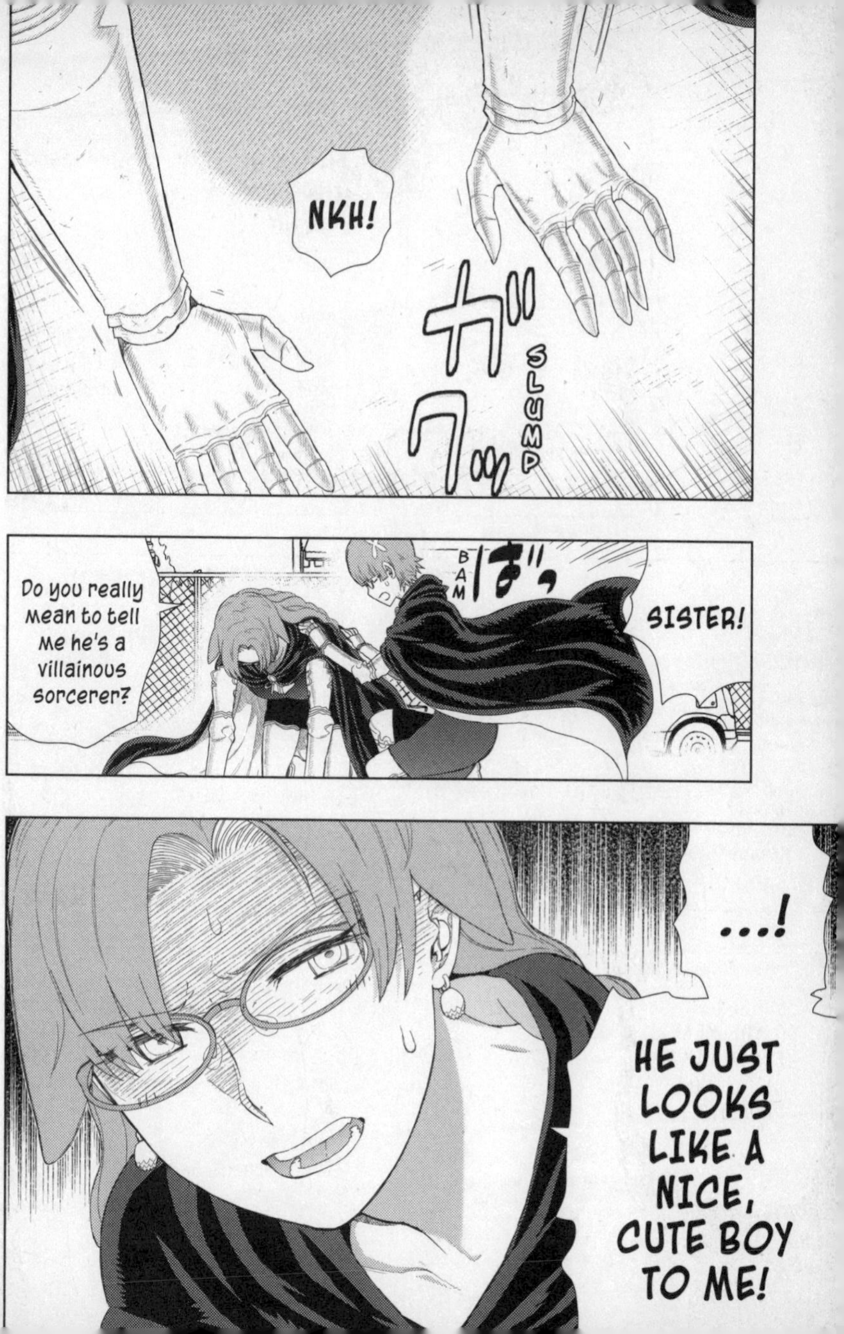
NKH!
ガクッ
SLUMP
SISTER!
BAM
ばっ
Do you really mean to tell me he's a villainous sorcerer?
...!
HE JUST LOOKS LIKE A NICE, CUTE BOY TO ME!

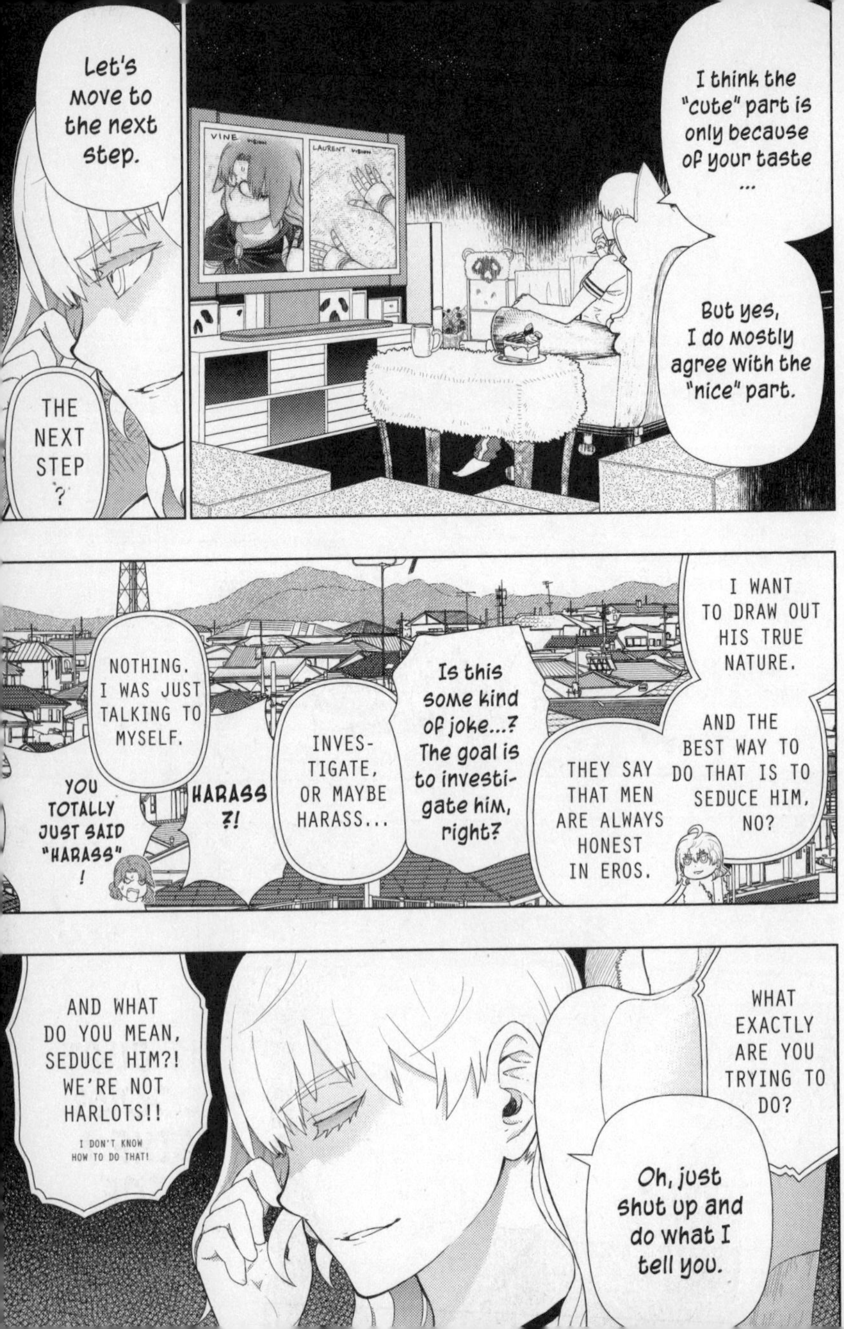
I think the "cute" part is only because of your taste ...
But yes, I do mostly agree with the "nice" part.
VINE VISION
LAURENT VISION
Let's move to the next step.
THE NEXT STEP?
I WANT TO DRAW OUT HIS TRUE NATURE.
AND THE BEST WAY TO DO THAT IS TO SEDUCE HIM, NO?
THEY SAY THAT MEN ARE ALWAYS HONEST IN EROS.
Is this some kind of joke...? The goal is to investigate him, right?
INVESTIGATE, OR MAYBE HARASS...
HARASS?!
NOTHING. I WAS JUST TALKING TO MYSELF.
YOU TOTALLY JUST SAID "HARASS"!
WHAT EXACTLY ARE YOU TRYING TO DO?
Oh, just shut up and do what I tell you.
AND WHAT DO YOU MEAN, SEDUCE HIM?! WE'RE NOT HARLOTS!!
I DON'T KNOW HOW TO DO THAT!

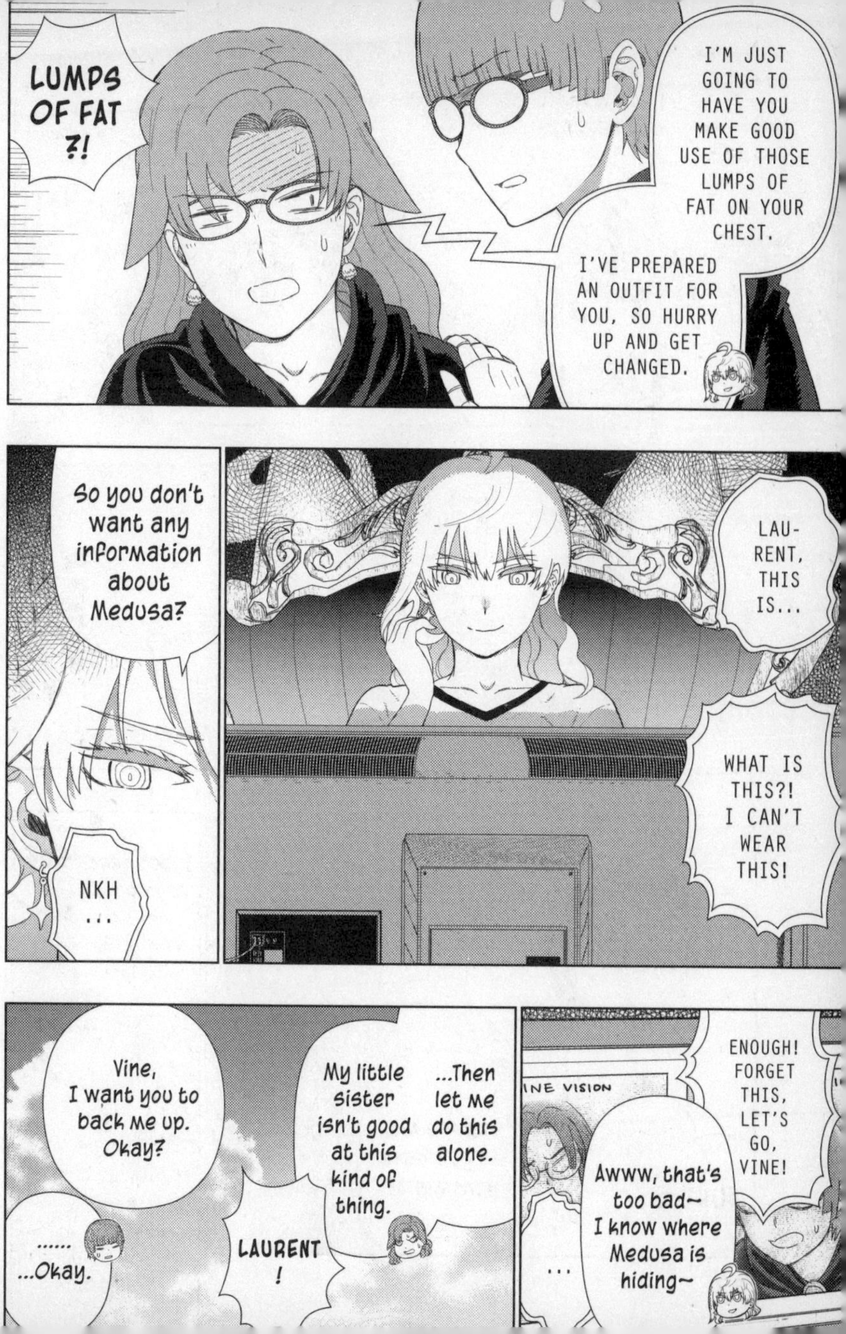
I'M JUST GOING TO HAVE YOU MAKE GOOD USE OF THOSE LUMPS OF FAT ON YOUR CHEST.
I'VE PREPARED AN OUTFIT FOR YOU, SO HURRY UP AND GET CHANGED.
LUMPS OF FAT ?!
LAURENT, THIS IS...
WHAT IS THIS?! I CAN'T WEAR THIS!
So you don't want any information about Medusa?
NKH...
ENOUGH! FORGET THIS, LET'S GO, VINE!
Awww, that's too bad~ I know where Medusa is hiding~
...
...Then let me do this alone.
My little sister isn't good at this kind of thing.
Vine, I want you to back me up. Okay?
LAURENT!
......
...Okay.

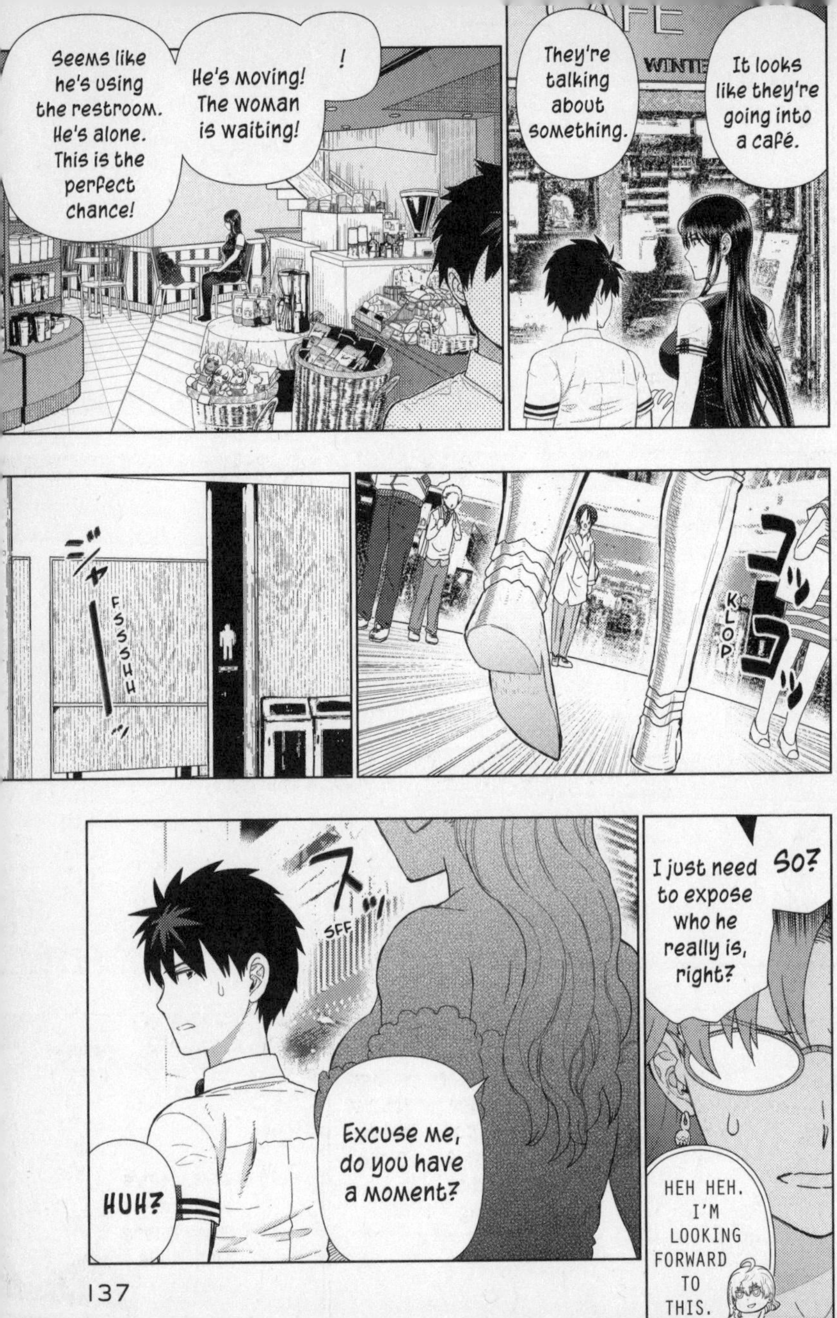
It looks like they're going into a café.
They're talking about something.
!
He's moving! The woman is waiting!
Seems like he's using the restroom. He's alone. This is the perfect chance!
KLOP
FSSSHH
So?
I just need to expose who he really is, right?
HEH HEH. I'M LOOKING FORWARD TO THIS.
SFF
Excuse me, do you have a moment?
HUH?

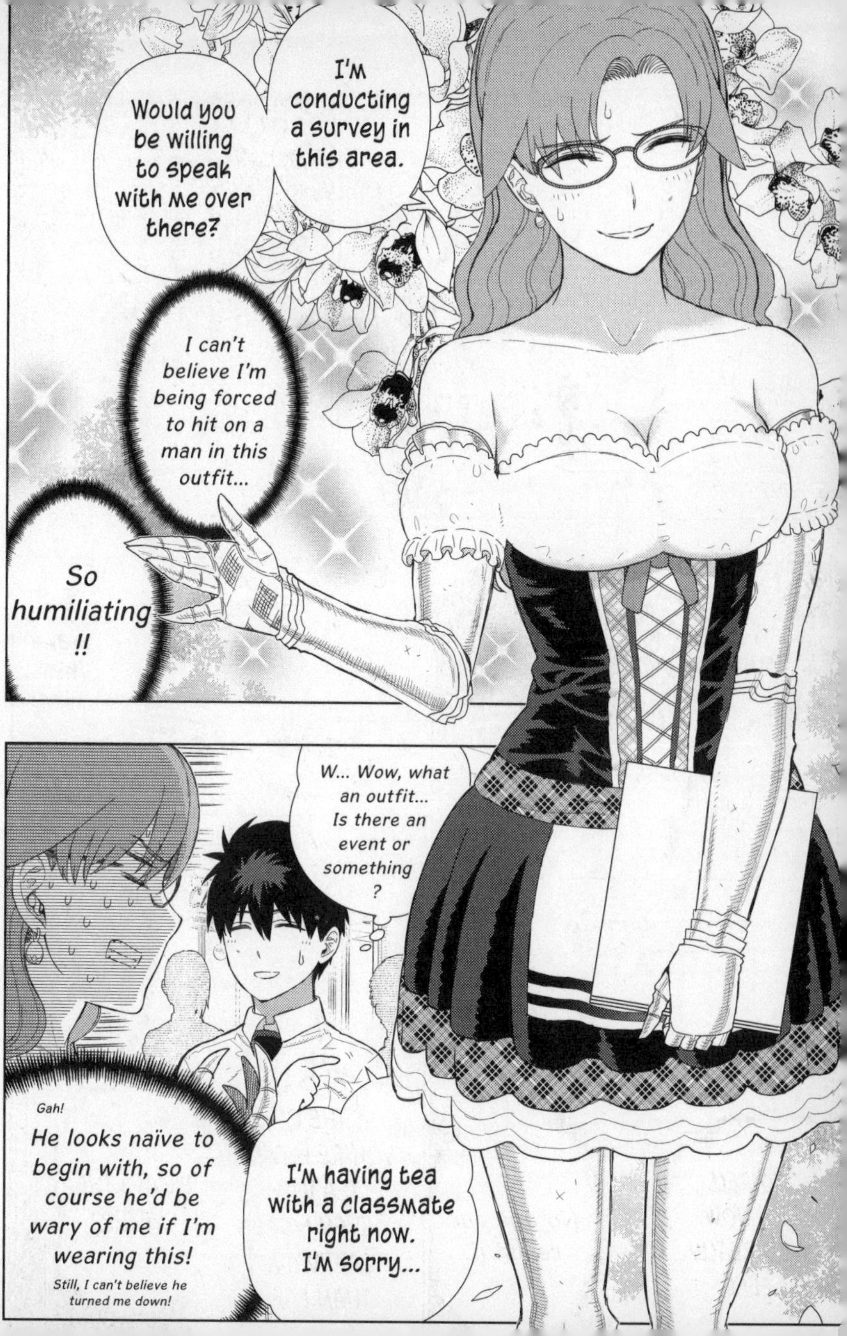
I'm conducting a survey in this area.
Would you be willing to speak with me over there?
I can't believe I'm being forced to hit on a man in this outfit...
So humiliating!!
W... Wow, what an outfit... Is there an event or something?
I'm having tea with a classmate right now. I'm sorry...
Gah!
He looks naïve to begin with, so of course he'd be wary of me if I'm wearing this!
Still, I can't believe he turned me down!

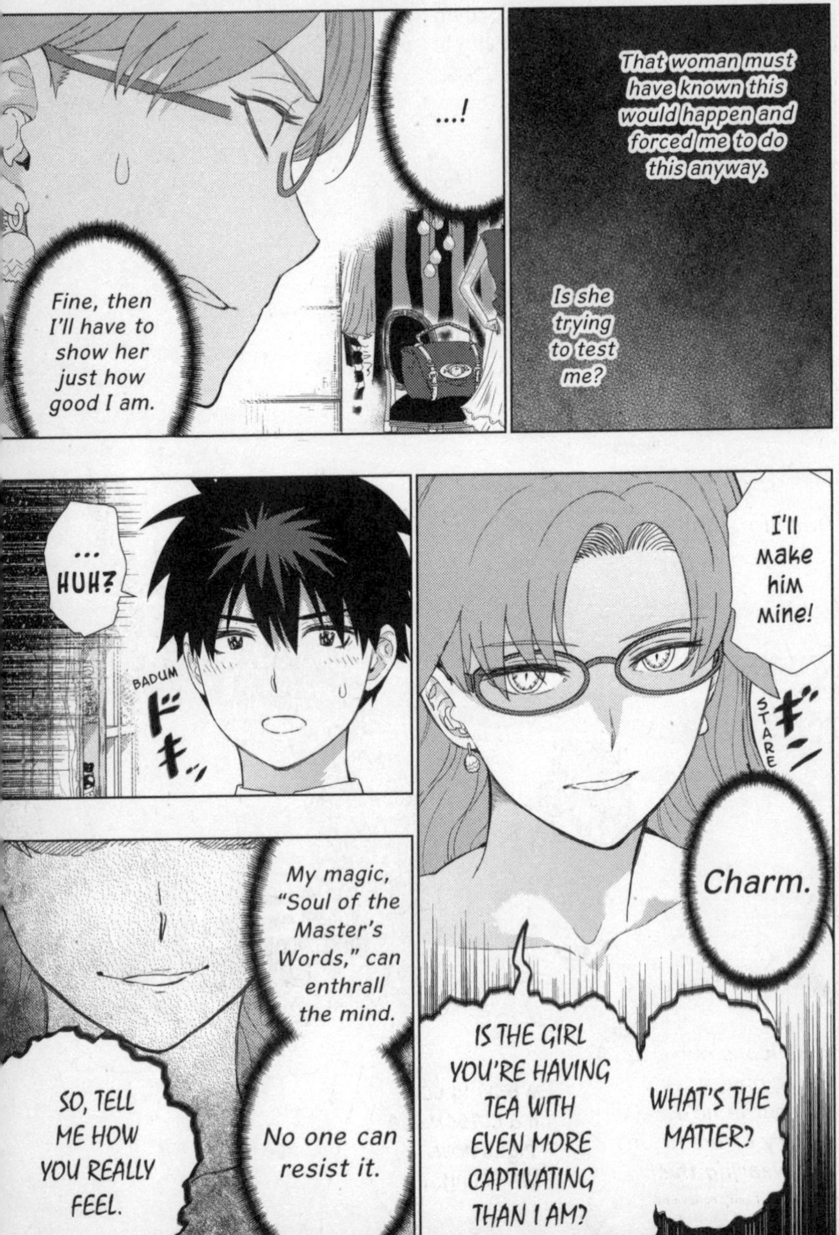
That woman must have known this would happen and forced me to do this anyway.
Is she trying to test me?
...!
Fine, then I'll have to show her just how good I am.
I'll make him mine!
STARE
Charm.
WHAT'S THE MATTER?
IS THE GIRL YOU'RE HAVING TEA WITH EVEN MORE CAPTIVATING THAN I AM?
... HUH?
BADUM
My magic, "Soul of the Master's Words," can enthrall the mind.
No one can resist it.
SO, TELL ME HOW YOU REALLY FEEL.

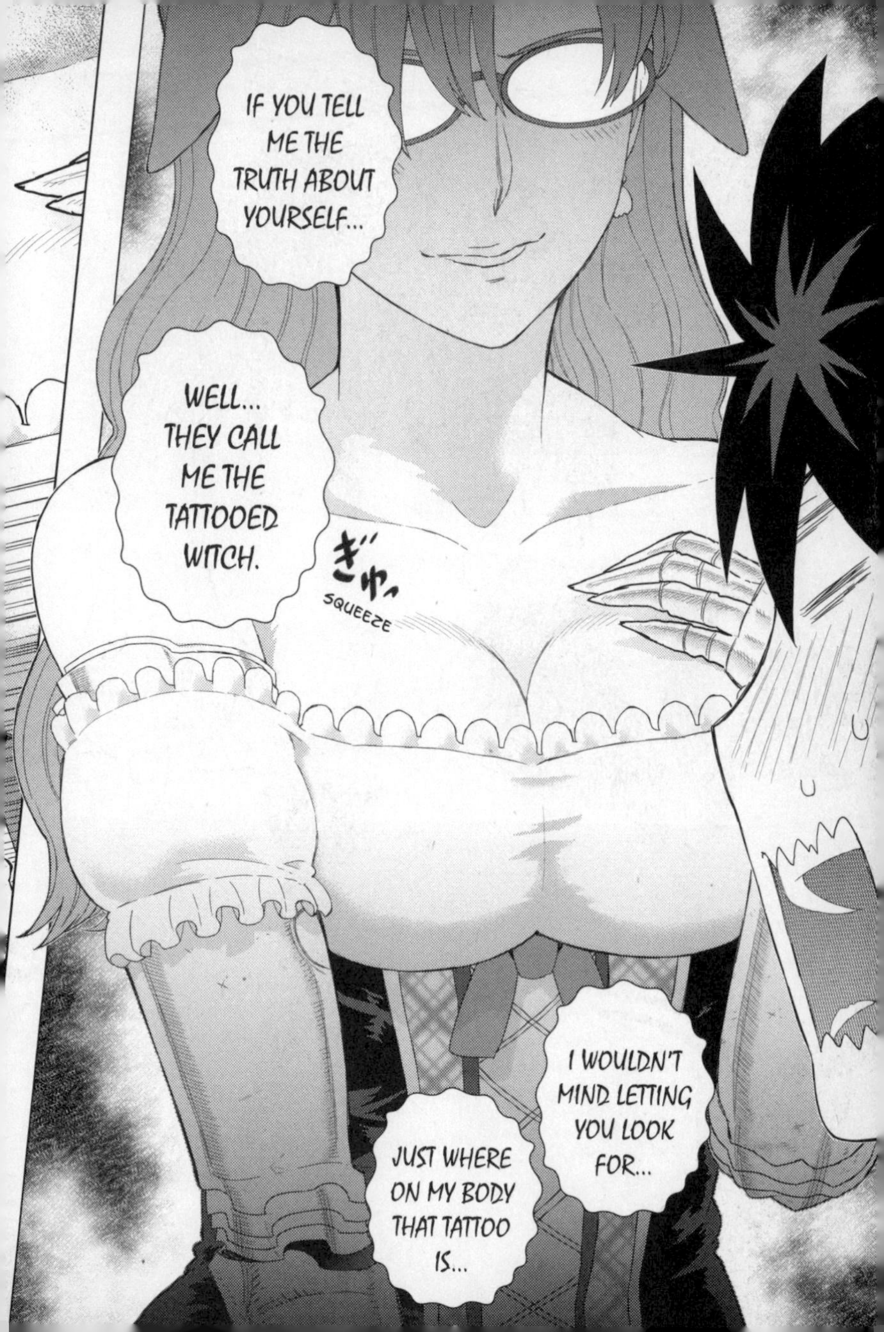
IF YOU TELL ME THE TRUTH ABOUT YOURSELF...
WELL... THEY CALL ME THE TATTOOED WITCH.
ぎゅ SQUEEZE
I WOULDN'T MIND LETTING YOU LOOK FOR...
JUST WHERE ON MY BODY THAT TATTOO IS...

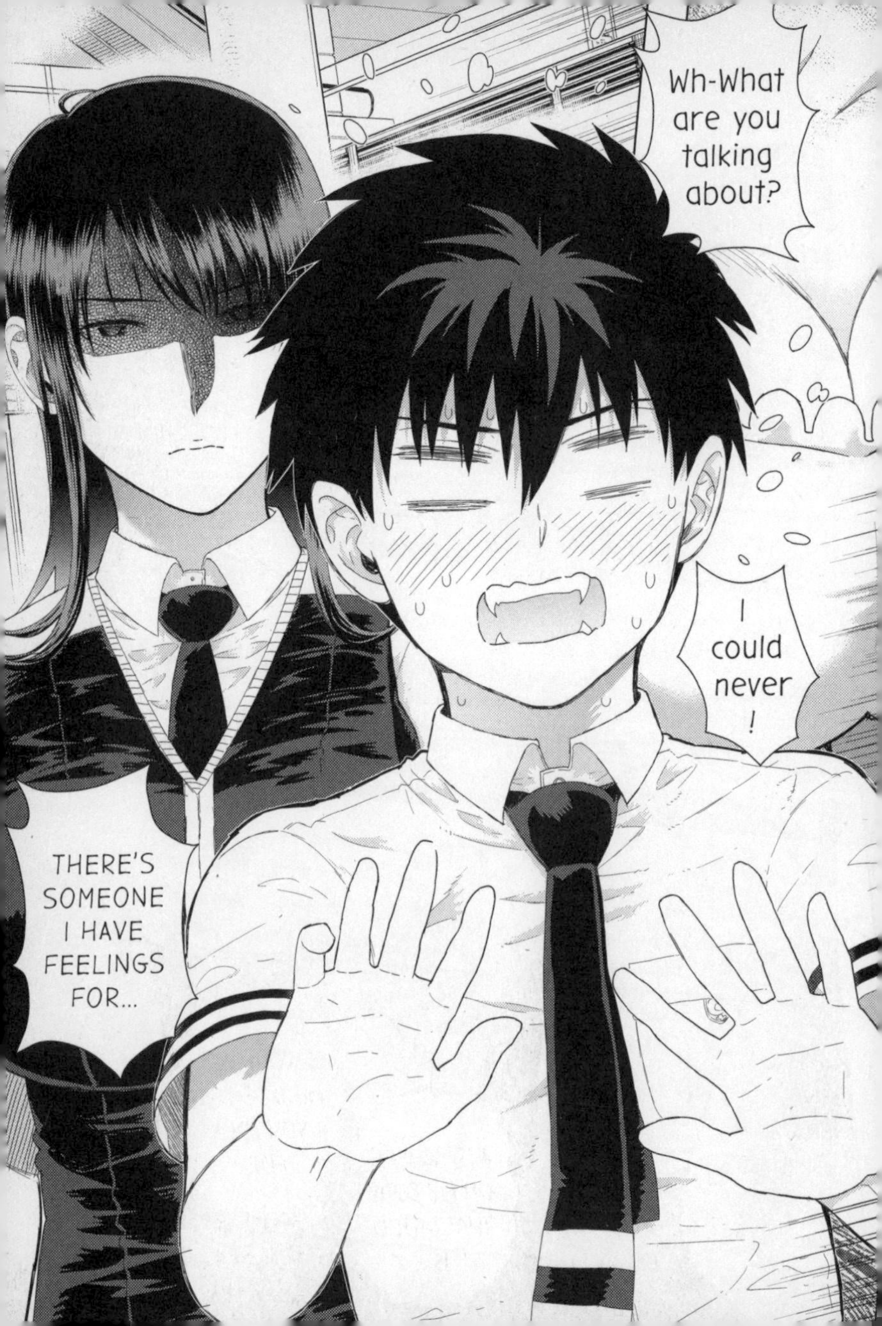
Wh-What are you talking about?
I could never!
THERE'S SOMEONE I HAVE FEELINGS FOR...

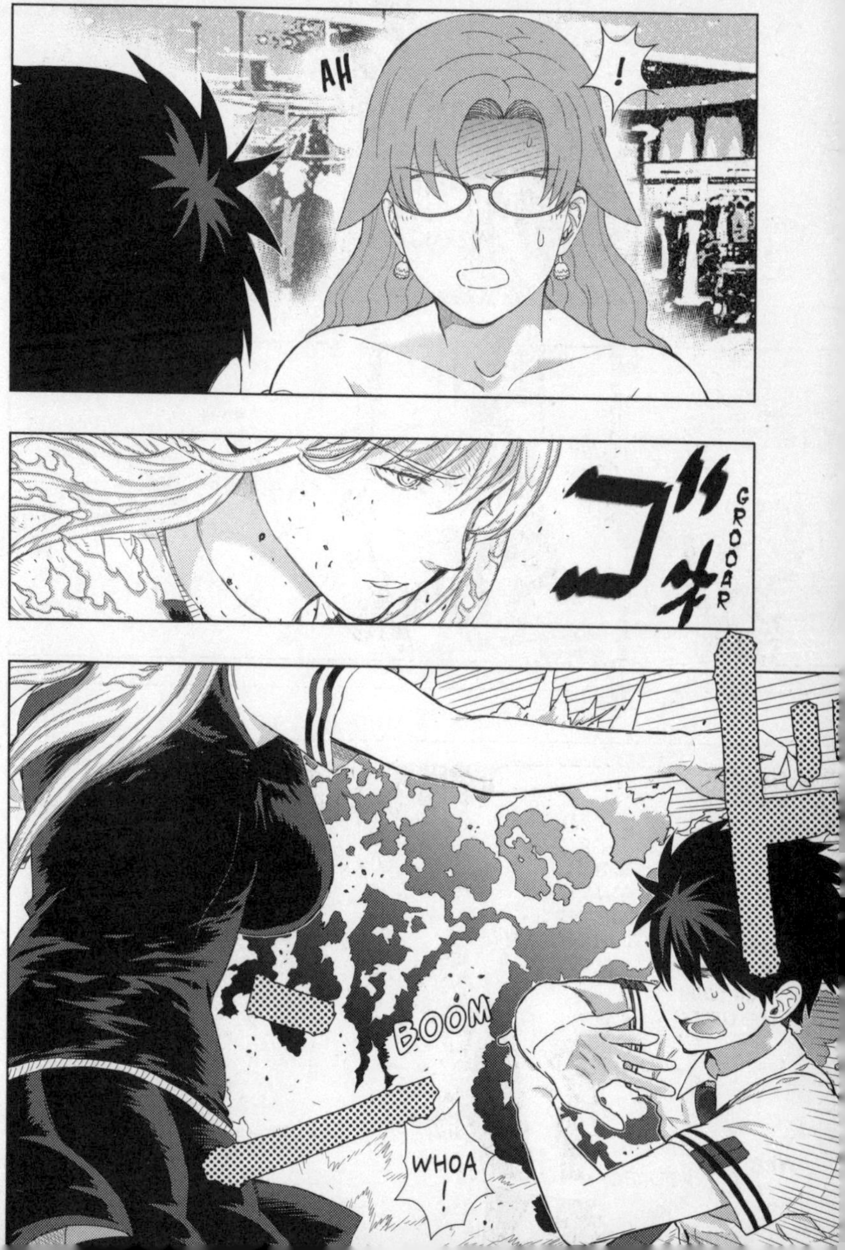
!
AH
ゴッ
GROOOAR
ド
BOOM
WHOA
!

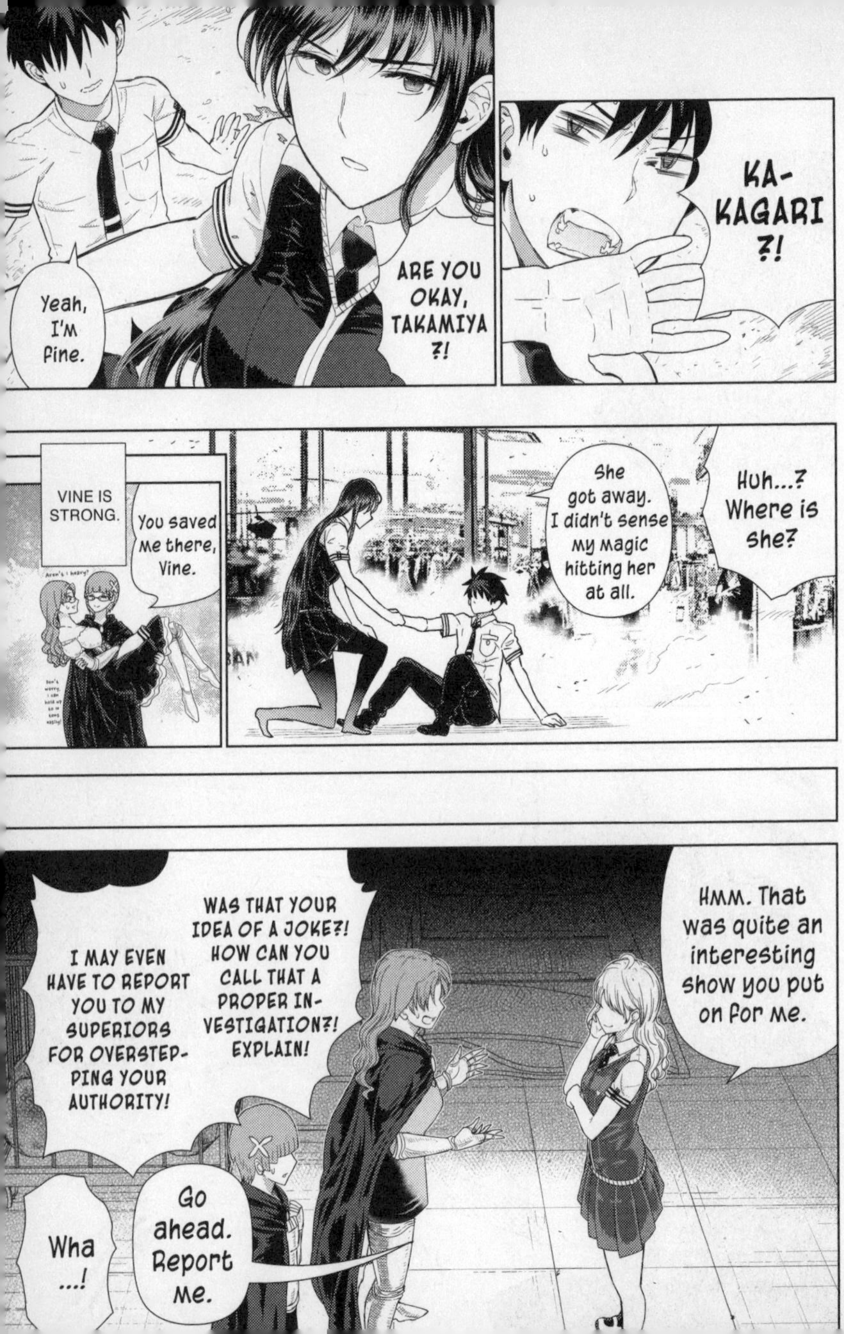
KA-KAGARI?!
ARE YOU OKAY, TAKAMIYA?!
Yeah, I'm fine.
Huh...? Where is she?
She got away. I didn't sense my magic hitting her at all.
VINE IS STRONG.
You saved me there, Vine.
Aren't I heavy?
Hmm. That was quite an interesting show you put on for me.
WAS THAT YOUR IDEA OF A JOKE?! HOW CAN YOU CALL THAT A PROPER INVESTIGATION?! EXPLAIN!
I MAY EVEN HAVE TO REPORT YOU TO MY SUPERIORS FOR OVERSTEPPING YOUR AUTHORITY!
Go ahead. Report me.
Wha...!

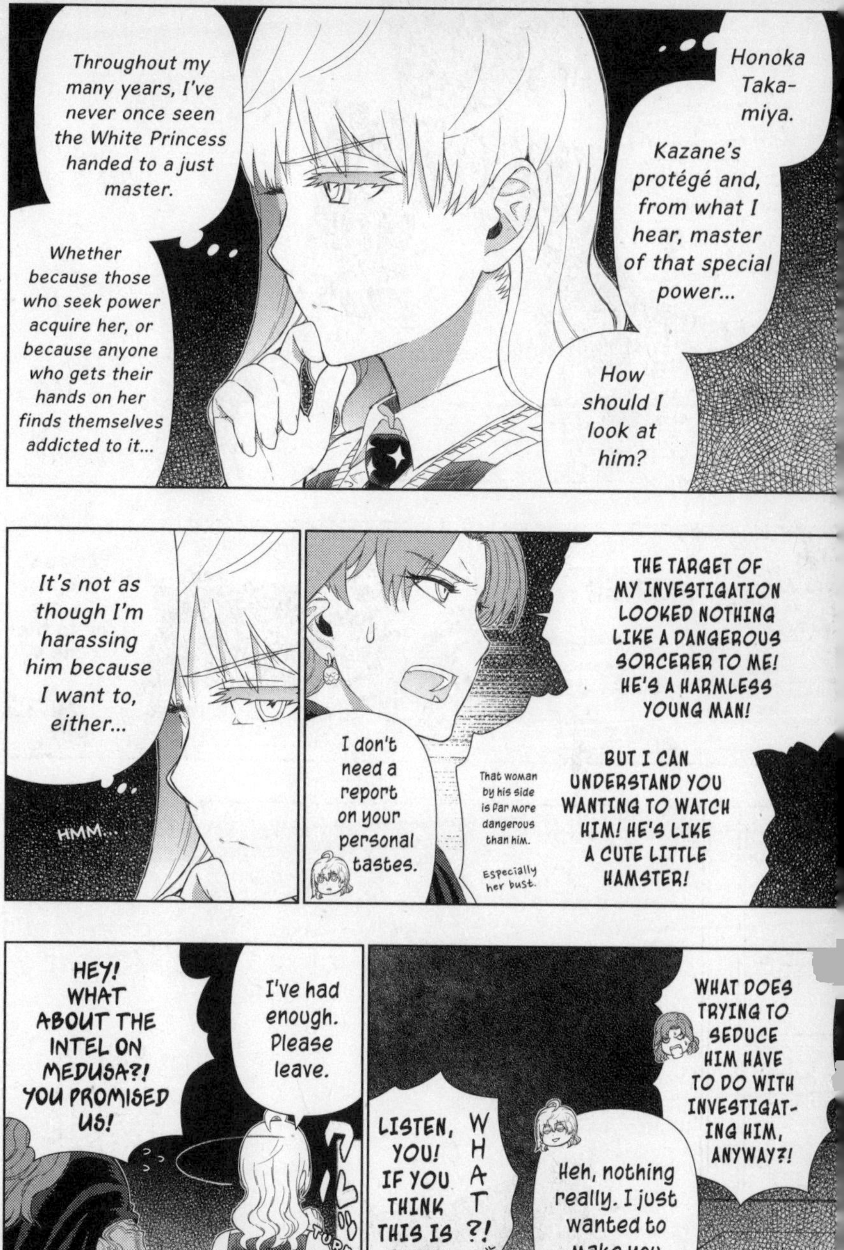
Honoka Takamiya.
Kazane's protégé and, from what I hear, master of that special power...
Throughout my many years, I've never once seen the White Princess handed to a just master.
Whether because those who seek power acquire her, or because anyone who gets their hands on her finds themselves addicted to it...
How should I look at him?
THE TARGET OF MY INVESTIGATION LOOKED NOTHING LIKE A DANGEROUS SORCERER TO ME! HE'S A HARMLESS YOUNG MAN!
BUT I CAN UNDERSTAND YOU WANTING TO WATCH HIM! HE'S LIKE A CUTE LITTLE HAMSTER!
That woman by his side is far more dangerous than him.
Especially her bust.
I don't need a report on your personal tastes.
It's not as though I'm harassing him because I want to, either...
HMM...
WHAT DOES TRYING TO SEDUCE HIM HAVE TO DO WITH INVESTIGATING HIM, ANYWAY?!
Heh, nothing really. I just wanted to make you do it.
WHAT?!
LISTEN, YOU! IF YOU THINK THIS IS FUNNY...
I've had enough. Please leave.
HEY! WHAT ABOUT THE INTEL ON MEDUSA?! YOU PROMISED US!
TURN

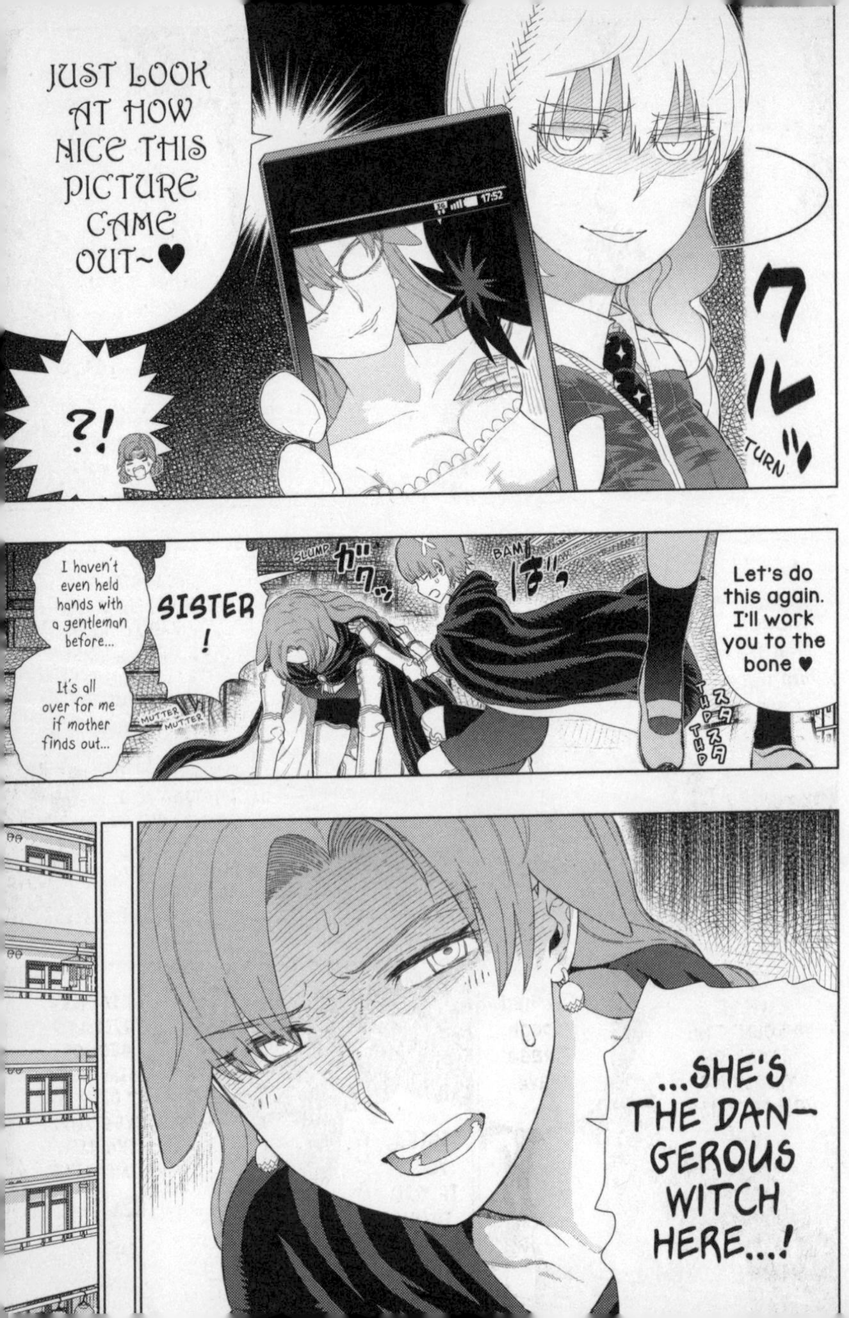
クルッ
TURN
JUST LOOK AT HOW NICE THIS PICTURE CAME OUT~♥
?!
Let's do this again. I'll work you to the bone ♥
スタスタ
THUD THUD
ぱっ
BAM
ガクッ
SLUMP
SISTER!
I haven't even held hands with a gentleman before...
It's all over for me if mother finds out...
MUTTER MUTTER
...SHE'S THE DAN-GEROUS WITCH HERE...!

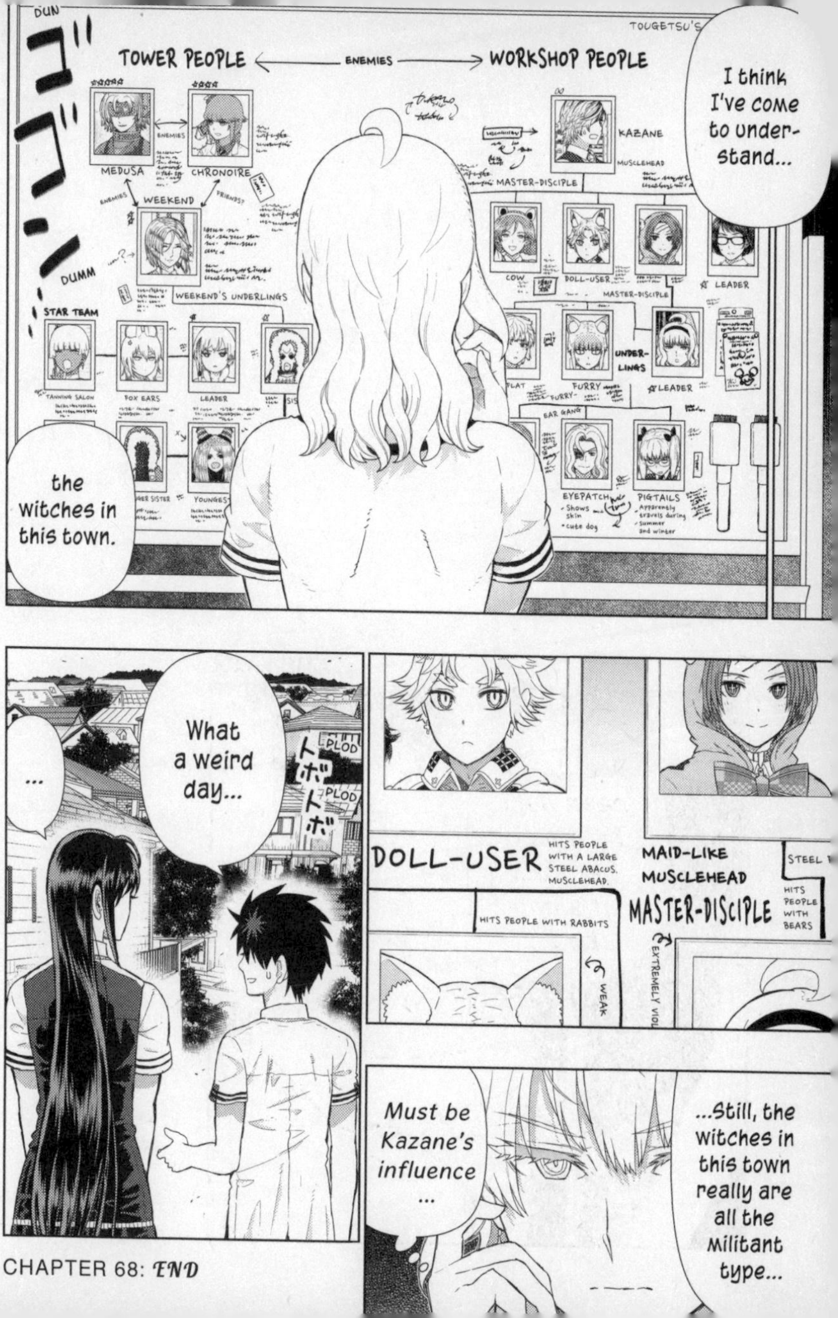
DUN
ゴゴン
TOUGETSU'S
TOWER PEOPLE
ENEMIES
WORKSHOP PEOPLE
I think I've come to understand...
KAZANE
MUSCLEHEAD
MASTER-DISCIPLE
COW
DOLL-USER
LEADER
MASTER-DISCIPLE
FLAT
FURRY
UNDER-LINGS
LEADER
EAR GANG
EYEPATCH
- Shows skin
- cute dog
PIGTAILS
- Apparently travels during summer and winter
MEDUSA
ENEMIES
CHRONOIRE
ENEMIES
WEEKEND
FRIENDS?
DUMM
WEEKEND'S UNDERLINGS
STAR TEAM
TANNING SALON
FOX EARS
LEADER
YOUNGEST
the witches in this town.
MAID-LIKE MUSCLEHEAD
DOLL-USER
HITS PEOPLE WITH A LARGE STEEL ABACUS. MUSCLEHEAD.
HITS PEOPLE WITH BEARS
MASTER-DISCIPLE
HITS PEOPLE WITH RABBITS
WEAK
...Still, the witches in this town really are all the Militant type...
Must be Kazane's influence...
What a weird day...
トボトボ
PLOD
PLOD
...

CHAPTER 68: *END*

Vine (Cat)

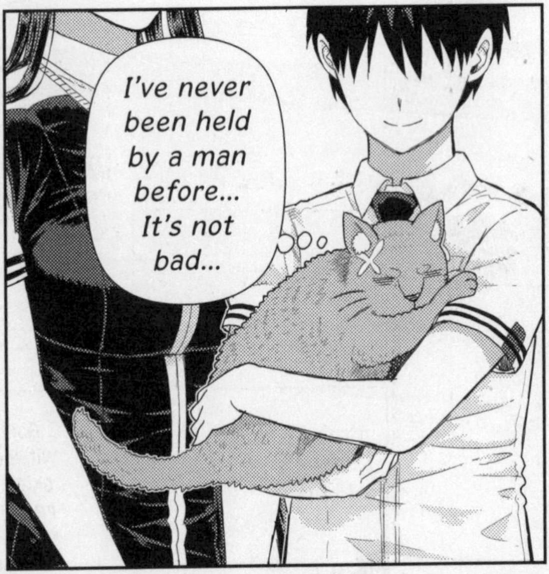
I've never been held by a man before... It's not bad...

Witchcraft Works

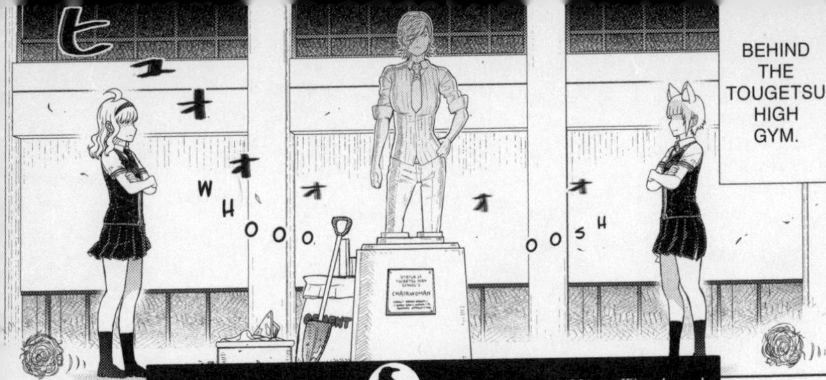
BEHIND THE TOUGETSU HIGH GYM.
WHOOO OOSH
CHAIRWOMAN
CEMENT

CHAPTER 69 Takamiya and Miss Weekend

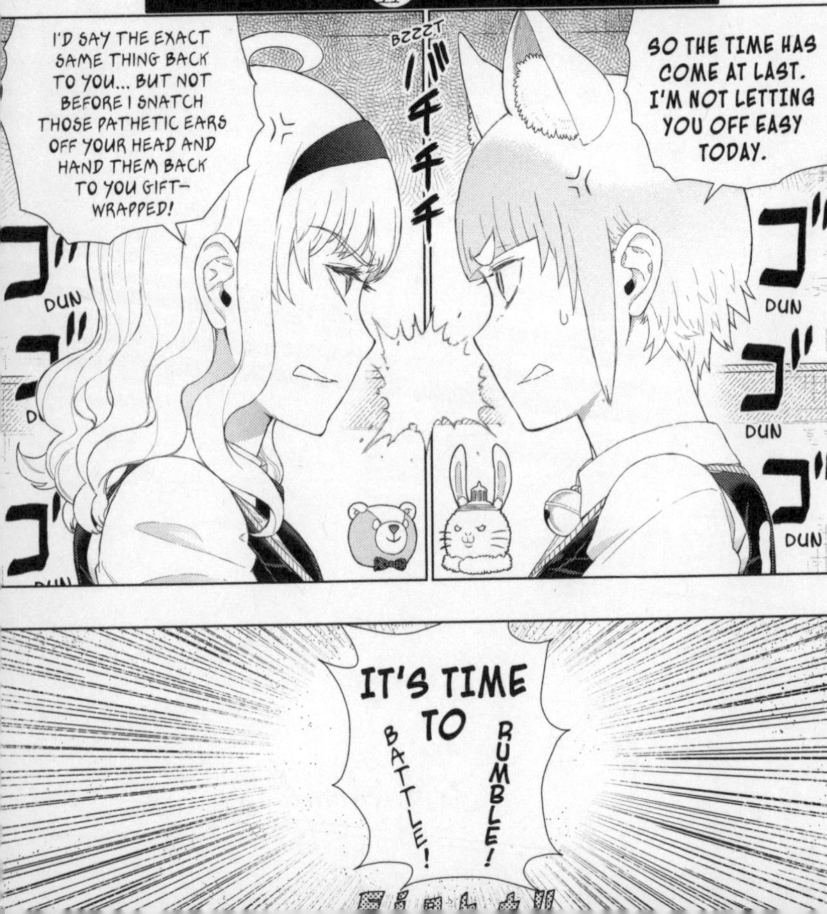
SO THE TIME HAS COME AT LAST. I'M NOT LETTING YOU OFF EASY TODAY.
BZZZT
I'D SAY THE EXACT SAME THING BACK TO YOU... BUT NOT BEFORE I SNATCH THOSE PATHETIC EARS OFF YOUR HEAD AND HAND THEM BACK TO YOU GIFT-WRAPPED!
DUN
DUN
DUN
DUN
IT'S TIME TO
RUMBLE!
BATTLE!

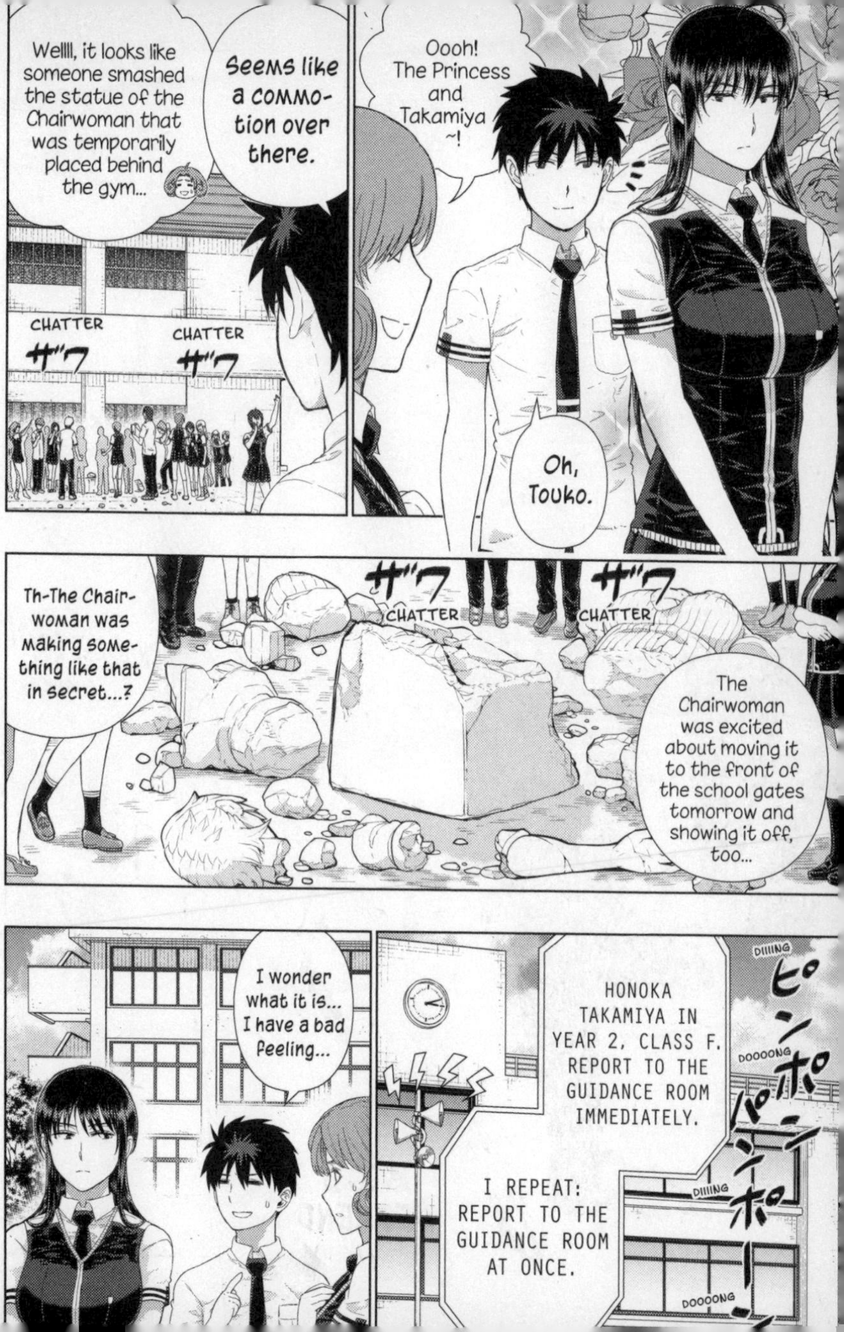
Oooh! The Princess and Takamiya ~!
Oh, Touko.
Seems like a COMMOTION over there.
Wellll, it looks like someone smashed the statue of the Chairwoman that was temporarily placed behind the gym...
CHATTER
ザワ
CHATTER
ザワ
ザワ
CHATTER
ザワ
CHATTER
The Chairwoman was excited about moving it to the front of the school gates tomorrow and showing it off, too...
Th-The Chairwoman was making something like that in secret...?
DIIIING
ピン
DOOOONG
ポーン
DIIIING
パーン
DOOOONG
ポーン
HONOKA TAKAMIYA IN YEAR 2, CLASS F. REPORT TO THE GUIDANCE ROOM IMMEDIATELY.
I REPEAT: REPORT TO THE GUIDANCE ROOM AT ONCE.
I wonder what it is... I have a bad feeling...

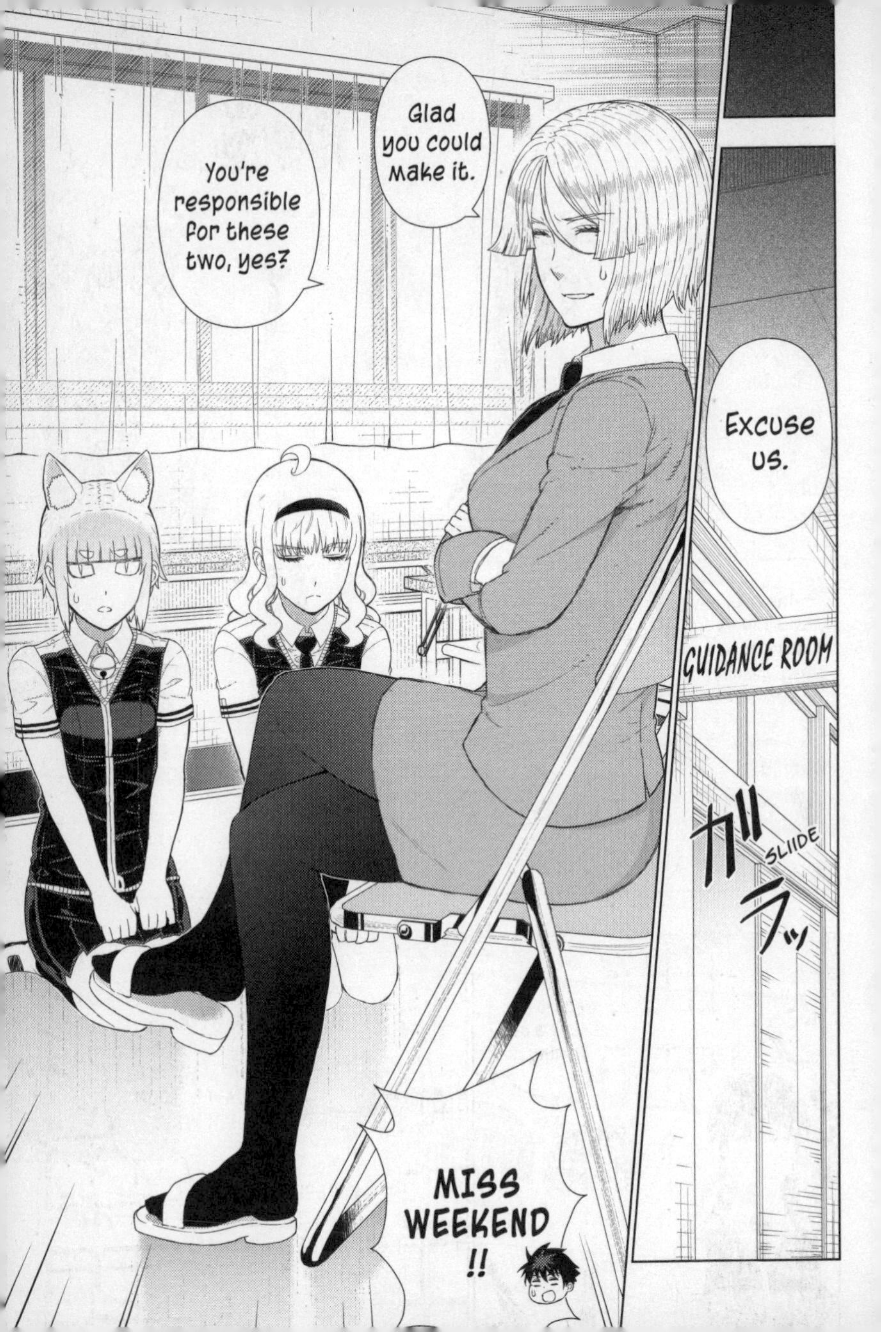
Excuse us.
GUIDANCE ROOM
ガラッ
SLIIDE
Glad you could make it.
You're responsible for these two, yes?
MISS WEEKEND !!

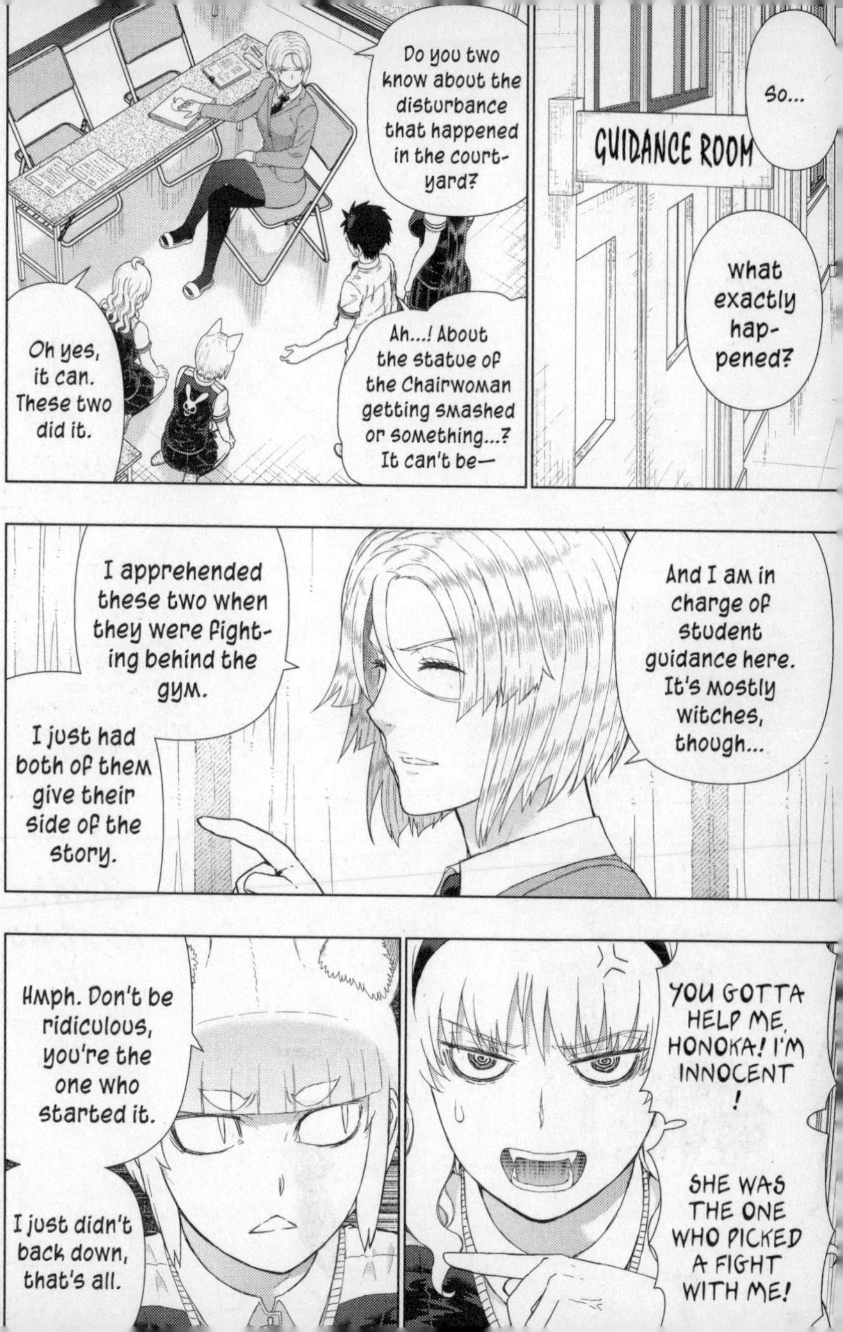

So...
GUIDANCE ROOM
what exactly hap-pened?
Do you two know about the disturbance that happened in the court-yard?
Ah...! About the statue of the Chairwoman getting smashed or something...? It can't be—
Oh yes, it can. These two did it.
And I am in charge of student guidance here. It's mostly witches, though...
I apprehended these two when they were fight-ing behind the gym.
I just had both of them give their side of the story.
YOU GOTTA HELP ME, HONOKA! I'M INNOCENT!
SHE WAS THE ONE WHO PICKED A FIGHT WITH ME!
Hmph. Don't be ridiculous, you're the one who started it.
I just didn't back down, that's all.

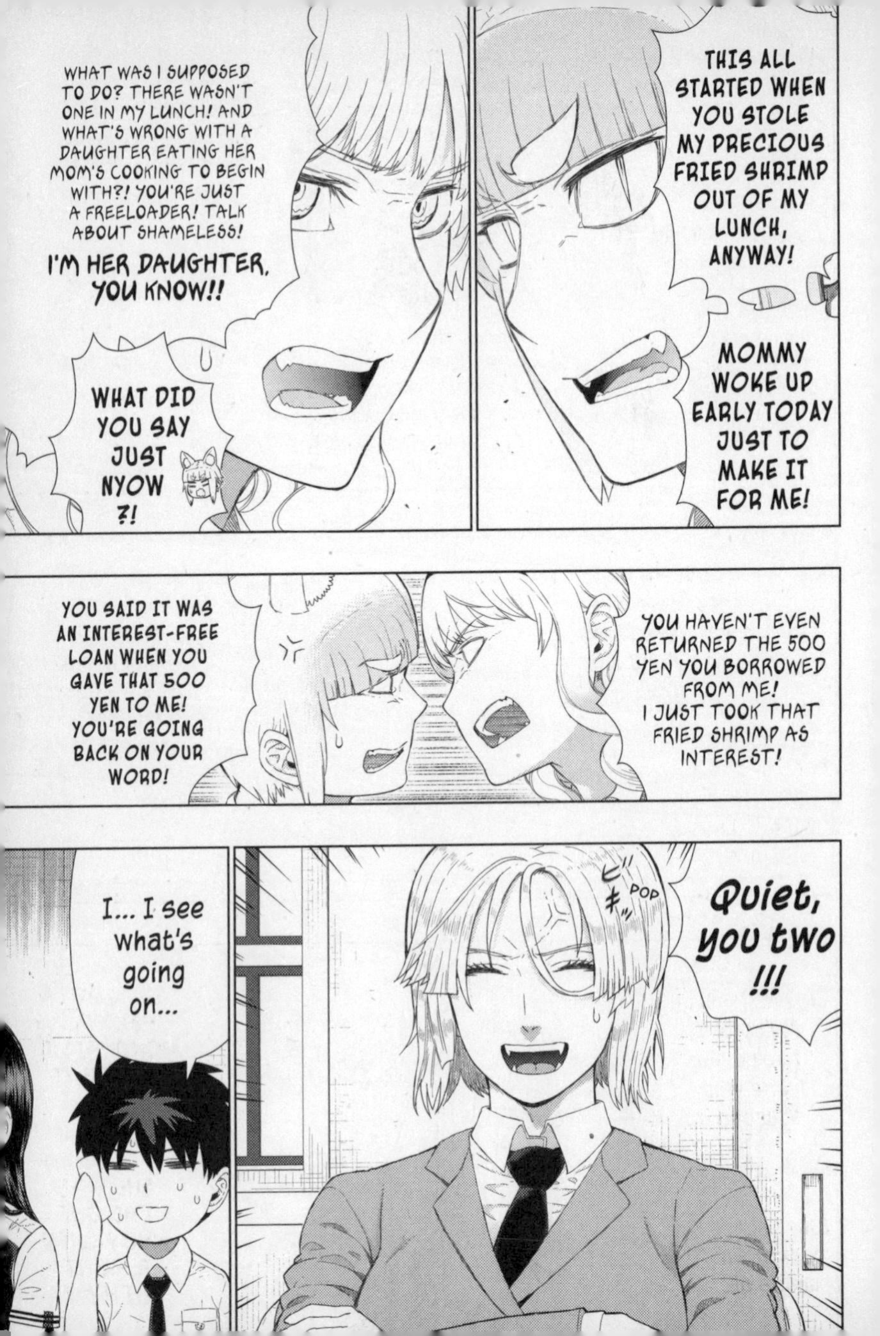
THIS ALL STARTED WHEN YOU STOLE MY PRECIOUS FRIED SHRIMP OUT OF MY LUNCH, ANYWAY!
MOMMY WOKE UP EARLY TODAY JUST TO MAKE IT FOR ME!
WHAT WAS I SUPPOSED TO DO? THERE WASN'T ONE IN MY LUNCH! AND WHAT'S WRONG WITH A DAUGHTER EATING HER MOM'S COOKING TO BEGIN WITH?! YOU'RE JUST A FREELOADER! TALK ABOUT SHAMELESS!
I'M HER DAUGHTER, YOU KNOW!!
WHAT DID YOU SAY JUST NYOW?!
YOU HAVEN'T EVEN RETURNED THE 500 YEN YOU BORROWED FROM ME! I JUST TOOK THAT FRIED SHRIMP AS INTEREST!
YOU SAID IT WAS AN INTEREST-FREE LOAN WHEN YOU GAVE THAT 500 YEN TO ME! YOU'RE GOING BACK ON YOUR WORD!
ビキッ POP
Quiet, you two!!!
I... I see what's going on...

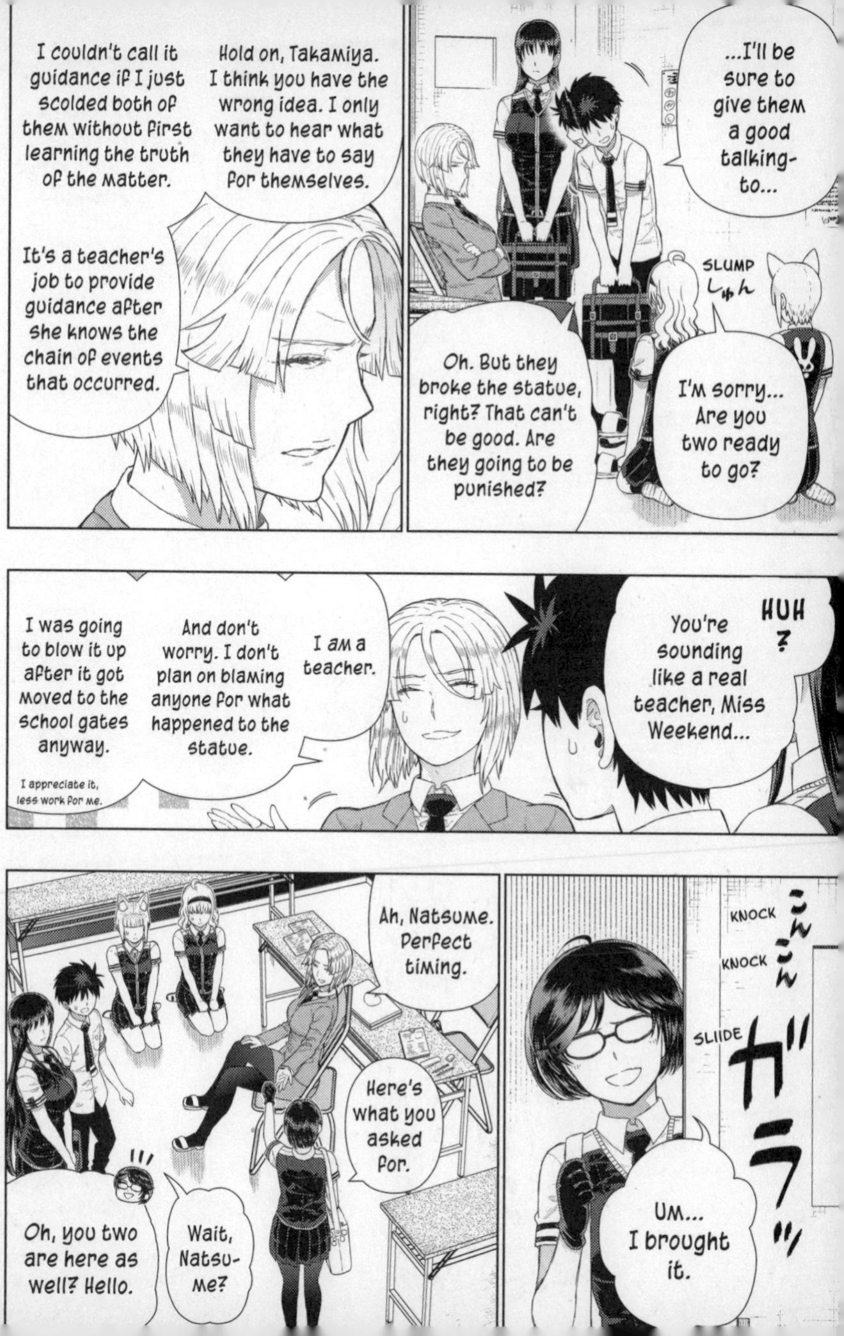

...I'll be sure to give them a good talking-to...
SLUMP
しゅん
I'm sorry... Are you two ready to go?
Oh. But they broke the statue, right? That can't be good. Are they going to be punished?
Hold on, Takamiya. I think you have the wrong idea. I only want to hear what they have to say for themselves.
I couldn't call it guidance if I just scolded both of them without first learning the truth of the matter.
It's a teacher's job to provide guidance after she knows the chain of events that occurred.
HUH?
You're sounding like a real teacher, Miss Weekend...
I am a teacher.
And don't worry. I don't plan on blaming anyone for what happened to the statue.
I was going to blow it up after it got moved to the school gates anyway.
I appreciate it, less work for me.
KNOCK
こん
KNOCK
こん
SLIIDE
ガラッ
Um... I brought it.
Ah, Natsume. Perfect timing.
Here's what you asked for.
Wait, Natsu-me?
Oh, you two are here as well? Hello.

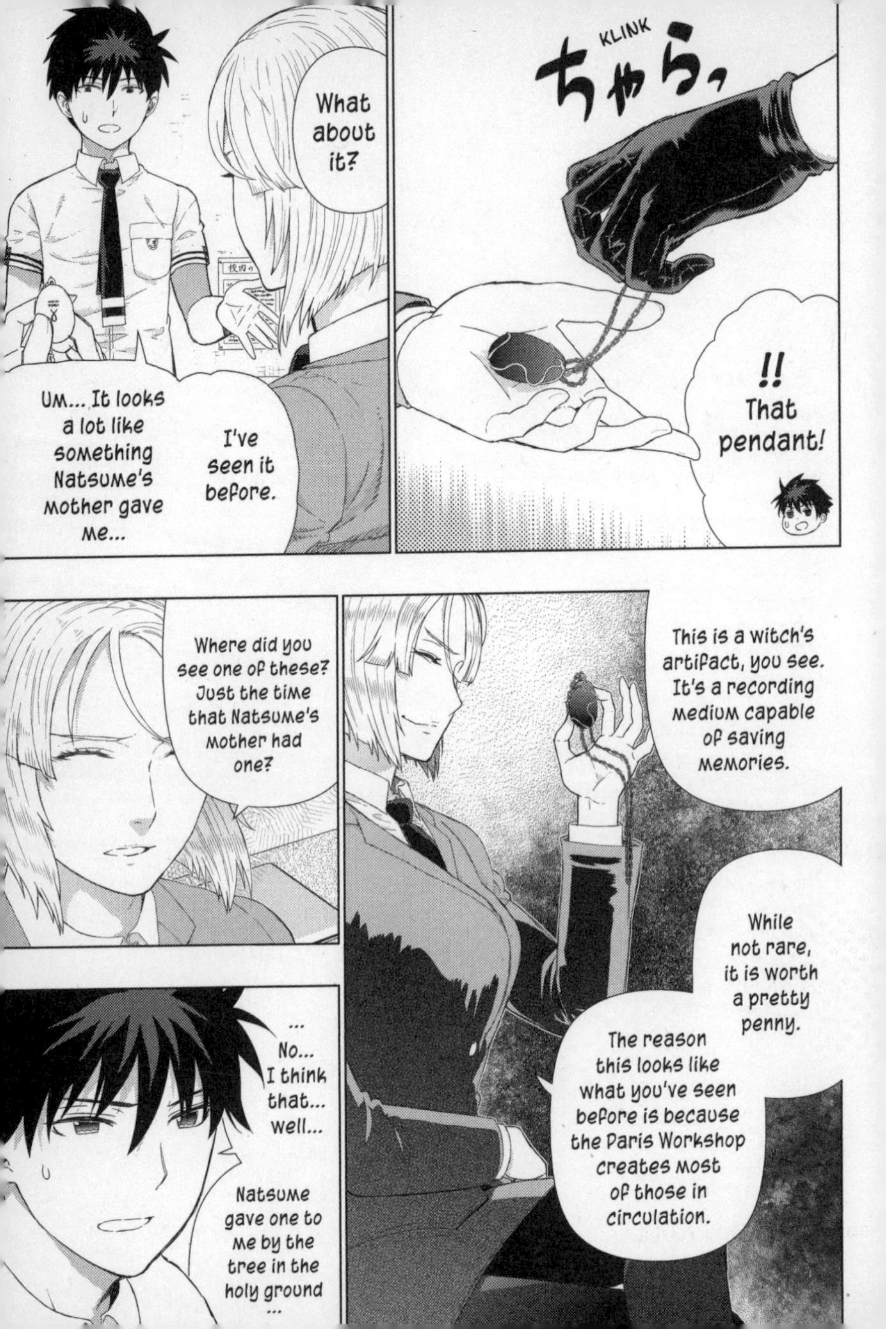
KLINK
ちゃらっ
!! That pendant!
What about it?
I've seen it before.
Um... It looks a lot like something Natsume's mother gave me...
This is a witch's artifact, you see. It's a recording medium capable of saving memories.
While not rare, it is worth a pretty penny.
The reason this looks like what you've seen before is because the Paris Workshop creates most of those in circulation.
Where did you see one of these? Just the time that Natsume's mother had one?
... No... I think that... well...
Natsume gave one to me by the tree in the holy ground ...

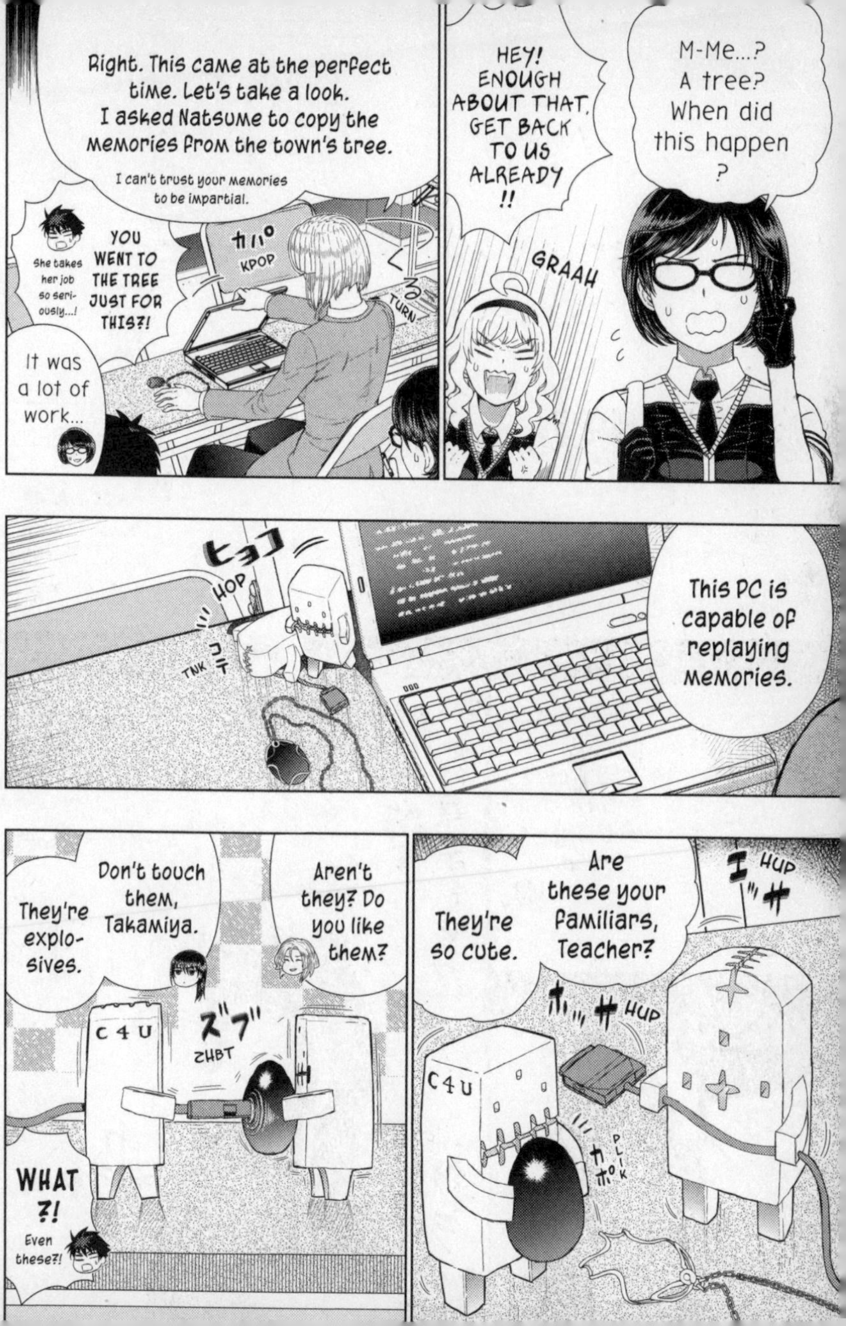
M-Me...? A tree? When did this happen ?
HEY! ENOUGH ABOUT THAT. GET BACK TO US ALREADY !!
GRAAH
Right. This came at the perfect time. Let's take a look. I asked Natsume to copy the memories from the town's tree.
I can't trust your memories to be impartial.
TURN
KPOP
YOU WENT TO THE TREE JUST FOR THIS?!
She takes her job so seri-ously...!
It was a lot of work...
This PC is capable of replaying memories.
HOP
TNK
HUP
Are these your familiars, Teacher?
They're so cute.
HUP
PLIK
Aren't they? Do you like them?
Don't touch them, Takamiya.
They're explo-sives.
ZHBT
C 4 U
WHAT ?!
Even these?!

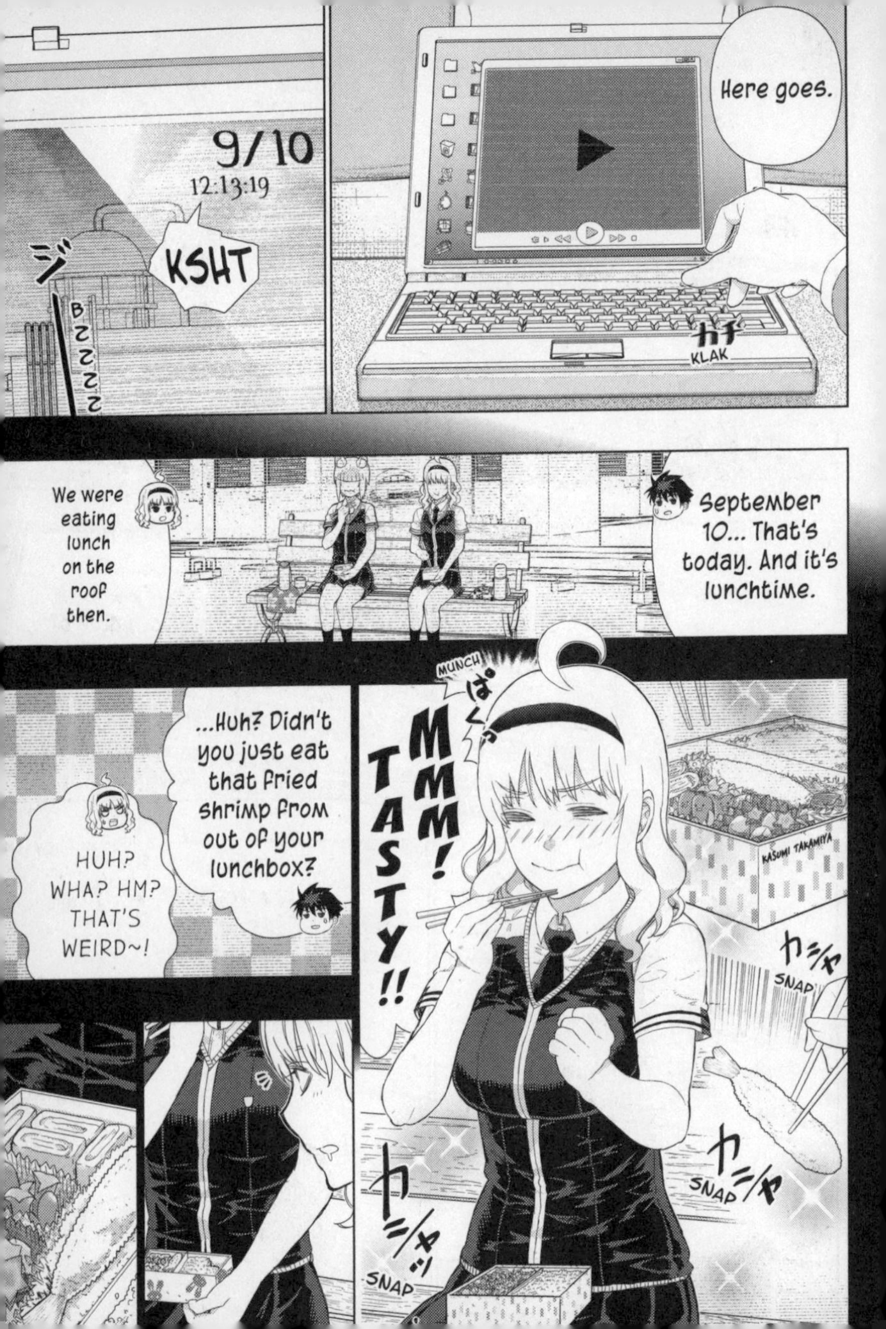

Here goes.
カチ
KLAK
9/10
12:13:19
KSHT
ジ
BZZZZZ
September 10... That's today. And it's lunchtime.
We were eating lunch on the roof then.
MUNCH
ぱくっ
MMM! TASTY!!
KASUMI TAKAMIYA
カシャ
SNAP
カシャ
SNAP
...Huh? Didn't you just eat that fried shrimp from out of your lunchbox?
HUH? WHA? HM? THAT'S WEIRD~!
カシャッ
SNAP

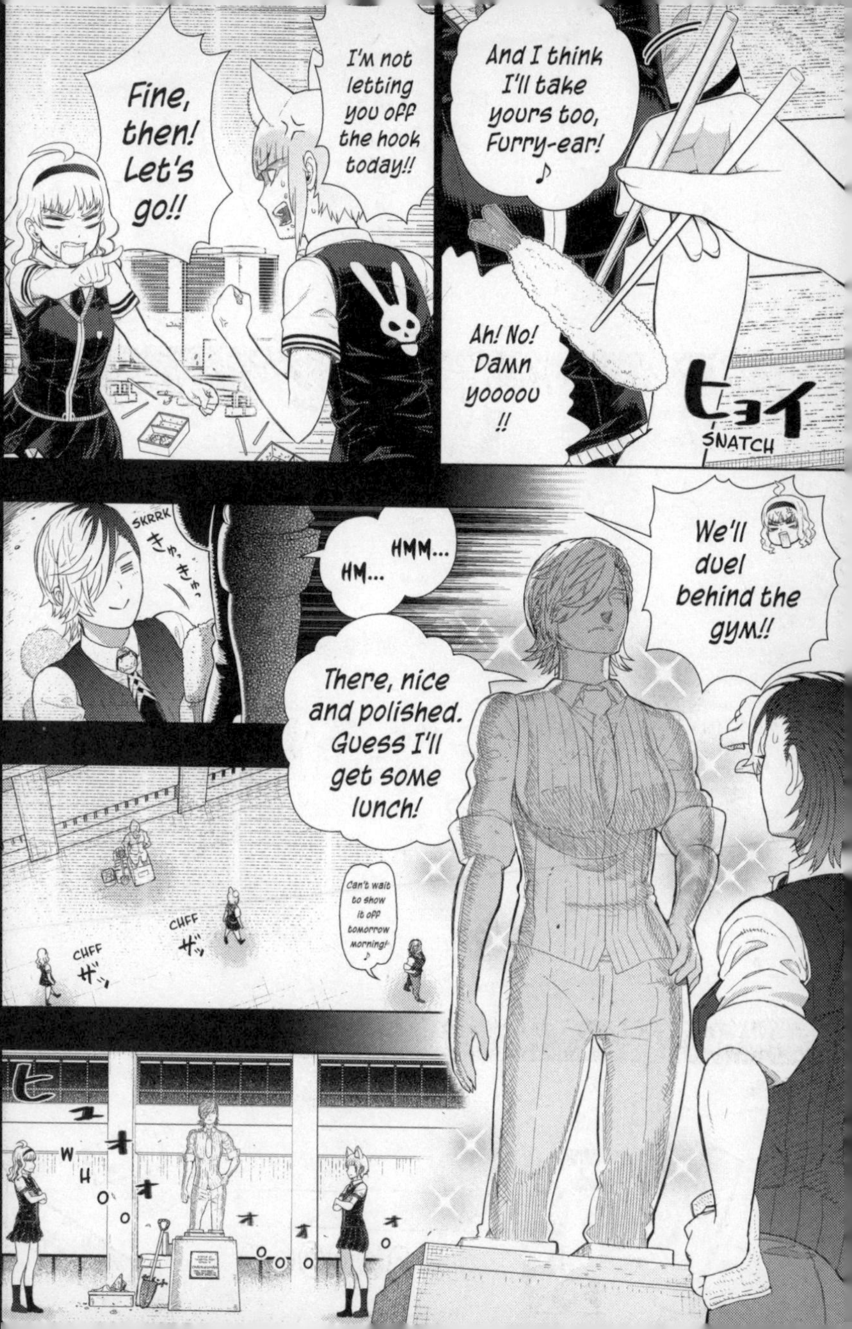
And I think I'll take yours too, Furry-ear! ♪
Ah! No! Damn yoooou!!
ヒョイ
SNATCH
I'm not letting you off the hook today!!
Fine, then! Let's go!!
We'll duel behind the gym!!
SKRRK
きゅ、きゅっ
HMM... HM...
There, nice and polished. Guess I'll get some lunch!
Can't wait to show it off tomorrow morning! ♪
CHFF
ザッ
CHFF
ザッ
WHOOOO
ヒューオオオオオ

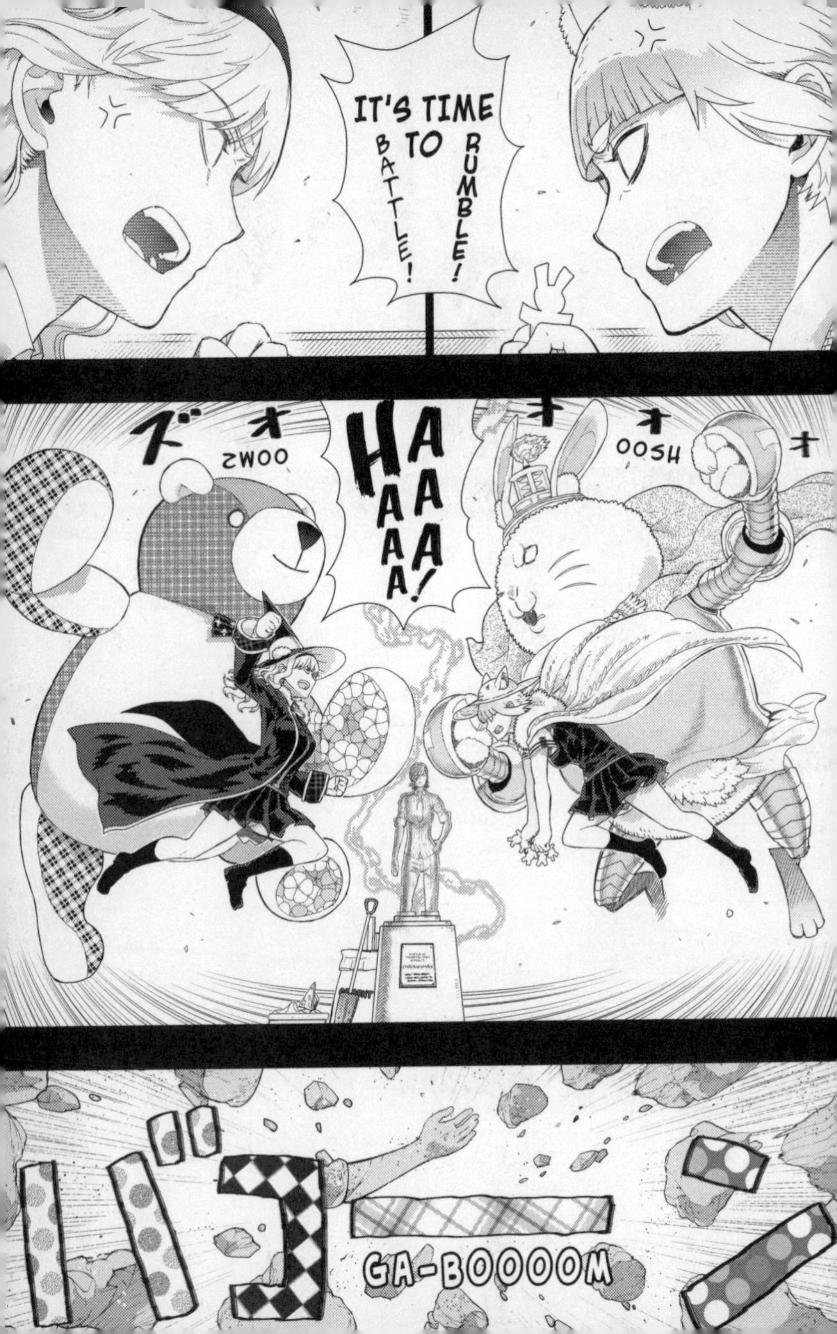
IT'S TIME TO RUMBLE! BATTLE!
ズオ
ZWOO
オオオ
OOSH
HAAAAAA!
ババコー
GA-BOOOOM

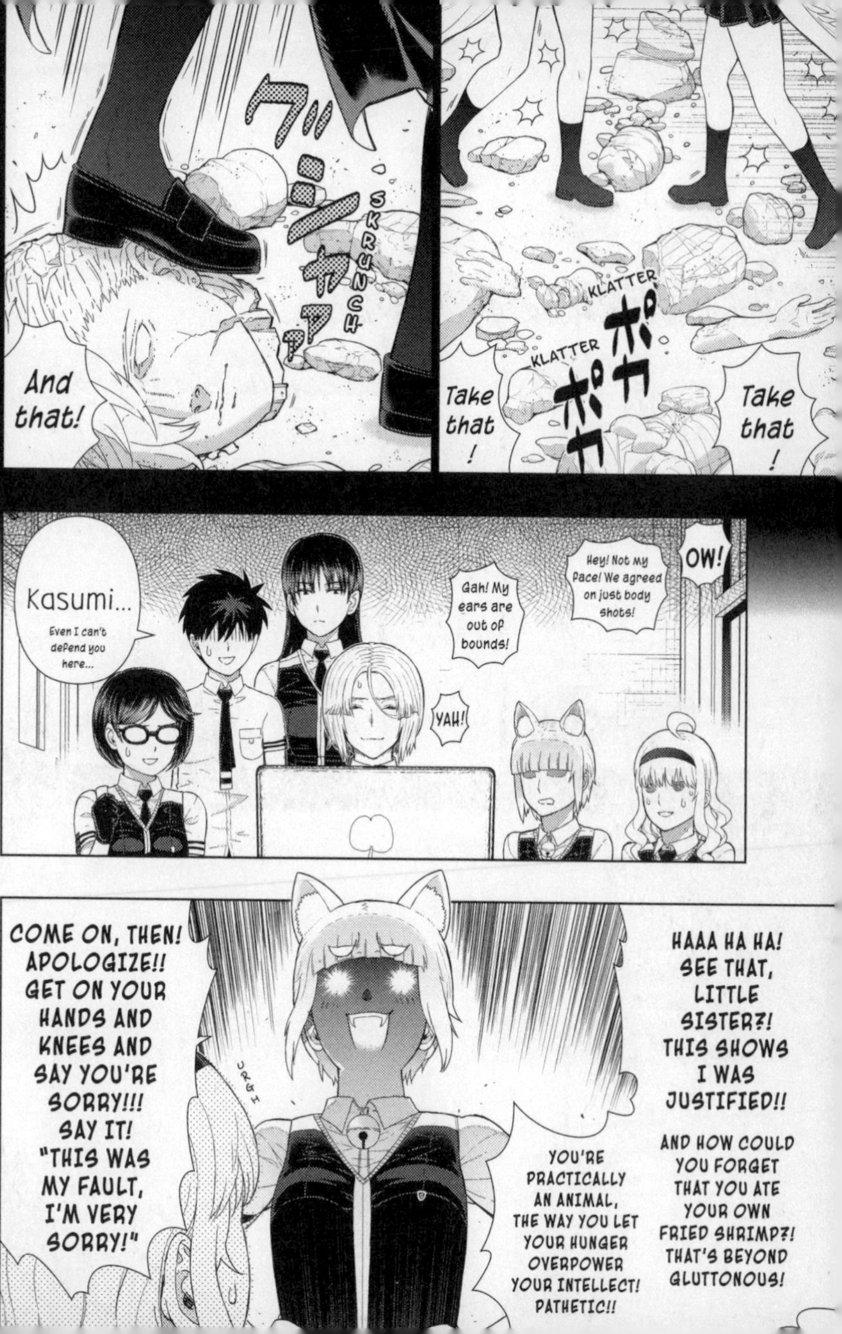
Take that!
Take that!
KLATTER
ポカ
KLATTER
ポカ
SKRUNCH
グシャァ
And that!
OW!
Hey! Not my face! We agreed on just body shots!
Gah! My ears are out of bounds!
YAH!
Kasumi...
Even I can't defend you here...
HAAA HA HA! SEE THAT, LITTLE SISTER?! THIS SHOWS I WAS JUSTIFIED!!
AND HOW COULD YOU FORGET THAT YOU ATE YOUR OWN FRIED SHRIMP?! THAT'S BEYOND GLUTTONOUS!
YOU'RE PRACTICALLY AN ANIMAL, THE WAY YOU LET YOUR HUNGER OVERPOWER YOUR INTELLECT! PATHETIC!!
COME ON, THEN! APOLOGIZE!! GET ON YOUR HANDS AND KNEES AND SAY YOU'RE SORRY!!! SAY IT! "THIS WAS MY FAULT, I'M VERY SORRY!"
URGH

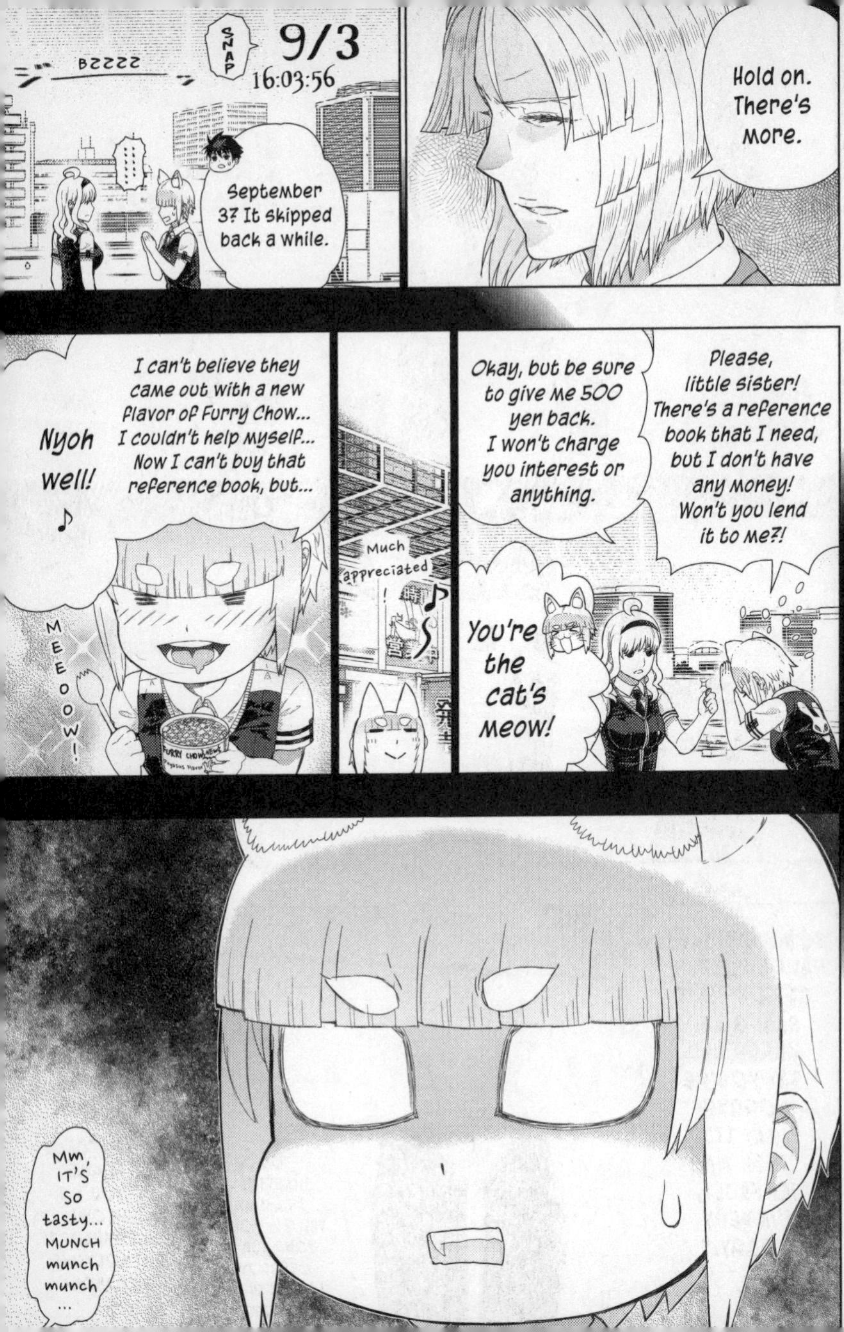
Hold on. There's more.
9/3
16:03:56
SNAP
BZZZZ
September 3? It skipped back a while.
Please, little sister! There's a reference book that I need, but I don't have any money! Won't you lend it to me?!
Okay, but be sure to give me 500 yen back. I won't charge you interest or anything.
You're the cat's meow!
Much appreciated
I can't believe they came out with a new flavor of Furry Chow... I couldn't help myself... Now I can't buy that reference book, but...
Nyoh well! ♪
MEEOOOW!
FURRY CHOW NEW
Mm, it's so tasty... MUNCH munch munch ...

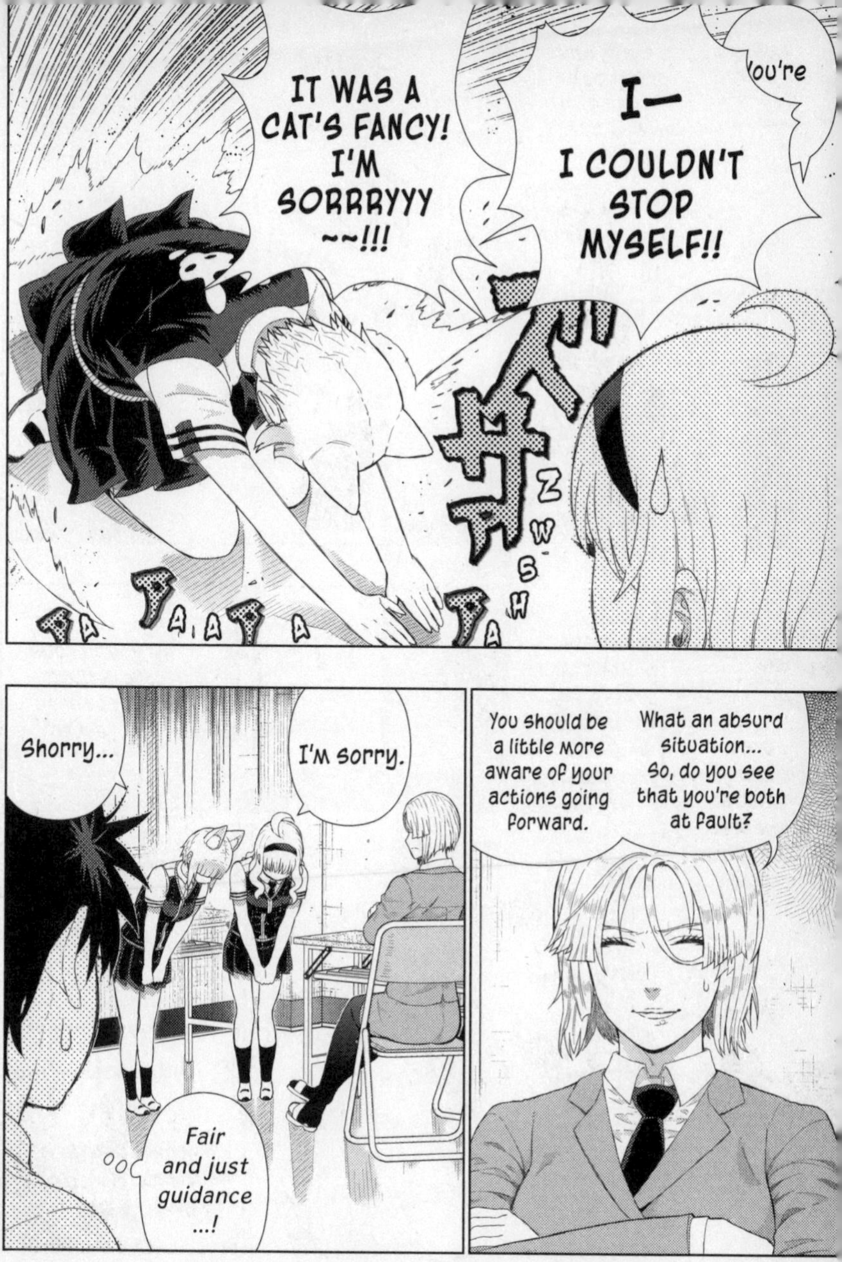
ou're
I— I COULDN'T STOP MYSELF!!
IT WAS A CAT'S FANCY! I'M SORRRYYY ~~!!!
ZWSH
What an absurd situation... So, do you see that you're both at fault?
You should be a little more aware of your actions going forward.
I'm sorry.
Shorry...
Fair and just guidance ...!

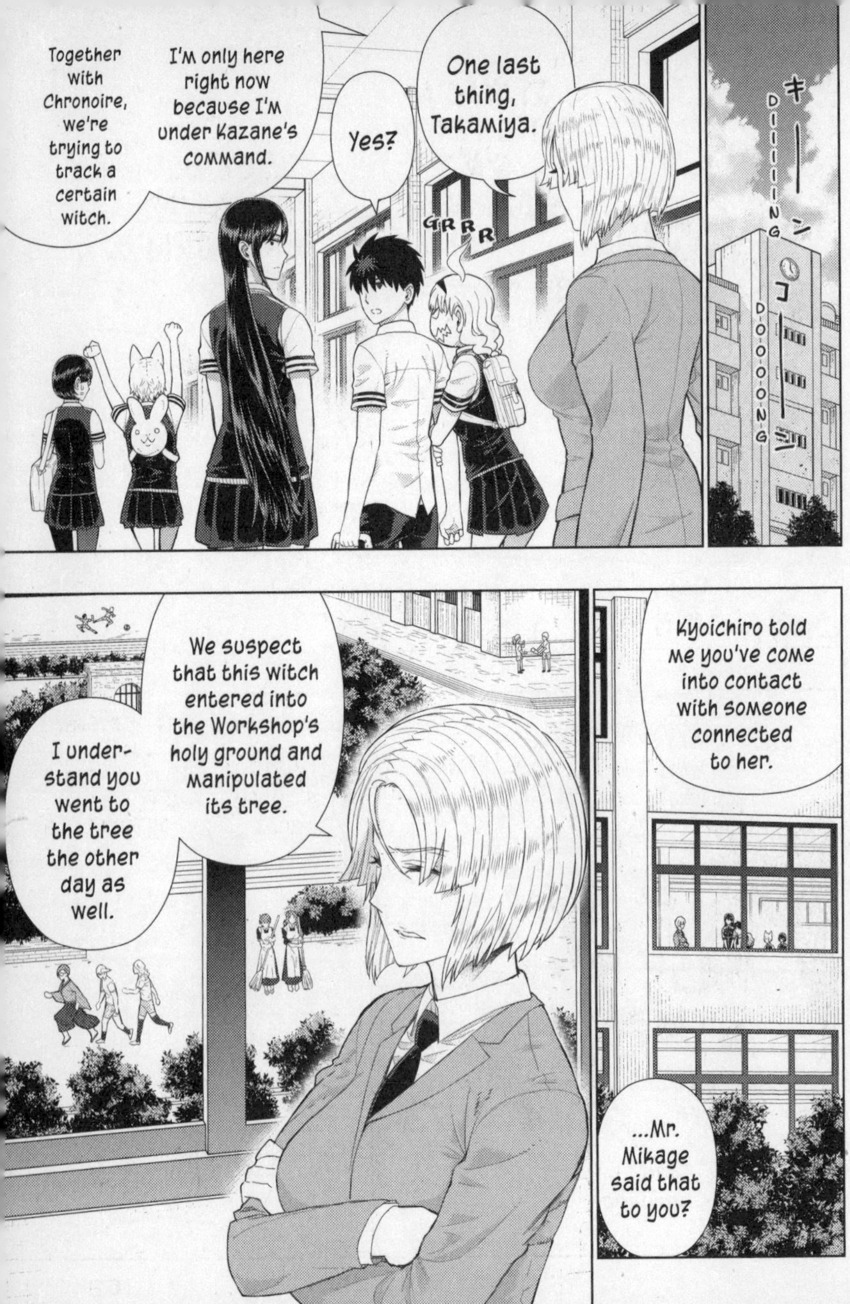
キーン
D-I-I-I-I-N-G
コーン
D-O-O-O-O-N-G
One last thing, Takamiya.
Yes?
GRRR
I'm only here right now because I'm under Kazane's command.
Together with Chronoire, we're trying to track a certain witch.
Kyoichiro told me you've come into contact with someone connected to her.
...Mr. Mikage said that to you?
We suspect that this witch entered into the Workshop's holy ground and manipulated its tree.
I understand you went to the tree the other day as well.

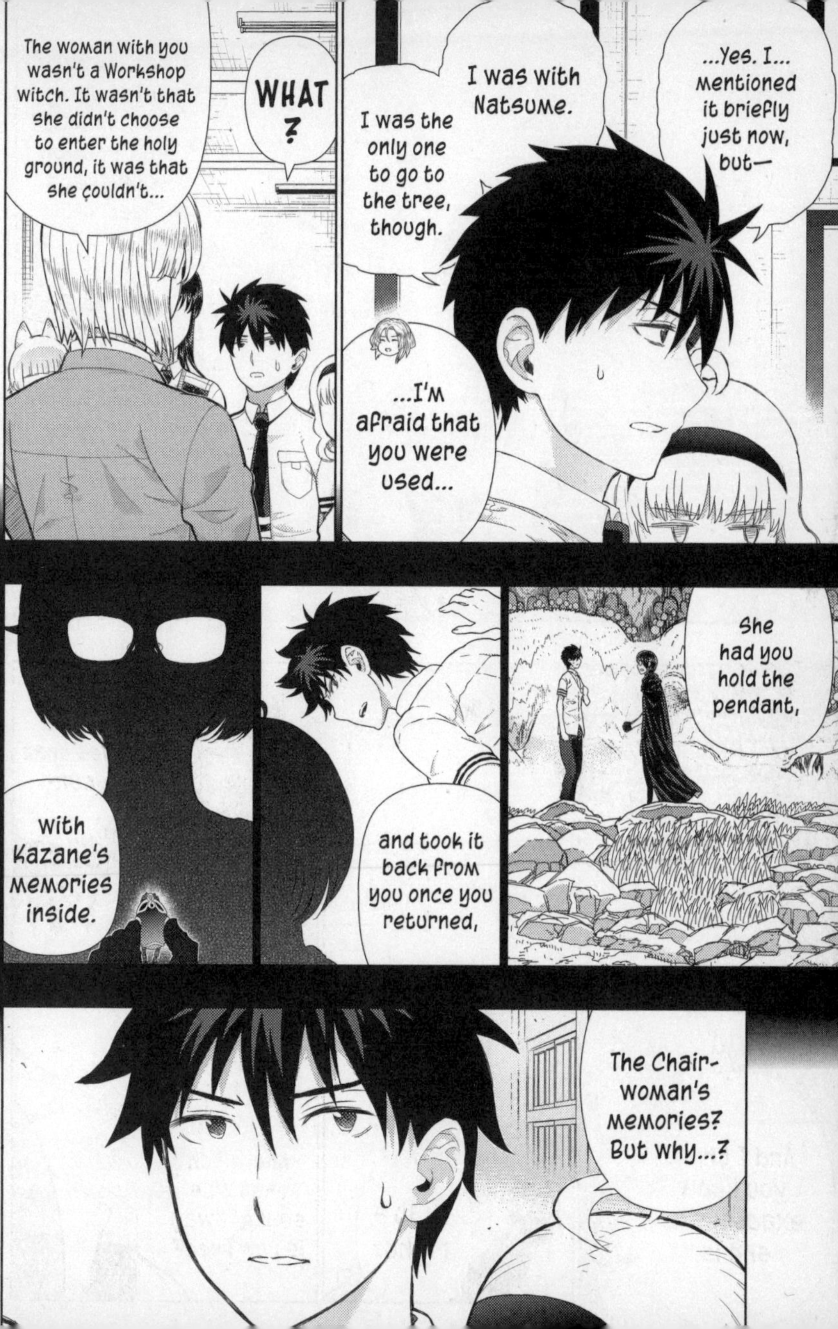
...Yes. I... mentioned it briefly just now, but—
I was with Natsume.
I was the only one to go to the tree, though.
...I'm afraid that you were used...
WHAT?
The woman with you wasn't a Workshop witch. It wasn't that she didn't choose to enter the holy ground, it was that she couldn't...
She had you hold the pendant,
and took it back from you once you returned,
with Kazane's memories inside.
The Chair-woman's memories? But why...?

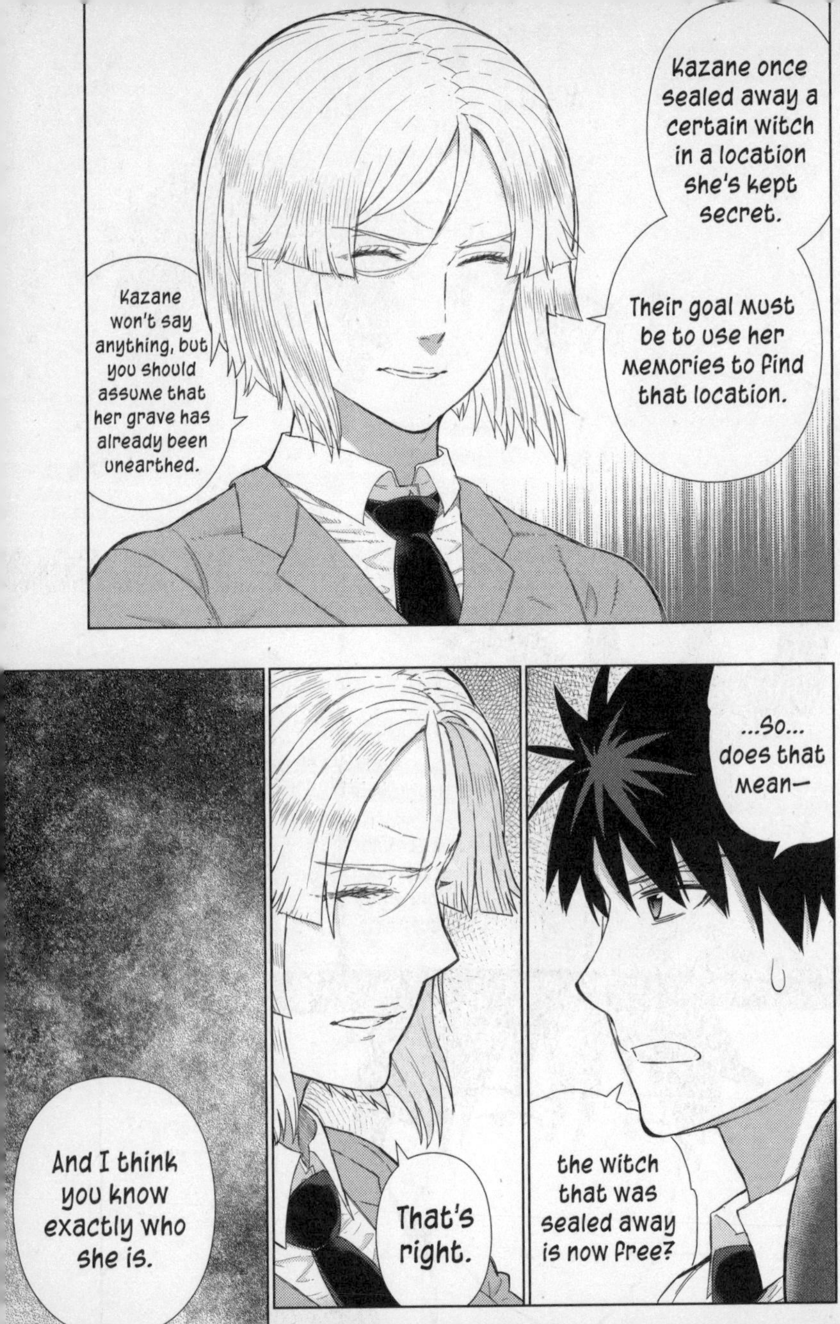
Kazane once sealed away a certain witch in a location she's kept secret.
Their goal must be to use her memories to find that location.
Kazane won't say anything, but you should assume that her grave has already been unearthed.
...So... does that mean—
the witch that was sealed away is now free?
That's right.
And I think you know exactly who she is.

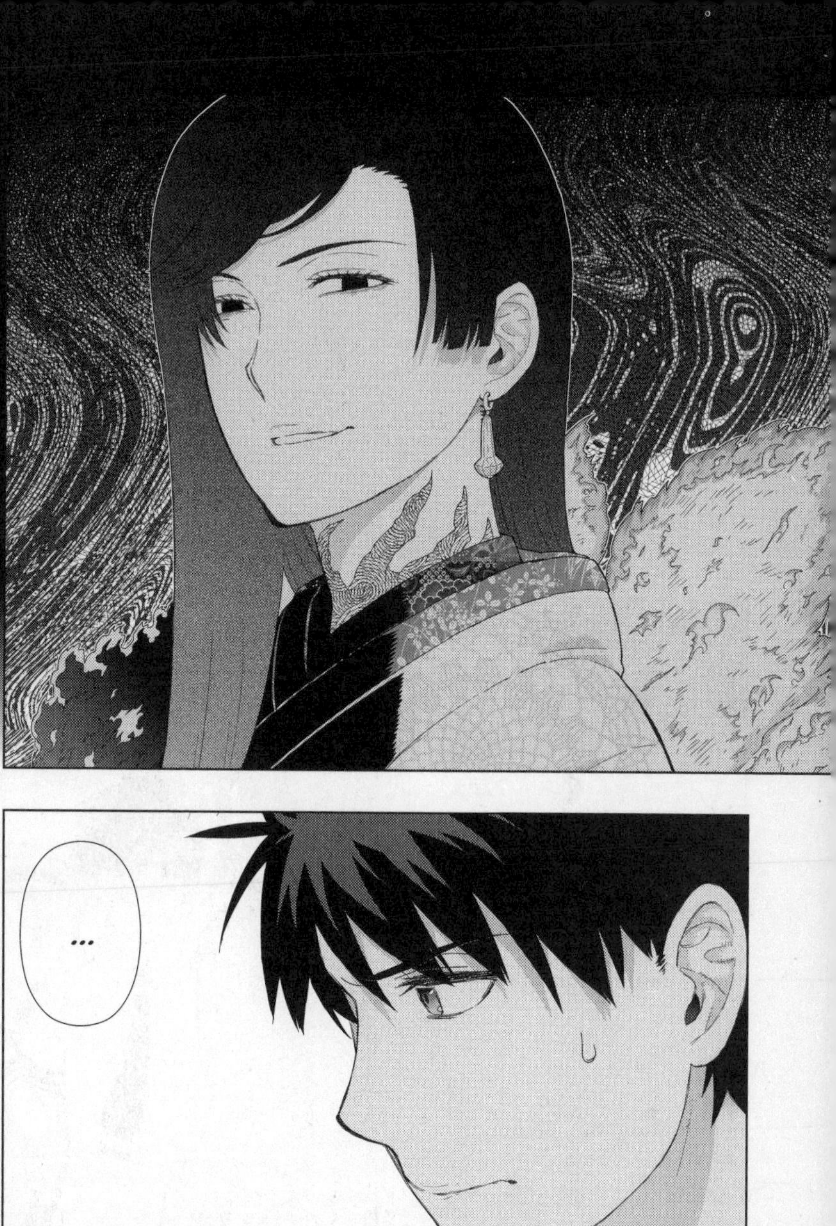
...

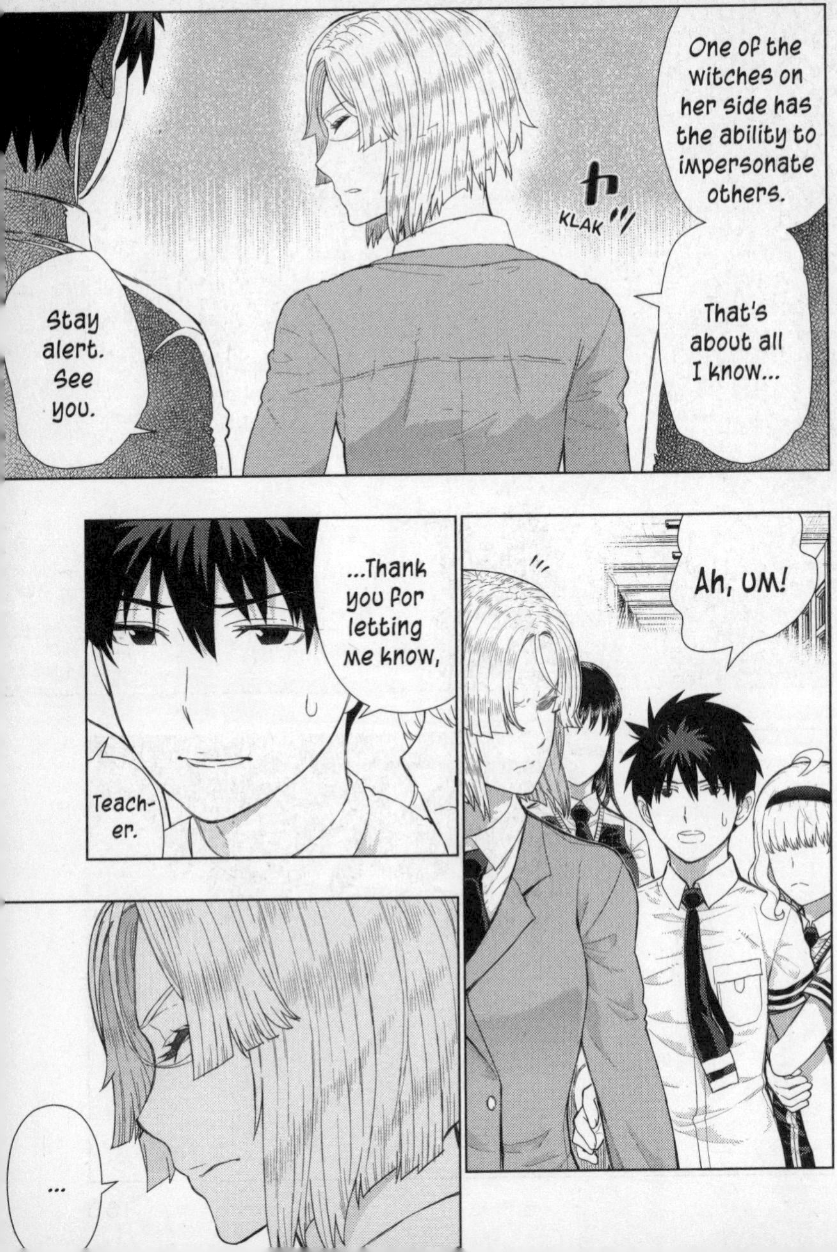
One of the witches on her side has the ability to impersonate others.
KLAK
That's about all I know...
Stay alert. See you.
Ah, UM!
...Thank you for letting me know, Teacher.
...

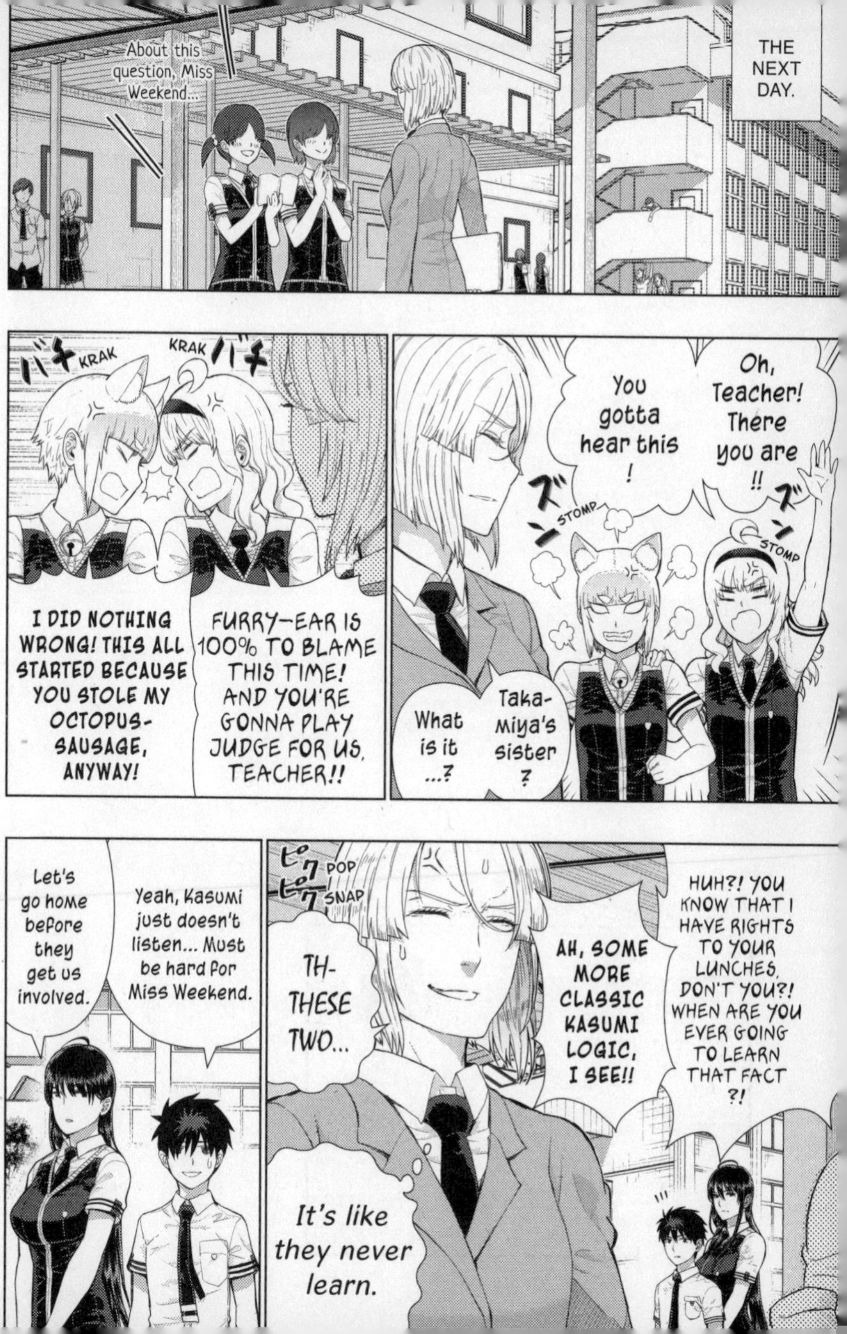
THE NEXT DAY.
About this question, Miss Weekend...
Oh, Teacher! There you are!!
You gotta hear this!
ズン STOMP
ズン STOMP
Takamiya's sister?
What is it...?
バチ KRAK
バチ KRAK
FURRY-EAR IS 100% TO BLAME THIS TIME! AND YOU'RE GONNA PLAY JUDGE FOR US, TEACHER!!
I DID NOTHING WRONG! THIS ALL STARTED BECAUSE YOU STOLE MY OCTOPUS-SAUSAGE, ANYWAY!
HUH?! YOU KNOW THAT I HAVE RIGHTS TO YOUR LUNCHES, DON'T YOU?! WHEN ARE YOU EVER GOING TO LEARN THAT FACT?!
AH, SOME MORE CLASSIC KASUMI LOGIC, I SEE!!
ピク POP
ピク SNAP
TH- THESE TWO...
It's like they never learn.
Yeah, Kasumi just doesn't listen... Must be hard for Miss Weekend.
Let's go home before they get us involved.

CHAPTER 69 END

The Suspect: Weekend

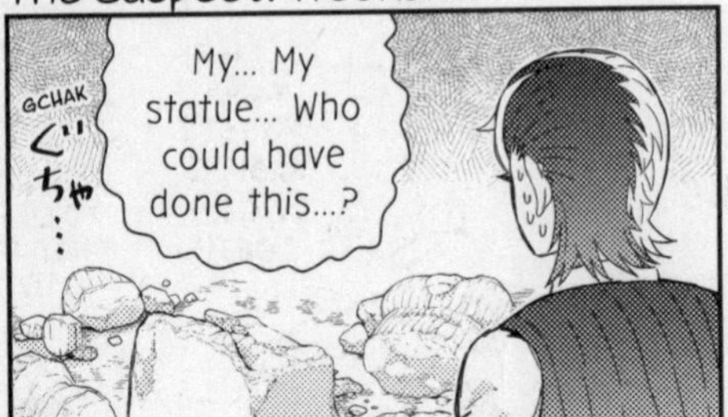
My... My statue... Who could have done this...?
GCHAK
ぐちゃ…

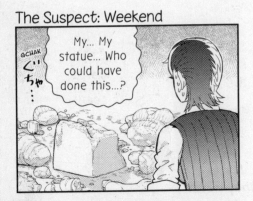

Witchcraft Works

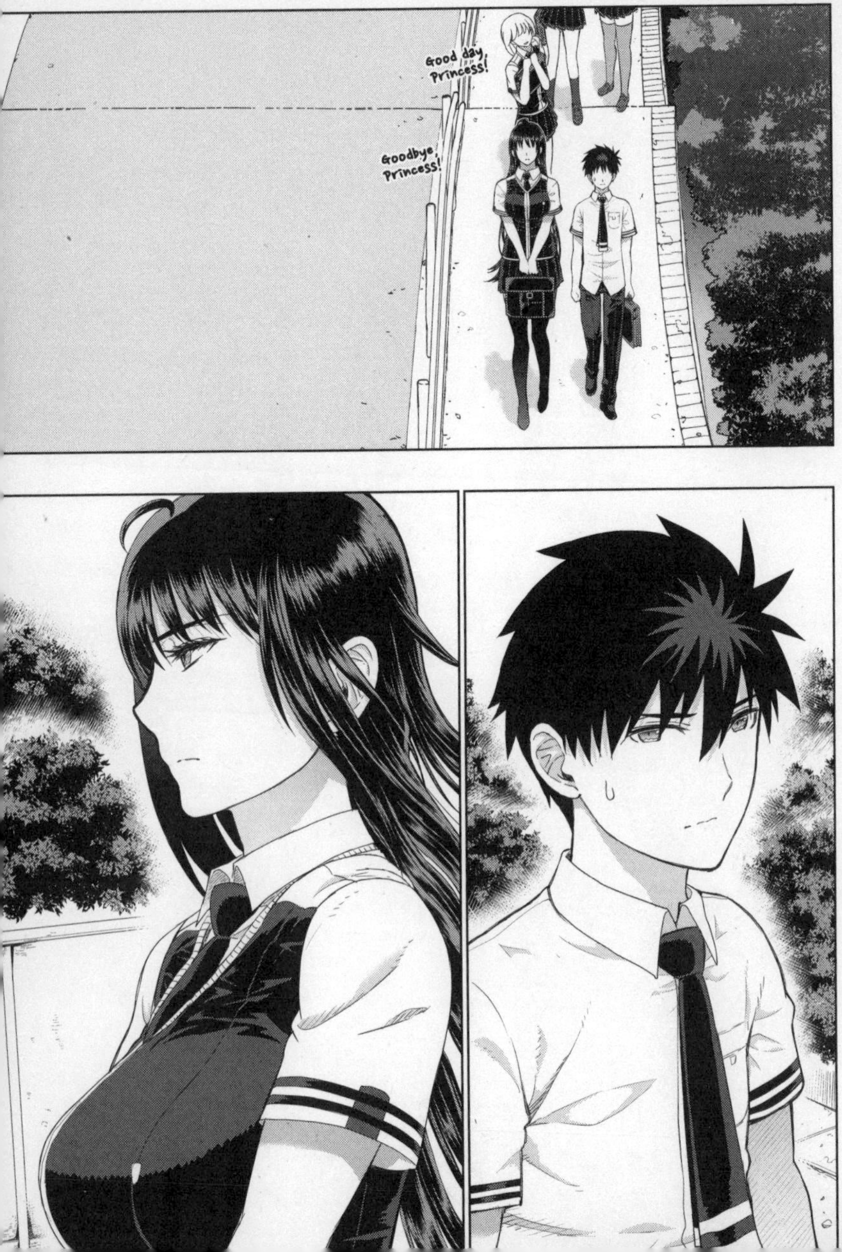
Good day, Princess!
Goodbye, Princess!

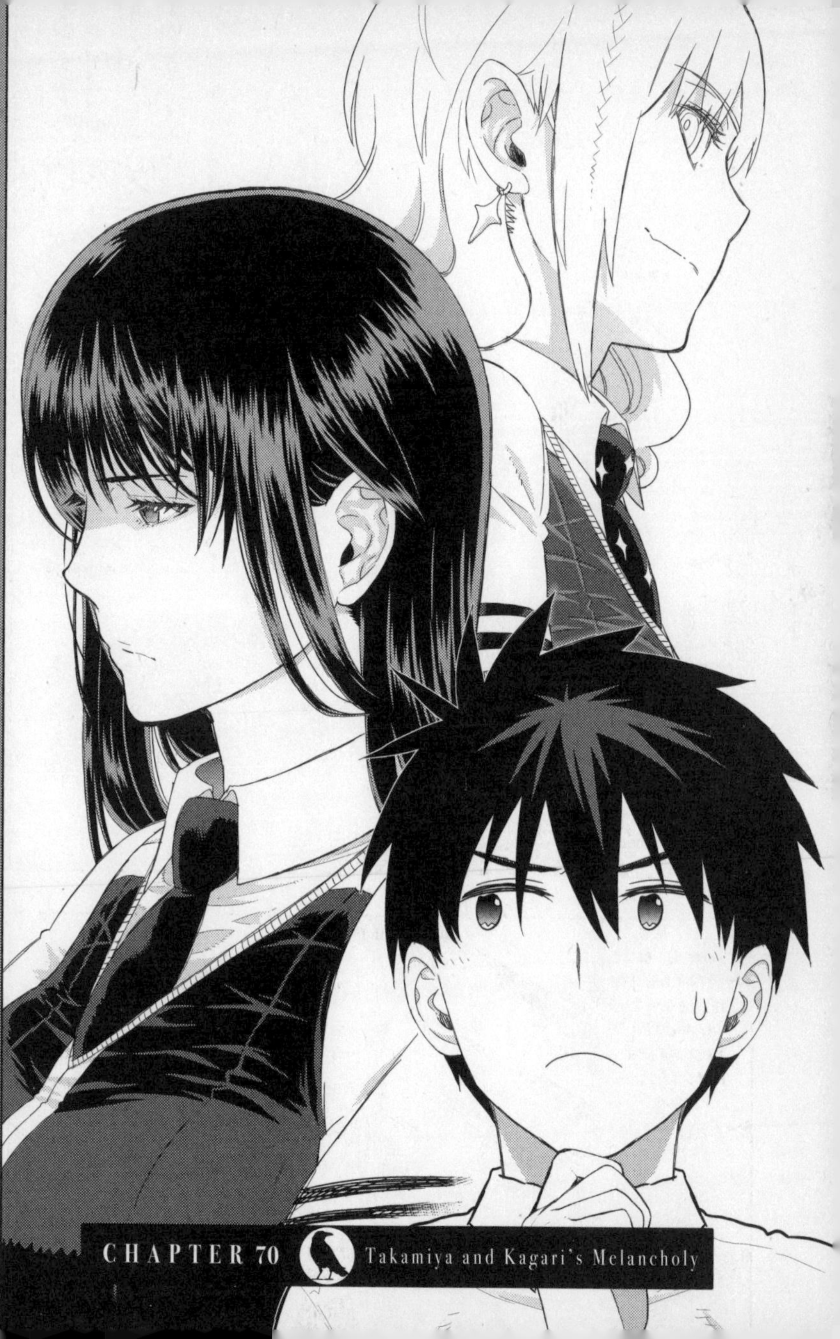

CHAPTER 70 Takamiya and Kagari's Melancholy

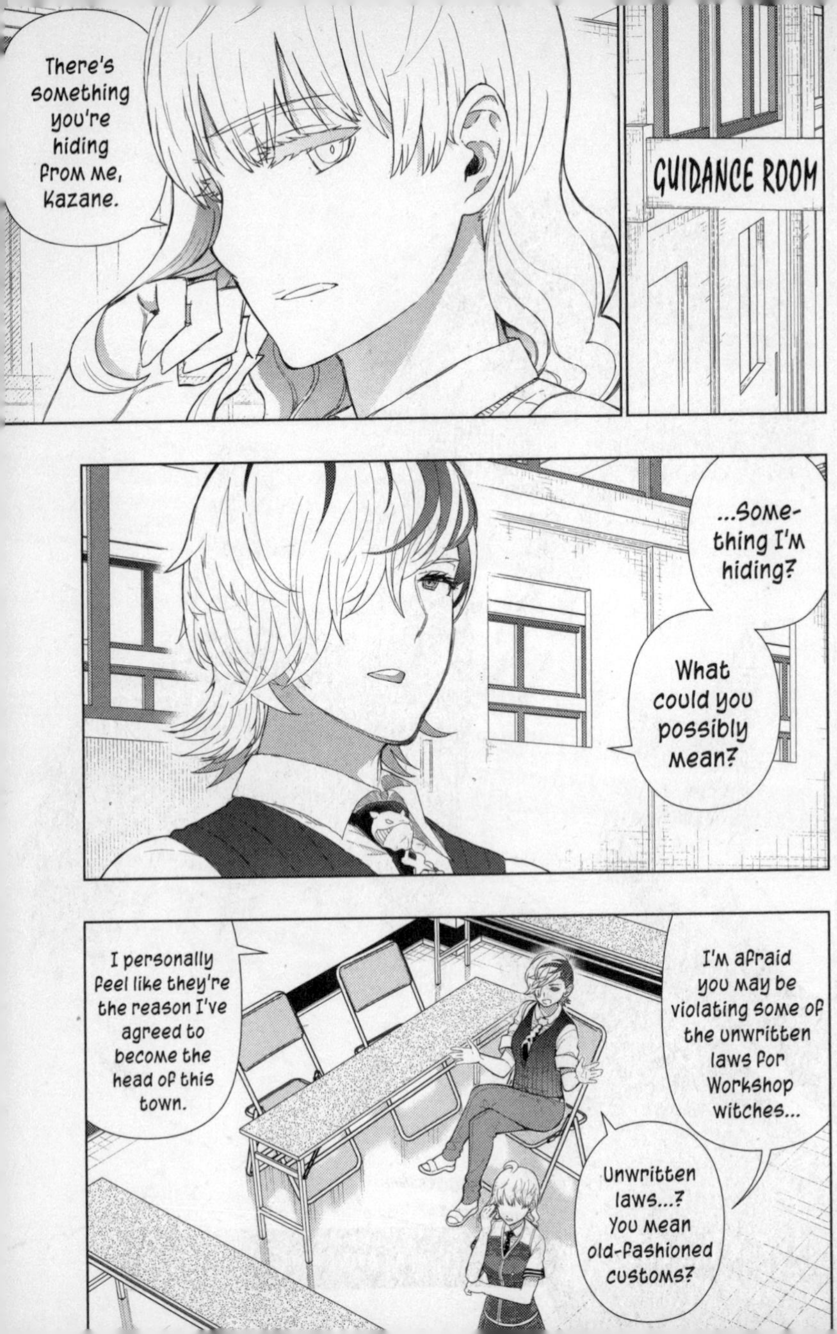
GUIDANCE ROOM
There's something you're hiding from me, Kazane.
...Something I'm hiding?
What could you possibly mean?
I'm afraid you may be violating some of the unwritten laws for Workshop witches...
Unwritten laws...? You mean old-fashioned customs?
I personally feel like they're the reason I've agreed to become the head of this town.

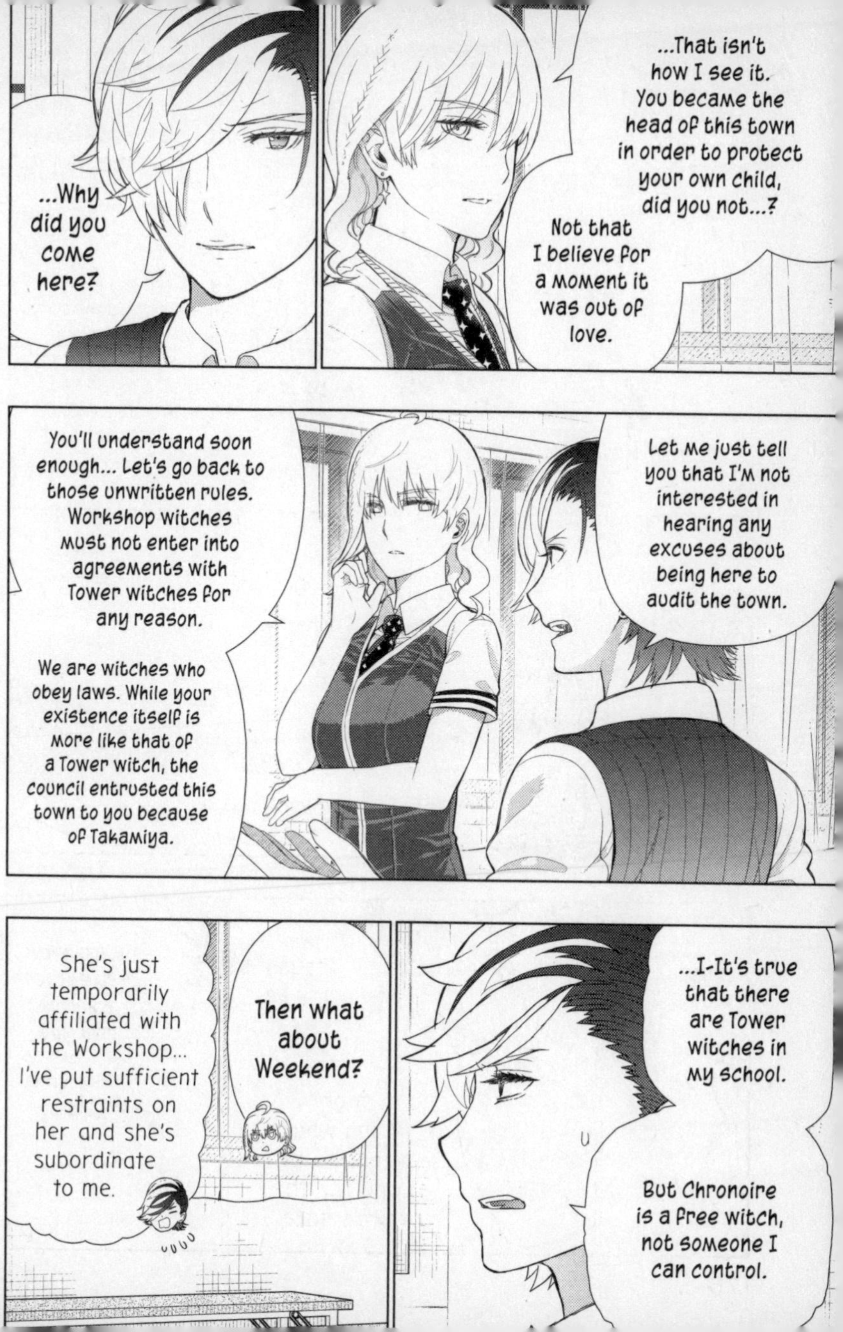
...That isn't how I see it. You became the head of this town in order to protect your own child, did you not...?
Not that I believe for a moment it was out of love.
...Why did you come here?
Let me just tell you that I'm not interested in hearing any excuses about being here to audit the town.
You'll understand soon enough... Let's go back to those unwritten rules. Workshop witches must not enter into agreements with Tower witches for any reason.
We are witches who obey laws. While your existence itself is more like that of a Tower witch, the council entrusted this town to you because of Takamiya.
...I-It's true that there are Tower witches in my school.
But Chronoire is a free witch, not someone I can control.
Then what about Weekend?
She's just temporarily affiliated with the Workshop... I've put sufficient restraints on her and she's subordinate to me.

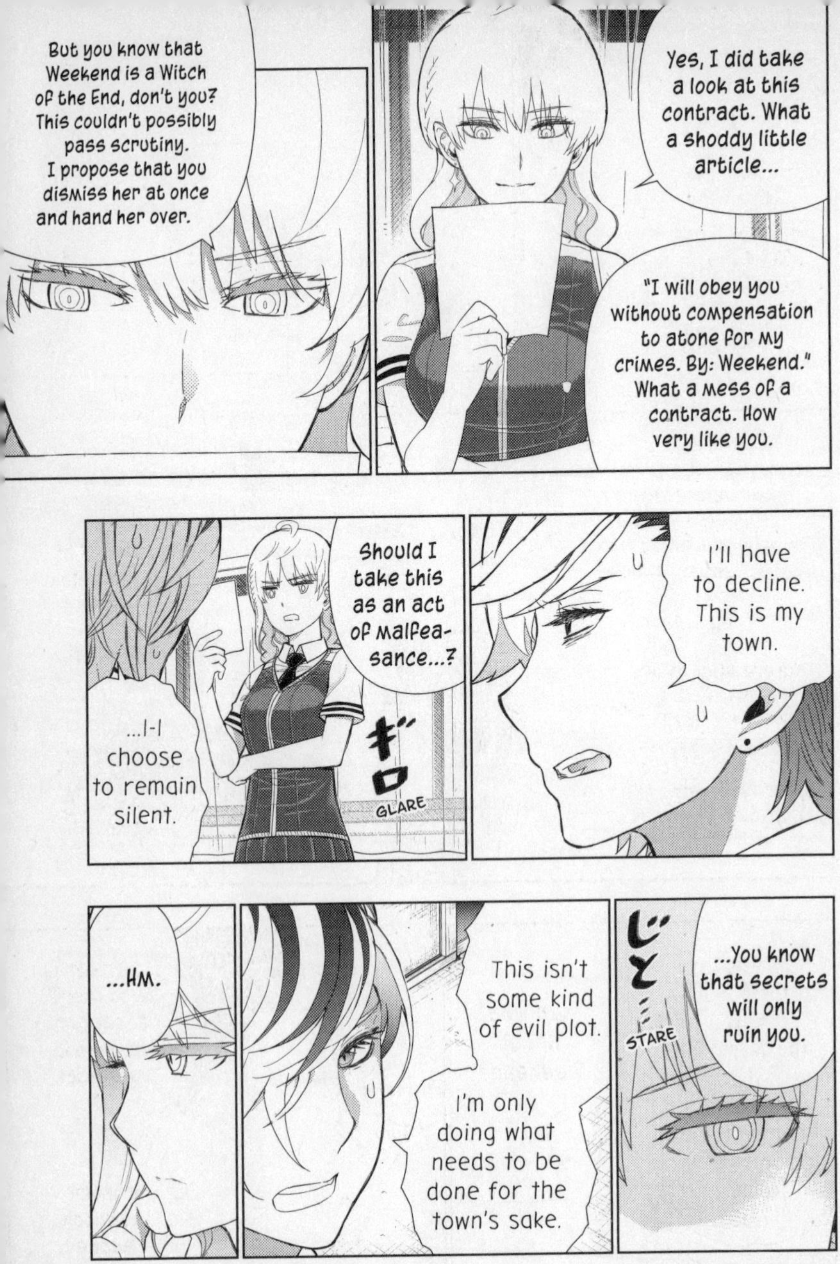
Yes, I did take a look at this contract. What a shoddy little article...
"I will obey you without compensation to atone for my crimes. By: Weekend." What a mess of a contract. How very like you.
But you know that Weekend is a Witch of the End, don't you? This couldn't possibly pass scrutiny. I propose that you dismiss her at once and hand her over.
I'll have to decline. This is my town.
Should I take this as an act of malfeasance...?
ギロ
GLARE
...I-I choose to remain silent.
じと
STARE
...You know that secrets will only ruin you.
This isn't some kind of evil plot.
I'm only doing what needs to be done for the town's sake.
...Hm.

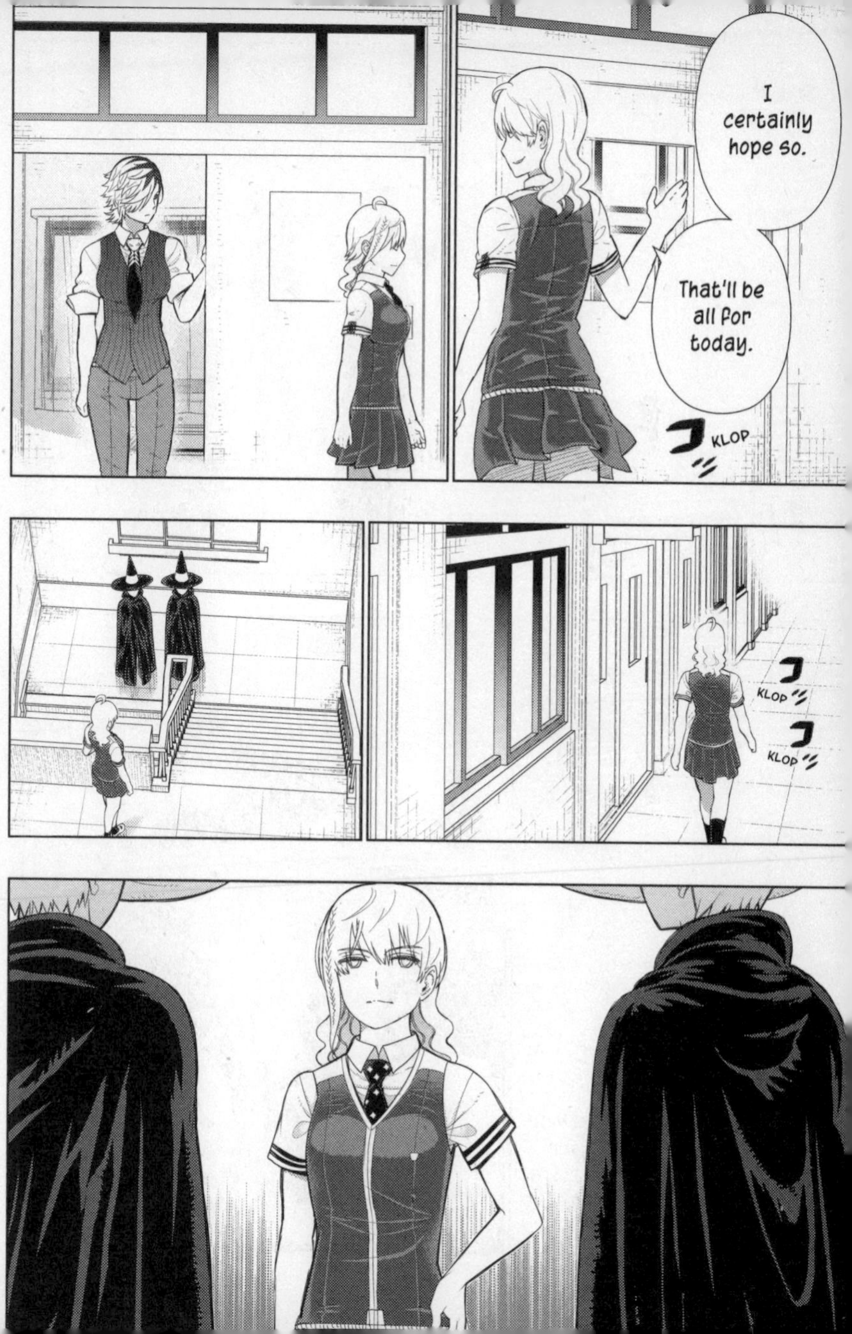
I certainly hope so.
That'll be all for today.
コ KLOP
コ KLOP
コ KLOP

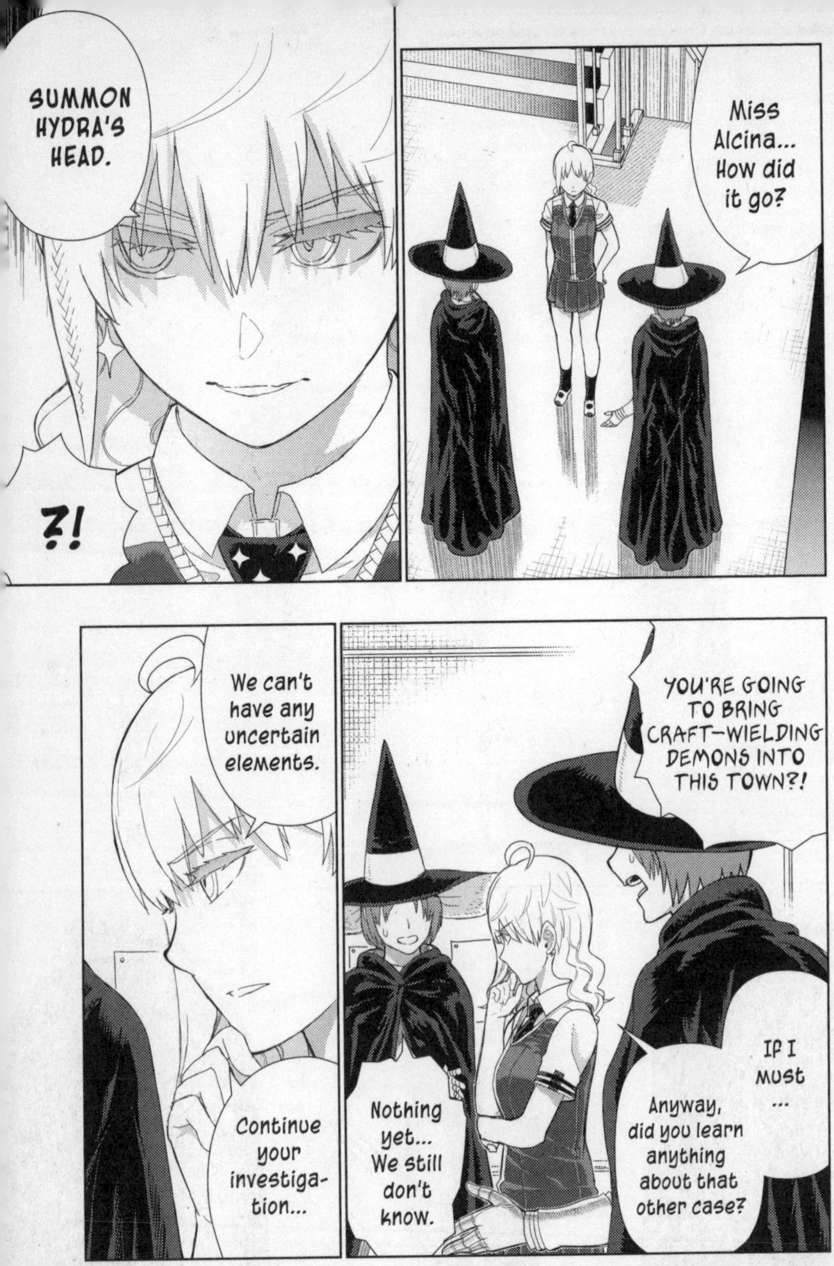
Miss Alcina... How did it go?
SUMMON HYDRA'S HEAD.
?!
YOU'RE GOING TO BRING CRAFT-WIELDING DEMONS INTO THIS TOWN?!
If I must...
Anyway, did you learn anything about that other case?
Nothing yet... We still don't know.
We can't have any uncertain elements.
Continue your investiga-tion...

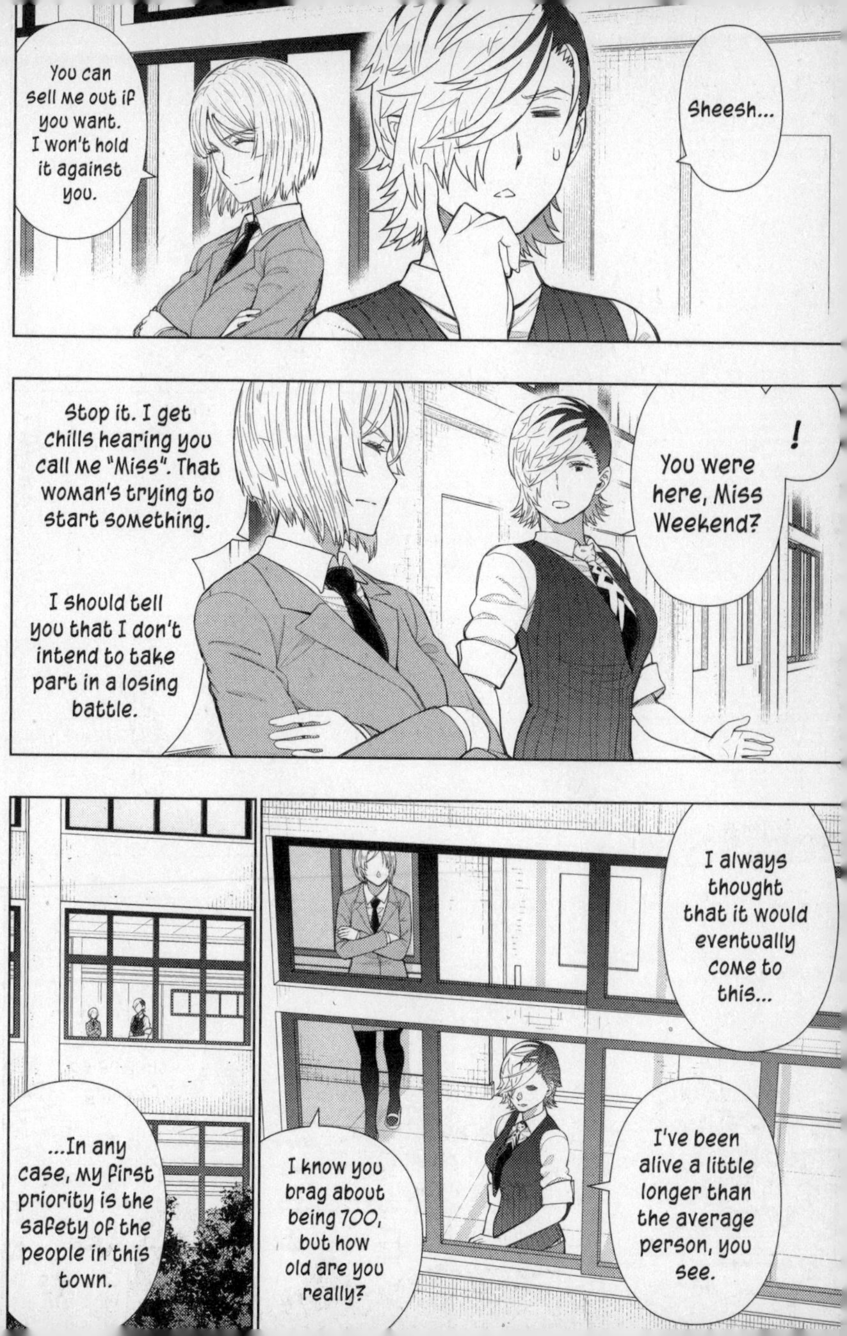
Sheesh...
You can sell me out if you want. I won't hold it against you.
!
You were here, Miss Weekend?
Stop it. I get chills hearing you call me "Miss". That woman's trying to start something.
I should tell you that I don't intend to take part in a losing battle.
I always thought that it would eventually come to this...
I've been alive a little longer than the average person, you see.
I know you brag about being 700, but how old are you really?
...In any case, my first priority is the safety of the people in this town.

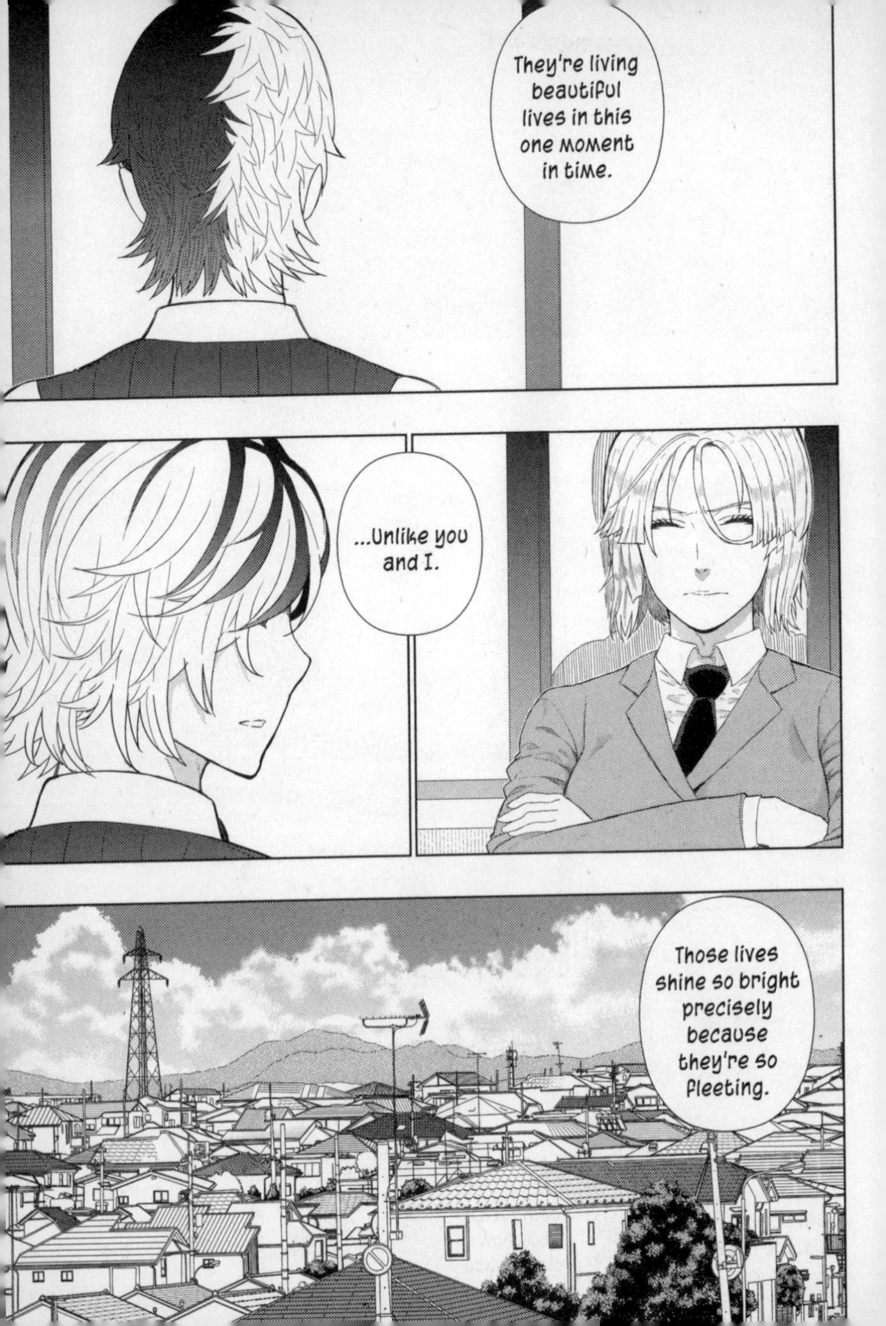
They're living beautiful lives in this one moment in time.
...Unlike you and I.
Those lives shine so bright precisely because they're so fleeting.

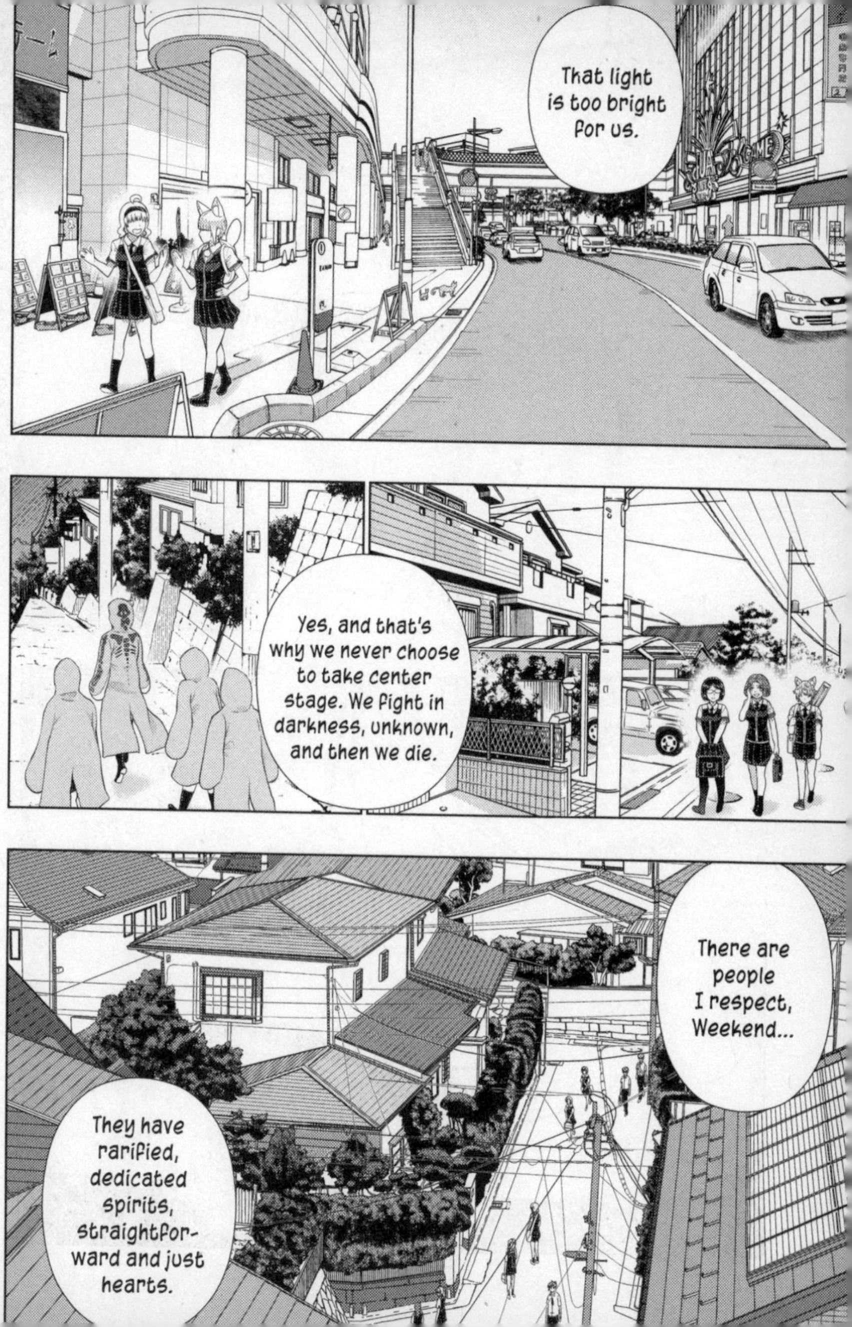
That light is too bright for us.
Yes, and that's why we never choose to take center stage. We fight in darkness, unknown, and then we die.
There are people I respect, Weekend...
They have rarified, dedicated spirits, straightfor-ward and just hearts.

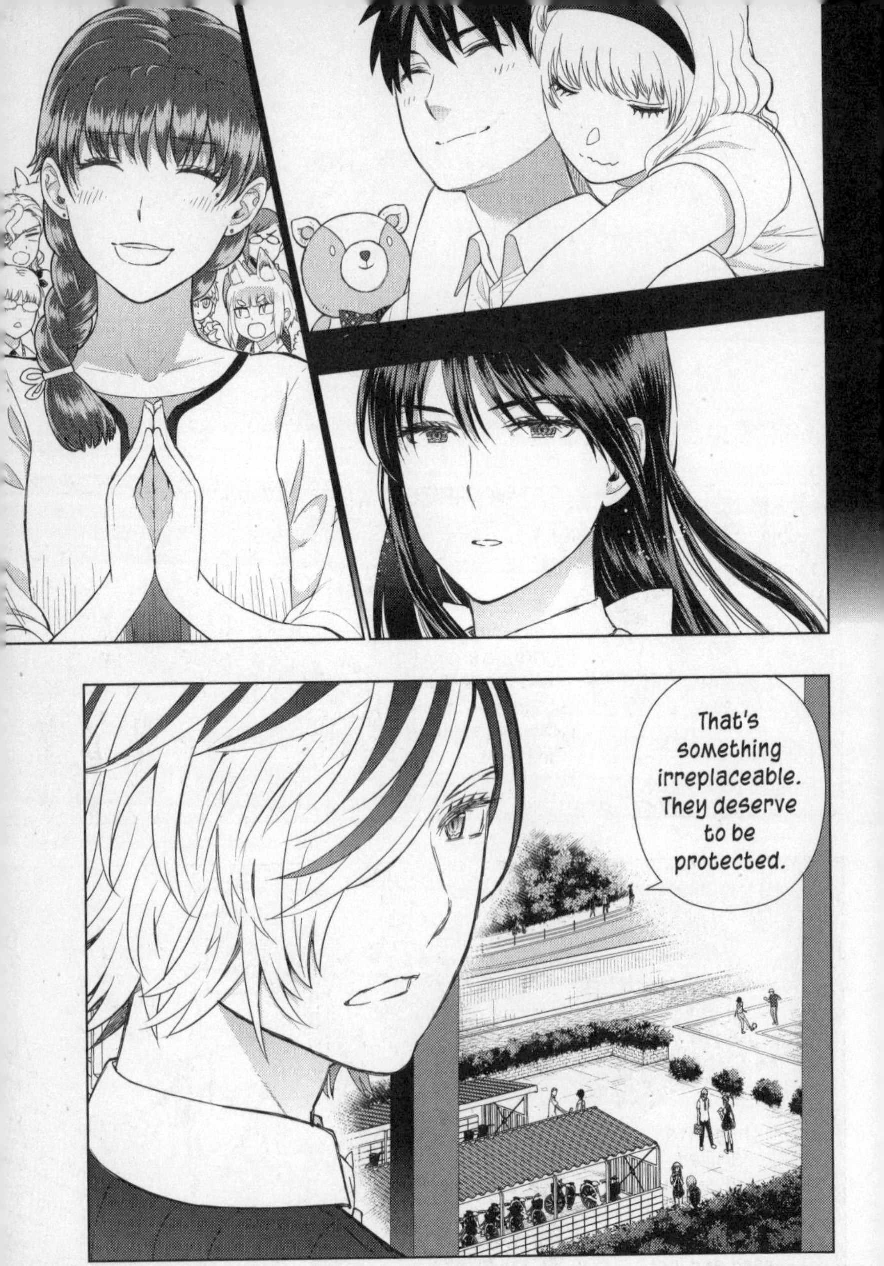
That's something irreplaceable. They deserve to be protected.

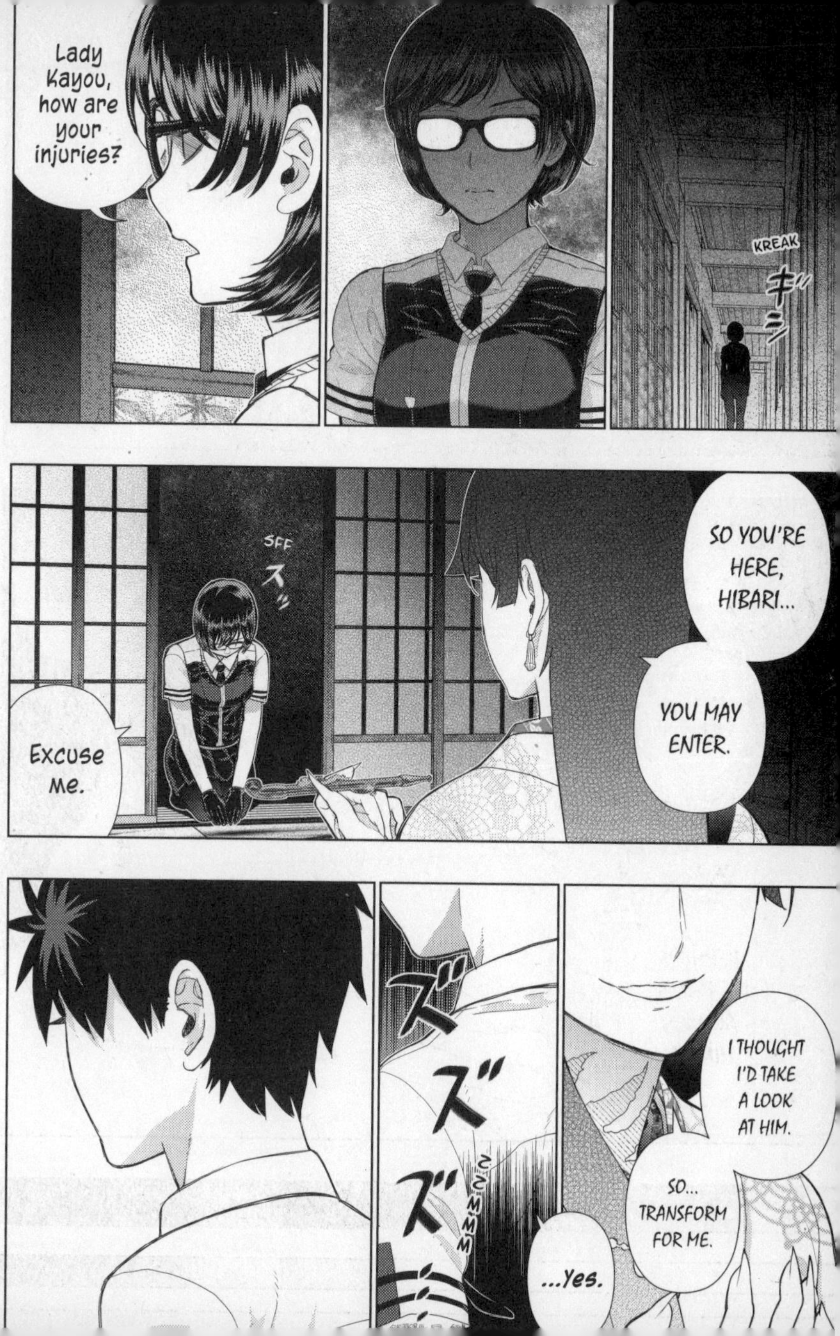
KREAK
Lady Kayou, how are your injuries?
SO YOU'RE HERE, HIBARI...
YOU MAY ENTER.
SFF
スッ
Excuse me.
I THOUGHT I'D TAKE A LOOK AT HIM.
SO... TRANSFORM FOR ME.
...Yes.
ZZMMMM
ズズズ

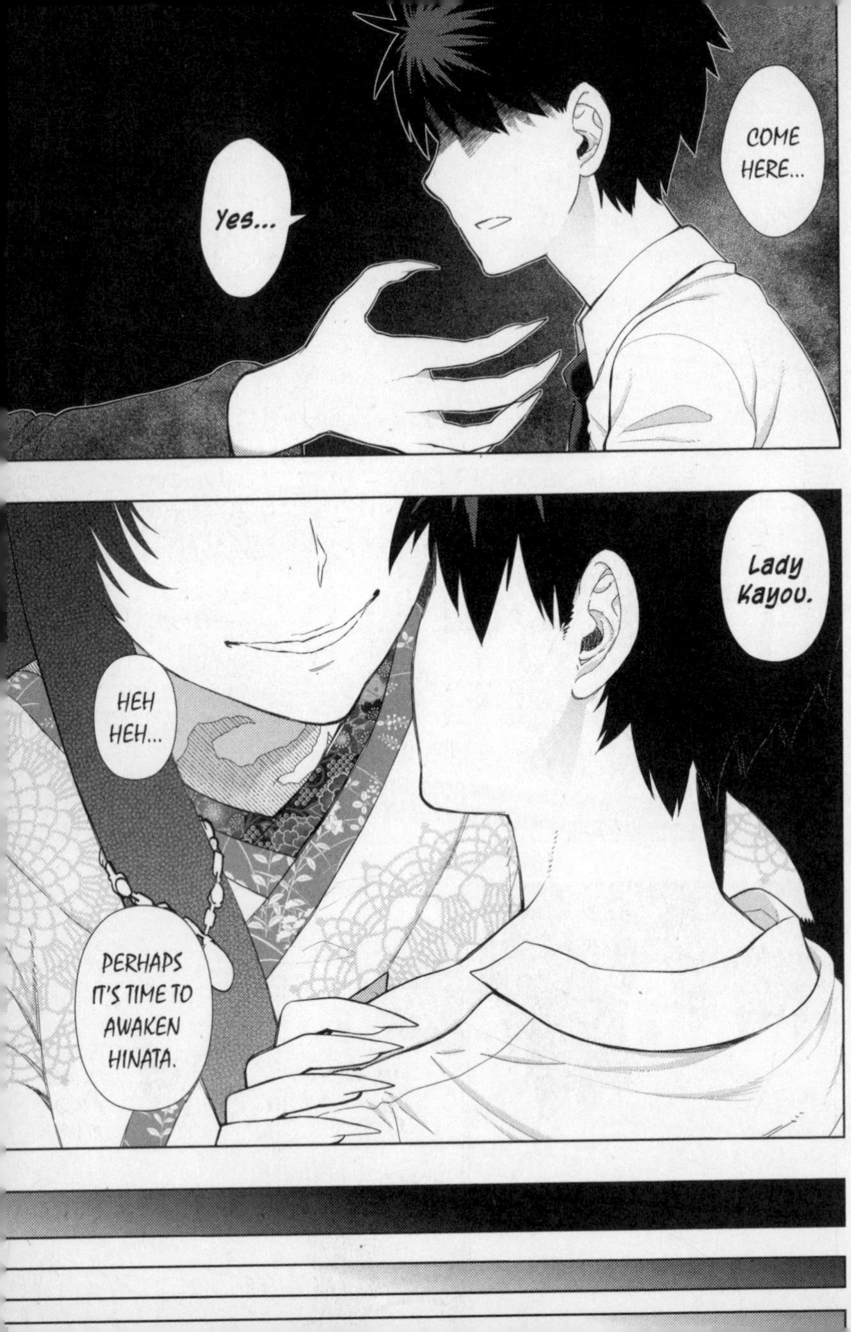
COME HERE...
Yes...
Lady Kayou.
HEH HEH...
PERHAPS IT'S TIME TO AWAKEN HINATA.

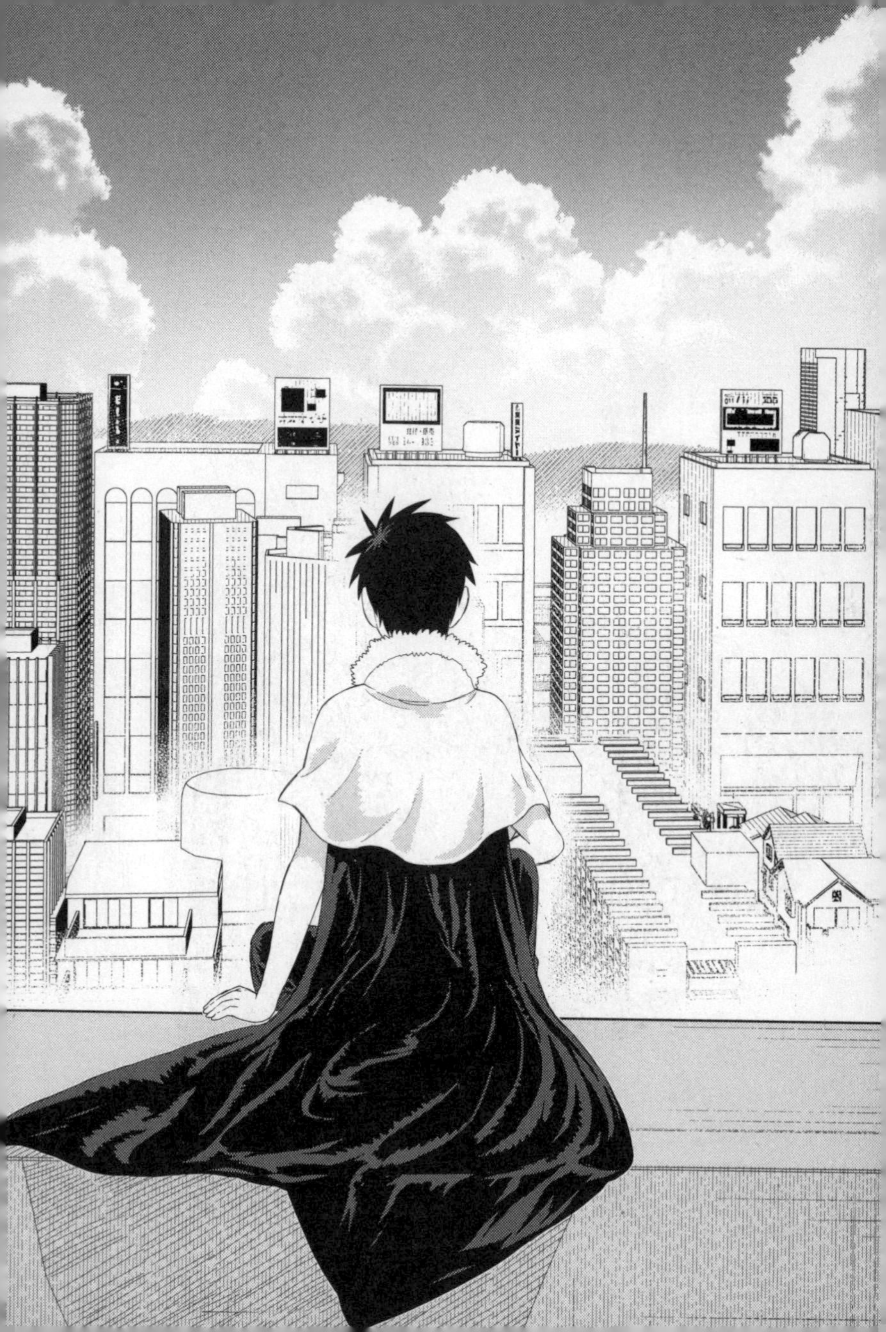

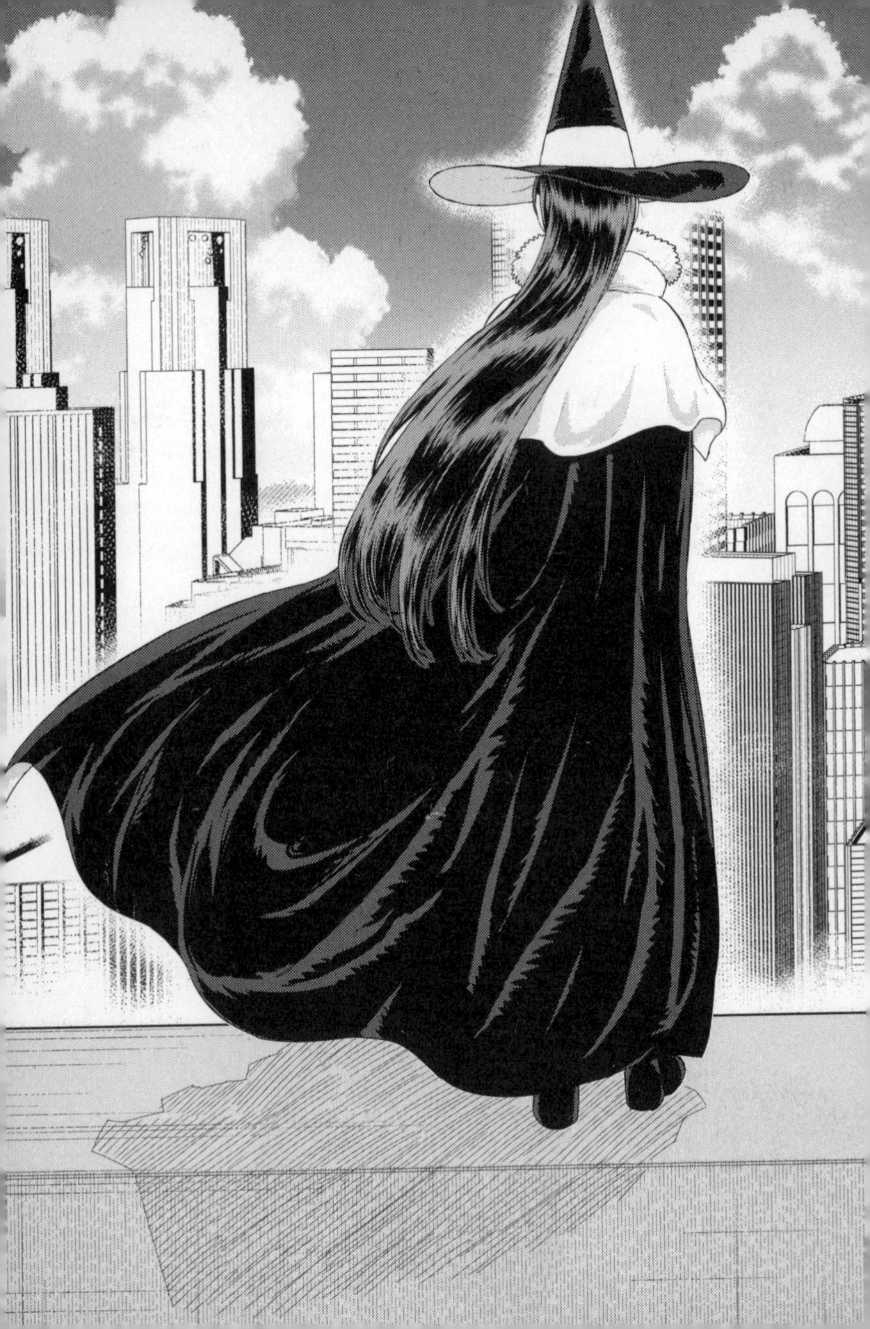

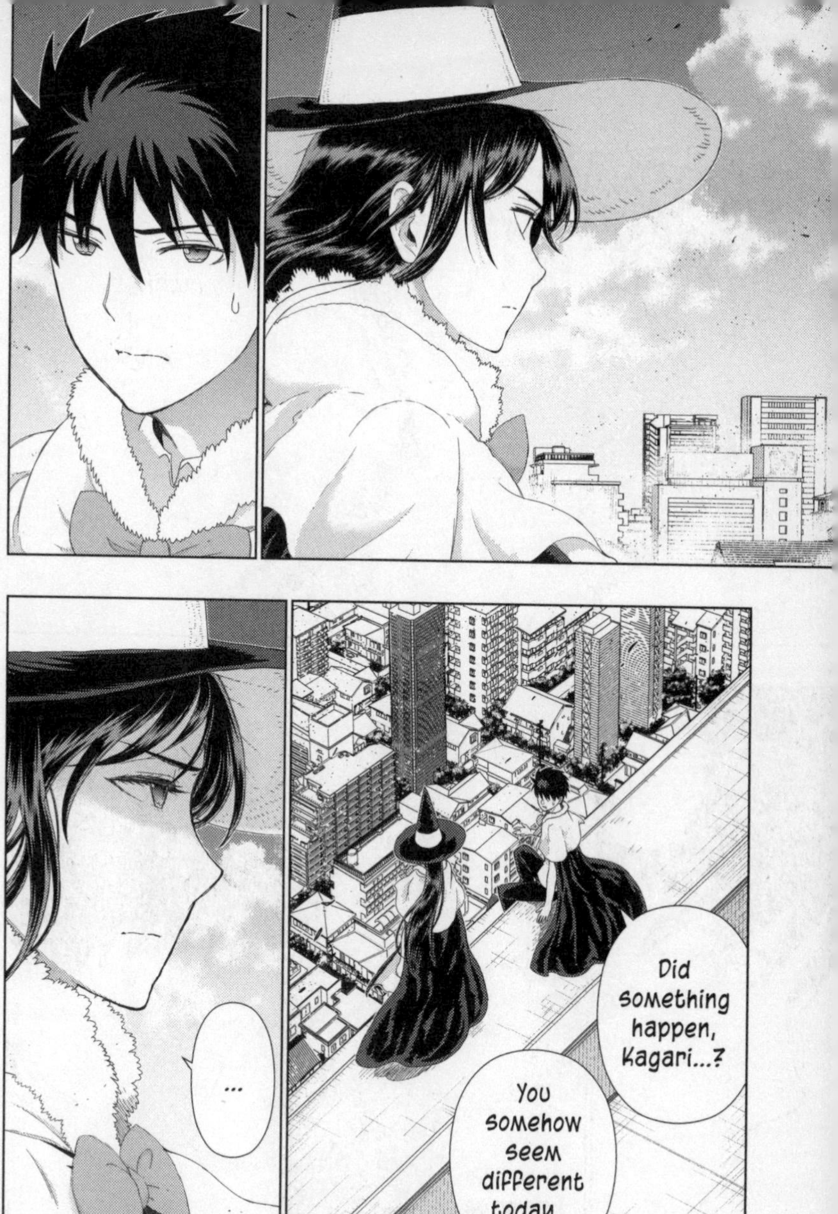
Did something happen, Kagari...?
You somehow seem different today...
...

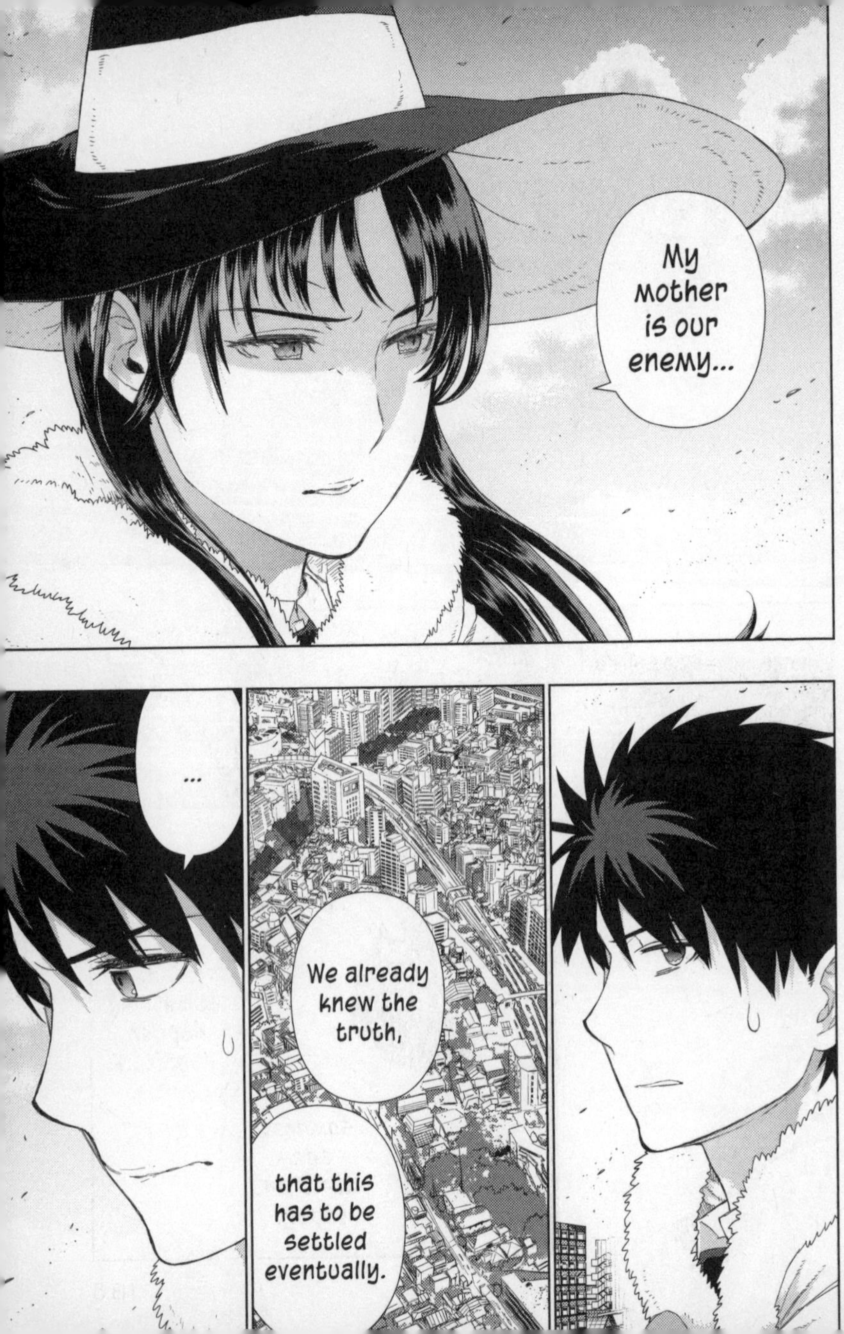
My mother is our enemy...
We already knew the truth,
that this has to be settled eventually.
...

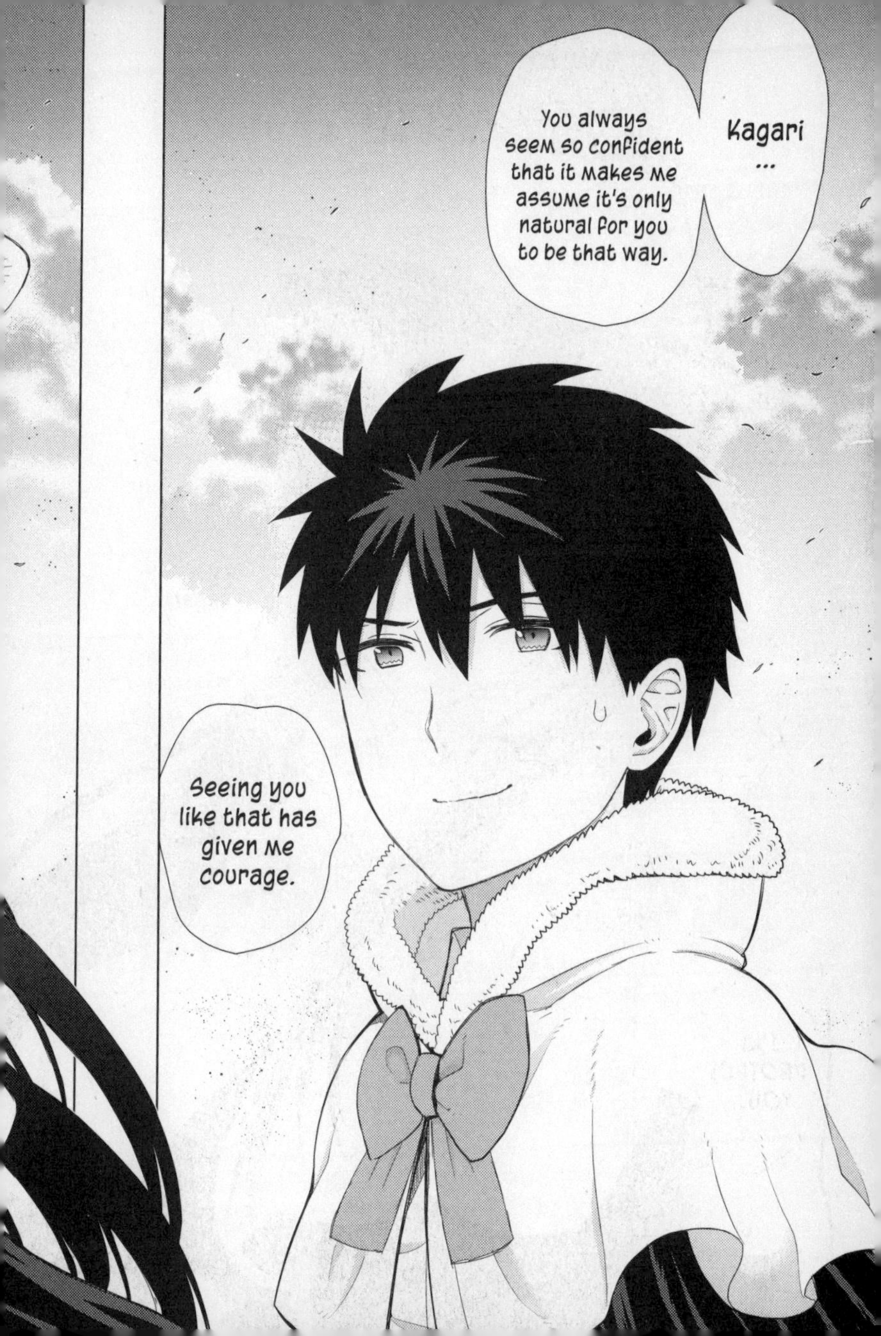
Kagari ...
You always seem so confident that it makes me assume it's only natural for you to be that way.
Seeing you like that has given me courage.

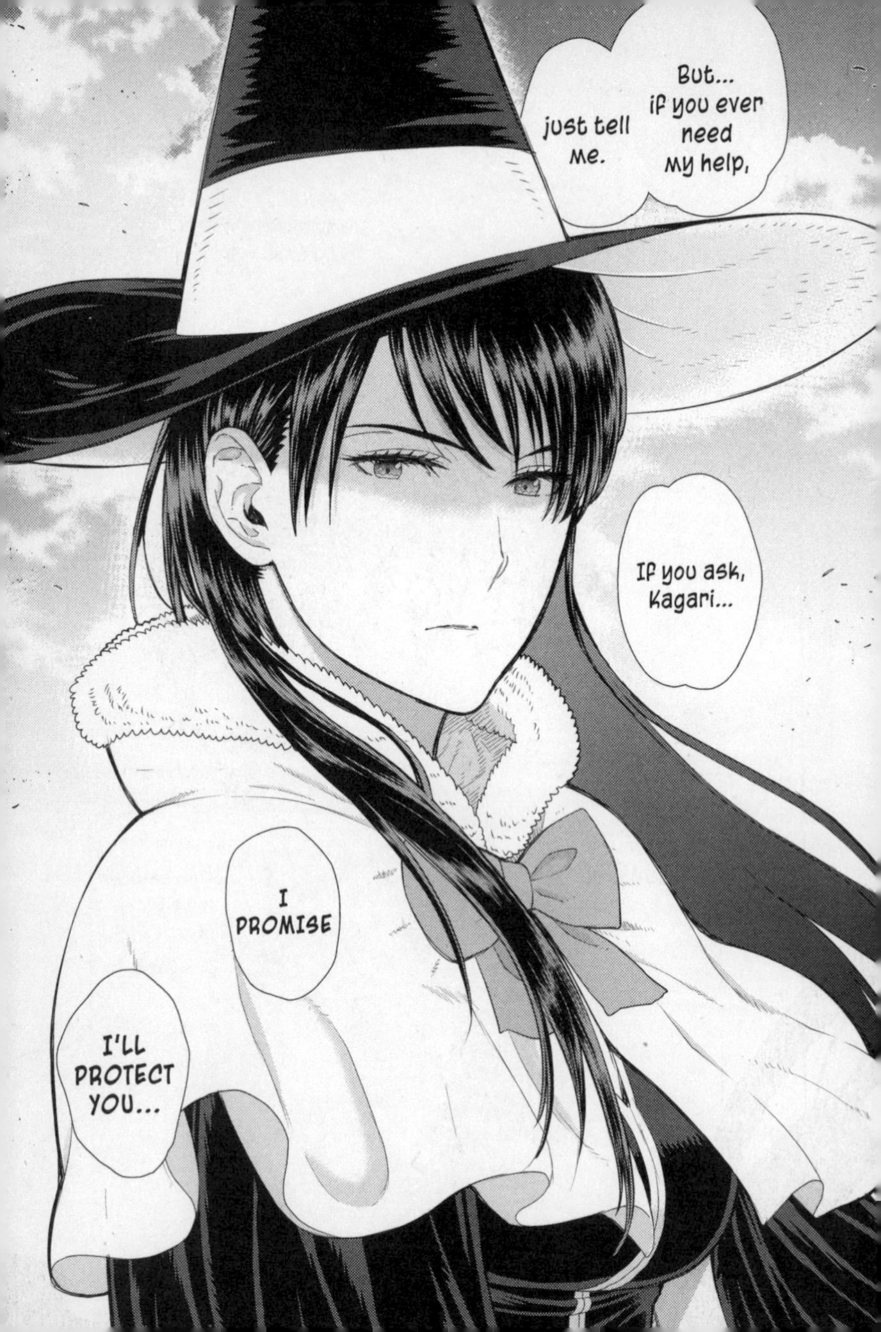
But... if you ever need my help,
just tell me.
If you ask, Kagari...
I PROMISE
I'LL PROTECT YOU...

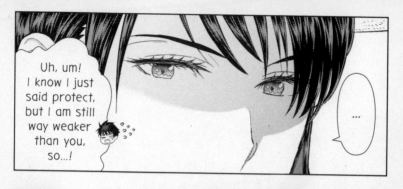

...
Uh, um! I know I just said protect, but I am still way weaker than you, so...!
I just, uh... don't want you to take everything on yourself, I guess...?
Worrying isn't a bad thing, anyway!
...
...It's almost time for dinner. Let's go home.

WITCHCRAFT WORKS 12: END

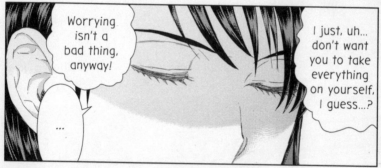

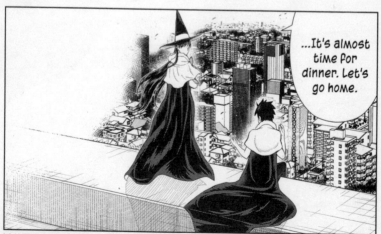

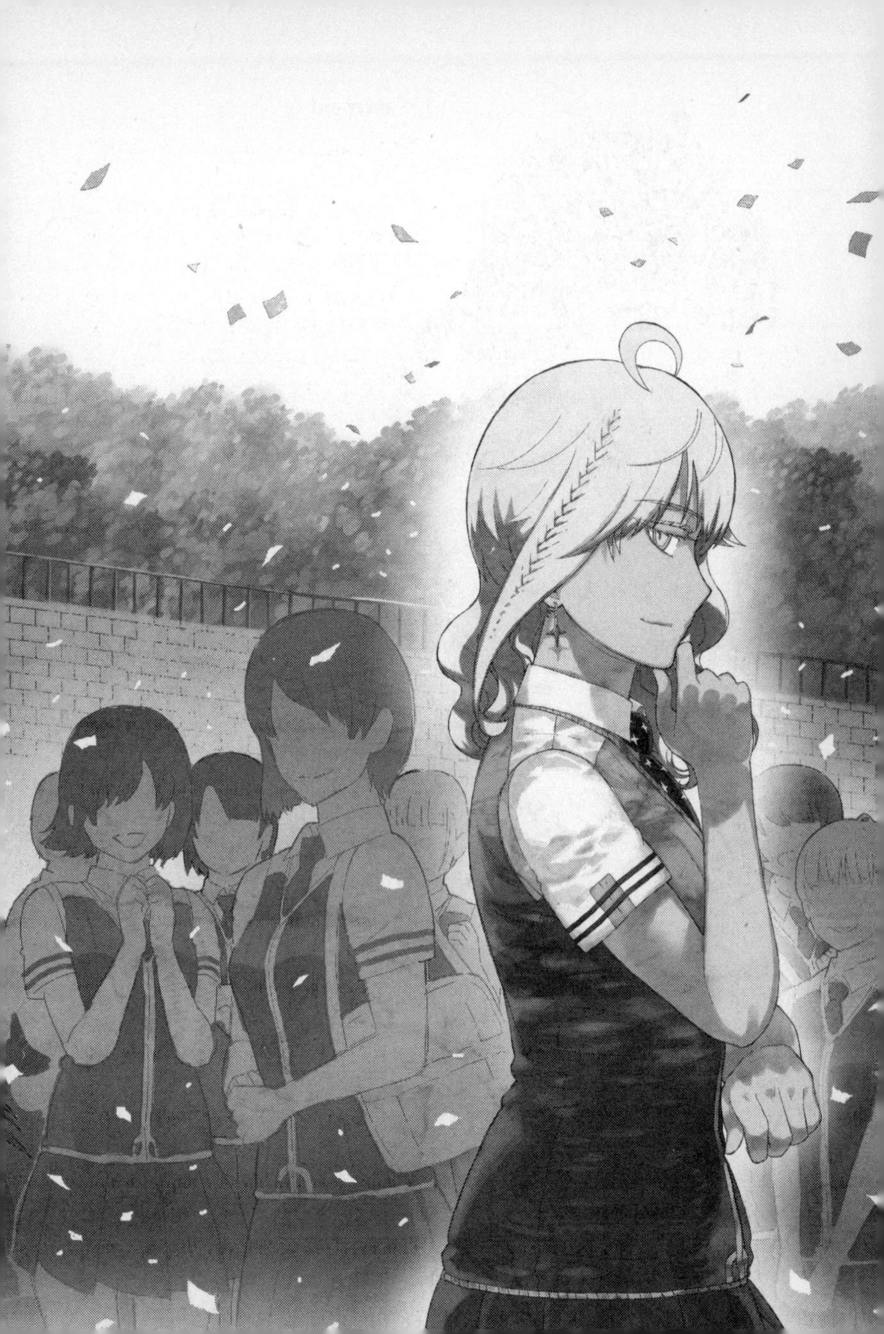

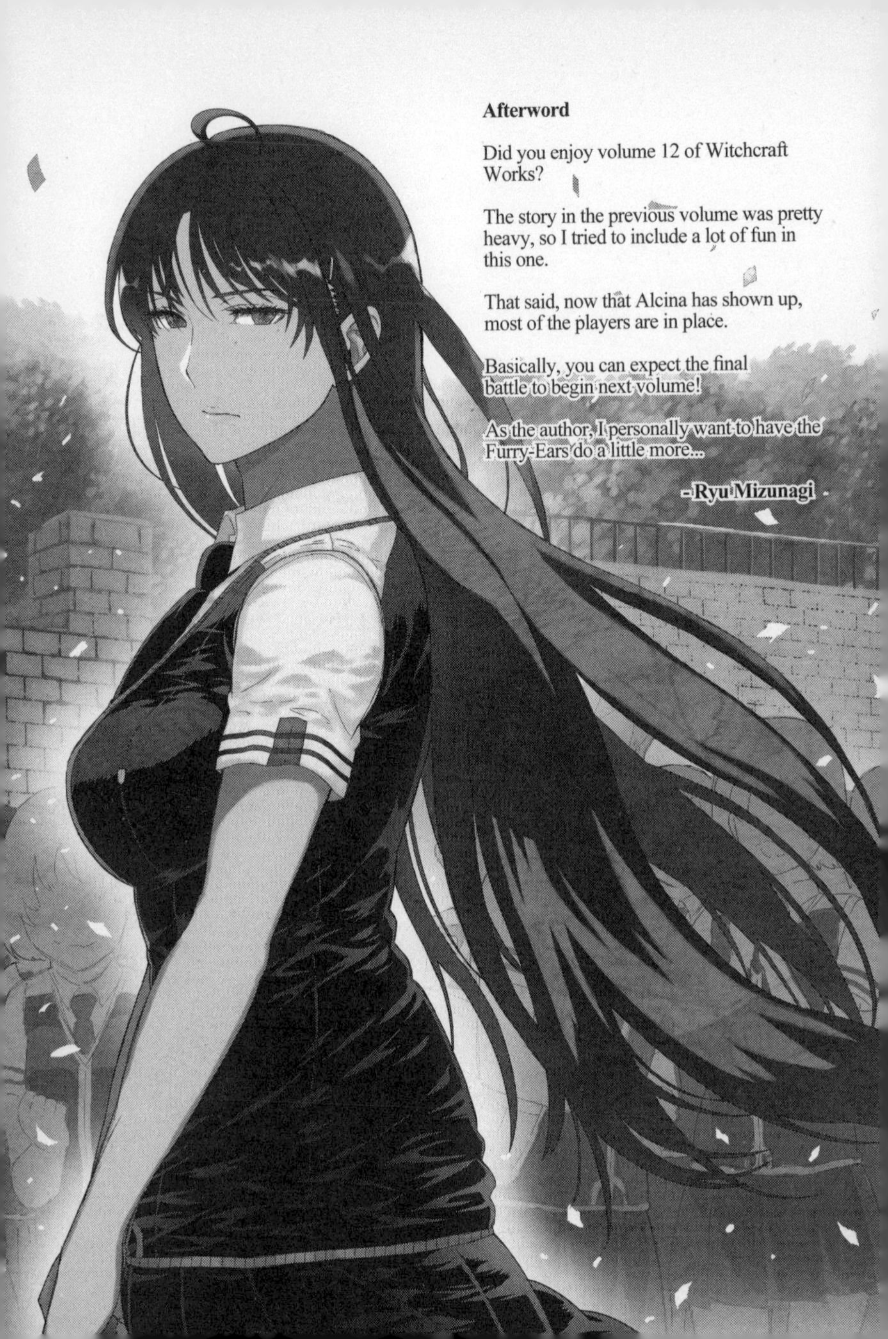

Afterword

Did you enjoy volume 12 of Witchcraft Works?

The story in the previous volume was pretty heavy, so I tried to include a lot of fun in this one.

That said, now that Alcina has shown up, most of the players are in place.

Basically, you can expect the final battle to begin next volume!

As the author, I personally want to have the Furry-Ears do a little more...

-Ryu Mizunagi

Witchcraft Works

Teach Me, Miss Weekend!

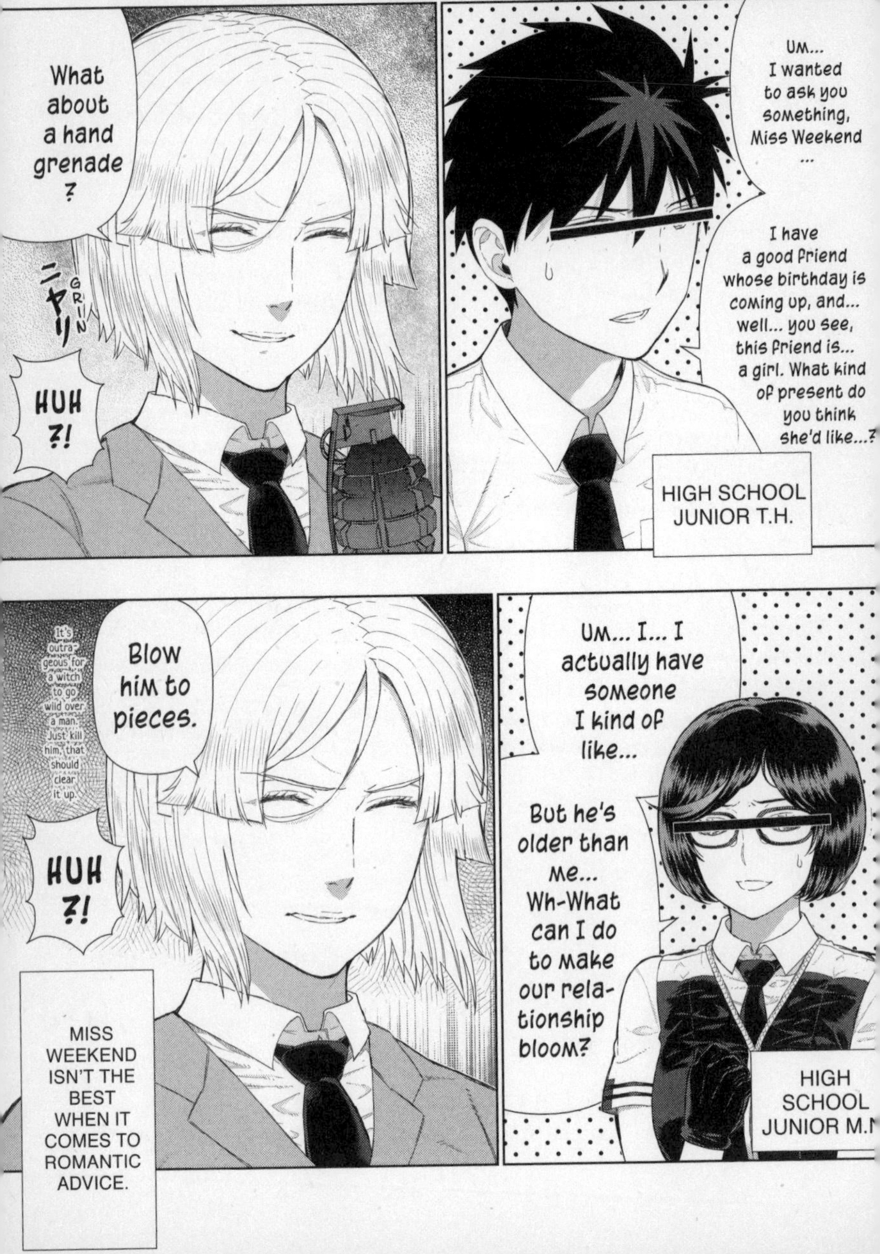
Um... I wanted to ask you something, Miss Weekend ...
I have a good friend whose birthday is coming up, and... well... you see, this friend is... a girl. What kind of present do you think she'd like...?
HIGH SCHOOL JUNIOR T.H.
What about a hand grenade ?
ニヤリ GRIN
HUH ?!
Um... I... I actually have someone I kind of like...
But he's older than me... Wh-What can I do to make our relationship bloom?
HIGH SCHOOL JUNIOR M.N
Blow him to pieces.
It's outrageous for a witch to go wild over a man. Just kill him, that should clear it up.
HUH ?!
MISS WEEKEND ISN'T THE BEST WHEN IT COMES TO ROMANTIC ADVICE.

Witchcraft Works

SETTING + SECRETS

This page is a collection of behind-the-scenes character and story elements that probably won't affect or appear in the main story, as well as comments by the author. If you finish reading the story and think, "I want to know more!" then we hope you enjoy the information here.

Chapter 62: Takamiya and the Summer Break Dinner

The tattooed Workshop witch sisters whom the readers have probably forgotten about reappear.

• Laurent and Vine
Witches belonging to the Rothenberg Workshop. Laurent is Vine's older sister. The two show up in Kazane's town while tracking Medusa after she escaped and disappeared. While they know that Medusa is hiding somewhere in the town, the two are still unable to find her and are at their wits' end. The armor that covers their limbs is specially made to reduce the effects of petrification. As they are specially trained to handle Medusa, they're often useless when it comes to other tasks. While we've discussed depicting their personal lives multiple times, I haven't had a chance to do so yet, possibly because they're low on the priorities list.

• Alcina
Her first appearance. Alcina is a very important Workshop witch. You can tell by her attitude toward Laurent and Vine that she outranks them.

Chapter 63: Takamiya and the Last Day of Summer Break

I remember my editor remarking how unusual it was to have Mei in the first panel of two chapters in a row. Now that I think about it, I guess it is kind of notable!

• The Furry-Ear Gang and Kasumi

Kasumi seems to have become one of the Gang. Together, they plot to sneak into Kagari's room and steal her summer break homework. Nothing ventured, nothing gained, right? They all end up falling without putting up much of a fight. Kasumi paid the lion's share of the bill at the karaoke parlor, and the Furry-Ear Gang owes her big-time. As they're always low on funds, they even find themselves having to borrow money from her.

• Tanuma

Tanuma is a little worried about Kasumi making lots of rough, mysterious friends. Tanuma loves being of use to Kasumi more than anything, so she's happy that she's being relied on for her homework.

Chapter 64: Takamiya and the Start of the New Semester

It seems like Natsume's having a pretty tough time. You know, with her mom and all.

• Natsume and Mr. Mikage

Natsume doesn't learn that her mother was attacked until a few days later. She doesn't hear from her mom very often, which can make her a little sad. Mr. Mikage feels sorry for her.

• Shiori

Takamiya is probably in whatever dream she's having.

• Miss Weekend

After various twists and turns, Weekend is now a teacher at Tougetsu High. She looks as embarrassing as ever under her suit. There are only two types of things in the world: those that explode and those that don't.

• Laurent and Vine

The sisters are being worked to the bone as school janitors by Alcina.

• Alcina Kagari

After transferring, Alcina is placed in Kasumi's class, making her Takamiya's junior by one year. She gets Kazane to agree to say that she's part of the Kagari family.

Chapter 65: Takamiya and the Mysterious Transfer Student

Alcina vs. the Furry-Ear Gang, featuring Kasumi.

• Alcina
It's revealed here that Alcina is a witch with the power to turn her targets into objects. Chronoire says that she turns those she doesn't like into furniture that she then surrounds herself with, but this isn't quite correct. She only keeps furniture that she likes. She'll destroy or dispose of any furniture she doesn't need. It's also revealed here that she is one of the Workshop's founding members, a Witch of the Beginning. The Furry-Ear Gang and Kasumi challenge her to a fight, but they get turned into furniture in the blink of an eye. It looks like she didn't fancy any of them, since she didn't take any furniture home.

Chapter 66: Takamiya and the Disenchantment Spell

Natsume does her best.

• Kazane and Chronoire
The two rush to the roof after getting a message from Atori. The battle has already ended, and everyone has been turned into furniture before being abandoned there. They call for Natsume and instruct her to undo the curse. Kazane isn't good at work that involves using her head.

• Natsume
Natsume somehow manages to analyze Alcina's curse and undo it. It seems that Alcina placed the curse assuming that it would be broken, though.

Chapter 67: Takamiya and the Mikage Family's Circumstances

Shiori's recovery and Kayou's plot.

• Shiori and Kazane
The fact that Shiori was attacked by a perfect Natsume imposter together with what happened to Takamiya makes it seem likely that Kayou has returned. Kazane visits the place where she had been sealed only to find it an empty shell. Part of Kayou's plan comes to light. The majority of the Kagari family witches were purged by Kazane in the past, and few remain in the present. This happened because so many of them had been won over by Kayou.

Chapter 68: Takamiya and Alcina's Scenario

Alcina shakes up Takamiya using Laurent and Vine.

• Laurent and Vine
Now under Alcina's orders, the two sisters neglect their job of tracking Medusa in order to investigate Takamiya. However, all that's discovered in their investigation is that Laurent likes younger men. You can see how mean Alcina is by how she forces Laurent to wear the traditional garb of her hometown. While they believe that the White Princess's masters are greedy witches who generally cause harm, the fact that Kazane was willing to protect him with her own body forces them to acknowledge that he may be different. Perhaps they even expect him to be a good man. They're not catching everything, though, as they believe that the Furry-Ear Gang are Workshop witches.

Chapter 69: Takamiya and Miss Weekend

The author enjoys the sound of the phrase "Miss Weekend." A great teacher is born!

• Weekend
Unexpectedly, the Tower witch Weekend is actually acting like a teacher, and her students adore her. Even when Kasumi and the others bicker, she doesn't fail to hear from both sides and gather evidence before handing down a fair judgment. The poor woman is then suspected by Kazane to be the one who destroyed her statue.

Prepare to be Bewitched!

Makoto Kowata, a novice witch, packs up her belongings (including a black cat familiar) and moves in with her distant cousins in rural Aomori to complete her training and become a full-fledged witch.

"*Flying Witch* emphasizes that while actual magic is nice, there is ultimately magic in everything." —Anime News Network

The Basis for the Hit Anime from Sentai Filmworks!

Volumes 1-7 Available Now!

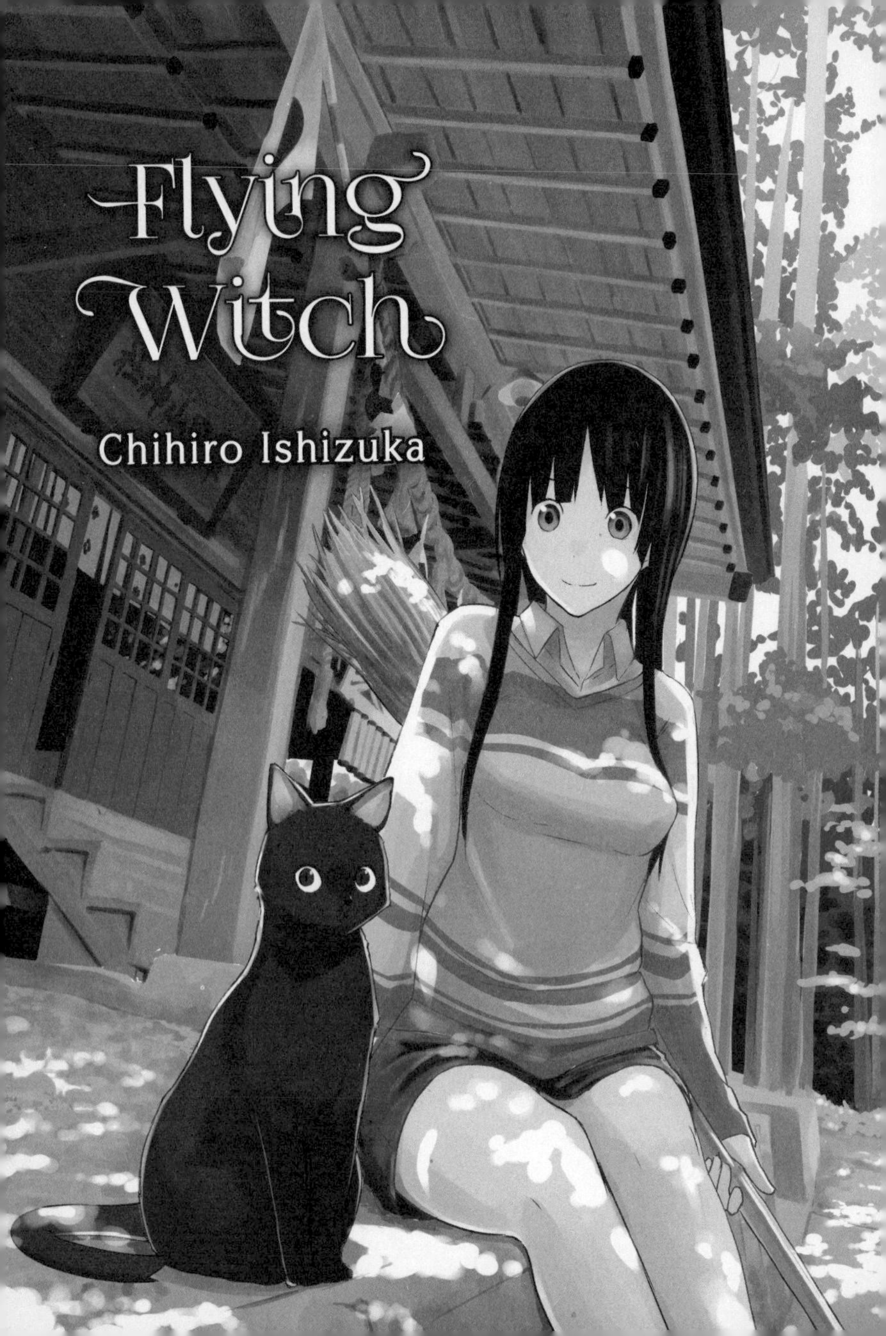
Flying Witch
Chihiro Ishizuka

Witchcraft Works, volume 12

A Vertical Comics Edition

Translation: Ko Ransom
Production: Risa Cho
Melissa DeJesus

First published in Japan in 2018 by Kodansha, Ltd., Tokyo
Publication rights for this English edition arranged through Kodansha, Ltd., Tokyo
English language version produced by Vertical Comics, an imprint of
Kodansha USA Publishing, LLC.

Translation provided by Vertical Comics, 2019
Published by Kodansha USA Publishing, LLC, New York

Originally published in Japanese as *Uicchi Kurafuto Waakusu 12* by Kodansha, Ltd., 2018
Uicchi Kurafuto Waakusu first serialized in *good! Afternoon*, Kodansha, Ltd., 2010-

ISBN: 978-1-947194-67-0

Manufactured in Canada

First Edition

Kodansha USA Publishing, LLC.
451 Park Avenue South
7th Floor
New York, NY 10016
www.vertical-comics.com

Vertical books are distributed through Penguin-Random House Publisher Services.